THE HERO'S FAREWELL

Jeffrey Sonnenfeld, a professor at the
Harvard Business School for the past decade,
is now Professor of Organization and
Management and Director for the Center for
Leadership and Career Change at Emory
University. He has twice won the Academy of
Management's annual award for outstanding
research on social issues, and was named to
their Board of Governors in 1988. He is the
author of three other books, including
Managing Career Systems, and numerous
articles on executive careers.

THE HERO'S FAREWELL

WHAT HAPPENS WHEN CEOs RETIRE

JEFFREY SONNENFELD

Harvard Business School

OXFORD UNIVERSITY PRESS
New York   Oxford

Oxford University Press

Oxford   New York   Toronto
Delhi   Bombay   Calcutta   Madras   Karachi
Petaling Jaya   Singapore   Hong Kong   Tokyo
Nairobi   Dar es Salaam   Cape Town
Melbourne   Auckland

and associated companies in
Berlin   Ibadan

Library of Congress Cataloging-in-Publication Data
Sonnenfeld, Jeffrey A., 1954–
The hero's farewell.
Bibliography: p.   Includes index.
1. Chief executive officers—United States—Retirement.
2. Chief executive officers—United States—Succession.   I. Title.
HD38.U6S66   1988   658.4   88-1542
ISBN 0-19-505091-6
ISBN 0-19-506583-2 (PBK.)

PREFACE

The year of this book's publication—just as in the prior year, and no doubt in the following year—will see the publication of at least two dozen autobiographies of prominent business leaders. These books give the authors an opportunity to put their interpretations of the meaning of their careers into the permanent record. At the same time, other management books, both scholarly and practical, will celebrate these leaders for their vision, words, and achievements.

Business leaders have long been lionized (and sometimes vilified) in American society, giving them a significance that can transcend their daily jobs. Some of them have become national folk heroes while others have gained heroic stature only within the walls of their own organizations. As a result, many of these top business leaders have come to think of themselves as embodying a heroic ideal not unlike the mythic heroes of earlier ages.

This is a book about how the management succession process involving chief executive officers of major corporations is affected by the heroic view that CEOs have of themselves. Some plan carefully and choose wisely who will succeed them. Others fight the process and must be forced out in what can be traumatic episodes for the CEOs and the organizations.

I have found in my studies that top business leaders judge their lifetime of service in different ways from the rest of us. These differences determine when a leader decides that a mission is completed. They determine how a decision to depart is made. It is essential to understand this process so that firms can plan for an orderly and productive management succession at the top.

But this is not a personal guide for executive retirement or a policy manual for designing corporate succession programs. Nor is it a book about management style. Curiously, a CEO's style of management by itself is a poor predictor of succession style. Some of the great autocrats have stepped down gracefully and some of the most paternal leaders have had to be forced out by their boards of directors. It is instead a conceptual examination of the leader's role in late career.

Over a decade ago I became interested in the area of retirement while working as a personnel researcher at IBM. The firm was concerned about possible changes in mandatory retirement far ahead of any actual changes in the laws covering retirement. After studying the IBM data, reading the available research on other companies, and looking into the research in psychology on aging and abilities, I was struck not by the danger, but by the many advantages of retaining older people in the work force. In 1978 I put these findings into an article in the *Harvard Business Review* entitled "Dealing with an Aging Work Force," in which I discussed age as an asset.

The response to this article led to a busy lecture circuit to executives since the laws on age and retirement were changing just as the article was published. The talks were well received up to a point. But the more senior the executive audience, the more skeptical they were about the validity of my argument applied to top management. They wondered if it were true that age is an asset at senior management levels. They thought that top-level turnover was essential. I was suspicious that their reaction resulted from self-interest. Perhaps they wanted top-level change to increase their own career opportunities.

As a result, I began this study expecting to find that older top-level executives were no different from other older workers. But I was wrong. This book explores the crucial differences and is a testimony to the wisdom of those executive audiences several years ago. I thank them for provoking me to look into the question in detail.

My own research involved fifty personal interviews with prominent leaders of generally the same generation of American business executives, a systematic analysis of surveys of these leaders, and an investigation of concurrent corporate performance of their firms. I also conducted an extensive review of related scholarly work on leadership and aging.

The study took five years in research and writing. Each interview required difficult negotiation to arrange and conduct since the central topic is so sensitive. Not only were these executives still busy, but I was asking for their cooperation in my look at one of their most prized possessions—their public reputations. They had made many sacrifices in their lives and had made enormous contributions to their organizations. Some greeted my study with warm enthusiasm and arranged many follow-up discussions. Others responded with anger and correspondence from their libel attorneys.

Among the sacrifices that these top leaders made in the course of their successful careers, the one that many still resent having made was the loss of personal privacy. Their life dreams became the public property of their firms and the impact of their personal lives on their decision making became a topic of understandable public speculation. I am therefore grateful to all of these leaders for making yet one more contribution to society through their candor in this book. Many volunteered painful recollections and relived moments of triumph in the interest of scholarship, not gossip.

I would like to thank several research assistants who have had a large impact on this work over the past few years. First, Paula Carlson Alexander of Sears Holdings, a former student of mine, joined me on the original five field interviews and helped gather the background data for the profiles of six or seven of these leaders. Paula's courage and colleagueship were critical to the early days of this study as we cautiously began this study which intruded into the personal lives of some powerful public figures. This study grew beyond our wildest dreams.

Next, Dr. Cynthia Ingols, a researcher at the Harvard Business School, was an enormous help in the preparation and the organization of the survey effort. Locating these retired leaders was often a challenge in itself as they have gone off to new lives often with limited trails behind. Many of them were still quite busy and many were no longer in good health. Gaining the participation of roughly 300 chief executives and chief operating officer level executives was a difficult undertaking. Cynthia's patient assistance was critical to this effort. She was assisted in the coding of the questionnaires by Rita Perloff and Jill Harris of the Harvard Business School.

James Phills, a doctoral student at the Harvard Business School, mastered the difficult challenge of blending very different data bases from Compustat financial performance data with this original survey data and with extensive coded data from the proxy reports of 150 companies over 25 years. Audrey Halfant of the U.S. State Department, while a researcher, labored with a research team for over a year to code this proxy data. Alice Morgan of the Cambridge Research Institute helped prepare the Flowtrol Case in Chapter 11. Patty Marx, Meredith Lazo, and my current research assistant Maurey Peiperl have been very helpful in the proofreading of the manuscript. The complex flow of correspondence and drafts was artfully guided by my secretary Gloria Buffonge, Rose Giacobbe of Harvard, and Wordsmith Wordprocessing.

I would like to thank several of my faculty colleagues for their time and ideas over the years. First, I would like to thank Dean John H. McArthur of the Harvard Business School for his initial suggestion in 1983 to seek these executives out for candid interviews. Next, I want to thank Professor Richard F. Vancil of the Harvard Business School for his comments on my draft and our collaboration on the data base he began which was drawn from corporate proxy reports. Also, I'd like to thank Associate Professor Richard S. Tedlow, editor of the *Business History Review* for his detailed and thoughtful commentary on each page of the manuscript. Ms. Michele Marram of the Baker library set up a pipeline for a rich flow of recent relevant publications. Professors Walter J. Salmon, Paul R. Lawrence, Rosabeth Moss Kanter, E. Raymond Corey, Howard H. Stevenson, Jay W. Lorsch, John P. Kotter, John J. Gabarro, Andrall E. Pearson, Thomas K. McCraw, Joseph L. Bower, Chris Argyris, Kenneth R. Andrews, and Hugo Uyterhoeven, all of the Harvard Business School, also provided me with valuable advice on this project over the past few years. Professors David Riesman and George Homans of Harvard's sociology department offered insightful comments on earlier drafts. Professors Manfred Kets de Vries of INSEAD, Donald Hambrick of Columbia University, Warren Bennis of the University of Southern California, Harry Bernhard of the University of Southern California, Douglas T. Hall of Boston University, Susan Ornstein of Suffolk University, Dr. Robert Kaplan of the Center for Creative Leadership, Dr. Harry Levinson of the Levinson Institute, and Herbert J. Addison of Oxford University Press have all given generously of their time, insight, and enthusiasm.

Boston   J. S.
May 1988

CONTENTS

CHIEF EXECUTIVES INTERVIEWED

Charles F. Adams Raytheon Company
Marvin Bower McKinsey & Company
Thornton F. Bradshaw RCA Corporation, Atlantic Richfield Company
John F. Burditt ACF Industries, Inc.
Philip Caldwell Ford Motor Company
Thomas S. Carroll Lever Brothers Company, Inc.
Roger C. Damon Bank of Boston
John D. De Butts AT & T
William P. Drake Pennwalt Corporation
Douglas A. Fraser United Auto Workers
Albert H. Gordon Kidder, Peabody Group, Inc.
Jerome S. Gore Hartmarx Corporation
Harry J. Gray United Technologies Corporation
W. L. Hadley Griffin Brown Group, Inc.
Bruce D. Henderson Boston Consulting Group, Inc.
Lenore Hershey *Ladies' Home Journal*
Richard D. Hill Bank of Boston
Arthur A. Houghton, Jr. Corning Glass Works
Winthrop Knowlton Harper & Row, Publishers Inc.
Edwin H. Land Polaroid Corporation
Robert W. Lear The F. & M. Schaefer Corporation
Royal Little Textron Inc.
Rene C. McPherson Dana Corporation
Jack Nash Oppenheimer & Co., Inc.
Paul Oberkotter United Parcel Service
Russell S. Reynolds, Jr. Russell Reynolds Associates, Inc.
David Rockefeller The Chase Manhattan Bank, N.A.
William Rosenberg Dunkin' Donuts Incorporated
Peter G. Scotese Springs Industries, Inc.
Irving S. Shapiro E. I. du Pont de Nemours and Company
William H. Wendel The Carborundum Company
Thomas J. Watson, Jr. International Business Machines Corporation

The remaining 18 interviewed requested anonymity

THE HERO'S FAREWELL

1

HEROES IN LATE CAREER

Everybody's a dreamer, everybody's a star,
And everybody's in movies, it doesn't matter
    who you are.
There are stars in every city, in every house,
    on every street,
And if you walk down Hollywood Boulevard,
    their names are written in concrete . . .
I wish my life was a non-stop Hollywood
    movie show,
A fantasy world of celluloid villains
    and heroes.
Because celluloid heroes never feel any pain,
And celluloid heroes never really die.

from "Celluloid Heroes,"
Ray Davies of the Kinks

Top leadership succession is largely influenced by the heroic self-concept of the departing leader. Fifty years ago the psychologist Otto Rank suggested that the age-old struggle of humanity is to conquer the fear of the seeming meaninglessness of life, a fear that arises from the certainty that life will end in death. The heroic drive, according to Rank, is an expression of our effort to survive our own death—to achieve immortality—by leaving a lasting imprint or heroic legacy upon society.[1]

Society has come to recognize the leaders of modern corporations, among many others, as heroes. As men and women take high corporate office today, they are expected to play a kind of heroic role in guiding the destinies of their firms. Most eagerly seek and accept this role and serve with enthusiasm during their term of office. But when the time comes to step aside for newer, and almost always younger, leaders, many high corporate officers are beset with the fears that Otto Rank described: Leaving office means a loss of heroic stature, a plunge into the abyss of insignificance, a kind of mortality.

3

Of course, not all leaders react in the same way to this loss. The heroic self-concepts of leaders in late career, tempered by the corporate settings, give rise to distinctly different departure styles. These departures have a large impact on the firms these leaders guided. Consider the cases of two very different leaders, retiring at the same time from the two leading firms in the same industry.

Coca-Cola was invented by an Atlanta druggist in 1886 as a combination thirst quencher and nerve and headache tonic. Pepsi-Cola was invented by a North Carolina druggist in 1893 as a stomach tonic.[2] Both elixirs grew beyond their origins as medicinal kola nut derivatives to become the world's leading soft drink beverages. Despite these similarities, however, the leadership transitions in these firms could not have been more different.

In the case of Coca-Cola, for example, Robert Woodruff became president in 1923, retired in 1955, and continued to exert his forceful influence far beyond his term of office. Though he was neither the founder of the firm nor its first marketing genius, it is Woodruff who will be remembered as "Mr. Coke" because of his revolutionary approach to sales. His major contribution was to equate sales with servicing customers, a concept he expanded to international markets. Woodruff appreciated that in the future, Coca-Cola needed to be sold not only as a fountain beverage but also in a canister or a bottle.

When Robert Woodruff retired as chairman and chief executive of Coca-Cola in 1955, he remained active as a board member. The company he had guided so expertly for three decades continued to occupy the center of his life, and the company continued to dominate the marketplace. For the next thirty years, until his death, he was the guardian of product consistency and the kingmaker of the succession process.

Walter Mack became president of the Pepsi-Cola Company in 1939, after Pepsi had had a long and rocky history of acquisition, merger, two reorganizations, and two rounds of bankruptcy procedures. But Mack brought it into a serious second place in competition with Coca-Cola, and after World War II, guided it to its very successful entry into the supermarket revolution. In 1950, however, Mack became entangled in a vicious proxy fight between the bottlers, his board, and his own convictions.

> I had gone about as far as I possibly could with Pepsi. I wouldn't be able to modernize because I was stuck with the franchise system. So I told them to go ahead and work out a contract for me as a chairman . . . and I allowed myself to be kicked upstairs. They gave me a contract of $110,000 to do very little except stay out of the industry and out of their hair, but I only stayed around for about a year and then I got out for good. I still had a lot of friends at Pepsi, and remained a consultant so they could come to me for advice from time to time, but I never went back to company headquarters.[3]

After leaving Pepsi, Mack turned to the rescue of many other enterprises in financial trouble, including ABC Vending, Nedick's, Great American Industries, and National Power and Light. But by 1962, he was back in the soft-drink business, having purchased the rights to an old Irish tonic-water firm called Cantrell & Cochran. With one of his Pepsi-Cola chemists, Mack used Cantrell & Cochran to create a new cola called C&C, which is a strong regional beverage in the New York area, though it has not succeeded in getting shelf space in other parts of the country. In 1978, at the age of eighty-three, Mack founded yet another cola beverage, King Kola—another competitor to his former firm's product.

These two cases illustrate that how a leader chooses to leave a company cannot be predicted on the basis of a firm's age or industry, as is often assumed. In trying to understand the forces that motivate departing leaders, and thereby to begin to find ways of ensuring that leadership transitions are as smooth and as least detrimental as possible, let us explore in greater depth the heroic analogy proposed by Rank as it applies to business leaders. Today, we transform business leaders into popular heroes. In fact, in a discussion of modern visionary giants, management scholars Warren Bennis and Burt Nanus include Thomas J. Watson (IBM), Edwin Land (Polaroid), Alfred P. Sloan (General Motors), and Lee Iacocca (Chrysler) among such world shapers as Winston Churchill, Mahatma Gandhi, and Franklin Roosevelt.[4] To compare history-making international statesmen with the leaders of private corporations is to take a big leap across value systems and magnitudes of human impact. Nonetheless, despite different scales of accomplishment, all of these inspired public figures have the common characteristic of being able to mobilize others through their imagination and commitment. Emerging research on top leadership corroborates that leaders' day-to-day management activities are less important than their broader agendas of action, and some recent studies of successful chief executives even describe these figures as having long-term "heroic missions." In order to understand why some business leaders are being seen in larger-than-life contexts, it may be appropriate to examine the concept of hero as illustrated in mythology and folk literature.

The Chief Executive as Mythic Hero

In literature and folk tales, the basic functions of leaders involve both demonstrations of codes of honor valued by a society and the deliverance of the group from collective dangers; they have both a symbolic function and a practical role. Joseph E. Campbell's classic anthropological survey of heroes across centuries, continents, and cultures has labeled deliverance from future hazard the "monomyth" of the hero.[5]

As Campbell sees it, these leaders' goals represent a concept of existence that is expansive, not self-enriching. The hero battles beyond personal and historical limitations to a valid, human solution to the community's problems and conflicts. The visions, ideas, and inspirations come from the "primary springs of human life and thought" and have the effect of enriching the human experience. For example, Aeneas in Virgil's *Aeneid* overcomes superhuman obstacles to found Rome. Similarly, Buddha is instructed by the god Brahma to become a leader and to teach and proclaim the life path for all humanity to follow. In the Old Testament, Joseph's interpretations of the Pharaoh's dreams save the Israelites, as do Moses' revelations, which led the people of Israel out of Egypt to the Promised Land. The wisdom and leadership of Jesus, Mohammed, the Aztec god Tezcatlipoca, and other ancient religious heroes also characterize them as dreamers or visionaries who aid people to reach their highest destiny.

What business heroes have in common with the heroes of myth and religion is that they not only symbolize dreams and aspirations to their firms, and even to general society, but also are accomplishers of pragmatic goals. Society, it seems, admires inspirational leaders who can translate hazy visions into concrete realities. But when the vision becomes passé, so does the reign of the leader. This explains a source of tension between the corporate leader and his organization on retirement: he perceives the corporate community as rejecting his dream and all that he stood for.

Among retiring leaders, chief executives experience the greatest tensions and must face an especially challenging retirement transition, for over their careers their purpose and self-worth have become increasingly linked to the well-being of the firm. The chief executive, as the personal symbol of the institution, defends the firm from public attack, constantly monitors the flows of disparate streams of activity toward a collective purpose, and maneuvers to see that the expectations of the corporation's owners, workers, and neighbors are addressed. In short, within his or her own organization, the chief executive becomes a folk hero.

In making a contribution to the corporation through leadership service, chief executives' visions and dreams become group property and as such are criticized, modified, and adapted to serve the whole corporate community—a process some leaders find more difficult than others. And just as surrendering one's goals and visions to public revision is more difficult for some than for others, so too is retirement more painful for some than for others.

Some retiring chief executives cling to their positions in late career, and others eagerly leave. Some are content with the impact they have had during their careers. Others seek greater impact and prolonged personal reassurance of their significance.

In the film *Cocoon,* aliens from outer space offer residents of a retirement community an escape to a land of eternal *productive* life. Most members eagerly accept this escape from their deteriorating, purposeless existence. However, Bernie, one of the older residents, firmly declines the gift: "I was dealt my hand of cards from the start, and played as well as I could; it's not fair to want to reshuffle the deck."

Like Bernie, some retiring leaders are content with the contribution they have made and have no desire to continue playing the role. But others want to relive and rework their careers, especially if they feel they did not achieve the truly great heights that were within their grasps. They want to serve as lifelong net contributors to society, rather than as mere consumers in their old age.

This book examines the return to mortal dimensions of those whose lofty careers transcended the norms of recognition and impact. The way these careers end is of genuine interest as an index to the culture of a wider community. All of us are concerned with the process of anointing new leaders. Many aspire to reach top leadership. And most of us are anxious to see that our conditions at work and at home benefit from the reign of new leaders. For these reasons, it is important to understand the thinking of departing leaders. This book will examine the perspectives of just one segment of public figures: the older generation of business leaders who moved to the top of the American corporate ladder before the generation of baby boomers began to aspire to the executive suite. Many studies have examined the rise of this generation to top management; I will look at the neglected half of the equation, their exit.

The theory of this book is that a leader's heroic self-concept leads to different styles of departure. The heroic self-concept is composed of two features: one's identification with leadership stature and one's quest for immortal contribution. Departure styles can be classified into four categories: monarch-like exits; general-like exits; ambassador-like exits; and governor-like exits. These departure styles are different from management styles. For example, both autocratic leaders and participative leaders can be found in each category of departure style. Departure styles, however, do influence corporate strategies and the effectiveness of executive succession. Corporate renewal plans are tied to a late-career leader's personal agenda. Whether we are leaders or not, we are all affected by leaders' retirements.

The first half of this book presents new theory and research findings, while the other half presents candid profiles of executive exits. Chapter 2 discusses how older leaders are different from other older workers throughout the job spectrum. Prominent figures with great discretion over their work conditions may face particular occupational challenges in late career that result from declining powers. It introduces us to the world of all older workers, so that we may appreciate what aging leaders may yet be able to contribute and understand the trials of late career common to all workers, regardless of whether they are top-level executives or not. We will consider the myths that underlie biases against older workers, as well as the psychological and the organizational research about late-career workers, which challenges much of our conventional wisdom regarding the role of older workers in the firm.

In Chapter 3 we examine the different tensions that arise in corporate leaders as they face the end of their careers: tensions about loss of status, tensions between departing leaders and their successors, and tensions between leaders and their constituencies beyond the organization.

Chapter 4 explores the question of whether it is even fair to consider corporate leaders as cultural heroes and seeks to determine whether top leaders are different from other older workers through prominence alone. It is argued that one quality that sets leaders apart is their career development as folk heroes.

Chapter 5 suggests special psychological barriers to career exit that business heroes face. These barriers can be lessened or heightened depending on the environment of the heroes' firms. This chapter introduces four types of departure styles of retiring business leaders, covering a variety of methods for overcoming these barriers to retirement. This chapter contains key findings from my chief executive survey and my analysis of Compustat data.

The next four chapters present an extended description of the four departure styles, with accounts of a number of executive careers. Chapter 6 describes the monarch-type leaders who choose not to leave office voluntarily. The monarch's reign is interrupted by death in office or by overthrow from within. Chapter 7 deals with generals, leaders who leave office very reluctantly and spend much of their "retirement" plotting a return to active service. Chapter 8 examines the ambassador-type—that is, those who leave office gracefully but retain an active and close, though low-key, relationship with their old firms. Finally, Chapter 9 focuses on the governor-type, those who willingly leave office to pursue very different new interests.

We turn from these examples, all drawn from large, *Fortune* 500 firms, to the family business in Chapters 10 and 11. It will be argued that the family business presents special challenges that further complicate the considerations of retiring leaders. In Chapter 12 we will review some survey research on a group of ninety family businesses and look at a detailed case study of one actual family firm and the retirement process of its leader.

The final chapter focuses on the link between corporate renewal and personal renewal, including how individual leaders can guide their own self-renewal and how firms can usefully sponsor late-career revitalization. Parallels are drawn between the plateau reached by some in mid-

career and the career ceiling faced by an ambitious, seemingly successful top executive. The new goal for these leaders should not be to guide
others' futures but to create a future for themselves.

The data underlying this book represent five years of study and the
gathering of information from a wide variety of primary sources as well
as from secondary sources in order to capture several ingredients of the
succession process overlooked by researchers and journalists. First, I
wanted to encourage chief executives to offer a rich and candid personal explanation of their own retirement process. Far too often the
perspective of the chief executive is presumed to be unreliable or inac-
cessible. Researchers turn instead to statistical data on succession, with
an espoused statement of purpose to inform the studies. Second, I wanted
to compare these chief executives' perspectives using comparable aspects of departure. Leaders' own accounts in biographies and autobiographies often emphasize different topics, so that it is hard to compare
their departures. One may choose to discuss personal challenges while
another may prefer to focus on corporate trials. Third, I wanted to
anchor these perceptions of the chief executives both by factual events
and by the perceptions of others close to the same events. Leadership
changes reflect personal decisions and personal consequences.

To accomplish these three goals, I gathered and synthesized twelve
classes of data. My eight primary sources include (1) intensive day-long
interviews and follow-ups a year later with fifty recently retired prominent chief executives who had achieved legendary status within the
business community; (2) personal interviews with family members or
work associates of these fifty chief executives; (3) a survey of one hundred
randomly selected *Fortune* 500 chief executives from manufacturing and
service industries; (4) a survey of one hundred retired top officers (e.g.,
chief operating officer, chief financial officer, etc.) who reported to the
chief executives; (5) a twenty-five-year history of succession information
contained in the proxy statements of each of the one hundred firms
these officers worked for, tracked year by year; (6) a study of the Compustat pool of financial performance indices of each of the one hundred
firms for the length of these top officers' reign and the two years after-
wards; (7) a survey of ninety chief executives of smaller, family businesses; and (8) surveys of the alumni of three forty-fifth reunion classes
of the Harvard Business School and their spouses. The four published,
or secondary, sources of data include classic biographies of leaders, media accounts of succession struggles, psychological research on aging
and career renewal, and anthropological studies of leadership and heroism. All twelve classes of data converge to provide personal depth and
corporate breadth in examining the leadership exits.

2

AGING LEADERS AND OTHER AGING WORKERS

Do not go gentle into that good night,
Old age should burn and rave at close of day;
Rage, rage against the dying of the light.

Dylan Thomas

Resisting Retirement

Burrell Ball, an eighty-nine-year-old bookkeeper, has worked for the same boss in the same job for seventy years. Ball's boss is ninety-eight-year-old Willis Farris, president of his own lumber company in Nashville, Tennessee. Neither Ball nor Farris has been forced to delay retirement to forestall poverty. Both work because they want to. "Retirement?" Ball remarked, when asked to comment. "Don't figure I've ever been thinking much about that kind of stuff."

Large-scale surveys of top executives find that almost three-fourths of the respondents would continue in their jobs even if they were financially independent.[1] Polls by Louis Harris and Associates indicate that over half the respondents would continue to work beyond age sixty-five. Among retired workers, 46 percent wish they were working full- or part-time.[2] Some new studies indicate a reversal in trends toward early retirement.[3] An oft-cited study of stressful life events ranks retirement as number 10, just after being fired (8), and marital reconciliation (9).[4] The only events in life considered more stressful were death of a spouse, divorce, marital separation, jail, death of a close family member, personal injury or illness, and marriage. Retirement was found to be 50 percent more stressful than changes in financial status and the death of a close friend.

Two recent reviews of research on retirement suggest that the study of retirement has really been a surrogate for the study of the trauma of aging.[5] This makes sense, for many people measure their lives by their career accomplishments. The eight or nine decades we hope to live can be calibrated by changing relationships, family developments, personal growth, geographic moves, community involvements, and career events. For many of us in our modern achievement-oriented society, career transitions mark how far we have come and how much opportunity in life may still lie ahead. For many, it is through our careers that we prove that our existence has had value. By extending our careers into old age, perhaps we minimize the trauma of aging. Thus Burrell Ball and Willis Farris, by resisting retirement, may be resisting giving in to aging itself.

Retirement Patterns of Top Leaders Versus Other Occupations

Top leaders, performers, self-employed professionals, independent artisans, and others with high personal discretion and involvement in their work are less eager to quit than are workers in routine, repetitive jobs requiring little initiative and autonomy. Many executives do retire early, but they tend not to be chief executives. The retiree faces different challenges, depending on his or her personality and the position he or she has held. A bookkeeper like Burrell Ball can find part-time employment after retirement that utilizes his skills. It would be harder for his older employer, Willis Farris, to find useful employment, for a retired chief executive's work skills are not so easily utilized, even if he or she is much younger than ninety-eight. For example, violinists in retirement can still offer solo performances or play with small ensembles. A conductor, however, needs the full orchestra to be employed, and thus a conductor's skills are not usually portable into retirement.

The lack of portability of their skills makes retirement especially threatening to chief executives. In conducting this study I found that many aging leaders, when asked about their intended retirement dates, were resentful of the suggestion that their time had passed. As long as they were healthy, they responded curtly, they would stay in office. Even in interviewing forty retired leaders, I found most shuddered each time I used the word "retirement." This seemed odd for a group who had

already said farewell to office in addresses to shareholders and employees, who were listed in corporate documents as retired, and who had
accepted their companies' retirement pensions. It was only when I re-
described the project as a study of chief executive exit and succession
that their discomfort was eased.

Similarly, many of the one hundred retired chief executives I surveyed by mail went out of their way to write back that they had not
really retired. Whether they were fifty-five or eighty-five years old, they
wanted to be recognized as busy and important people. Most of this
group greeted this study enthusiastically. They wanted to contribute to
what they felt was a worthy academic project and a useful management
resource. But they also saw it as a forum to make a statement to the
world about their own continued professional worth.

Why was this so important? Are aging leaders different from others
in their need for late-career contribution? This chapter will examine
these issues by considering the bind of older workers who, on the one
hand, are pressured to "act one's age" and conform to retirement expectations but, on the other hand, know that they retain the ability to
perform. Through these discussions, we will explore the common prop-
erties of aging leaders as aging workers.

Acting Your Age

Scientific investigations of physiologists and psychologists over the past
two decades have revealed that chronological age, the time that has
passed since birth, is an inadequate measure either of one's functional age (what one can do) or one's social age (what one is obligated
to do).

Social pressures to act one's age are vividly painted by filmmaker Paul
Mazursky in *Harry and Tonto,* a moving tour through an older person's
world. The protagonist, Harry, lives in a community of lonely people
of limited means. A retired schoolteacher, Harry tries to bring warmth
and humor to his empty life through his companionship with his cat
Tonto and through visits with other "lone rangers" on the frontier of
old age. These older persons, dismayed over the changes in their lives
ranging from lost loved ones to lost purpose, blame their problems on
those still able to control their own fate: new neighbors, politicians, celebrities, even their own offspring. At first, we laugh at the eccentrici-
ties of Harry and his friends, later we pity their evident disengagement
from life, and finally we share their anger as we come to see the world
through their eyes. By the end, they are no longer anonymous ciphers
in an urban landscape, but familiar people whose histories we have come
to understand.

Harry initially tries to resist the change around him by withdrawing into the protective shell of his memory-drenched apartment. Here, amidst the clutter of old photographs and furniture from his former happy life, he is comforted by the reminders of better days. As he arrives home one day, after having been almost hit by a car and then mugged on the street, he hums the tune "Boulevard of Broken Dreams" to his cat Tonto and settles into an easy chair to sleep, muttering:

> Would you believe it Tonto? Mugged four times this month. You know I'm glad that Annie isn't here to see it now. She loved this neighborhood . . . like Shakespeare's London, bristling with energy. Today it's still bristling, but without the energy. There were trolleys, cobblestones, the aroma of corned beef and cabbage, the tangy zest of apple strudel. . . . Had to hand crank the cars. Names like Reos, Franklins, Hudsons. These days you don't know if you're driving a car or an animal—Mustangs, Cougars. I used to drive Burt around on his paper route, help the boy make a little money. It *was* a wonderful neighborhood. It's running down. It all runs down sooner or later. Where would I go and live? I still know a lot of people around here. If you know people, that's home.

Harry drifts off to sleep only to be awakened by the sounds of sirens, police bullhorns, and shouting crowds outside his window. He is being forcibly evicted just moments before his house is razed. Harry's embarrassed middle-aged son rushes in from the suburbs to retrieve his father. When the son scolds, "Pop, act your age!" Harry shouts back, "I am acting my age!"

Homeless now, Harry is free to act his age as he chooses and not how it was chosen for him by others. Disliking airplanes and buses, he takes to the road in his car on his own odyssey. As he travels, he renews old personal skills, meets new friends, and learns techniques for adapting to a changed world. By the end of the film, he has relocated and begun working again, tutoring young people. Harry has touched many lives in the meantime and brought joy back into his own. Rigid and bitter in the beginning, his adventures on the road change him. By the film's close, he is, in fact, the youngest person in spirit, if not actually so in chronological age. Children and adolescents applaud Harry's renewal and instantly connect with him. Though patronized throughout by middle-aged people who see him only as a confused and stubborn old man, by officials in airports, casinos, nursing homes, and morgues who treat him as a bother, and by his own middle-aged offspring who persist in reenacting with him the conflicts of their adolescence, Harry ignores the admonitions to act his age, acts young, and hence becomes young. He decides not to quit living until his human machine has given out.

Friction between the middle aged on the one hand and the young and the aging on the other is commonly observed in the nearly conspiratorial union of grandparents and grandchildren. As author Ronald Blythe commented in *The View in Winter*, "The old challenge authority because they have exercised its pretensions, the young because they cannot believe they will ever have to." The middle aged, meanwhile, see both groups unconsciously as a personal threat:

> The middle aged frequently find themselves timidly—yet compulsively— measuring their assets against those of youth to see what they have left, and against those of old age to see what has yet to go. It is often a great deal in both cases. There can be then a spiritual and physical drawing back from the old, as if they possessed some centrifugal force to drag the no longer young into their slipstream decay. Many . . . have to disguise their loathing of old people. . . . The old do not fear the young, but they are ever conscious of the lengths to which self-preservation in the not-so-young will go, and they frequently fear them.[6]

Exposure to the elderly reminds the middle aged of future loss. At mid-life we undergo a painful and profound reorientation to time. No longer do we look at our lives in terms of how long life has been. Instead we begin to see just how little time remains.

Chapter 1 suggested that such intergenerational hostilities are aggravated within managerial hierarchies. That each cohort sees the other as the source of its own diminished opportunity was demonstrated in a pioneering study of age bias drawn from a broad-based sample of managers who read the *Harvard Business Review*.[7] The managers were asked to recommend actions regarding three employees: (1) a manager responding too slowly to customer complaints; (2) a manager requesting permission to attend a production seminar; and (3) a candidate requesting a promotion. In each case a paragraph or two was provided that described the employee's general background. For half of the study participants, the employee was described as older, and for the other half he was described as younger. The participating managers who thought the employee was younger were far more willing to provide him with opportunities for training, promotion, and helpful feedback than were those who thought the employee was older, even though he had identical qualifications (see Figure 2.1). Older respondents were far less likely to be influenced by the candidate's age. Yet despite their age-biased recommendations, most participants overtly claimed to *favor* improved treatment of older workers! I have replicated this study with almost a thousand of my students and consistently found that those who thought the employee was younger were more willing to help him or her and provide opportunities.

We have not always forced older workers into retirement at prescribed ages. A decade ago, Congress passed legislation extending the mandatory retirement age from sixty-five to seventy. Many employers and journalists of that time expressed alarm that vibrant enterprise was about to be strangled by senescent old hands. For example, columnist William Safire cautioned in a *New York Times* article, "The Codgerdoggle," that

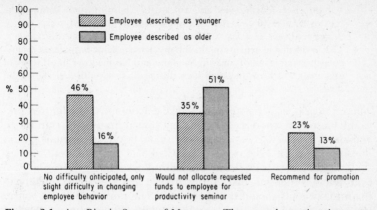

Figure 2.1 Age Bias in Survey of Managers. Three employee situations were described. Half the 1,570 respondents thought the employee was old in each situation, and half thought the employee was young. (Source: Benson Rosen and Thomas R. Jerdee, "Too Old or Not Too Old," *Harvard Business Review* 55, November–December 1977, pp. 96–106.)

old people get older and usually less productive, and they ought to retire so that business can be better managed and society more economically served. We should treat the elderly with respect, which does not require treating them as if they were not old.[8]

Five years later, after losing a $2-million-lawsuit brought by three fired employees in their late fifties and early sixties, Norman Wexler, the chairman of I. Magnin department stores and sixty-eight years old himself, defended the firm:

> With all due respect, I'm different. . . . [Most] old people don't want to work as hard. . . . The young people are better. . . . It's an evolutionary fact . . .[9]

By 1983, only three people had ever qualified for the I. Magnin pension plan because so many left before reaching eligibility. Such common conceptions about older people are not consistent with scientific research, however, or with the experience of many companies.

Retirement is a twentieth-century practice. Company policies requiring older people to cease working did not exist prior to 1900. Until then, older workers were appreciated for their wisdom and experience and were regarded as guides to youth and pillars of moral stability in a dynamic society.[10]

A new era began at the turn of the century when, in a 1903 farewell speech, William Osler, the chief physician of Johns Hopkins University Hospital, charged that:

The effective, moving, vitalizing work of the world is done between the ages of 25 and 40 . . . the uselessness of men above sixty years of age [suggested] that as a matter of course, men stop work at this age . . . That incalculable benefits might follow such a scheme is apparent to any-one who, like myself, is nearing the limit and has made a careful study of calamities which might befall men during their seventh and eighth de-cades.[11]

These remarks set off a storm of public debate, for they captured pre-viously unspoken tensions as employment shifted from farms, craft shops, and small mills to large factories with new, fast-paced technologies in the workplace. In 1904, while most Civil War veterans were in their sixties and seventies, President Theodore Roosevelt amended the Civil War veterans' pension plan to declare old age a disability, qualifying them for benefits should they quit work. The purpose, in part, was to encourage their exit.[12] In the early decades of the century, a spirit of efficiency and control derived from the principle of scientific manage-ment, along with the influence of the Progressive movement's humani-tarian concern for the conditions of workers, pervaded the nation and drove older workers from dangerous manufacturing jobs. Through the 1920s, the nation's cultural fascination with youth began to show in overtly preferential personnel policies. In the 1930s, the massive un-employment of young people unable to find jobs and heads of families unable to keep jobs led to collective bargaining agreements and New Deal legislation that established formal retirement provisions. In the Social Security Act of 1935, age sixty-five was earmarked as the national retirement age, based upon Bismarck's use of the same age cutoff in his German social-welfare system decades earlier. Participation in the U.S. labor force by men over sixty-five fell from 68.3 percent in 1890 to 55.6 percent in 1920, 41.8 percent in 1940, and 19.1 percent in 1980 (see Figure 2.2).[13]

By the 1960s, pronounced age discrimination by some employers was affecting workers and concern grew to the point that President Lyndon Johnson led Congress on a crusade against what he termed a "shameful waste of human resources and unemployment payments through arbi-trary age discrimination." In 1967 the Age Discrimination in Employ-ment Act was signed into law, providing protection for workers be-tween the ages of forty and sixty-five from discrimination in hiring, discharge, compensation, career opportunities, or conditions in em-ployment on the basis of age. In 1978, Representative Claude Pepper led a successful legislative blitzkrieg to extend this protection to age seventy for all employees. The amendment also abolished mandatory retirement for federal employees.

Much litigation has taken place since the passage of this legislation, and though employers were successful in 73 percent of the cases over

Figure 2.2 Labor Force Participation for Those 65 and Over: 1890–1986.
(Sources: U.S. Bureau of the Census, *Historical Statistics of the United States, Colonial Times to 1970*, Bicentennial Edition, Part 1 [Washington, D.C.: Government Printing Office, 1975], p. 132. U.S. Bureau of the Census, "Population Profile of the United States, 1980," *Current Population Reports*, Series P-20, No. 363 [Washington, D.C.: Government Printing Office, 1981]. For more detail see Judith Treas, "The Historic Decline in Late-Life Labor Force Participation in the U.S.," in James Birren et al., *Age, Health and Employment* [Englewood Cliffs, N.J.: Prentice-Hall, 1986].)

the past decade, many multimillion-dollar age-discrimination lawsuits were lost by employers, including Eastern Airlines, Chevron, Consolidated Edison, Hartford Insurance, Liggett and Myers, Pan American World Airways, The Equitable, Home Insurance, United Airlines, I. Magnin, TransWorld Airlines, and AVCO.[14] By the mid-1980s, 40 percent of the *Fortune* 500 companies had withdrawn personnel policies calling for mandatory retirement. In 1984, state judges in some states could no longer be forced to retire at age seventy, and by 1986, sixteen states had passed laws banning mandatory retirement at any age for all employees. Similar federal legislation has now been passed.

These legislative changes are inspired, at least in part, by the shifting of power to older workers. From 1985 to 1990, the eighteen- to twenty-four-year-old portion of the population will shrink by 10 percent while the number of those over sixty-five years of age will grow by 10 percent.[15] By the year 2020, one-third of the U.S. population is expected to be over age fifty-five.

Households headed by someone over age fifty now control more than one-half of all the discretionary income in the United States, or roughly $150 billion. It has been suggested that Florida, with 17 percent of its population over age sixty-five and 33 percent over age fifty, provides a glimpse into the year 2000 for the rest of the nation.[16] Older people have startled consumer marketers by their purchasing behavior, and

Florida, with its older population, has become a principal laboratory for consumer research. The major packaged goods firms now market new foods, cosmetics, and health items for this age segment, and advertisements regularly feature active, healthy older people as models.[17] Major Hollywood studios have found box-office success with films starring "senior" citizens, including *Cocoon* with septugenarians Don Ameche, Jessica Tandy, and Hume Cronyn; *Harry and Tonto*, with Art Carney as a retired teacher; *On Golden Pond* with Henry Fonda and Katharine Hepburn as a retired couple; and *Going in Style*, with George Burns, Lee Strasburg, and Art Carney as restless retirees.

Similarly, where once television broadcast only youth-oriented adventure series and family comedies, several shows, such as "Golden Girls," today have a far older audience in mind. Brandon Tartikoff, president of NBC Entertainment, explains this change to his subordinates: "Take women around 60. Society has written them off and has said they're over the hill, but we want to show them to be feisty as hell and having a great time."[18] "Golden Girls" deals explicitly with themes that address such "late life" trials as new romantic relationships, faltering health, and death. When the show opened on September 14, 1985, it was the week's highest rated program, and the ratings have stayed strong.

Such changes in attitudes toward the elderly in general and toward mandatory retirement in particular have been part of a larger transformation. Leading gerontologists suggest that a quiet revolution has taken place that has liberated people from having to "act their age." The rigid timetable for guiding major life events has been reset. In the next section, we will consider what increased opportunity may mean given changing abilities with age.

Abilities and Aging:
From Mountaineering to Management

Just as attitudes toward older workers are changing, so is rigidly enforced age-grading disappearing. Gerontologist Bernice Neugarten comments:

> The whole internal clock I used to write about that kept us on time, the clock that tells us whether we're too young or too old to be marrying or going to school or getting a job or retiring, is no longer as powerful or compelling as it used to be.[19]

Does this mean that older workers will be able to perform well at all tasks merely because they may be provided with the opportunity to stay around? Or does it mean that the work force will be burdened by determined but exhausted older workers unable to keep up with the needed pace of change to master new strategies and technologies?

Individual Variation in Minds and Bodies

The press regularly tantalizes us with paradoxical answers to the concern over age limits to job competence. For example, *USA Today*, a nationwide newspaper, ran a story in the summer of 1986 about pitcher Steve Carlton, age forty-one, and his refusal to recognize that he may have passed his peak. While a pitcher for the Philadelphia Phillies, Carlton had struck out 4,000 batters, won 319 games, and was the only pitcher in baseball history to receive the sport's Cy Young Award four times. As his performance fell off, however, the team president pleaded with the aging pitcher to retire, but Carlton refused. Finally, the president fired Carlton, calling this the "most agonizing time I spent in baseball."[20] Rehired by the San Francisco Giants, Carlton's performance failed to measure up to anyone's expectations, and he quit midseason in quiet embarrassment. It seems that in this case age was a barrier to continued participation.

But in the same issue of the paper was an article on Hilda Crooks, a ninety-year-old mountain climber just returned from her twenty-third ascent up Alaska's Mount McKinley. She had first scaled the 14,494-foot mountain in 1962 at age sixty-six and has climbed roughly a hundred peaks since.[21] Here age was no barrier.

As these two cases point out, the will to continue participating is not the only determinant, for there are many individual variants in minds and bodies. Albert H. Gordon, the vibrant eighty-four-year-old chairman of the investment bank of Kidder Peabody, has stressed the importance of physical activity to keep mind and body active. Gordon has continued to run ten miles a day and recently ran in the London Marathon. "People don't realize the potential of the human mind or body," he commented to me in a 1984 interview. "You have to keep yourself active physically and mentally. Physical health greatly affects your occupational flexibility. You must prepare to fight physical decline by planning regular challenging exercise."

Another example of the physically fit elderly is found in the unlikely ranks of the Guardian Angels. The famous street-smart, rugged neighborhood civilian crime patrols now boast that their youthful numbers have been penetrated by volunteers approaching eighty years of age. These crime fighters are trained in self-defense, cardiopulmonary resuscitation, and the laws on citizens' arrests.[22]

Not all aging persons are capable of physical activity on this level, but we often develop a deep bias against older workers, because we associate decays in performance in some with aging in all. Even career-stage theorists label late career a time for "decline and disengagement." For example, MIT management professor Edgar H. Schein has pointed out that organizations expect older workers to adjust to their circumstances by:

1. Learning to accept reduced levels of power, responsibility, and centrality.
2. Learning to accept and develop new roles based on declining competence and motivation.
3. Learning to manage a life that is less dominated by work.[23]

Similarly, the prominent adult life development theorists Erik Erikson, George Vaillant, Roger Gould, and Daniel Levinson discuss the later years not as a time for career opportunities, but for coping with reduced physical capacity, reacquaintance with family and friends, and reviewing one's life work and contribution.[24] Erikson describes late life as a time for resolving the balance between a sense of integrity and completeness in life versus a sense of despair and regret over mistakes and lost opportunity.

Such social expectations are important in understanding the emotional needs of older workers. But an exclusive reliance upon Erikson's approach may lead to a dysfunctional preoccupation with the future. Older people are closer to the end than younger people, and their long-range outlooks thus may be a bit less cheerful. But their lives are not limited to these concerns. By prematurely emphasizing the need to prepare for the end of work or the end of life, we rob individuals of full life in the present.

Controlling Physical Decline

Placing emphasis upon more fully utilizing present capabilities is not to gainsay the genuine ravages of age, particularly those physiological changes that are the most pronounced signs of age: atrophy of skin tissue, hair loss, and stooped posture. A decline in sensory processes, particularly vision, failures of the immune system, which exacerbate cardiovascular and kidney problems, and degenerative diseases such as arthritis all afflict the elderly. But although 85 percent of workers over sixty-five suffer from chronic diseases, most develop them or signs of them well before this time.[25] In fact, 75 percent of those between sixty and sixty-four suffer from these diseases, which, however, can be treated and controlled through modern medicine.

The MacArthur Foundation has funded a multidisciplinary project on successful aging headed by Harvard physician John N. Rowe for the purpose of studying the tremendous variation in how people age. And in a related area, Robert Butler, the physician who heads Mt. Sinai Hospital's geriatrics department in New York, has highlighted ways people can limit or compensate for age-related disabilities.[26] It seems that people differ more as they age and that disuse accounts for half of the functional decline that occurs between the ages of thirty and seventy. People who maintain regular exercise can set the clock back twenty-five years, according to research by Herbert de Vries of the Andrus Gerontology Center at the University of Southern California. His studies suggest that a seventy-year-old man, in a moderate physical conditioning program, can enjoy a 35 percent increase in work capacity.[27]

Psychological Changes

Some psychological changes related to these physiological changes are also subject to a degree of control. For example, neurological decay has been linked to random brain activity or "neural noise," which distracts the brain from responding promptly to proper neural signals. In older persons, this increased neural noise can lead to a higher percentage of errors if not compensated for by a greater degree of caution. In fact, older people have been found to employ far more rigid criteria for making a decision than younger people. Older people also require a 75 percent chance of certainty before committing themselves to respond, whereas younger people leap into action despite high risks. If time pressure is not a relevant factor, the performance of older people tends to be at least as strong as that of younger people. For example, self-paced learning and self-paced tests, where individuals do not have to trade off speed for accuracy, are free of age-related declines in performance. Bias-free intelligence tests show no decline in skills involving problem solving, number facility, or verbal comprehension.[28] A major review of the studies on human perception concludes with an especially encouraging inference:

> It is important to emphasize that while some perceptual processes exhibit age-related declines in adulthood, other processes, such as higher order selectivity, may come to play a more significant role in accounting for perceptual experience.[29]

Perception, of course, is a psychological as well as a physiological process. Expectations and needs have a large impact on what is perceived. Older workers may actually have some advantages, given their increased experience.

Learning may also suffer from the effects of neural noise in that short-term memory is crowded. Most of the learning difficulties of older people relate to acquisition and recall failures. The human memory system is thought to be a two-step process involving, first, information entry and then information storage. Older people have more trouble holding newly entered information in short-term memory. In retrieval as well, short-term memory blockages cause problems. Training in appropriate mental techniques, such as rehearsal and the usage of mnemonic devices (memory cues), can overcome many of these memory blockages.[30] New research from MIT, Harvard, Tufts, and the National Institute of Mental Health suggests that memory loss may be curtailed by diet. While brain damage may not be reparable, the addition of choline, which can be found in the food additive lecithin, for example, may increase the amount of the vital neurotransmitter acetylcholine, which carries brain signals across nerve synapses.[31]

Furthermore, actual brain capacities may be enhanced through an enriched psychological environment. Researchers at the University of California, Irvine, and Harvard Medical School have found that the brain continues to grow in late life if a person is presented with a stimulating situation. Learning a new language, for example, can lead to significant growth of nerve dendrites.[32] Psychologist Ellen Langer has found that many supposedly natural consequences of aging result from aged people allowing themselves to be put into a helpless state. She found that nursing-home patients with greater control over their situation showed significant improvement on measures of alertness, happiness, active participation, mental well-being, and actual physical health.[33]

By the same token, shaping one's environment to conquer age-related challenges to physical and intellectual performance may also apply to work attitudes of older employees. Continuous activity in the workplace instead of planned disengagement and gradual withdrawal is now thought to account for the strikingly high morale observed among many older workers, and a recent government study has suggested that the lower turnover and lower absenteeism among older workers follows from high morale.[34] In fact, research on all sectors of the American work force has found that age and job satisfaction are positively related.[35]

Thus, increasing monetary benefits, but not expanding opportunities for job variety, could be a serious mistake that encourages the less productive, staid older workers to remain instead of the more vibrant. The desired workers are more interested in personal growth and achievement than in financial incentives. Mastery and achievement on the job are closely correlated with job satisfaction, and sudden changes in job structure and social networks can be threatening to older workers, whose niche in society, outside their families, is defined largely through their contribution at work. The older employee's job represents friendship, routine, a sense of self-worth, and an identity. Surprise job changes and sudden alterations in the work environment may be frightening prospects for some older workers. For instance, a colleague and I recently completed a three-year study of middle-management retraining in the financial services industry.[36] In this industry, where the threat of obsolescence is prevalent because of changing strategic markets, business operations, and technologies, we found that older workers were generally as receptive as younger managers to retraining. But although older workers viewed retraining as relevant to their jobs and the changes in the company, they did not find it relevant to their own career progress.

Their age was not related to their motivation to learn, as they did not feel that their learning would enhance their career opportunities as much as younger people felt. Thus in addition to updating and retraining skills, older employees should have the opportunity to develop through new assignments.

Age in Various Occupations

In reviewing studies of performance in different occupations for different age groups, it is important to be aware of biases built into the performance appraisals themselves. The use of "potential" in performance appraisals often measures time remaining more than anticipated productivity or likely advancement. In addition, many of the studies are cross-sectional and do not compare the same individuals over a lifetime. It is possible that older workers who remain on the job are somehow different in their skills or interests than their age cohort who left the job. Fifty scholarly studies of age and work performance over the last two decades report no substantial overall relationships between them, with the exception of slight variations corresponding to occupation and methods of performance assessment.[37]

Many well-publicized reports from companies that have never introduced mandatory retirement and that employ workers in their seventies and eighties substantiate these findings. The president of Globe Dye Works commented, "as long as a man can produce, he can keep his job."[38] The eighty-seven-year-old president of a small General Foods subsidiary, where the average age is seventy-one, commented, "older people are steadier, accustomed to the working discipline."[39] Sales workers at Macy's and at Hartmarx have never faced mandatory retirement and show no decline in performance attributable to age. Banker's Life and Casualty proudly promotes its tradition of open-ended employment and retains top executives, clerks, and secretaries through their eighties. The company reports that these workers show more wisdom and are more helpful to others, and also have lower absenteeism, than younger workers. Polaroid and U.S. Steel have both had good experiences with older workers. Joe Perkins, the manager of retirement programs at Polaroid, commented that both performance and attendance are exemplary: "Older workers often apologize for having missed work one day three years ago because of a cold. There is a fantastic social aspect, as people look forward to coming to work." No one is shifted from job to job at Polaroid, unless the worker requests a change. Even among older workers whose jobs entail heavy demands, high performance is maintained. At Travelers Insurance Company, older workers have been so valuable that the company has been begging them to return from retirement. Of the roughly 1,100 people who have retired from the Travelers home office in Hartford over the past five years, two hundred have signed up for a job bank. On any given day, roughly one hundred of those retirees are called in to work, thereby filling over half that office's need for temporary help.

Age has surprisingly little effect on manual workers. In several studies, job performance remained steady through age fifty. After that, decline in job performance was less than 10 percent of peak performance. Attendance was not significantly affected, and the separation rate (quits, layoffs, discharges) was high for those under age twenty-five and very low for those over forty-five. Labor studies of clerical workers show more variation within age brackets than between age brackets. Generally, older workers show a steadier rate of work and accuracy than younger workers.[40] Attendance records were as good for older workers as for younger workers, and rates of turnover were lower.

Older workers seem to have superior performance in sales positions. Insurance companies, auto dealers, and large department stores regularly report that age, if a factor at all in performance, is clearly an asset.[41] Accumulated technical knowledge and interpersonal skills are most evident at this career stage. A notable exception to this trend is the older salesperson's experience in several high-technology companies. Here morale frequently plummets with length of service. These organizations often use sales as a traditional entry position for managerial development. Those employees remaining on the job over ten years begin to perceive the frustration of their personal goals of managerial development.

Studies of professionals generally concentrate on scientists and engineers. Perhaps this is because their output is relatively easy to measure. Such studies show that there are two peaks in one's performance in these fields, one at around age forty and the second at around age fifty.[42]

In managers, a relationship between age and risk taking has been found, and also a relationship between age and the value placed upon risk. A study of 1,484 managers in two hundred corporations found older managers less willing to take risks and holding lower estimates of the value of risk in general. A study of eighty lower-level decision-makers also found that older managers tended to take longer in reaching decisions and were less confident of them. However, older managers were better able to appraise the value of new information.[43]

Additional research suggests that younger managers tend to be the most autocratic, making quick decisions without consulting their coworkers, while middle-aged managers are more consultative. However, it is suggested that older managers are most efficient in that they can act as decisively as the young autocrats but take better advantage of information-gathering activities than do younger managers.[44] Thus, older managers may be more cautious and slow, but they can make firm decisions based on superior information.

Work-Intensive Occupations and Late Career

In addition to this reserve of underutilized potential in late career, many older workers maintain the drive for fulfillment through their work. For example, performers who do not submit to the discouraging pressures of age bias and charges of declining performance believe they still have more to give. Pianist Claudio Arrau commented in his eighties: "Age is biological, but psychologically when I am playing, I feel like a young man. My muscles have acquired a wisdom of their own and I think they are working better than ever."[45] Though these performers may realize that their contribution may not be immortal, and though they may be bothered that their fame may die with them, they still possess the ability to be net producers in life, and that is why they persist.

Aging artists, performers, and corporate and national leaders represent a vast array of professional skills and individual personalities. Some achieved recognition early in life; others were not successful until later. Some were gregarious and popular, while others were aloof and reclusive. Some were most creative in team settings; others have needed more solitary conditions. But though these people differ in so many fundamental ways, their late-career attitudes toward their work are surprisingly similar and present a forceful contradiction to the well-documented national trend toward early retirement.

Running counter to this powerful overall trend toward early retirement is another phenomenon. Recent research on large numbers of workers throughout the spectrum of jobs and industries suggests that occupations vary in terms of their age profiles, and the records of the Social Security Administration and the U.S. Bureau of the Census corroborate that the trend toward early retirement is not found in all jobs.[46] Some fields are sparsely populated by older workers, whereas others have a rather large population of older workers. For example, the performing arts, law, medicine, sales, and domestic service are more likely to have far higher concentrations of older people (6–16 percent) than the general work force.[47]

The National Longitudinal Survey, a fifteen-year study by the U.S. Bureau of the Census to track the retirement behavior of more than 5,000 civilian males aged forty-five to fifty-nine, found that, despite eligibility for pensions and/or social security, 18 percent stayed at their jobs after age sixty-two for at least thirty-six hours of work a week.[48] Contrary to expectations, those eligible for greater pension income and those with higher educations tended to stay on longer. Those shunning retirement were more likely to be found in agriculture, finance, and miscellaneous services, and less likely in manufacturing, transportation, and utilities.

Further insight is gained from sociological studies that indicate that occupations that reward experience, have greater job complexity, and exhibit higher rates of growth tend to have greater proportions of older workers.[49] In other words, older workers are more committed to their jobs if the reward structure, whether it be salary, hierarchical power, or public recognition, recognizes their record of achievement. Also, in industries or occupations with a fast rate of growth in opportunities, older workers feel less competitive with younger workers, and hence they are not resented as "blockers."

On the other hand, those occupations characterized by high levels of late-career exit are those requiring heavy physical exertion, quick reflexes, and manual dexterity. In these occupations, especially when the economy or the industry is contracting, older workers are often pushed out by younger workers with the carrot of early-retirement incentives.

Psychological studies have found that an individual's occupational status is a good predictor of his or her willingness to retire and prepare for exit. They also report that workers with high status—those who report greater amounts of control over their work, such as chief executives—are less willing to retire than those in the lower ranks. Chronic health problems and financial well-being are other important predictors of very early retirement. But financial, health, and even family situations have been found to have very little significant impact on the decision to not retire at the "normal age" and to continue working through late life. In addition to having control over one's work situation, research suggests that personality type and job skill obsolescence may lead to different retirement patterns. In particular, those with a "Type A" personality— that is, one characterized by aggressive, hard-driving, impatient activity and a willingness to put in long hours—are less likely to retire than the calmer "Type B."[50]

In sum, a driven personality type in a challenging job is in a "work-intensive" situation. "Work-intensives" are highly motivated people engaged in personally involving work, who reach for bold goals for life accomplishment. Because they have an inner need to *create* (not to be confused with the workaholic's external orientation to keep up), work-intensives do not greet the prospect of retirement as an escape. Instead of a reward for a lifetime of toil, retirement for these work-intensive people represents defeat and even death.

Summary on the Assets of Age

The important findings of the research reviewed in this chapter are that older workers' performances reflect a potential for decline, especially as noticed in the use of greater caution in judgment and slight drops in manual dexterity. Conversely, increased work commitment, high-quality decision-making, greater expertise, reliability, equal volume of output, and improved interpersonal skills suggest that older workers may still have a great deal to offer. Physiological and psychological deterioration associated with age can be minimized in most cases through challenging physical and mental exercise. Theories that older workers want to disengage and need to disengage may reflect the situation of some people, but certainly do not capture the sentiments or skills of all late-career workers. This theory of disengagement leads to self-fulfilling prophecies when translated into corporate personnel policies. Older people are often denied advancement opportunities and the retraining needed to revitalize skills. They are put into positions leading to obsolescence. Psychologist B. F. Skinner mentioned to me in a 1984 interview that his eighties were his most productive decade:

> This is very encouraging for my ninth decade. You have to work to shape your physical world so that you can create. If artists realize their work is getting a little too tight, they should try a new touch in what they put on the canvas and paint with a longer brush.

Conclusions

To understand the motivation of aging leaders to continue working, we must first understand the impact of age on work. Any discussion of the psychological meaning of retirement is really a discussion of the psychological meaning of work. Work provides more than financial compensation. It provides many of the same functions as family and community—namely, personal identification, group belonging, and a purpose for our efforts. For some, such as leaders, work is so important in providing such benefits that a life without work appears to be impossible. The lessons of this chapter are that retirement is not necessarily a desirable or a desired institution for all. It is largely a twentieth-century invention created for at least three reasons. First, there was increased concern over the ability of people to perform, especially given the stepped-up production technologies of this century. Second, the emphasis upon retirement grew as a way to bypass rigid minds that had become fearful of unnecessary risk. Third, there was a concern that older workers might clog vital channels of promotion and growth for

younger people. Related to this third point is the tendency, during retrenchments, to favor the young, with their longer presumed potential
future employment in the firm. Therefore, encouraging retirement allows the firm to retain valuable future resources at the expense of current talent.

These concerns all have some validity, but there are drawbacks as
well. Some jobs are better suited to an eighteen-year-old than they are
to a sixty-eight-year-old or even a thirty-eight-year-old. The reverse is
also true. Some positions benefit from the wisdom and caution of a
more experienced person. The great choreographer Martha Graham,
at age ninety-one, described the adjustment between age and occupation:

> That today is yesterday and tomorrow is today you can't stop. The body
> is your instrument in dance, but your art is outside that creation, the
> body. I don't leap or jump anymore. I look at young dancers and I am
> envious. More aware of what glories the body contains. But sensitivity is
> not made dull by age.[51]

Physical deterioration cannot be halted, but its occupational impact
can be minimized. A challenging physiological and psychological environment for older workers prevents the common self-fulfilling proph-
ecy of obsolescence. These conditions do not require older workers to
monopolize power and opportunity. Job changes through lateral moves
and demotions can sometimes help the older worker find needed new
challenges, while creating job vacancies for younger successors. Geron-
tologic research on the mind, the body, and the behavior of older workers suggests that age can be an asset. If companies atrophy, it is through
poor utilization and revitalization of resources and not because of demographic shifts.

In general, this chapter suggests that we all look more closely at the
frontier of possible contributions that can be made by the thoughtful
assignment of older workers to appropriate jobs. Individual variation in
work vitality, misplaced paternalism, and the eagerness of ambitious
younger people threaten our chances of using more imaginative methods to reinvigorate aging minds and bodies. When it comes to the leadership of our organizations, however, the problems may be quite different. In the next chapter, we will see how the situation and the psychology
of chief executives and other prominent public figures present future
complications to the special challenges of late career.

We have identified in this chapter what we call work-intensive people. These are people not merely deeply involved in their job or committed to their employers, but fully immersed in work as a way of life.
For them as for many of us, an occupation is not merely a source of
livelihood and compensation; it is more important as a symbol of accomplishment than for its ability to raise one's standard of living. For

them, as also for many of us, work provides a sense of belonging to a wider society. But to the work-intensive, work provides more than membership in society. Highly work-intensive people seek to have a profound influence in shaping their society. Whether they be leaders shaping institutions from within, or artists providing perspectives from without, their mission is to make a transcendent contribution that separates them from their "mortal" peers. Through their work, they reach for an immortal legacy. This is why psychologist Otto Rank grouped artists and leaders together as heroic figures.[52]

For work-intensives, work provides a sense of purpose in life. They live to work instead of working to live. Unlike workaholics, who are afraid of falling behind others, work-intensives do not feel compulsively driven to meet the expectations of others and do not fear others' expectations and accomplishments. Instead, they have an inner drive to excel and to stand apart from others through the magnificence of their contribution. Rank pointed out how even seemingly socially isolated artists chose to work in the prevailing medium of their culture, whether it was paint, clay, stone, musical instruments, unusual styles of composition, musical styles, or film, because they intended to influence that culture. In the same way, work-intensives want to be different from their mortal peers by making a lasting contribution. According to seventy-two-year-old painter Robert Motherwell:

> One wonderful thing about creativity is that you're never wholly satisfied with what you're trying to do. There's always the anguish, the pleasure-able challenge. For me to retire from painting would be to retire from life.[53]

This quest for lasting impact is so compelling that it is difficult to know whether it has been attained when retirement, whether "early" or "on time," motivates the work-intensive to fight the implied threat to his or her life's mission.

3

EXECUTIVE RETIREMENT AND THE PARADE OF FUTURE LEADERS

We are the music-makers,
    And we are the dreamers of dreams,
Wandering by lone sea-breakers,
    And sitting by desolate streams;
World-losers and world-forsakers,
    On whom the pale moon gleams:
Yet we are the movers and shakers,
    of the world for ever, it seems. . . .
One man with a dream, at pleasure,
    Shall go forth and conquer a crown;
And three with a new song's measure
    Can trample an empire down. . . .
For each age is a dream that is dying,
    Or one that is coming to birth.

Arthur William Edgar O'Shaughnessy

When older top executives are confronted with retirement, their reaction results more from how they feel about themselves than from their perception of their jobs.[1] Those who feel young, healthy, and effective are most likely to continue working later in life. The reluctance of chief executives to leave office may be misunderstood in the light of their specific occupational and psychological qualities. The job is generally characterized by officeholders as attractive and enjoyable, albeit wearing. The hours are long, the demands are exhausting, and many life sacrifices must be made in the climb to the top. Nonetheless, as with the work-intensives in the last chapter, most research indicates that the chief executive job is a source of great satisfaction for those who attain it.

Unlike the pride of accomplishment of a mountain climber, however, satisfaction for the chief executive is not solely in the quest for the peak. Instead, it is the fundamental tasks of the job after arrival that are gratifying. In a recent survey of 237 chief executives conducted by the Conference Board, the respondents reported satisfaction in seeing the growth of subordinates and in playing a significant role in the strategy and performance of their companies.[2] These chief executives, whether of small firms (under 1,000 employees), medium-sized firms (1,000–15,000 employees), or large firms (15,000 employees and more), expressed astounding exhilaration with the everyday "fun" of the job. They were hard-pressed to elaborate on any pains and frustrations beyond government-imposed barriers, paperwork, executive succession, and overly dependent personnel.

This study, as well as others by the American Management Association, by Gordon Donaldson and Jay Lorsch of the Harvard Business School, and by executive recruiters Korn/Ferry International, also indicates that people seek the chief executive position and choose to remain in it for reasons far more compelling than financial reward.[3] In fact, the 1985 Korn/Ferry survey of 1,362 top executives of *Fortune* 1000 firms (500 manufacturing and 500 service) found that fewer than 10 percent of the senior executives surveyed included increased compensation as a stated reason for changing employers. Instead, most reported changing employers for increased responsibility and increased challenge. The Conference Board's survey of current CEOs also found that most cited "challenge" as the primary reason for seeking this top job.

Although most chief executives report working close to sixty hours per week on average and taking fewer than two weeks' vacation in the course of the year, this does not extinguish their enthusiasm for the work. Recent stress research suggests that strain from the high psychological demands of top executive positions may be ameliorated by the increased discretion or "high decision control" intrinsic to the job. Public health researchers who studied 5,000 workers found that strain is reduced in those occupations where individuals can translate energy into action. It is possible that those workers with high psychological demands placed on them but with little control accumulate excess adrenaline. Bosses, this research concludes, may experience less stress than their subordinates.[4]

Thus, we can view the job of chief executive as an attractive one. Those who hold the position generally enjoy their work. Those one step down from the chief executive aspire for the top job. Only a third of senior executives are content not to reach the chief executive's job.

What are the characteristics of individuals who hold these desirable jobs? Those interviewed report having worked a lifetime to reach the position, and most describe long hours, hard work, functional skills, and the readiness to take advantage of chance opportunities as their prominent features according to data collected by the Conference Board, the American Management Association, and Korn/Ferry, and reported in scholarly psychological studies of chief executives.

One intensive study of six prominent chief executives by psychoanalysts Harry Levinson and Stuart Rosenthal concluded that these individuals have a very strong self-image and an "ego ideal" toward which they strive.[5] In other words, they work to close a gap between how they see themselves in actuality and how they would like to see themselves. In their research on top corporate decision-makers, Gordon Donaldson and Jay Lorsch found among chief executives an especially strong drive to excel.[6] The executives themselves often describe this drive in strongly emotional and competitive terms, comparing themselves to chief executives, peers, and friends at other firms. They also often sized themselves up in relation to the accomplishments of leaders they did not personally know. One CEO complained that merely picking up a newspaper and seeing a report on a competitor getting bigger was enough to drive him into a rage.

Another characteristic of chief executives emerges from a recent psychological study of 171 *Fortune* 500 chief executives, which found an extremely high incidence of Type A behavior among them.[7] The Type A behavior pattern is an action-emotion complex observable in people who are aggressively involved in a constant struggle to achieve more and more in less and less time. Though this may suggest a potential for the accumulation of great stress among U.S. top executives, it is interesting that Japanese chief executives score lower on measures of Type A behavior, but higher than U.S. executives on stress. The highly competitive and ambitious U.S. chief executive apparently has an easier time discharging tension than his or her Japanese counterpart. Perhaps Japanese cultural norms favoring group control over individual control are frustrating to Japanese chief executives. Not surprisingly, U.S. chief executives report significantly higher job satisfaction and a greater sense of accomplishment than Japanese chief executives, perhaps because the U.S. chief executives feel more able to exert their individual judgment and to attempt new methods.

The chief executives' characteristic drive to excel and to continually reach new heights makes it hard for them to contemplate retirement. These people enjoy their work, feel they have much to offer, and often reset their goals for even greater accomplishment as they age. A Conference Board survey suggests that chief executives with less than a decade of service may feel that they have had less than an optimal tenure.[8] In fact, the younger the chief executive, the longer his or her optimum time in office seems to be.

A Korn/Ferry survey of 1,362 top executives reported that fully 16 percent intend never to retire.[9] A striking example is Armand Hammer, still running Occidental Petroleum at the age of ninety. Hammer has denied any plans to retire: "I'm in excellent health. There's no reason for me to retire."[10] His daily swim and steady globe-trotting might almost convince him of his immortality.

Such leaders see nothing attractive in retirement and much to avoid. In interviews and surveys they often mention how retired leaders of giant firms had become shrunken men soon after leaving office. In contemplating their own retirement, they see only losses: loss of power; loss of attention; and loss of a life mission.

In my own survey of one hundred recently retired chief executives, I found a pronounced resistance to the very term "retirement," which seemed to carry a connotation of a retreat from the boardroom to the golf course. In fact, retirement as an opportunity for recreation was rarely mentioned. Most chief executives were extremely reluctant to walk away from a successful career. As work-intensive, ambitious seekers of challenge with a great deal of control over their work conditions, they did not eagerly anticipate their own exit. This finding is presented in Table 3.1. Parts A and B of Table 3.1 note significant differences between attitudes of chief executives toward retirement and those of the rest of the senior management team.

In Part A, we see that the top leaders were far less interested in even contemplating the end of their reigns than were other senior managers. They preferred not to discuss retirement and avoided planning for it. In Part B, we see that chief executives were more likely to retire as a response to company pressure than from their own volition. Other officers, however, were more likely to retire as an escape from the job, to "take life easier," and to respond to the attraction of other activities. Part C of the table presents impressive evidence that chief executives are far less willing to sever ties with the firm than are other senior managers. Seventy-two percent of CEOs, as compared to 9 percent of senior managers, for instance, remained on the board of directors. Also, 52 percent, as compared to 5 percent of other managers, retained a formal position in the firm, and 57 percent, as compared to 23 percent, maintained an office in company headquarters for at least two years. Chief executives were also more likely to be influenced by the manner in which their predecessors retired.

Finally, once they left office, the chief executive and his top officer corps seemed to experience retirement quite differently. Chief executives tended to stay active in organizations, causes, and firms in need of their expertise. The other top executives tended to be tired and slightly more interested in recreation and relaxation.

The Tensions of Approaching Retirement

As top leaders face a decision on retirement, conflicts and tensions arise within themselves and with others in their organizations. For a corporate officer, retirement is especially difficult, for as visionaries, business leaders are identified with the plans of the institution that they led.

Table 3.1 Retirement Behavior of Chief Executives Compared with Other Senior Managers

	Chief Executives (%)	Senior Managers (%)
A. *Retirement Planning*		
Did not prepare at all for retirement[a]	30	16
Developed personal financial plans	47	74
Solicited advice on retirement from friends[a]	4	14
Earlier preparations would have been helpful[b]	31	9
Should have identified successor sooner[b]	22	6
B. *Retirement Timing*		
Left office because of company tradition[b]	22	6
Left office to provide opportunity for younger executives[c]	56	20
Left office to take life easier[a]	12	28
Left office because of loss of pleasure in jobs[a]	12	19
Left office for activities outside the firm[c]	25	60
C. *Continued Company Contact after Retirement*		
Continued to hold a formal position[d]	52	5
Remained on board of directors[d]	72	9
Left board immediately on retirement[d]	12	59
Kept office in company headquarters for 2 years[d]	57	23
Left office immediately on retirement[d]	36	73
Continued to seek to represent firm externally[a]	26	12
Followed example of predecessor[a]	32	7
Followed example of outside leader[a]	17	0
Influenced by prominent leaders' poor examples[a]	30	48
D. *Outside Involvement after Retirement*		
More time for family and friends[a]	25	48
Declined corporate boards[c]	61	27
Declined public office[a]	28	17
Declined opportunities due to lack of interest[a]	15	32
Declined opportunities due to burnout exhaustion[a]	5	20
Tough times characterized by boredom[a]	10	1
Miss being in center of attention[a]	21	9
Now experience less pressure or stress (NS)	22	33
More time for recreational activities[a]	28	40
More time for civic activities[a]	40	22

[a]Significant at p<.05.   [d]Significant at p<.00001.
[b]Significant at p<.01.   NS = Not Significant
[c]Significant at p<.001.

Their departure from the institution involves more than their own personal fate; it involves the fate of the firm itself. A determined aging leader, desperately clinging onto the throne, may deny other potential leaders their future, as well as prevent society from experiencing alternative leaders. A leader who frustrates the goals of followers will lose the support of those followers, and hence, the legitimacy of his or her position and the goals of the firm he or she led.

For every corporate leader, the years of power and prestige must ultimately end, which is why it is every bit as important to understand the leader's style of departure as his or her rise to power and the qualities of his or her "reign." The decision to retire affects not only the individual leader, but also the relations between successors on lower rungs of the hierarchical ladder and the larger community to whom the leader feels a responsibility. Thus, the departure of leaders involves three sets of tensions: (1) those within the leader, (2) those across generations of leaders, and (3) those between leaders and the wider community.

Tensions Within the Leader: The Personal Retirement Decision

There are many examples of reluctance to give in to old age among corporate leaders: Armand Hammer of Occidental Petroleum is ninety years old; seventy-five-year-old William Norris ran Control Data for twenty-nine years; J. Peter Grace of W. R. Grace is seventy-four; Florence Eiseman oversaw the manufacture of the stylish clothing bearing her name from 1931 until her death in 1988 at the age of eighty-five. The empire builder Cyrus Eaton died at age ninety-five as the chairman of the Chesapeake and Ohio Railroad, Cleveland-Cliffes Iron Company, the Kansas City Power and Light Company, and the Sherwin-Williams Company, owner and operator of two large cattle farms, and a fellow of the American Academy of Arts and Sciences.

Another long-tenured chief executive, Justin W. Dart, who built Dart Industries, a diversified consumer products and chemical company, out of the struggling drugstore chain United-Rexall Drugs, announced at age seventy-two, "I want my death and my retirement to be simultaneous."[11] Three years later, after having merged his company with Kraft Inc., and while serving as chairman of the new corporation's executive committee, he died.

At age seventy, Ben W. Heineman, the chairman of Northwest Industries, shelved his initial retirement plans to perform a major corporate overhaul. "I'm not ready to retire from life," he explained. "I'm not going to sit around with a blanket over my knees."[12] Two years later, still with no clear successor identified, his company was acquired by Chicago investor William F. Farley.

In these examples, we see the fierce spirit of determination in highly prominent people not to abdicate their earned positions while they are alive and their health is still strong. Like many public figures, business leaders can become almost addicted to their energizing prominence and influence. Thus we see many resisting retirement.

But the personal dilemma older leaders face—to hold on or to quit— is fraught with dangers on both sides. Those who choose to hold on claim that they maintain their strength and energy through continued performance and thus benefit both themselves and the firm. Those who choose to retire claim they either want to maintain the reputation built in their prime or desire to put the interests of succeeding generations of leaders and those of the community above their own interests.

Whichever course they take, leaders must meet the organization's need for a sustaining vision. Whichever course is chosen—maintaining performance or maintaining a reputation—both are avenues to individual immortality through the organizational legacy.

Tensions Across Generations of Leaders: Opportunities for Successors

Psychoanalytic theorist Daniel Levinson has argued that business leaders remaining in the firm over age sixty-five retard the development of future leaders. Levinson thought the late-aged executive should leave office, stating:

> If he [remains in office] . . . he is "out of phase" with his own generation, and he is in conflict with the generation of middle adulthood who need to assume greater responsibilities. . . .
> [Even] when a man has a high level of energy and skill he is ill-advised to retain power into late adulthood. He tends to be an isolated leader in poor touch with his followers . . . or hated by them. The continuity of the generations is disrupted.[13]

The isolated and disgruntled leader can sabotage his firm's own executive development programs, especially by reasoning that, if the company's mission no longer includes the fulfillment of his own dreams, why work to fulfill the collective dreams of the company? A boss filled with despair over his or her fading career may be a destructive mentor. Resenting his own lost opportunity, he might neglect to cultivate new leaders, whom he regards as potential threats, and discourage training others for longer term goals by putting a greater emphasis on immediate performance. Such bosses signal subordinates to meet today's performance and leave career dreaming for later. They dismiss initiative as foolish naïveté and view ambition as opportunism.

When this happens in a firm, it is often interpreted by the lower ranks as selfishness and stodginess, with the unfortunate result that vast reservoirs of accumulated wisdom remain untapped as the young seek to bypass those who obstruct the free flow of the career stream. Older supervisors are viewed as impediments, not as experts, and intergenerational hostility intensifies as the manager realizes that he or she is perceived as merely a blocker of the careers of others. A common response is to intensify the campaign to prove one's centrality and ensure survival, thus perpetuating the cycle.

This tension between generations leads to a discovery by all age groups that hard work and commitment do not always guarantee the rewards anticipated. As each group blames the other for overlooking its accomplishments, intergenerational scapegoating may result, which will be fueled even further by the career frustrations of the younger generation.

Tensions Between the Leader and the Firm: A Succession of Heroes

The firm, as a community, is led by a parade of leaders, who can be viewed as a procession of passing generations, each displaying its finest efforts as it marches past the reviewing stand. As it ages, a particular generation's performance has less fervor, and in time it seems to be no more than a stale, rehearsed routine, at which point the baton passes to the leader of the succeeding generation. Each new leader inspires his own generation with his visions of glory as he implements his strategies, sets the pace of the organization, and institutes plans for continuity of leadership.

What lessons can be found in the exit of a departing leader? The manner and circumstances of departure affect the continuity of achievements, the respect held for the leader's accumulated experience and wisdom, the quality of succeeding executive management, and the degree of trust and harmony among the work force. A smooth transition, where the leader is treated fairly and honorably, instills loyalty among the firm's workers; a rocky one gives rise to uneasiness and distrust.

Unfortunately, the parade of leaders through firms is not inherently smooth. Conflicts of interest abound. Having spent years promoting the company's interest, the departing leader desires to impart the lessons learned to his or her successor and to make sure the successor will be able to carry through ongoing projects. The leader wants the option of training that successor, of timing his or her own exit, and of enjoying a sense of fulfillment. But such ambitions are often thwarted when departing leaders, treated with impatience and resentment by their peers, must accelerate their termination.

Corporate leaders, like other public figures, have difficulty retiring, because it means the loss of an audience upon whom they have come to rely. Furthermore, leaders enjoy public influence, including the public's acceptance of their visions for the future prosperity of the corporate community. Rejection by the community can affect a retiring leader's self-esteem.

Business leader Siegmund Warburg warned that corporate officers have even more compelling reasons to leave the stage than do other public figures. The founder of S. G. Warburg and Co., a prominent merchant banking firm, Warburg declared that he wanted to retire before his doctor said he must. After beginning his career at Rothschild & Sons in London, he trained in Boston with Lybrand, Ross, Montgomery and in New York with Kuhn & Co. In 1930 he opened the Berlin office of M. M. Warburg. Four years later, he fled the Nazi rampage, and, with less than $5,000 to his name, he rebuilt in London the old Warburg firm confiscated by the Nazi government. Yet, on reaching age sixty-three in 1963, Warburg felt that the organization should regard him as dispensable:

> Leaders in industry and finance are often inclined not to step down before the decline of their capabilities becomes manifest, holding on too long to their positions and thus preventing the formation of a strong chain of potential successors. . . . I am convinced that stepping down will not weaken, but on the contrary, will strengthen our group.[14]

Corporate leaders who leave office positively and enthusiastically may meet both their personal needs for renewal and the needs of their firm and society.

4

CORPORATE FOLK HEROES: LIVING LEGENDS OR BUSINESS CHEERLEADERS?

The metamorphosis of his reputation from didactic writer for boys to Progressive moralist, economic mythmaker, and finally political idealogue—seems to have been dictated less by the content of his books than by the context in which the books were read or remembered.

The Lost Life of Horatio Alger,
Gary Scharnhost and Jack Bales

There is a parallel between the folk hero of literature and the modern-day work-intensive corporate leader. Both pursue their "mission" in life (or would like to) until their deaths. In the novel *Lonesome Dove,* two retired Texas Rangers, folk heroes of the late 1870s, drift aimlessly across the disappearing frontier in search of a lost purpose. When an opportunity arises to lead an epic cattle drive to Montana, their self-pity evaporates with their perspiration, and with career renewal comes the pride in themselves and their public image as they rediscover the courage, loyalty, and strength needed to survive the trip and regain their heroic standing.[1]

In the same way, the prospect of retirement means a loss of a heroic public identity for the work-intensive corporate leader. Empty and unsure of his or her future private identity, like the lonesome out-of-work cowboy, each holds on tightly to the reigns of power. The industrialist Henry Ford, for instance, was in many ways an authentic folk hero. Born into the modest home of Irish immigrant farmers, he was a self-made success and a relentless efficiency expert who used cost-saving mass-production techniques to bring automobile purchases within the price range of the average American. With the encouragement of Thomas Edison, another industrialist who fits the folk hero description, Ford brought America into a new automobile age. Both his introduction of the Model A automobile in 1903 and his benevolent, paternalistic labor practices made this industrialist a national legend. And true to form, when it came time to retire, Ford, like the folk hero who dies with his boots on, stoutly resisted his own demise.[2]

In this chapter, I will develop the argument that corporate leaders should be seen as folk heroes. Some critics have held that the image of corporate leaders as folk heroes is only the result of empty corporate public relations campaigns which sell unconvincing puffery and empty myths. In their view, chief executives are colorless, anonymous bureaucrats with limited power. I challenge this school of thought and will explore the "heroic" activities of modern-day chief executives, their role in concrete decision-making, and their symbolic representations of corporate leadership. After establishing that chief executives may, at the least, serve heroic roles within the cultures of their own firms, I will consider the powerful tradition of heroes in American culture from the cornfield to the battlefield, arriving eventually at the door of the executive suite. Finally, I will discuss five personal qualities common to American business heroes and how they satisfy society's thirst for such heroism.

Corporate Heroes or Empty Legends?

Before looking at their difficulties in exiting, we should first consider why we should even care about who fills the chief executive's office. Books and articles about corporate events often portray complex corporate processes as the consequences of one individual's decisions. According to Ralph Waldo Emerson, "An institution is the lengthened shadow of one man."[3] Certainly the "great man" view of history has been applied to the corporate world by recent writings of management enthusiasts.

But others feel that perhaps the accumulated power of a single person, whether a corporate chieftain or national leader, is overstated, and that the "great man" theory oversimplifies the underlying institutional complexities that shape society. It has been suggested that we create the myth of powerful individuals to provide us with the illusion that we can fully understand and influence abstract forces.

Who runs American business? Some critics charge that, rather than being strong-willed, colorful, hands-on captains of industry in the executive suites, business leaders are actually "faceless oligarchs" who administer efficient corporate bureaucracies. This is the view according to Robert Reich:

> There is an overwhelming tendency in American life either to lionize or pillory the people who stand at the helms of our large institutions—to offer praise or level blame for outcomes over which they may have little control. This tendency is particularly apparent in regard to the performance of large corporations, whose legitimacy in our political and economic system continues to be an open question. The current infatuation with successful CEOs offers an illustration. The unfortunate result is that we are distracted from deeper questions about the organization of our economic system. In personalizing these exciting tales, we overlook much bigger stories.[4]

Reich believes that the dynamic chief executive profiles presented in such books as *Iacocca, Managing,* and *In Search of Excellence* are misleading. He argues that most chief executives are dull, hardworking negotiators whose public pronouncements are largely ignored.

John Kenneth Galbraith supports this view that the leaders of today's corporations are anonymous bureaucrats. As evidence of this belief, he points out that since the disappearance of the charismatic tycoon of the nineteenth and early twentieth centuries, the stock market reacts with refined indifference to the passing of command in the great corporations.[5] The modern business executive, according to Galbraith, may present his ideas to a wide variety of groups, but his or her statements are rarely attended to and are merely the bland and measured words of the organization he or she leads, not its leader. Galbraith views the concept of powerful individual executives as a social invention.

This school of thought, which I will challenge later, can be traced back to economist Joseph Schumpeter's prediction in 1942 that capitalism's very success would create the seeds of its own destruction. The evolution of innovative entrepreneurships into stable bureaucracies, Schumpeter argued, would virtually replace innovation with routine, as the irresistible drift toward bureaucracy bulldozed individual initiative and leveled the impact of individual destinies. Earlier, the German sociologist Max Weber had predicted that executive charisma would eventually be routinized into rational economic organization.[6]

Such skepticism about the impact of top executives can be found among two management theory schools of thought currently in vogue. Both minimize the role of executive discretion. One, the "population ecology" school, suggests that organizations survive through a process of random natural selection. Thus the current character of firms is thought to represent those conditions existing at the time of their inception that have survived trials for fitness.[7] A second group of management scholars, the "resource dependent school," suggests that firms change over time, but not as a result of management initiative. The firms' changing strategies are largely a response to such external forces as the availability of supplies, changes in markets, and legal regulation.[8]

And outside the economic world, there are those who wish to debunk the theory of the powerful leader changing history. Novelist Leo Tolstoy had battled with the romantic notion of great men in history as propounded by such novelist peers as Alexander Dumas and Walter Scott. In Tolstoy's classic *War and Peace,* he attacked the personality worship of leaders:[9]

> In historical chronicles, the so-called great men are mere labels used to designate events but having no closer relation to them than labels do. (Volume I, Book IX, Chapter 1)

> The king is history's slave. (Volume II, Book IX, Chapter 1)

> Throughout the entire period, Napoleon was like a child holding a pair of ribbons attached to the inside of a coach and imagining that he is driving the horses. (Volume II, Book XIII, Chapter 10)

> The history-book hero does not command the masses; he is constantly commanded by them. (Volume II, Book XIII, Chapter 1)

Tolstoy intended to debunk idol-makers and remind his audience of the role of the unsung warriors, forgotten by history, as well as the impact of situations and events outside the leaders' power. But he, like the aforementioned more recent political economists, neglected the significance of the leader as a source of inspiration for the anonymous warriors and as a catalyst for social change through symbolic as well as real attributes.

Entrepreneurial Leaders or Bureaucratic Managers?

Both the Schumpeter thesis and the more recent theories of Galbraith and Reich overlook important factors. First, it is clear that capitalism has not been destroyed by its own success through the process of stultifying bureaucratization. Older firms are often capable of renewal through innovative, turnaround management. Examples include IBM, Xerox, and Polaroid, where vital and dynamic men who took control of long-established, atrophying firms made disproportionately large contributions to the development of new technology.

Furthermore, new enterprises continue to appear and challenge the dominance of existing ones. We have only to look at such *Fortune* 500 manufacturing and service firms as Digital Equipment, Wang Laboratories, Hewlett Packard, Apple Computer, Control Data, Intel, Dunkin' Donuts, Texas Air, Hospital Corporation of America, Capital Cities/ABC,

Wal-Mart, and The Limited to appreciate that new entrepreneurs can join the ranks of major U.S. firms while still under the reign of their founders. When Armand Hammer took charge of Occidental Petroleum in 1957, it had three employees and a net worth of $34,000. It now ranks nineteenth on the *Fortune* 500 list of leading firms. In 1986, *Fortune* described Digital Equipment founder Ken Olsen as "the most successful entrepreneur in the history of American business," having taken his firm from no assets to a net worth of $7.6 billion in three decades.[10] *Fortune* pointed out that even allowing for inflation, Digital's growth under Olsen exceeded that of Henry Ford's automobile company, Andrew Carnegie's steel company, and John D. Rockefeller's oil company. In another instance of a new entrepreneur rising to power in recent decades, Sam Walton, the founder of Wal-Mart stores, had amassed a larger fortune than any other entrepreneur, owning $4.7 billion in his firm's stock, before losing $1 billion in the crash of October 1987.

Entrepreneurs Olsen, Walton, and Hammer, along with Edwin Land of Polaroid, H. Ross Perot of Electronic Data Systems, An Wang of Wang Laboratories, Mitch Kapor of Lotus, Frank Lorenzo of Texas Air, and Steve Jobs of Apple Computer, serve as ready reminders of the inaccuracy of Schumpeter's prediction of the death of entrepreneurship.

Another factor overlooked by Schumpeter, Reich, and Galbraith is that innovative leaders can appear from within large bureaucracies. Those whom Galbraith regards as colorless organization men are viewed by some historians as "managerial capitalists."[11] Managerial capitalists, in contrast to the financial capitalists who preceded them, were neither founders nor controlling owners in the institutions they led, but that did not prevent them from having a major impact on their companies' future and on business in general. For instance, Alfred P. Sloan, Jr.'s imaginative and successful overhaul of General Motors in the 1920s brought this firm to industrial dominance, and Sloan's transformation of GM was a model for many other firms, even though Sloan was not the entrepreneur who built the company and never had a controlling interest in it. William C. Durant had formed the company in 1908, but he provided little central authority over his sprawling auto empire and lost control of it to debt holders such as Pierre du Pont.[12]

Three other prominent examples of such leaders appearing within established companies deserve to be mentioned. Theodore Vail, a powerful and brilliant capitalist, joined the Postal Service in 1868 as a telegraph operator and was so successful in improving operations and routing that by 1876, at age thirty, he was made general superintendent of the U.S. Rail Mail Service.[13] Vail then took charge of AT&T, transforming this enterprise through his support of patent-protected research, acceptance and encouragement of regulation of long-distance lines, stock ownership of operating phone companies, and licensing of phone and switchboard equipment. His concept of the firm largely shaped its destiny from 1900 through the 1970s. Another managerial capitalist, Robert Wood, left Montgomery Ward, which did not appreciate his strategic vision, to lead rival firm Sears, Roebuck in the late 1920s into its highly successful department store business. Yet another example, Thomas Watson, Sr., of IBM, neither founded nor owned a controlling interest in the firm he led to international greatness. The company was founded in 1884 by Herman Hollerith, who patented the automatic punch-card tabulating machine. Watson joined the firm in 1914 and led it for the next forty-two years.

Such great industrial enterprises as IBM, AT&T, Sears, and General Motors have suffered difficulties over the years. However, their days of greatest glory were not under the reign of the founding entrepreneurs, but under the professional managers disparaged by Schumpeter, Galbraith, and Reich.

By the mid-twentieth century in America, salaried top managers of large mass-retailing, mass-manufacturing, and mass-transportation enterprises directed the flow of goods and services from production to the ultimate destination, the consumers. A managerial caste as such did not exist before this time, but the new technologies and expanding markets called for enhanced administrative expertise and leadership vision.[14] According to business historian Harold Livesay:

> Bureaucracy, I think, has not inevitably obliterated the entrepreneurial spirit necessary to the maintenance of capitalist business systems. In the hands of the right protagonists, it has become an instrument to cope with the complexities of doing business in the modern world. Bureaucracy thus has not inevitably become the nemesis of the entrepreneur: it has rather become a necessary tool of his trade. Enough individuals capable of turning bureaucracy to their own purposes continue to emerge to provide capitalism with a constant source of regeneration, confounding the expectations of Marx, Weber, Schumpeter, and others.[15]

Both sociologist Rosabeth Kanter and management expert Peter Drucker concur that innovation and dynamism are possible in virtually all large modern enterprises.[16]

It seems perverse, indeed, to argue that the individual who can harness and direct the might of a large bureaucracy so that it enhances rather than smothers individual will, whether he creates his own firm or rehabilitates one that already exists, is not in the tradition of the original captains of industry. The observer who doubts the potential of individual leaders to affect the fate of entire firms has only to consider how top executives like Thomas Watson at IBM and Robert Wood at Sears, Roebuck affected those giant enterprises.

Even the stock market recognizes the impact a chief executive can have. Far from reacting with refined indifference to the passage of command in the great corporation, as Galbraith has charged, the stock market is very sensitive to changes in the highest ranks of corporate America. Researchers Stewart D. Friedman and Harbir Singh of the Wharton School at the University of Pennsylvania studied the stock market prices of a number of companies from four hundred days before CEO succession announcements to eight hundred days afterward. They also looked at published indications of the reasons for the chief executives' departures, later contact between the firms and the outgoing chief executives, and the sources from which the new chief executives were chosen. They found that when a chief executive was forced out of office because of poor firm performance, the company's stock rose at the time of his exit. Stock price was not affected, however, when the succession was a routine, planned retirement. In short, the information about the change of individuals in command was sufficient to influence investor decisions.[17]

Political Leadership and the Management of Symbols

Another charge of the critics is that the role of the chief executive is largely symbolic. Top managers, in their view, deal with sentiments, not substance. Such management writers suggest, much like Tolstoy's view of Napoleon, that substantive corporate action is principally the result of external factors rather than of executive vision.

I believe a more accurate view of the chief executive's role is that it combines both symbolic aspects and actual power. In his pathbreaking study *Presidential Power,* Richard Neustadt suggested that even the power of the U.S. presidency is both symbolic and actual—the president is both visionary leader and day-to-day administrator.[18] Neustadt sees the ability of a president to use persuasion to influence action as at least as important as the ability to exercise power through overt command.

Management scholar Joseph L. Bower found that the chief executive uses his symbolic power to persuade, along with his actual power to command, in order to initiate action.[19] This common characteristic of both political and business leaders was pointed out by former Schlumberger chief executive Jean Riboud when he stated that "running a company is like politics, you are always balancing interests and personalities and trying to keep people motivated."[20] Management scholar Philip Selznick labeled this symbolic leadership function "institutionalization," whereby a firm's values are infused through the leader's efforts to navigate the firm beyond immediate tasks toward larger common purposes.[21]

Symbolism Versus "Substance"

Although a chief executive's influence is not merely symbolic, truly powerful leaders rely heavily on the prestige and clout of their office to rule. For over fifty years, both academicians and chief executives have emphasized the importance of the symbolic functions of leadership.[22] Yet the chief executive who gets things done because he is a cultural symbol with political dependencies is almost always one who also rules by substantive action. His role is to interpret the organization's context for its members in order to create a shared meaning of action, and he does this by using both his symbolic power and his substantive power.

One of the first researchers to identify the symbolic and substantive roles that managers must master, researcher Henry Mintzberg, has pointed out that the chief executive must act out such roles as figurehead, liaison, spokesperson, resource allocator, and negotiator.[23] And often he is flexible, innovative, and nontraditional in the techniques he uses to attain his goals. Leadership expert John Kotter has found, for instance, that rather than relying upon the formal chain of command, top executives often tend to create informal networks to gather information across hierarchies and to continuously reorder priorities as the agenda changes. The overt issuing of formal orders to initiate executive decisions was rarely observed in those he interviewed; conversation was the main vehicle for persuasion and change.[24] Other researchers of management styles have also found that top executives place a great reliance upon political coalition-building and personal networks, and that it is first-line supervisors and middle managers who are more concerned with the traditional management activities of coordination, planning, and decision-making.[25]

Thus most chief executives are not rugged autocrats who pound their fists and command results. Instead they rely upon many forms of executive action beyond the channels of formal authority to strengthen their actual power. For them, the symbolic actions are the substantive tools of leadership. The chief executive, though he or she may be the leader of a formal bureaucracy and tied to a limited bureaucratic role, operates, as we shall see, as the reigning hero of the corporate culture. In this role, he or she embodies the spirit and values that provide others with a sense of collective purpose and group membership.

Kotter, Mintzberg, and others have described the specific activities that top executives follow to circumvent their own bureaucracies. Organizational theorist Edgar H. Schein has described how the consequences of such managerial behaviors shape the underlying culture of a firm.[26] Leaders shape corporate culture by: (1) what they pay attention to through measurement and control; (2) how they react to specific incidents and crises; (3) their recruitment, selection, promotion, and dismissal policies; (4) the overt authority structures and flow of information they establish; (5) the design of the physical space they administer (e.g., building architecture and office layout); (6) their creation or circulation of stories, legends, and myths that convey the firm's core values; and (7) their formal statements of company philosophy.

The leader's personality is often identified with the firm's collective personality. But it is not only positive qualities of personality and style that are imprinted on a corporation. Researchers Manfred Kets deVries and Danny Miller have found that the personification of the chief executive's charisma by a firm's culture can lead to the institutionalization of dysfunctional personality styles (e.g., paranoid-persecuted, defensive-depressive, compulsive-ritualistic, dramatic-impulsive, schizoid-politicized) of the chief executive by the entire firm.[27] This tends to happen in those cases where the chief executive's personality type is more extreme and where the firm is highly centralized. Several other studies of the psychodynamics of leaders, conducted by such noted psychoanalysts as Abraham Zaleznik, Harry Levinson, Michael Maccoby, and Elliot Jacques, have consistently demonstrated the profound impact of the defensive behaviors of a leader upon the culture of the entire organization.[28]

Whether chief executives have founded a new company, transformed an existing enterprise, or maintained the firm's momentum, their individual imprint on the culture is felt in both real and symbolic terms within the company.

I submit, then, that the chief executive is a hero within his own corporation, for he is capable of creating or transforming the firm's strategic purpose while shaping the culture of the membership.

Legendary American Heroes

There is a corporate heroism that can transcend the corporation itself. In our time, we have seen the emergence of corporate leaders as folk heroes. American society has long balanced admiration and fear when considering business leaders. Folk heroes serve as a barometer of the social aspirations and expectations of individuals in society. In different periods of American history, different heroes have reflected these aspirations and expectations.

The anthropologist Richard Dorson and the historian Dixon Wector have each related social aspirations in different periods of American history to the kinds of figures who became heroes to their contemporaries.[29] During the colonial period, the nation took as its heroes George Washington, Thomas Jefferson, and Benjamin Franklin, men who were identified with the emerging republic. In the early national period, there was a move toward the common man, personified by actual or fictitious figures such as Daniel Boone, Kit Carson, Davy Crockett, and Mose the Bowery B'hoy. In Dorson's words:

> My view is that they were indeed the cherished popular folk heroes of the young American nation, catching perfectly the brash humor and daredevil impudence of the Jacksonian period, yet comparable to the legendary creation in other cultures. A case can be made . . . for Crockett as an Heroic Age Champion, the blood-brother to Achilles, Siegfried, Grettir, Cuchulain, Arjun, and Antar even though in the United States the conditions of Heroic society and the bardic reworking of the oral legends were enormously compressed and condensed.[30]

During the later national period there was a persistence of admiration for rugged individuals such as William Cody (Buffalo Bill), Sam Bass, and the legendary Paul Bunyan. Dorson suggests that both the values and conditions of the lumberjacks echo those of the cowboys as prerequisites for an American folk hero. He says:

> Both are sturdy individualists belonging to a golden age, roughly 1870–1900, when their skills and *machismo*, on range and trail for one and in the woods and on rivers for the other, contributed indispensably to the early success of the cattle and lumber industries.[31]

But a new breed of heroes also emerged in the later national period. It included figures who combined inventive talents with business acumen. Among these were Samuel F. B. Morse, Alexander Graham Bell, Luther Burbank, the Wright brothers, Henry Ford, and Thomas Edison. Of the last, Dixon Wector has said:

> The inventive vein that ran through Franklin and Jefferson and Lincoln, but was submerged by public duties, bubbled to the surface in the industrial age, and in the person of Edison, shot skyward like a geyser of spectacular achievement.[32]

Still later in this period, in response to the crises of the Depression and World War II, America's thirst for heroes was quenched by figures like President Franklin D. Roosevelt, and generals George C. Marshall, Omar Bradley, Douglas MacArthur, and Dwight D. Eisenhower, who was both a general and a political leader.

In the contemporary period, in the midst of the tragic domestic and international consequences of the Vietnam War and the highly publicized Watergate political scandals, political leadership lost its heroic mantle. The major periodicals carried cover stories on the "Vanishing American Hero."[33] Statesmen were no longer cast in the traditional heroic mold. It was a period without heroes.

In what we might call the post-industrial period, society looked elsewhere for heroes and found the business leader. This was apparent from opinion surveys, magazine articles, and bestselling books.[34]

Before looking at the characteristics of the modern business hero, it is instructive to see how myth and reality come together in the works of Horatio Alger. His name is synonymous with the epitome of business success, but his life and work are largely a social invention. The heroes of the Horatio Alger stories made career success seem accessible to the average person. His "rags to riches" formula was a conscious heavy borrowing from the works of Charles Dickens, Herman Melville, Mark Twain, and Benjamin Franklin. His formula stories were not justifications of wealth nor even of meritorious behavior. These stories are not, as is often thought, accounts of poor boys who, by honesty and industry, became millionaires. The stories described moral heroes who were only moderately successful in business, rather than successful business heroes who were moderately moral. Alger's heroes rose to middle-class respectability through personal loyalty following a lucky break.

The frequently inaccurate portrayal of Alger's stories is exceeded by the mistaken view of his life. His early biographers in the 1920s wrote wholly fictionalized accounts of Alger's life because he and his family had destroyed most of his personal records. Only a half century later, after his work received critical attention from such literary giants as Malcolm Cowley and Mark van Doren did the leading biographer, Herbert Mayes, acknowledge the hoax. A new investigative study has revealed that Alger, in fact, was a former minister from Brewster, Massachusetts, who was a fugitive from several charges of child molestation.[35] In mid-March of 1886, he fled to New York City in disgrace. He tried in vain to succeed as a newspaper writer. Alger's life was mostly a series of failures and near-successes, soaring briefly with the publication of *Ragged Dick* in 1887. But he soon slid backward again, continually struggling to recapture that success with the same formula. He served as a private tutor to help make ends meet. Toward the end, he hired Edward Stratemeyer as a ghost writer. At his death in 1899 at age sixty-seven, his total accumulated wealth, despite the popular myth to the contrary, was $950 and a gold calendar watch. A recent biography of Alger concluded that "the metamorphosis of his reputation from didactic writer for boys to Progressive moralist, economic myth maker, and finally political ideologue seems to have been dictated less by the content of his books than by the context in which the books were read or remembered."[36]

As with Alger's heroes, American business heroes can be regarded as social creations to help construct and maintain a national identity. Perhaps the emergence of business heroes in the late 1800s and early 1900s, and then again eighty years later, has to do with the perceived threat to individual mastery of a complex and changing economic system. In both eras, new technologies and major structural shifts changed occupations and institutions. Business heroes, like other heroes, help us to personalize the system and make it seem more familiar to a worried population. Like the folk hero of literature and legend, the business hero reduces social uncertainty by triumphing over adversity. Just as heroes in ancient cultures provided answers to the most fundamental questions of human existence, such as mortality, the metaphysics governing the universe, territorial stability, and concepts of honor and loyalty, the modern business hero is admired for providing visions of the firm's future.

Characteristics of the Modern Business Hero

The modern business heroes who must accomplish this social agenda have five typical characteristics: they are of humble origins; they suffer career setbacks; they offer a novel sweeping vision; they are strong promoters; and they have a strong spirit of civic responsibility. Recent books and articles portray top executives as swashbuckling iconoclasts, triumphing over humble beginnings and career setbacks to achieve national prominence as industrial titans. After navigating bureaucratic mazes, breaking through traditional definitions of markets, and introducing new products and services, they promote sweeping change in their firms and in society at large.

To consider the first characteristic, most of the modern industrialists, like the rags-to-riches protagonists of Horatio Alger's fiction, have modest origins. Computer pioneer An Wang was an immigrant from Shanghai. Chrysler's savior, Lee Iacocca, was the son of an Italian immigrant. Texas Air chairman and founder, Frank Lorenzo, was the son of a Spanish beautician in New York City. H. Ross Perot, the billionaire founder of Electronic Data Systems, was the son of a horse trader.[37] Perot was an IBM computer salesman before launching his own firm with $1,000 in personal savings. By 1984, when it was sold to General Motors for $2.5 billion, Electronic Data Systems employed 15,000 dedicated workers. Inventor-industrialist Thomas Edison, who founded the General Electric Company and invented the electric light, the phonograph, and motion pictures, was the son of a rural lumber mill operator. Self-taught in chemistry, electricity, and industrial management, he began his own career as a telegraph operator. Another turn-of-the-century industrial hero was self-educated Andrew Carnegie, the immigrant son of a Scottish weaver, who died as one of the greatest figures in the American steel industry and one of the world's leading philanthropists. Henry Ford grew up on a farm and was himself a farmer until his mechanical interests drove him to the world of machines.

A second common quality of these industrial heroes is that most triumphed over major career setbacks, their resilience providing them with a further opportunity to demonstrate their leadership valor. Iacocca was fired from the Ford Motor Company for what he claims was, in part, his insistence on the need for the firm to produce smaller cars.

In 1974, H. Ross Perot lost $60 million when two Wall Street investment houses he owned both collapsed. Computer maker An Wang in 1986 recalled his resentment of IBM's clever strong-arm practices that had forced him to sell them his patented magnetic core memory thirty years earlier. Both of Henry Ford's first two automobile firms, the Detroit Automobile Company of 1899 and the Henry Ford Motor Company of 1901, were financial and market failures. Even the genius Thomas Edison was decisively outmaneuvered by tycoon Jay Gould in 1873 and lost the rights to compensation for his substantial telegraphic inventions, such as the one providing the capability of simultaneously transmitting several messages on a single wire.

A third quality of business heroes, past and present, is that after they introduced new technologies of production, revived old businesses, discovered new markets, and changed the standards of business conduct, their sweeping strategic visions were subsequently emulated and copied in other firms and adopted across industries. After failing to convince his employer, Montgomery Ward, of the strategic value of expanding beyond the catalog business into suburban department stores, Robert Wood led competitor Sears, Roebuck into this important new market. H. Ross Perot left IBM in 1962 when he became convinced of the importance of selling integrated information-system design and software rather than merely hardware.

Henry Ford's vision of bringing the automobile into the hands of the average American through his process of mass production on the assembly line was adopted worldwide, as was Apple Computer founder Steven Jobs's dream of bringing new technology into the average household with his notion of an inexpensive user-friendly personal computer. Thomas Edison opened the doors to vast new industrial frontiers in the fields of electricity, appliances, entertainment, and communication through the creation and commercialization of his inventions. Andrew Carnegie's revolutionary approach to the manufacture of steel toward the end of the nineteenth century facilitated new advances in transportation and construction, and his awareness of the importance of cost control to the production process was influential throughout the industrial world.

Some business heroes have triumphed by redefining businesses threatened by regulatory changes. Frank Lorenzo, for example, built the nation's largest air carrier in the aftermath of air deregulation. The new trail he blazed in this once-stodgy industry, through his emphasis on cost-cutting and consolidation, was followed by all major carriers. William G. McGowan, the founder of MCI Communications, similarly turned litigative and legislative changes to positive results. He pioneered in competing with AT&T for long-distance phone service through the use of expanded services and lower prices.

These business leaders, whether they created their own firms or assumed the throne of an existing empire, whether they were owners or employees, managed to transform their enterprises so profoundly that their competition and customers had to reorient themselves as well. Steelmaking was never the same after Andrew Carnegie. The auto industry was never the same after Henry Ford. The U.S. airline industry will never be the same after Frank Lorenzo.

A fourth common quality of these leaders is that all have displayed a remarkable talent for self-promotion. They have accomplished a great deal, and they are rarely modest about their contributions. In public statements by Apple founder Steven Jobs and Chrysler chairman Lee Iacocca we can readily hear their bold claims to indispensability in the creative shaping or overhaul of their firms. Dozens of chief executives have heralded their own accomplishments in autobiographies. The list includes Remington's Victor Kiem, cosmetics entrepreneur Estée Lauder, ITT conglomerator Harold Geneen, computer pioneer An Wang, financier Guy de Rothschild, 1940s Pepsi restructurer Walter Mack, and Sony founder Akio Morita.

The auto industry has provided its share of such reflective narratives on the success of its top executives, John DeLorean's *On a Clear Day You Can See GM* a maverick's vision of corporate life in the 1970s. Lee Iacocca's blockbuster autobiography reports on his rise from modest origins to the presidency of the Ford Motor Company, as well as on his resiliency upon his dismissal, and finally his inspiring "can do" attitude in turning around Chrysler. Perhaps one of the most educational and influential chief executive autobiographies was Alfred P. Sloan, Jr.'s 1963 account, *My Years with General Motors,* in which Sloan described his reorganization of the firm in the 1920s. The new miltidivisional decentralized structure he developed and proudly promoted was widely copied elsewhere as a solution to growing friction among line, staff, and general managers of multidivisional enterprises.[38]

Another automaker's autobiography, Henry Ford's 1922 *My Life and Work,* was especially successful, considering the questionable presentation of his childhood family life and his disputed role in the technological innovations he claimed. According to one business historian:

> The growth of the Ford "image" is in itself one of the prodigies of American communications history. The singular thing about Ford's self-apotheosis is that a great many believed it all and Ford achieved a fame and esteem nearer to Lincoln's than Edison's. In Ford's prime, in the early 1920s, he must have been more widely known than any other American.[39]

Ford's role model, Thomas Edison, was also an effective booster of his own accomplishments. Ignoring the parallel work of inventor Alexander Graham Bell and the important contributions of Edison's anonymous researchers at his lab in Menlo Park, New Jersey, Edison sold himself as a solitary, heroic wizard. According to historian Jonathan Hughes, Edison thrived on others' discoveries, which inspired his own inventive energies, and he regarded victory over his competitors as sweeter than any monetary reward:

> He was a compulsive achiever. There is little evidence that he cared for anything more than the fame and prestige which came from his highly publicized triumphs of invention. Edison was his own and his most constant publicity agent. It was the case, moreover, that he did not like to share his fame with other claimants.[40]

This propensity for self-promotion in leaders is not new. It is not even peculiar to American business executives. For example, Alexander III of Macedonia turned himself into "Alexander the Great" by consciously imitating the popular features of such mythological heroes as Achilles and Odysseus and drawing overt parallels between his battles for personal prestige and family honor, and those of these heroes.[41]

A fifth common quality of American business heroes is their sense of civic responsibility. The vision they hold for transforming their firm and even their industry may tie into a larger societal mission. Through personal philanthropy and political involvement, they often display an evangelic zeal to transcend the boundaries of the corporation and reach a wider audience. Their books and personal statements ring out with loud proclamations of their own approaches to manufacturing, finance, marketing, and human resource management as a suitable model for many other U.S. enterprises.

One individual who demonstrates the civic sense of business leaders is Lee Iacocca, who, among many other projects, serves as a frequent spokesman for national industrial policy regarding "smokestack industries," and in 1986 chaired the committee that planned the Statue of Liberty–Ellis Island Centennial Commission. Many other contemporary chief executives court active public leadership roles. J. Willard Marriott, Jr., divides his time between running his $3-billion company, his deep involvement with the Mormon Church, and his chairmanship of several conservative business lobbying groups. H. Ross Perot is well known for his patriotic public activities, his conservative political involvements, his leadership of educational reform efforts and toughened drug laws, and his daring rescue mission to free U.S. citizens held hostage in Iran. William C. Norris, the founder of Control Data and one of the founders of the Microelectronics and Computer Technology Corporation, a consortium of high-technology companies, continually allocated a generous portion of company profits to progressive social programs, including providing computer-based services for the needy and employment for inner-city residents. An Wang is an influential figure in the

Massachusetts High Technology Council, a backer of many liberal social issues, and a major philanthropist, as evidenced by Boston's Wang Center for the Performing Arts.

Perhaps the greatest philanthropist among American business heroes was Andrew Carnegie, who in late life gave away virtually the entire fortune he had amassed from building and selling the company that became U.S. Steel. The Carnegie Corporation of New York, founded in 1911 with $125 million of Carnegie's own U.S. Steel bonds, was the first great open-ended foundation and served as a model for the later foundations of Rockefeller and Ford. The Carnegie Institute of Washington received $23 million from the Corporation, the Carnegie Institute of Technology in Pittsburgh received $22.3 million, and the Carnegie Foundation for the Advancement of Teaching received $29 million. Carnegie personally donated $10 million to the Hero Funds and $10 million to the Carnegie Endowment for International Peace, built 2,811 free public libraries, donated 7,689 church organs, and allocated tens of millions of dollars to various institutions around the world, including Scottish universities, the Sorbonne, and the Koch Institute of Berlin. In addition, he created a novel pension system for retiring steel workers and college professors and maintained a substantial private pension fund that supported retired presidents Grover Cleveland and William Howard Taft as well as the widows of Teddy Roosevelt and Cleveland. He also provided retirement pensions for many childhood friends and benefactors and for the telegraphers of the Civil War, a group neglected for veterans' pensions by Congress. Politically, Carnegie was personally involved in major world peace initiatives. He spent much of 1907 in Europe, negotiating as a private citizen with major national leaders, and led peace crusades across Europe until World War I broke out in 1914. He then sadly retreated from Europe to support the United States.

Henry Ford shared Carnegie's passionate involvement in the antiwar movement. On December 4, 1915, he commissioned the steamship *Oscar II* as a peace ship bound for Europe in a last-ditch effort to halt the approaching world war. His delegation included clergy, journalists, and students. Though roundly ridiculed for this quixotic gesture, he continued to fund this mission for peace until the United States actually entered the war. In 1918, Ford ran for the U.S. Senate and narrowly lost. He subsequently funded a major investigation of the corrupt election practices of his Republican opponent, who consequently resigned his seat in disgrace. A strong supporter of President Woodrow Wilson, Ford himself was frequently mentioned as a dark horse Democratic candidate for the U.S. presidential election and actually began an abortive campaign in 1924. Ford's third major great cause, aside from his virulent support of anti-Semitism, which he espoused in articles he wrote for his paper, the *Dearborn Independent,* and his concern for world peace, was to promote the virtues of manufacturing and warn of the villainy of financiers. Like Carnegie, Ford saw manufacturers as the salvation of the republic and financiers as the curse.

Thomas Edison shared the pacifism of Ford and Carnegie, though by 1916 he had joined public marches in favor of preparedness for war and spoke publicly in support of President Wilson's call for a realization of the inevitability of war. He joined the Naval Consulting Board and worked long hours conducting experiments with explosives and submarine-detecting devices. He frequently commanded the national spotlight with his pronouncements on religion, politics, education, and money.

Public Acceptance of Corporate Heroism

A final factor in defining corporate folk heroes is the system of account-ability and rewards. Both are associated with a CEO's heroic image and power. If he or she does not come up to expectations, the chief execu-tive must go. According to research by Eugene Jennings of Michigan State University, chief executive turnover has more than doubled in the past ten to fifteen years, a result of increased pressure from the invest-ment community as well as generally heightened public scrutiny of cor-porate behavior.[42] The demands placed upon the chief executive are intensified by responsibility for the employment of thousands of work-ers, long work days, and events over which he or she may have little control.[43]

As compensation for these responsibilities, on the other hand, the chief executive frequently earns the same wages as top athletes and entertainers. According to a 1988 *Business Week* survey, chief executives of large firms earned $1.8 million, on average, in salary, bonus, and long-term compensation.[44] Often, these monumentally high wages are agreed to by board members who themselves have similar salary expec-tations as top executives at other large firms. Board members may also lavish heroic rewards upon chief executives to induce them to remain in their positions, because they find it safer to placate a leader with whom they are familiar rather than to face the risks of a new one.[45]

Despite the cries of some union leaders and dissident stockholders, these wages are met with little public disapproval. As institutional sym-bols, CEOs are expected to maintain royal lifestyles. This widespread public acceptance of the CEO's heroic-sized paycheck was anticipated by political economist Thorstein Veblen decades ago when he pointed out that the average American does not want to overthrow the wealthy but instead wants to become one of them.[46]

Conclusions

This chapter has examined how corporate leaders become heroes within their organizations and in the larger society. The five qualities common to business heroes are found among today's leaders, as they were among the business tycoons at the turn of the century. And although often portrayed as greedy robber barons, these earlier tycoons, as well as their modern-day counterparts, can also be seen as a link with the Jefferson–Jackson ideology of the "common man."

Early in this century, the introduction of mass production, electrical power, mass communications, and the automobile forever changed notions about time, travel, the marketplace, productivity, the spread of information, and manufacturing. Today, the impact of electronic information technology, bioresearch, abstract financial transactions, and newly competitive global markets have again introduced economic insecurity to our lives. Today, as a century ago, individuals wrestling with increasingly complex institutions and changes that threaten fundamental assumptions about the nature of work look for leaders with comforting visions of the social order and their role within it.

Industrialists who fearlessly conquer these threatening events and harness bureaucracies to meet their own needs, as well as society's needs, reassure all of us that a role for the lone individual still exists in mass society. Not only is Schumpeter's entrepreneur not dead, but he lives on to provide hope that people can control the incomprehensible institutional forces that threaten to smother them. If these leaders did not appear on their own, we would have had to invent them. The great sociologist Max Weber described "charismatic leadership" as an interaction of personal attributes and social needs. Charisma was observed to be "a certain quality of an individual personality by virtue of which he is set apart from ordinary men."[47] However, Weber continued, this quality is

> an extraordinary quality of a person regardless of whether the quality is actual, alleged, or presumed. The legitimacy of charismatic rule rests upon the belief [of the governed] in magical powers, revelations, and hero worship. The source of those beliefs is the "proving" of the charismatic quality through miracles, through victories, and through other successes, that is, through the welfare of the governed.[48]

The business hero's charismatic force is a product of the interaction between the community's need for miracles and the leader's success in meeting that need. The corporation provides legitimacy for that exchange.

Heroic American business leaders' common qualities of humble origins, prominent career setbacks, triumphant visions, self-confident promotion, and ambitions for broad societal impact are five mutually agreed upon attributes set by popular figures and their constituents. Facing retirement, the hero loses a sense of self, independent of this mutual definition of his or her own identity. When the corporation does not renew this contract, the hero is suddenly left without a ready personal identity, for the work-intensive executive does not see a job as a mere form of livelihood, but as an extension of his or her self-concept. Sometimes, retirement provides the leader with an opportunity to prove his heroic potential to himself, as well as to others, by rising above it, perhaps by seeking a new community where he can promote his vision and reconfirm his self-image. But in other cases the business hero is forced to retire permanently from the stage, for the conferral of heroic status by society is a reward that can be and often is repossessed.

Stanford sociologist William Goode has theorized that a society's celebration of heroes is a mechanism of social control and that the heroes selected are those who have demonstrated core values of the society.[49] When the core values change, old heroes will be forsaken and new ones chosen. The hero is still obliging group needs. The shift in glory across occupations, from frontiersman, to soldier, to noble toiler, to cowboy, to detective, to spy, to government leader, to industrial titan, reflects American society's dynamic process of redefining its heroic needs.

In Chapter 5, we will explore specific barriers to the heroes' exit from office. We will also look at four distinct departure styles and suggest that barriers to exit can be overcome by heroes who learn to fortify themselves internally before they face retirement.

5

THE HERO'S RELUCTANT FAREWELL

I met a traveller from an antique land
Who said: Two vast and trunkless legs of stone
Stand in the desert. Near them on the sand,
Half sunk, a shattered visage lies, whose frown,
And wrinkled lip, and sneer of cold command,
Tell that its sculptor well those passions read . . .

'My Name is Ozymandias, king of kings:
Look on my works, ye Mighty and despair!'

Nothing beside remains. Round the decay
Of that colossal wreck, boundless and bare,
The lone and level sands stretch far away

"Ozymandias,"
Percy Bysshe Shelley, 1817

We have now come to see heroism as something more than a fixed occupational status. Its dynamism derives from the fact that it is a reality which emerges from a coincidence of illusions. That is, when an individual leader's illusions of his or her identity meet society's illusions of its identity, a star is born. The anointed hero may be a farmer, a warrior, a politician, a machinist, a consumer advocate, a physician, an actor, an environmentalist, or an industrialist, depending on the needs the society expresses. The society may be a national audience, a local community, a business firm, or any stable group. When the group's needs change, its hero usually changes. As his status fails and his honor is torn away, the hero is left exposed on the outside and empty within. His lifetime of accomplishment often affords no lasting comfort.

Consider the late-career despair portrayed in Billy Wilder's classic film, *Sunset Boulevard,* in which Gloria Swanson plays a retired star of the silent screen, Norma Desmond. Once a queen in Hollywood, Norma was cruelly left behind in favor of younger faces, newer voices, and the different talents required by the talkies. No longer a celebrity, she has withdrawn in depression to the seclusion of her mausoleum-like mansion, where she has buried herself in her memories of a long-lost adoring public. The phone no longer rings with the calls of agents, producers, and directors, and Norma spends her days autographing photographs for make-believe fans. She faithfully sits through repeated screenings of her long-forgotten films. She complains regularly about the poor quality of those who followed her. During one such screening she jumps to her feet and cries out, with the projector's beam upon her, "Have they forgotten what a star is? I'll show them. I'll return some day!"

A stranded motorist, played by William Holden, wanders in to use the telephone and challenges this has-been's delusions that she will someday make a comeback. Holden observed, "She was still sleepwalking along the giddy heights of a lost career! Plain crazy when it came to that one subject—her celluloid self, the *great* Norma Desmond. How could she breathe in that house surrounded by Norma Desmonds?" In the end, the spotlights return to Norma Desmond only when the press, accompanied by the glare of television cameras and reporters' flash cameras, follow the police to her mansion after she murders him.

Of course, this actress was portrayed as an exceptionally unbalanced, psychotic woman. We can readily think of similarly forgotten celebrities whose stardom declined and who never regained the fame they enjoyed early in their careers. By contrast others, such as Ruth Gordon and Henry Fonda, performed to the end of their lives, while Cary Grant, Grace Kelly, and Jimmy Stewart voluntarily left the stage decades before it was necessary.

When we look at chief executives, we find that some leave the stardom they have achieved more easily than others, although all feel some despair over missed opportunities and some anger at being unappreciated. Frequently in my interviews, chief executives would mutter that they had felt a sudden emptiness and sense of insignificance when they saw the same people cry, "The King is dead" and then moments later, "God save the King!" as a new leader took office. Five of them used the same line: "I felt like I'd been editorially shifted from *Who's Who* to *Who's That?*" Three chief executives claimed that they were unable to attend their going-away parties because they were not recognized by the custodian working in the executive suite.

Chief executives are in no hurry to flee the world of work. Like actors, authors, and other "work-intensive" professionals, they are different from many other types of workers in that they have enormous discretion over their work conditions, a nearly insatiable drive to create, and a reluctance to concede that their crusade is complete.

In this chapter, I will first consider the chief executive's reluctant farewell and the specific barriers executive heroes face in contemplating retirement. Then I will consider why some chief executives follow one path and others follow another. Finally I will introduce a typology that categorizes four distinct styles of departure from high office.

Despite their common dedication to a creative mission, leaders differ in the ways they come to terms with the finiteness of their career. Chief executive departure style is not a projection of leadership style. Whether they are impulsive or reflective, whether they are "hands-on" types or delegators, whether they are conciliators or antagonists, leaders' departure style is distinctly different from the way they have led the company. We must step into the leaders' self-concept and their situation to appreciate the differences in heroic departure. The key is to understand how differently they come to terms with the ultimate boundary of their reign.

Barriers to Exit: The Heroic Self-Concept

We have learned in the previous chapter of the ingredients which serve as a recipe for heroism. They are composed of the individual attributes of the person anointed a hero as well as the changing conditions that lead to the selection of heroes. Heroes believe that they have earned their stature through their deeds and sacrifices. Thus they do not realize until retirement is upon them that their position is, in part, a social creation. Their personal identities are so intertwined with their roles that retirement often represents a personal catastrophe, a void into which they are forced to step.

When Winston Churchill was elected as British prime minister in October 1951, he was seventy-seven, quite deaf, and had suffered two strokes. As a condition of his selection, he had promised his cabinet that he would stay in office for only a year, then pass control to the capable foreign secretary, Anthony Eden. But he reneged on this promise and, even though he suffered another stroke, he struggled on in the job for four-and-a-half years. Churchill felt that, as the most experienced world leader in office, with his sixty years of public service, for him to leave the world stage would be nothing but a waste. He saw himself as the reigning senior statesman in any major power forum and the man most capable of initiating a badly needed four-power summit. At the end, he felt embittered and hounded out of office by overambitious successors.[1]

Churchill's fear of wasting his unique talents is not in itself uncommon. While such fear is pervasive among political leaders, we can also find a comparable example in a distant field, the management of professional sports. New York baseball legend Casey Stengel showed no interest in finding another pursuit or niche for himself after his retirement as a reigning symbol of baseball management.[2] Stengel had begun his baseball career as a player with the Brooklyn Dodgers in 1912. After struggling through many career setbacks and humiliating exits, he was fired as manager of the Dodgers in 1935, and the Boston Braves in 1944. He came back to reign triumphant over the New York Yankees from 1949 to 1960. That year, at age seventy, he was pressed into retirement, but by the next year, he returned to power and prominence as manager of the newly created New York Mets. He led the Mets for five years until disabled by a hip injury, and maintained unrivaled energy and drive, as well as his renowned wit, through his eighties. For the last decade of his life, he continued to hover around the baseball clubs and to attend games and various formal Hall of Fame events, where he was always received as the elder statesman of the sport.

Despite the apparent vast differences in their heroic roles, parallels can be safely drawn between a great political leader such as Winston Churchill and a sports figure such as Casey Stengel—providing that we limit the comparison to the internal psychodynamics of heroism. What does it mean for someone who thinks of himself as a hero to face what he sees as an untimely career end? Anthropologists and folklorists have drawn parallels among even more disparate folk heroes across cultures and across ages. Anthropologist Joseph Campbell's classic study, *The Hero with a Thousand Faces,* uncovered universal patterns in the life stages of heroes.[3] In his discussion of the life stages, or monomyth, of the hero, Campbell discerned three components: a period of separation from society through calls to adventure and for the hero to realize superhuman talent; a period of continual trials through temptation, setbacks, and ultimate triumph; and finally, a period of reintegration into the mainstream of society.

It is this final stage of reintegration into society at large that the hero resists. Pressured to surrender the unique role that they feel they have created, some heroes fear that in their retirement, the past will catch up with them and those they vanquished will take revenge. Others fear that their constituents will see their retirement as a career collapse. And of those who resist their retirement, Campbell warned, the "hero of today becomes the tyrant of tomorrow." The tyrant's inflated ego is a curse to himself. Regardless of the outward signs of strength and prosperity, the hero who goes on to a late career lives in fear of threats to his power from the outside. The despotic defensiveness that marked the final days of such dictators as Philippine president Ferdinand Marcos and the Shah of Iran demonstrates this point well. In each case, self-styled reformers and professed humanitarians became overtly repressive and murderous martinets.

Even far more benevolent leaders can become panicked at the realization of a quickly approaching termination of office. The clever political scheming of the nation's only four-term president, Franklin D. Roosevelt, is a familiar reminder of self-styled heroes' temptation to extend their reign. Political scientist Richard Neustadt warned that leaders as democratically elected as the U.S. presidents can come to believe in the lasting supremacy of power and thus destroy themselves. He states, "No one saves him [the president] from himself."[4]

To master this fear of reintegration into society at late career, a top leader must come to terms with two barriers to exiting: *heroic stature* and *heroic mission*. Heroic stature refers to the special distinction a position of command has that allows a person to stand above the group and thus occupy a unique role in it. With the late-career loss of supremacy, declining heroes are uncertain as to how they still fit into their old groups, whether it be a team, a company, or society at large. The second addictive quality of leadership that proves a barrier to the hero's exit is the sense of heroic mission, a feeling that one has a unique role to fill and that only the hero is capable of carrying out the responsibilities of the job. Late career, in general, is a time for reflection upon one's accomplishments and requires coming to terms with the degree of success that has been reached. The chief executive, having established a superhuman yardstick by which to calibrate success, is often unable to appreciate an objective view of the magnitude of his or her triumphs.

Heroic Stature

The first of these barriers to exiting, the sense of heroic stature, provides the chief executive a place in the firm with a distinct identity, but it nonetheless places him or her outside the crowd. Thus the leader is never lost in the anonymity of mass membership. The perspective a chief executive has on the firm, as well as the relationships with subordinates, have been defined along the lines of "he or she is one of us, but different." Cultural conventions and trappings support the status distinctions between leader and subordinates. Some subordinates may project their personal feelings about past relationships with authority figures (e.g., parents, teachers, coaches, previous bosses) into this relationship. There are various priorities placed on the importance of perquisites of office, such as chauffeur-driven limousines, personal jet planes, platoons of administrative assistants, and offices in choice corner locations well appointed with luxury furnishings. The CEO's mildest requests and suggestions are often translated as imperial commands by attendant clerks. Respected and consulted by outside leaders and often quoted by the media, the chief executive is asked to serve on the boards of directors of other companies and is treated as near nobility in elite social circles. Chief executives can become so immersed in these trappings of office that it may be hard for some to imagine just how they will be able to interact with former subordinates and clients after they leave it.

Relinquishing leadership, then, leaves the chief executive without a ready identity in the firm. Research on group affiliations has suggested that we join groups for the purpose of submerging within a larger entity in order to gain such benefits as strength in numbers, the pooled variety of individual talents and knowledge, and the creation of norms or codes of conduct.[5] Membership in some groups also provides opportunities for approval and status that afford the individual high social visibility and identity. Thus groups not only can embrace individuals within a larger whole, but also can satisfy a need for personal recognition. This status is lost when the job is left behind.

Some theorists have suggested that the leader's need to be singled out by the group represents a narcissistic drive. Studies by political scientists Harold Lasswell and James David Barber, as well as by psychologist Erik Erikson, suggest that public leaders project many personality effects of childhood into their career drives.[6] For example, Barber has written:

> Intense political activity may represent either compensation for low self-esteem, usually resulting from severe deprivation in early life, or a specialized extension of high self-esteem, but seldom does it represent an ordinary or normal adaptation to one's culture.[7]

A desire for recognition has been traced through history. In *The Frenzy of Renown*, literary scholar Leo Braudy has argued that society always generates a subset of people eager to live their lives in the public eye.[8] These people court recognition on a grand scale in a belief that fame will ultimately liberate them from the suffocating expectations of their peers and offer them wide acceptance in society. To gain this greater fame, they recreate their private identities into more publicly salient images. Alexander III of Macedonia's self-metamorphosis into Alexander the Great demonstrates how heroes re-create themselves during their pursuit of adventure. Braudy observed that

> it hardly seems useful to separate the Alexander he created from the Alexander he became to others, or even from the Alexander he was to himself. Such distinctions assume that the inner nature is more real than the social self. . . . Kings have always been performers, but Alexander introduced the possibility that the king might be his own playwright and stage manager as well.[9]

The pursuit of fame is a manifestation of the urge to be unique. A famous person, however, is not only a successful person, but also a successful *public* person. As the would-be hero manufactures a larger identity to help reach his or her ambitions, he or she often loses contact with the original inner self. This split between an inner, more personal self-concept and an external one defined by group responsibilities and identification is not limited to leaders. Sociologist David Riesman's pathbreaking social commentary, *The Lonely Crowd*, described a generation of "inner-directed" and "outer-directed" types of people.

Developmental psychologists Jean Piaget, Lawrence Kohlberg, Abraham Maslow, and Robert Keegan have also identified similar stages of cognitive development that suggest that most of us vacillate between periods in life where our orientation is embedded within a group or an institution (parents, school, employers, etc.) and periods when we break free from these shackles and gain release from institutional roles. At one point, there is a self which seeks to operate within the organization, while at another time there is a self which seeks to escape the organization. Robert Keegan theorized that by late life, a person's career has become less central in that a person *has* a career but no longer *is* a career.[10]

But this gradual shift to an identity based more on an individual self-concept as opposed to an institutional identification is far more difficult for a leader than for others. The responsibilities of leaders' roles keep them trapped meeting the expectations of others. Leaders do not have the time or freedom to look after their own inner self to the same extent. The heroic self-concept can so overwhelm the leader's nonheroic, personal self-concept that some may lose touch with it forever.

An interesting illustration of this was provided by a 1983 meeting of former world leaders. In August of that year, former president Gerald Ford hosted a gathering that included former president of France Valéry Giscard D'Estaing; James Callaghan, former prime minister of Britain; and Malcolm Fraser, former prime minister of Australia. This group had governed a large slice of the industrialized world through the 1970s, but all were involuntarily retired by the 1980s. As they reminisced over the past, complained about the present, and speculated over future world events, each spoke wistfully about his lost identity. Later, Prime Minister Callaghan commented, "I had to pinch myself last night and almost pinch the rest of them to remind ourselves that we were no longer in power."[11] When President Giscard D'Estaing was asked by an inquiring reporter how it felt to be out of power, he responded, "How does it feel? About the same way you feel when you write a story that doesn't get in the paper!"[12] These world leaders emeritus knew, as many corporate leaders know, that even as "has-beens" they needed their institutional identities. Their words are reminiscent not only of Churchill's painful exit, but also of the bereavement in the portrayal of Gloria Swanson's forgotten retired film star.

Heroic Mission

Like the feared loss of heroic status, a second barrier to exit for a leader is the feared loss of the sense of heroic mission. The parting words of top executives frequently reveal the agonized confession of unrealized career goals. For example, consider the following final message to his shareholders by Donald C. Burnham, the retiring chief executive of Westinghouse:

> Inasmuch as I step down from the position of chief executive officer as of the date of this letter, perhaps I may be excused for taking one brief look back at the corporation of July 1963, at which time I assumed leadership. The $2.3 billion corporation of that date has increased more than two and a half times in size. The $48.5 million in earnings of 1963 reached nearly $199 million in 1972 but have been subpar during the two years just past.
>
> Naturally, I had hoped to yield the helm to my successor with profits at a record high. But I must be content with the knowledge that the company has taken bold steps to solve the energy, transportation, education, security, productivity, and other people problems of today. It has grown and developed into a far stronger organization than ever in its history, and the remedial groundwork laid during 1974 now provides a favorable platform for profit improvement.[13]

In this candid letter, we see Burnham's disappointment at the close of his career at Westinghouse. His references to the organization's history suggest his search for a niche in the records of Westinghouse that might last beyond his reign. Although his letter reveals that he had not achieved as much as he would have wanted, Burnham's statement also reflects a desire to prove that he had left Westinghouse in better condition than he had found it, and better prepared for its future.

We can find many similar sentiments expressed by other retiring chief executives when they reflect upon their record of accomplishment. Baron Guy de Rothschild, the chief executive of the venerable French merchant banking firm bearing his family's name, was forced into retirement in 1981 when the new socialist government of President François Mitterrand expropriated the House of Rothschild in the course of nationalizing all French banks. In his fury over his family's eviction from their 170-year-old office on the Rue Laffitte, Rothschild wrote a letter that appeared on the front page of the French newspaper *Le Monde* defending his proud family dynasty as well as his own personal dedication to the French nation. Four years later, he commented on the reasons why he wrote this letter:

> It obviously came at the right time as the interest it aroused surpassed what might have been attributed to myself or to my family. Besides, it served as proof that our name was still famous and above all, that it was associated with current events, enhanced and not enshrouded by its historic past.[14]

Thus Rothschild wanted some evidence of the continuity of family stature, but he also felt he had a personal mission to perform. The historical mantle of the family firm's dynasty had survived even after the

German invasion of France and the threat of the Nazi Holocaust had temporarily driven the family into exile. While Guy de Rothschild was at the helm, he kept the bank profitable and actively contributing to contemporary French life. But despite this, he could not hide from the nagging reminder that the family had lost the bank while under his command.

> By expressing my views, I got them off my chest, as they say; I fulfilled what seemed to me to be my duty. But I still had to live through the actual event. Everything I'd been able to create or helped to create during my lifetime . . . had been confiscated, my world demolished. I'd toiled for thirty-five years to no avail.[15]

Again, as with Burnham's reflections upon his responsibilities to the proud Westinghouse heritage, we see Rothschild concerned over whether he had met his historic responsibility to secure the future of his organization.

In part, his concern reflects what psychologist Erik Erikson has described as the late-life tension between "integrity and despair."[16] That is, in coming to terms with the gap between our life aspirations and our record of accomplishment, we either enjoy a feeling of "integrity" and completeness, or are plagued by feelings of disappointment and despair. Chief executives have tough going in this area, because they hold themselves to especially high standards of accomplishment. Psychoanalysts Otto Rank, Ernest Becker, and Robert Jay Lifton have described the unusual need of leaders to justify themselves as objects of primary value in the universe. In *The Denial of Death,* Becker wrote that the leader "must stand out, be a hero, make the biggest possible contribution to world life, show that he counts more than anyone or anything else."[17] This speaks to the very core motives of the hero—seeking to make a contribution that will not be readily eroded by the sands of time.

The narcissistic urge to have a unique impact on the world is not an isolated property of heroes. Ralph Waldo Emerson suggested that we all strive to re-create the world out of ourselves as if others did not exist or never had. Belief in our uniqueness allows us to bury our intellectual acceptance of our own mortality. Death threatens to wipe clean the slate which charts the significance of our daily labors, so the myth of our uniqueness allows us to believe that we can avoid death. Just as we regard holiday traffic mortality rates on actuarial tables as applying to someone else but not to ourselves, so our heroic self-concept allows us to believe that, somehow, we will survive.

Frequently, heroic myths actually describe a hero's return from the dead. In these myths, the hero has a heightened awareness of his mortality and struggles to overcome death by producing seemingly immortal creations or performing superhuman deeds. In reviewing the classic folk heroes Gilgamesh and Odysseus, Rank explained:

> The problem is fundamentally similar: namely to attain personal immortality. Neither in primitive man nor in classical times does he actually achieve it. But he finds it ideologically in that his deeds, which he subserved in his attempt to gain immortality, have made him a hero whose fame lives on in the song of other generations.[18]

A society encourages an individual's pursuit of a heroic legacy because the hero's vision is a collective perception of the society's immortality. In much the same way, the chief executive's strategy for a firm is not only a permanent record of the chief executive's individual effort, but a plan to ensure the company's immortality as well.

As chief executives sense the close of their careers, many fear for their heroic legacy. Will it survive the test of history? Will their dream outlive their reign, let alone their lifetime? These leaders did not hit mid-career plateaus, as do most workers. It is not until their late years that their career mobility slows. And it is then that chief executives begin to worry—not about whether they have reached their ultimate career peaks but whether they may have peaked prematurely. In fact, because their path to success has been a clear one, many face mid-life and mid-career dilemmas virtually at the same time as they confront their late-career history.

Their delayed realization of career limits, coupled with a heightened sense of their mortality, can lead chief executives to stubbornly assert their command. They feel a life's work endangered and seek to prove their visions to be immune to the effects of age. Scholars have suggested, for example, that Chinese communist chairman Mao Tse-tung's Cultural Revolution was, in part, a late-career assertion of his heroic mission.[19] Mao's career had been that of a revolutionary. His late-life recollections of his career showed his keen awareness of having been an "eternal survivor" to his people, narrowly avoiding being killed many times. Death had often come very close as his brothers, his first wife, and many colleagues were killed during the revolution. He led the famous Long March in 1934 and 1935, during which 80 percent of the original group perished along a six-thousand-mile trek. By the mid-1960s, however, the aging of his colleagues and the complacency of the institutions he had created indicated to Mao that his revolutionary works might not endure. Thus he announced the advent of the Cultural Revolution.[20]

Robert Jay Lifton has described this brutal, anti-hierarchical, and anti-intellectual Cultural Revolution, overtly intended to cleanse the system, as partially a struggle for revolutionary immortality by a septuagenarian ruler:

It is, as we have seen, the last stand of a great revolutionary against internal and external forces pressing him along that treacherous path from hero to despot. It is similarly the last stand of a collective expression of early revolutionary glory which he has epitomized. And it is perceived on several symbolic levels as a last stand against death itself—of the leader, the revolution, and the individual man in general.[21]

In sum, a chief executive's frustration in late career is especially difficult to master, because, unlike most of us, he or she selects far more difficult standards of accomplishment and does not experience final limits to personal abilities until late in life. The degree of despair that older persons feel as they reflect upon their past career often has more to do with the subjective goals they established earlier in life than with actual, objective successes. No aspiration could be more ambitious than the leader's heroic dream of an immortal contribution. It is no wonder that many depart office with such difficulty, given the low probability of realizing such a dream.

Exiting the Executive Suite

These barriers to exit can be measured by expressed attitudes. In my survey of retiring chief executives, their mastery of heroic stature as a barrier to exit was measured by their affirmative responses to twelve items that were derived from coded responses to open-ended questions that asked about the timing and description of one's retirement. Three independent raters coded "stature" items from the questionnaires, with 95 percent agreement among raters.[22] The more an executive reported retirement to be an opportunity to build an identity independent of his or her previous role as the leader of a corporation, the more the executive had mastered the heroic self-concept regarding stature. Their descriptions of an independent identity at retirement included such references to retirement as an opportunity to enjoy time for themselves, a chance to spend badly needed time with family members, a long-desired escape from public exposure of their private life, and a chance to begin enthusiastically community, recreational, academic, business, or various other new activities.

The second heroic barrier to exit, the sense of frustration with their heroic mission, was measured in the survey by five items, including regret for an uncompleted mission, regret over the firm's performance after they left, regret over the performance of an individual successor, regret over the timing of the retirement decision, and the feeling that their skills were underutilized. Three independent raters coded the questionnaires for "mission" items, with a 95 percent agreement among these raters.

An opposite scale—the measure of satisfaction with one's heroic mission, meaning the overcoming of a barrier to exit—was based on seven affirmative responses to items indicating that the chief executive had retired because he or she had found other compelling community or business interests, or that he or she had no expressed difficulty at any time after retirement.

These barriers to exit were significantly correlated in my study with the actual length of a chief executive's reign. The greater one's frustration with one's heroic mission, the longer the reign.[23] Similarly, the more attached chief executives were to the heroic stature of office, the longer they reigned.[24]

As with the data analyzed in Chapter 3, I surveyed one hundred chief executives and roughly one hundred other top corporate officers. Chief executives did not significantly differ from other top officers in their sense of a completed mission, but chief executives were far more significantly attached to heroic stature in the firm.[25]

This highly significant finding deserves some further reflection. It seems that those who were second-in-command of their firms, or at that level, shared the chief executive's drive to create a lasting legacy. In other words, both groups were of the same forest of executive timber. As aspirants to the chief executive's throne, they too were ambitious to have their accomplishments outlast their tenure. Those who ultimately became the supreme power in the firm, however, were showered with the trappings of office when they left it, perhaps because guilt-ridden boards of directors or boards seeking continuity of command often feel they make the transfer of power less painful to all by allowing the departing chief executive to retain more executive privileges than are allowed the second-in-command. Thus the chief executive often has to choose whether to remain actively engaged with the corporation in an effort to fortify links with a diminishing heroic role. The second-in-command is merely cut free. When asked how long it took to adjust to a life outside the executive suite, many top officers stated, "About the time it took for the elevator to get from the penthouse to the lobby!" Not a single chief executive responded in this fashion.

A Typology of Departure Styles

In addition to examining these barriers to exit from executive stardom, I studied chief executives' specific exit activities, classifying them into one of four departure styles based on the pattern of the actions leading up to and through retirement. Before I surveyed the one hundred chief executives and one hundred officers, I visited fifty recently retired prominent CEOs. These day-long interviews with chief executives were the source from which I developed the four categories. Some executives consistently spoke in imperial, autocratic ways with regard to succession; others spoke in combative and competitive terms; yet others spoke in paternalistic family tones; and finally a last group spoke in crisp, calculated political metaphors. Characteristic patterns of behavior were associated with the imagery they selected to tell their personal career stories. The four categories I derived from these interviews I have labeled *monarchs, generals, ambassadors,* and *governors.* These terms refer to their manner of exit rather than to their lifelong management style.

The data that I used later to sort my questionnaire survey of the one hundred *Fortune* 500 chief executives into the four departure styles included:

1. The purpose of the timing of the chief executive's exit.
2. The expressed emotions over leaving office (resentment, loss, loneliness, eagerness, exhaustion, etc.).
3. The time and energy spent on ongoing contact maintained with the firm.
4. The return to office after retirement.
5. The length of time serving on the board of directors.
6. The development of successors (periods of grooming, timing of identification of the successor, timing of announcement of retirement, etc.).
7. The magnitude of involvement in outside corporate board directorships.
8. The magnitude of involvement in new business ventures and officer positions.
9. The length of reign as chief executive and total years in the firm.

I not only used the individual questionnaires from the surveyed chief executives to make these judgments, but also gathered information from a twenty-five-year review of every annually published shareholder proxy statement for each of the firms. After the judgments were individually evaluated by three independent raters, with 85 percent agreement among them, I sorted the chief executives into one of four categories.

Monarchs do not leave office until they are decisively forced out through the death of the chief executive or through an internal palace revolt. This palace revolt may be in the form of ultimatums, the resignations of top officers, or the action of the board of directors.

Generals depart in a style also marked by forcible exit. Here, the chief executive leaves office reluctantly, but plots his return and quickly comes back to office out of retirement in order to rescue the company from the real or imagined inadequacy of his or her successor. The general enjoys being the returning savior and often hopes to remain around long enough to take the firm and himself toward even greater glory.

Ambassadors, by contrast, leave office quite gracefully and frequently serve as post-retirement mentors. They may remain on the board of

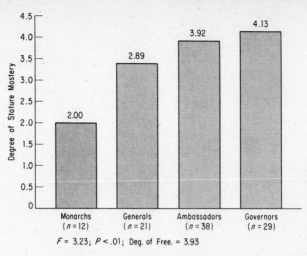

$F = 3.23; \ P < .01; \ \text{Deg. of Free.} = 3.93$

Figure 5.1 Mastery of Heroic Stature.

directors for some time, but they do not try to sabotage the successor. The ambassadors provide continuity and counsel.

Finally, *governors* rule for a limited term of office, then shift to other vocational outlets entirely after retirement. Despite their fairly graceful exits, the governors maintain very little ongoing contact with their firm once they have left.

In comparing the heroic barriers to exit in these four departure styles (Figures 5.1 and 5.2), we can see that both monarchs and generals are far more captured by the status of their positions and find it harder to relinquish the respect and influence of office than ambassadors and governors (see Figure 5.1). Ambassadors were especially untroubled by a loss of status and hence were able to remain on the premises after being stripped of their power. In their continued willingness to put the greater good of the group over their self-interest in status, they managed to preserve heroic respect from their former constituents.

Looking at the other barrier to exit, the fulfillment of one's heroic mission, again monarchs and generals were far less ready to depart from their calling (see Figure 5.2). Monarchs seemed to feel especially frustrated and generals somewhat less so. In contrast, ambassadors were particularly content with their record of accomplishment. They no longer felt the need to prove themselves in battle. Governors, while still as eager to satisfy a mission as were the generals, although less so than the monarchs, were least troubled by the loss of heroic stature in the firm. To understand why some chief executives manage to retire easily

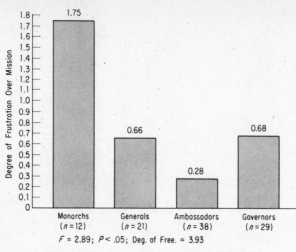

Figure 5.2   Frustration over Heroic Mission.

and others do not, we will have to look deeply into each of the four departure styles.

The Corporate Context

In addition to the heroic self-concept, the corporate context contributes to one's behavior on leaving high office. In my study of chief executives, length of term in office was significantly correlated with such factors as their ages, their lengths of service in the company, and the number of outside directors on the board. For example, those who were younger when named chief executive tended to remain in office far longer than those named to this top office as older executives.[26] Those chief executives with longer company service tended to remain in their top office longer.[27] Finally, those chief executives with longer reigns tended to have fewer outside directors on the boards of their companies.[28] This highlights the symbiotic relationship between the hierarchy of a company and its leader. Firms with older leaders, developed from within, and served by more insular boards are likely to have longer reigning leaders.

Each of the four departure styles also indicated dramatic differences in such features of the company as profitability in the leader's year of retirement, the career mobility of the chief executive, and the number of outside directors on the board. It is important to consider how such corporate factors as finance, organization, and cultural indexes set the

Table 5.1   Heroic Departure Style and the Corporate Context

	Monarchs	Generals	Ambassadors	Governors
Average firm income at year of retirement[a]	$58.0 Mil.	$117.4 Mil.	$113.3 Mil.	$448.2 Mil.
Average length of reign (in years)[b]	15	11	10	7
Percent of outside directors[c]	42.6%	58.7%	61.2%	66.5%
Average firm assets at year of retirement	$575.8 Mil.	$3.282 Bil.	$5.788 Bil.	$8.884 Bil.
Average firm sales	$1.864 Bil.	$2.398 Bil.	$3.673 Bil.	$7.665 Bil.
Number of employees at year of retirement	21,500	23,800	42,700	71,700
Average age at retirement (in years)	67	62	63.5	63.4
Number of jobs in company[d]	2.8	4.6	4.4	3.8
Number of chief executives	12	21	38	29

[a]Contrast test of means for significance of pooled variance $T = 2.016$, $p < .05$, degrees of freedom = 85

[b]Analysis of variance: $F = 2.613$, $p < .05$, degrees of freedom = 3,82

[c]Contrast test of means for significance of pooled variance $T = 2.88$, $p < .05$, degrees of freedom = 82

[d]$F = 5.3$, $p < .01$, degrees of freedom = 3,95

stage for enhancing or restraining the predispositions of leaders' heroic self-concepts.

Table 5.1 presents some noteworthy differences among the four departure styles as they are presented in increasing order of ease of separation from the firm. We can see that the larger the firm, the easier the leader's exit from office. Monarchs and generals measured lower than ambassadors and governors in the sales, assets, and employment figures of their firm at the time of retirement. Also, the more outside directors a firm had, the easier was the leader's exit from office. Monarchs and generals had significantly fewer nonemployees or "outside" representatives on their boards. One reason for those differences may be that the larger firms provide greater formalization of the succession process as well as more exposure to outside models of management practice from their boards.

The chief executive not only is shaped by the heroic context of the corporation, but also helps to shape it. In Figure 5.3 we can see the enormous emphasis on growth during the monarch's reign. Given that the companies were smaller, such proportionate increases over the base may seem easier, but the emphasis on asset growth over profits is a telling indicator of the relative emphasis on institution-building over short-term enrichment. Generals, in contrast, emphasized growth in

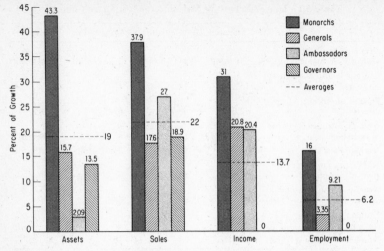

Figure 5.3 Average Annual Company Growth During Reign, by Departure Style.

profits relative to growth in assets, and ambassadors emphasized growth in sales relative to profits. The governors and generals had the lowest growth in employment in their firms, while the monarchs showed the largest growth in their work force over the length of their reign.[29]

These relative priorities shift. All the categories of departing leaders showed about a 25 percent growth in sales and in assets as the leaders approached the ends of their reigns. Looking at growth in profits, however, over these last two years in command, governors came from behind to lead with a remarkable 89 percent increase over the twenty-four months (see Figure 5.4). The others ranged between 20 and 46 percent. This is supported by the finding that the greater the increases in income and in earnings per share in the two years prior to the leader's retirement, the cleaner the break from the firm. Certainly the governors enjoyed the easiest exit from the firm. It seems that those leaders who achieved lower profit growth resisted retirement more. Those leaders whose companies had lower profit growth also tended to cling to an on-site office after retirement and to offer advice to their successor whether or not they were asked for it.[30] The longer the leader's reign, the lower the company's income growth in the final two years.[31] The older the chief executive is at retirement, the lower the company's income growth in the final two years.[32] These longitudinal, multifaceted data allow us to see that we can predict chief executives' departure styles, given their priorities in shaping their firm during their reign and their success in doing so.

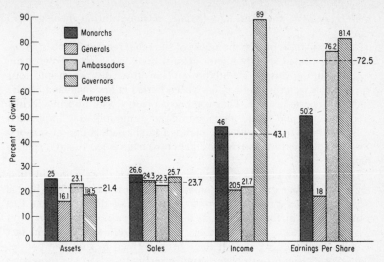

Figure 5.4   Average Company Growth over Last Two Years of Reign.

The differences in the accomplishments of these four types of leaders were also noted by the financial community. Table 5.2 summarizes what happened. Apparently the monarchs' visions of their companies were believed by investors who traded the stocks of their companies at about twice book value during the last two years of their reigns. This was the highest for all four types of leaders. Stocks of the companies of the other three types traded at, or just above, book value during the last two years of their terms of office. Also, the market-to-book ratio of monarchs' firms rose during the last two years, as did the ratios of the ambassadors' and governors' stocks. By contrast, though the stocks of generals' companies also traded slightly above book value at the time of

Table 5.2   Market Value of Stocks During Retirement Period

	Monarchs	Generals	Ambassadors	Governors
Market-to-book value at retirement	1.9	1.14	1.12	1.0
Change during last two years[a]	+12.5%	−4.3%	+15.9%	+14.1%
Market-to-book value two years after retirement[b]	2.3	1.1	1.3	.9

[a]Significant at $p < .05$
[b]Significant at $p < .01$

their retirement, the ratio had actually declined during their last two years.

After their retirements, the stocks of the monarchs' and ambassadors' companies traded slightly higher against book value, and those of the generals and governors slightly lower. This finer distinction into four types reveals patterns that may have been buried in Friedman and Singh's study, as reported earlier. They compared planned with unplanned chief executive exits and found increased market value following unplanned exits. My analysis suggests that planned (ambassadors and governors) versus unplanned (monarchs and generals) exits is too broad a split to make.

The data in this study allow us to project that those who end their reign with higher growth in profits leave office more cleanly, whereas those with lower growth in profits at the end of their terms tend to continue to fight for influence as a consultant, a board member, and even as an officer. Following their retirement, those who did in fact remain actively engaged with their firms seemed to continue policies that favored asset growth over income growth. That is to say, those who were thrown out of office because of their dedication to dreams of a future empire over current profits would continue to assert their cherished policies through every opportunity they could find.

Self-Concept, Corporate Context, and a Leader's Retirement

Departure style is influenced both by a leader's heroic self-concept and by the hero's corporate context. The subjective inner world of a leader's desire for social stature and for immortal contribution is either exacerbated or restrained by an objective outer world that evaluates his or her contribution to corporate performance. The leader's departure style results from a combination of these subjective and objective factors. We will now consider the convergence of these two sets of factors for each departure style.

Monarchs have tighter control over their slightly smaller domains and continue in office far longer. The support they receive is from those who believe in their campaign of institution-building. Generals, while equally captivated by their own dream, do not have so clear a vision, nor do they as credibly bring it to life. They are removed from office as their plans fail and their dreams fade. They struggle to regain a foothold through their attachments within the firm or in a lonely conspiracy to return. The ambassadors lead larger firms and show moderate strength in increasing sales, assets, employment, and profits through their reign. Their firms are the next most highly valued by investors after those of the monarchs. The governors serve the shortest reigns in office and come from the largest companies, with a large proportion of outside directors. Despite lackluster results through the course of their term, governors' corporations show a dramatic increase in profits before the governors leave office, either due to late-career galvanization or due to a delayed payoff of prior strategic moves.

Monarchs and generals share both a stronger attachment to the heroic stature of office and a zealous pursuit of a heroic mission. Monarchs, however, were especially frustrated with their degree of accomplishment of this mission. In looking at the kinds of corporations that fostered monarch-like departure styles, we found that monarchs led smaller firms for longer periods and enjoyed greater control over their boards. Their stubborn visions resulted in their firms' growth and captured the imagination of investors. Their ambition and control over their settings allowed them to set a continuous upward spiral of goals, but this may have led to their frustration and the sense of incomplete mission in late career, because they found themselves unable to hit a continuously moving target. In their retirement, they sought to maintain an on-site office, perhaps believing in their continued indispensability to the company.[33] With so much left to accomplish, they felt significantly more strongly than most other leaders that their retirement was premature and forced.[34] This no doubt explains their complete disinterest in retirement planning. Not a single monarch cared to contemplate life after the top office.[35]

The generals' exit profiles were similar, but not identical. They, too, were enamored of the heroic stature of high office, but frustration with their heroic mission was less than it was for the monarch. For the generals, the dominant trauma was the blow to their ego, their identity as the leader. Their firms were a little larger than those of the monarchs and showed average growth in profits. By the end of their reign, the generals had decided to make their mark by enormously boosting sales growth and market share. Like the monarchs, their departure behavior also showed a distinct disdain for retirement planning.[36] They, too, felt that their retirements were forced and premature.[37] Unlike the monarchs, however, the generals, like the ambassadors, were more likely to remain on the board of directors.[38] They did not build lasting monuments, as did the monarchs. Instead, they clung to the memories of power and the aura of their authority and status. Accordingly, they complained in their retirement of lost power, lost prestige, and the lack of a spotlight, which few of the other chief executives, including monarchs, lamented.[39] Furthermore, all retained a formal position and a title in the firm after their retirement.[40] The generals were unique in yet another way. Despite all the losses they mourned, they were the only group of leaders to describe retirement as a relaxation from stress.[41] Apparently, retirement eventually meant the end of a losing battle to stay in charge.

Ambassadors were the most comfortable with their performances in retirement; they were content with their stature and felt fulfilled in their mission. They had neither identity losses nor fear for the durability of their contributions. Their firms were large and profitable, with a record of moderate growth over their reign. They were happy to continue an association with their successful firms as board members. Unlike the generals, however, they scrupulously avoided circumventing their successors and imposing or offering their advice without explicit invitation.[42] They were content to assist quietly from the sidelines. No longer needing to prove their worth to the firm, they turned their wisdom and energies to civic causes.[43]

Finally, the governors displayed no evidence of any lingering desire for heroic stature in their firms, but they did exhibit a moderate degree of concern over a continued opportunity to make a lasting contribution. In their final years in office, they emphasized profit growth so that they would leave with a bang. They worked in the largest firms with established succession procedures and a large proportion of outside directors. Given such conditions they served shorter terms, and left both office and the board at once.[44] The governors accepted the constraints of their mature and stable institutions. To find new adventures, they knew that they would have to look beyond their firms, and through their large network of outside business contacts, they found new business opportunities. As turnaround leaders, entrepreneurs, or consultants, they were rejuvenated by new business involvements rather than by the civic activities that attracted the ambassadors.[45] Instead of entering into a less stressful period after retirement from the office, these leaders often replaced one set of stresses with another. Eager to begin new adventures quickly, they often reported that they would have liked to have retired sooner than they did.[46]

Conclusions

Some heroes, even in late career, often ride off into the sunset, not to obscurity, but in search of new adventures. But to others, retirement suggests an abdication of heroic status and an aborted heroic mission. Thus some chief executives resist exit, which they regard as a public confession of their limitations. Frequently they feel pressured into leaving office with talents and a reservoir of energy still underutilized.

Two exit barriers chief executives must conquer to overcome the retirement dilemma are the loss of heroic stature and the loss of heroic mission. Heroic stature refers to the chief executive's identification with the power and the status of office. The key to mastering this barrier to exit depends on how immersed one has become in one's heroic institutional role. Sometimes the energies required to nurture a person's public persona divert energies needed to maintain a healthy independent internal self-concept. Heroic mission refers to an executive's lifelong career purpose. The key to mastering this second barrier is to come to terms with one's own mortality and one's definition of "lasting contribution."

Executives vary in how they conquer these heroic barriers to exiting the executive suite. Some find new activities, others fight on, while still others accept their past records as a complete job well done. A comparison of chief executives with their second-in-command top officers showed the latter to have a similar dedication to the heroic mission, but a far smaller attachment to the heroic status of the executive role. Perhaps the job takes a greater toll on the personal identity of the chief executive than on any other executive in the firm.

Four patterns of departure characterize four distinct executive types: monarchs, generals, ambassadors, and governors. Monarchs were those who did not leave office willingly but were overthrown and strong-armed out, or else died in office. Generals left office reluctantly, but managed to mount campaigns for their own return to office. Ambassadors left, but remained actively involved in the firm, supporting their successors. Governors left the firm cleanly, severing virtually all continued formal contact with the firm.

In comparing exit barriers to departure style, we found that monarchs and generals were the most attached to the stature of the role and felt the least fulfillment in their role. Meanwhile ambassadors were the most content with their accomplishments and the least troubled by a loss of stature in the firm. Their companies different financial performance and their post-retirement activities correspond with different departure styles.

The retired chief executive of Du Pont, Irving Shapiro, offers a valuable insight that may help us to understand further the differences in these patterns: "Every CEO should remember that the position exists not for his benefit, but for the corporation's. It is his job to know when it is time to step down." Perhaps this is why some chief executives have managed to retire and yet preserve their heroic image, while others have unwittingly transformed themselves into late-career villains.

6

THE MONARCH'S DEPARTURE

**"I am the King himself . . . . Aye, every inch a king!
When I do stare, see how the subject quakes."**

King Lear, Act IV, Scene 6

A monarch's reign usually ends with the sovereign's death rather than with an abdication. Monarchs do not retire, but wear their crown until the end. As the 124th leader in an imperial line which, according to Japanese legend, began 2,645 years ago, the current Emperor Hirohito's sixty-year rule has set a record for longevity.[1] Hirohito has been an important symbol of Japanese national identity since he inherited the Chrysanthemum Throne on December 25, 1926, the day his father, Emperor Taisho, died. The 1947 constitution, imposed upon the Japanese by the United States after World War II, formalized his ceremonial role. Nonetheless, his spiritual significance continues, as the emperor remains the chief priest of the indigenous Japanese religion, Shinto. Furthermore, Hirohito signs documents and legislation and receives regular briefings on domestic and international affairs. His fifty-two-year-old son, Crown Prince Akihito, and his twenty-five-year-old grandson, Prince Hiro, wait in the line of succession.

Those corporate leaders who fall into the monarch category are not symbolic figureheads of limited governmental monarchies. They long to be admired, and often step beyond their corporation's mandate to rule in that they refuse to entertain seriously any thought of retirement until they are ready. This, like a sovereign, is not until they die. In more traditional times, other aspirants did not always accept the lengthy reign of a king. Princes or dukes could withdraw their fealty and challenge the reigning monarch. Julius Caesar's death at the hands of his inner circle and Napoleon Bonaparte's exile are examples of emperor exits that provide a metaphorical parallel to the exit of corporate monarchs through a palace revolt of their boards of directors or management committees.

In this review of corporate monarchs we will seek to dispel several common misconceptions about these leaders. Too often sensationalized accounts of boardroom intrigue have unfairly biased our assessment of their reign. By looking at a specific monarch we can infer the characteristics that distinguish monarchs from other types of retiring chief executives.

Bruce Henderson and the Boston Consulting Group

Bruce Henderson has often been called one of the founding architects of modern strategic planning. At least eighteen consulting firms have origins in Henderson's firm. Yet despite a world renowned reputation for brilliance, by age sixty-four in 1979 Henderson had effectively been "kicked upstairs" in the firm he had created sixteen years earlier.

Henderson started his career at Westinghouse in 1941, leaving the Harvard Business School just ninety days before graduation "after a long talk with my draft board . . . my favorite professor . . . and the Dean." He obtained a deferral from military service, given the importance of Westinghouse to the war effort. During those years at Westinghouse he raced through the hierarchy, serving on the management committees of several divisions, as general manager of purchases and traffic, and eventually as vice president of purchasing.

Ten years after Henderson started at Westinghouse, the man who had hired him originally, and for whom he was now working, suffered a heart attack and was off the job for about a year. Although not yet a vice president, Henderson was asked to step in and take his boss's place on the corporate management committee. As he was already fulfilling most of his boss's other responsibilities, this was a logical next step. When the boss returned and tried to regain his seat on the management committee, the CEO refused his request and instead accepted his resignation. Henderson went on to reorganize the transformer division. After returning to headquarters, he found his own protégé had replaced him in the purchasing slot. He then worked as a troubleshooter for a previous mentor—a group vice president—and took responsibility for a few small operations, including semiconductors. Finally, he was made general manager of the failing air-conditioning division, which had never been profitable and which Westinghouse eventually liquidated ("I was thrown to the lions"). He was unable to turn the division around and was fired in the recession of 1958.

After a job search lasting more than a year, Henderson joined the consulting firm Arthur D. Little as a senior vice president. He was awed by the firm's intellectual qualities but later came to feel that, as an organization, "they survived for reasons they don't really understand," referring to the internal marketplace of ideas. Four years later, the feisty and independent Henderson got caught in the middle of political skirmishes between some of the semiautonomous groups of professionals. He was senior vice president in charge of the management services division, which represented a third of the total company. He had become interested in corporate strategy, but this topic spanned different practice areas. After a clash over professional and personal matters with the man who had originally hired him, Henderson was again fired.

He then created the Boston Consulting Group (BCG) in 1963. The firm originated as a department of the Boston Safe Deposit & Trust Company (BSD&T), where it helped in the management of small firms contained in some private estates. In six years he established BCG's reputation for expertise and brilliance with a growth rate that doubled the firm's size every two years, and it was incorporated as a subsidiary in 1968. Under Henderson's forceful rule and imagination the firm prospered, but here again a power struggle flared up. In 1971, Henderson established three internal teams—red, blue, and green—"to provide coordinated professional leadership," but as he puts it, "I made one mistake—I didn't find a means for them to have any territory, so they started to kill each other." The first major challenge to the organization's stability occurred when an ambitious team leader, William Bain, left the firm, according to Henderson, frustrated by his inability to get Henderson to name Bain as his successor. Bain defected along with several other BCG professionals to form a rival consulting firm in 1972.

Henderson had hired Bain, a former Vanderbilt University official, and trained him in the field of strategic planning. Years later, Henderson still spoke emotionally of this incident. He was visibly angry at the disloyalty displayed by one in whom he had had so much faith:

> He told me . . . he was resigning to start a . . . consulting firm to apply some of the ideas [he] had developed. . . . He also told me that he would probably try to recruit a few people from BCG.
> Both Bain and I were scheduled to leave that evening to fly to a meeting in Madrid. . . . Bain did not go, of course, but I had to go. . . .

Unfortunately, coincidentally, or as a result of Bain's careful planning, both The Boston Company board [the parent of BSD&T] and the BSD&T board were meeting that day. I could get only ten minutes of [the CEO's] time before I had to go.

[I]n Madrid all of the talk was about Bain. . . . If Bain could recruit enough people from BCG, he could seriously damage BCG's image, and even worse he could put TBC [the parent] in a position so that they would almost have to financially back Bain in some way, and sponsor him publicly in order to protect their own image. . . . If that happened Bain's attraction for the younger staff would be irresistible. . . . Bain's negotiation leverage over TBC would be so great that almost anything could happen.

During the meeting in Madrid, Henderson learned from his secretary in Boston that Bain had obtained a commitment for financing from The Boston Company. He promptly raced back to contact Boston Company officials and dispatched his own loyalists to clients to prevent them from defecting to the new rival. After an "eight-day war," Henderson was able to dissuade The Boston Company from supporting the "renegades" and thereby kept control of his firm. Bain set up shop within a half mile of BCG's offices. Beyond the personal affront, Henderson was distressed that the trauma of Bain's pullout had destroyed so much trust within his organization.

With the closing of the chapter on Bain, Henderson turned his attention to the ownership of BCG. He wanted to negotiate an employee buy-out of BCG from the parent company. TBC, a conservative Yankee trust company, had lost face and millions of dollars in legal fees following the great Equity Funding insurance scandal. Furthermore the impatience of BCG people to form an independent firm and the embarrassment caused by the publishing of Henderson's high salary were troubling to already burdened TBC. In 1974, federal legislation (ERISA) made it possible for a company to structure its profit-sharing and retirement plans in such a way that it could be entirely owned by its employees. Henderson initiated this process in October of 1974. By the time the process was completed in 1975, BCG had grown to almost fifty officers and three hundred associates in seven offices.

Unfortunately, power struggles within the organization had not yet ceased. Boston Company officers, disgruntled with their lack of voice in the organization, were meeting out of hours to discuss "changes" to the BCG management structure. In discussing the buy-out, BCG's own officers became embroiled in disputes over the terms of employment and the power structure under the new ownership scheme. The BCG officers finally appointed a three-member task force to hammer out an agreement. Henderson and two senior officers eventually worked out a proposal saying that: (1) all current officers would become directors of BCG, and (2) Bruce Henderson would hold an employment contract that would give him a third higher salary than any other employee and twice as much as the average officer, until he reached the age of seventy. Henderson then removed himself from the negotiations and appointed two senior officers to hammer out an agreement with the parent company.

In a 1979 palace revolt organized by yet another leader of one of the three original teams, Henderson was dethroned from the kingdom he had created. According to Henderson, "control of the Boston office was control of the company at that time," and it was that control that was wrested from Henderson by Alan Zakon, leader of the group of disgruntled officers. After gaining enough influence over incoming business leads, Zakon "managed to obtain enough support to convince me that he should be appointed manager" of the Boston office. According to Henderson, "That was the end of my ability to have any significant influence over the company and its policies even though I remained CEO until my sixty-fifth birthday a year or so later."

At the time of Zakon's ascension, a three-member policy advisory committee was instituted to oversee the strategic direction of the company. The CEO would be a permanent member with the other two positions rotating among the officer group. From the start, the policy committee made it clear that they didn't want Henderson to play any part in their discussions. His central position in influencing the strategic directions and operating decisions of the firm was taken away. He was invited to continue generating his innovative theories, but he was shunned in his efforts to offer suggestions and observations regarding more substantive matters.

Henderson claims today that he never intended to be an entrepreneur but approached every company he ever worked for expecting to spend the rest of his life there—although it never worked out that way. According to Henderson, he's "been fired" from every company he's joined since business school, and it looked as if he were "being fired from BCG as well." But this time it meant a lot more:

> I think a lot of my problem with BCG is I care more about the company than I do about myself. I'll tell you, there is nothing more deadly than to have something that you put everything you have into—your marriage, your children, and all the other things—then you get told, "Get lost." Whatever you think is not only worthless, it's annoying. You can break somebody pretty easily that way.

From Henderson's perspective, his employment agreement should have kept him involved in some major role at BCG until he was seventy. But what he saw instead was a deliberate effort to change some things he stood for, just to prove he was no longer in power. Initially, Henderson bemoaned the fact that BCG was never going to be the kind of company he wanted it to be. Others in the firm may have said that was just as well, but the creator's vision had been destroyed nonetheless. More recently, Henderson has voiced the opinion that BCG, once again under new leadership, has gotten back on track. John Clarkson, the new CEO, had "kept his poise during a very turbulent period of political infighting." Now, the "intellectual fertility is being restored."

Interestingly, Henderson now says he believes there shouldn't *be* a CEO position in a consulting firm. Instead, he feels there should be a managing partner who is thought of as a partner willing to take on a rather "unwelcome burden for the good of the firm." Is Henderson now seeing what might have stopped a palace revolt years earlier? No, he says, "You will never stop palace revolts except by joining ranks to overcome a common enemy. Too much success always fuels palace revolts with their power struggles." As for his own firm's CEO post, Henderson says it continued to exist because they "wanted someone besides me and I had set the model." Unfortunately, the model that Henderson had set was perhaps too domineering for the democratic leaning of the intellectual free spirits that BCG had historically attracted. Had the roles been reversed, it is likely that Henderson would have felt equally as stifled. Henderson's view of management succession draws from the sociobiological explanations of ethologists. He believes that, as in wolf packs where one of the pack males looks for a chance to kill the alpha male, which leads the pack, succession in human groups is based on an urge to dominate. Furthermore, Henderson contends that professional service firms, with their tendency to form loyalties at the work unit level, are especially vulnerable to such power struggles.

Monarch Succession Characteristics

In this book I challenge the notion that the succession and departure styles of a leader are determined by industry. I believe that Bruce Henderson's loss of domain illuminates one form of departure—the monarch's. I contend that there are five common themes or characteristics of monarchs' exits that are found in the experience of Bruce Henderson. First, monarchs leave their thrones only through their death, ill health, or, as with Henderson, a palace revolt. Second, monarchs often rule over a kingdom of their own creation. They may or may not have founded the institution they head, but they have often radically reshaped it. Third, the reshaping is frequently made possible because they entered the scene during a time of great turmoil in the business environment and they presented a plan with both a collective purpose and an effective method for organizing the effort. Fourth, the monarchs themselves may become enslaved by their leadership plans. As times change, they often fail to change plans appropriately to the new conditions. The original mandate is enshrined as a sacred mission. Fearful of change in their career role, they cling to the familiar leadership vision that worked in the past. They worry that a change in their role may cause them to lose their footing. A monarch feels most competent when maintaining the continuity of the original mission. Fifth, the monarchs do not believe in a planned succession process. Powerful new leaders are not groomed, but instead they emerge as rival candidates and are left to fight among themselves.

As we saw in Chapter 5, monarchs have both a strong attachment to their heroic identity and an ongoing feeling of lack of fulfillment of their heroic mission. They believe that the course of history depends on the actions of a single person, and in the same way that the survival of their firm depends on one indispensable person.

Bruce Henderson is instructive in another way. He must be admired for his resilience. Monarchs are difficult to defeat and after his relegation to a subordinate role at the Boston Consulting Group, he joined the faculty of Vanderbilt University's business school. He retained his interest in doing "whatever I can to help [BCG]," yet he recognized the barriers to regaining the centrality and voice he once enjoyed and so desperately desires: "Of course I had a great identification with BCG, as I still do with my own children. [But] I know better than to offer unsolicited advice to either my children or BCG." He prepared for teaching by attending classes at Harvard's Advanced Management Program at age sixty-eight. Nonetheless, he reported two years later that the transition to teaching was tougher than he had imagined: "Those kids can be demanding—they really want to be heard and not just be listeners."

Despite his extraordinary accomplishments, Bruce Henderson is hardly a complacent man. He still looked for new challenges and had dreams of further accomplishment. Complete satisfaction for him may always be elusive. His drive to continually surpass earlier achievements may be inherited. Through door-to-door book sales, his father had worked himself up from poverty to the presidency of a publishing company. As a commissioned salesman, he was making more than the president of his firm, Southwestern Publishing. The elder Henderson eventually bought the firm and ran it until the late 1950s. At the age of seventy-two, faced with the imminent defection of several star salesmen, he sold the company to two employees in order to keep it intact, rather than pass it along to the family, one of whom had worked full time for the company. Henderson said that he himself could have just about bought the firm from his father—although they never discussed it—but was not interested in doing so:

> I did not want to buy the Southwestern Publishing Company under any condition, or at any price. I was already a vice president of Westinghouse in an environment I knew a lot about and was succeeding in. I detested house-to-house selling of books. . . . *I knew I could not manage that company and hold it together.* . . . I am convinced that Dad *wanted* to sell the

Southwestern Company to his key employees. He knew they would carry it on as he had. They did.

Was his father impressed with his son's accomplishments? Henderson reflected on his father:

> He just kept setting higher and higher expectations which I could never meet. He was very proud of my success in Westinghouse, but he could never bring himself to tell me; I heard about it secondhand from his friends.

As for his mother, she never quite comprehended it. He remembered her visiting him one day when he was in charge of procurement for Westinghouse's transformer division.

> She came over and said, "Why, Bruce, this office is much bigger than your father's." He only had an old broken-down desk and his office was eighteenth century. He was not pretentious about his office.

Henderson went on discussing this parental influence:

> A strong, successful father is bound to have some influence upon you. It makes you feel like you can never live up to him. He's ten feet tall. He doesn't look that way quite so much now, but I'm sure he did accomplish a lot more than I have ever accomplished. It's a long way from Hard Rock Farm with eight children and no education to what he accomplished.

Because of the media coverage and drama surrounding monarch departures, many of us have formed harsh theories about the nature of monarchs. Monarchs' exposed vanities are captured in the stories in the media, but their business genius and frailties as human beings are rarely explored further. When I have presented my studies to both managers and scholars, I have been struck by their haste to seize on a single descriptive feature as the universal cause of monarch exit patterns. For example, I regularly hear, "That's just what happens in family businesses." Other times I hear, "This is how entrepreneurs are. They have an unresolved oedipal struggle and are fighting the ghosts of their fathers." Yet still other times, "These selfish curmudgeons are really only common to those industries such as show business, where flamboyant personalities prevail." The following examples of monarchs provide a wide spectrum of executive profiles that challenge the simplicity of such preconceptions—including the common assumption that all monarchs are male.

Media Moguls

The communications industry has long represented changing tastes, technologies, and leaders. It is also an industry that is hard for a leader to abandon. The glamour, power, and excitement give one's career a mesmerizing quality. It is not surprising that we could find that the communications industry, particularly the media of motion pictures and television, frequently gives rise to monarchs.

Lew Wasserman provides an example of a monarch-founder who shows no sign of stepping down from his long reign. He became president of the Music Corporation of America in 1946 at age thirty-two. The firm was then a talent agency that had been founded in 1923 by Jules Stein, a Chicago eye doctor. Wasserman had previously worked for Stein for a decade, having begun as a theater usher. Over the next forty-two years, Wasserman transformed the firm into a major film studio. Today, he owns 7 percent of MCA's stock and is an active trustee of trusts that control an additional 8 percent. In 1952, one of his clients, Ronald Reagan, then president of the Screen Actors' Guild, allowed MCA both to represent actors as their agents and to produce television shows in which they appeared. Following a Justice Department antitrust investigation in 1962 of the MCA domination of television programming, MCA signed a consent decree to leave the talent-agent business. That same year Wasserman bought Universal Pictures and its parent, Decca Records, having already moved into filmmaking through the purchase of Universal's studio and a lot three years earlier. At seventy-four years of age and still in firm control of the company he has built, Wasserman does have a probable successor in fifty-four-year-old Sidney J. Sheinberg, but there has been no public plan for Wasserman to wind down his triumphant long run.

Another moviemaker, Louis B. Mayer, did not have the luxury of choosing when to terminate his reign. He was born in Russia in 1885 and emigrated to Canada at age three. Mayer came to the United States in 1907, leaving his father's ship salvage business. He bought a theater in Haverhill, Massachusetts, and alternated film showings with live stage shows. Mayer ultimately built a large chain of New England theaters and helped form a New York film distributorship called Metro Pictures. By 1918, Mayer decided to become further involved in production and founded Mayer Pictures in Culver City, California. Another entrepreneur, Marcus Loew, merged Mayer's two firms with Goldwyn Pictures to form Metro-Goldwyn-Mayer. MGM was the largest motion-picture company in the world by the 1940s, largely through the creative genius of its production head, Irving Thalberg. After World War II, revenues at MGM and its parent company, Loew's, dropped sharply. Mayer was forced to resign amidst a battle with Loew's chief executive, Nicholas Schenck, in 1951. Years later, under its new owner, Laurence Tisch, Loew's sold off MGM and left filmmaking. Tisch later bought control of CBS.

In television, Leonard Goldenson is a prime example of the monarchical leader and shows many of the heroic qualities of the business leader as well. The son of a Russian-born merchant, he entered Harvard at age sixteen, eventually graduating from Harvard Law School. He got his start in the media when he left a New York law firm to help Paramount Pictures reorganize its New England theater operations. In 1938 he was given responsibility for all of its 1,700 theaters and became a director of the company. In 1944 Paramount was forced to divest its theater operations. Goldenson then became president of United Paramount Theaters, which he merged with the newly independent American Broadcasting Company, which RCA had been forced to spin off from NBC. Eventually, ABC liquidated the theaters and began to show feature films on television. By 1980, Goldenson had brought ABC entertainment and sports programs to a leading position in the industry. The internal succession politics during this thirty-four-year rule were often fierce, but they ended when he approached his eightieth year and the company agreed to be acquired by Capital Cities Communications in late 1985. The only place for him was to remain on the Capital Cities board with no other corporate position. His heir apparent, Frederick Pierce, whom many had expected to succeed Goldenson before the sale, did not succeed him after it, and, like Goldenson, he retains a seat only on the Capital Cities board.

Though Goldenson does not embody all of the characteristics of the monarch, he has enough to qualify. Like many, he was more willing to sell his firm than to see it pass to an independent leader from within. He has attributed much of his ambition to his mother's inspiration:

> The drive I have . . . I think it comes from my mother. She had great drive. She died at 96½ years of age and up until two years before her death, she was up every morning at 6:30, active in charity and doing things. . . . She wanted to know what was going on in Washington, about politics. She had read every book that ever came and more.[2]

Publishing—The "Gentleman's" Profession

In publishing, there have been long dynastic reigns of prominent newspaper families, such as the Sulzbergers of the *New York Times*, the Mayer/Graham family of the *Washington Post*, the Cowles of the *Des Moines Register*, the Taylors of the *Boston Globe*, the Pulitzers, and the Hearsts. But instead of being the saga of a given leader's career, however, the dramas and lessons of these succession experiences are in the family setting. We will defer dealing with the special challenges of mastering transitions in the family enterprise until Chapters 10 and 11.

The genius of magazine publishing monarch Henry Robinson Luce, founder of *Time, Life,* and *Fortune,* is an often-told story. Less widely known is the interesting life and death of Cyrus H. K. Curtis, the founding publisher of the *Ladies' Home Journal*, whose magazine empire, while he lived, was the largest in the world. Curtis began this popular magazine in 1883 as a supplement to his weekly magazine, the *Tribune and Farmer*. Initially, his wife edited this supplement. Curtis attracted the leading literary and political figures of the day as regular contributors, boosting circulation to 700,000. With much fanfare, he brought in a new editor to attract and handle these celebrity authors. The editor was Edward W. Bok, a Dutch immigrant and former Scribner's editor. Bok served as editor for thirty years.

Curtis then purchased the dying *Saturday Evening Post* in 1887. He and his new editor, George Horace Lorimer, built circulation up from 2,000 subscribers to three million, which made the *Post* the largest selling weekly magazine in the world. Their editorial policy focused on interpreting everyday life for middle-class families. These two magazines, the *Post* and the *Ladies' Home Journal*, made Curtis the world's wealthiest and most successful magazine publisher. He earned two dollars out of every five dollars spent on magazine advertising. Curtis's later efforts as publisher of the *Country Gentleman*, the *Public Ledger*, and the *Philadelphia Inquirer* were less successful. He served as president of his company until the age of eighty-two, when he made himself chairman. He died the next year, and his death was soon followed by those of his long-time editors Lorimer and Bok. In fact, the entire publishing operation almost followed Curtis to his grave. Within a decade, all of its magazines were overtaken in circulation by rival publications. Eventually, the *Journal* was sold and the *Post* ceased publication, to be revived years later by another organization. As with other monarchs, Curtis did not create an organization that could survive his exit. He was succeeded by his old friends who were good editors, but were not the general managers to lead this publishing house for later generations.

Lenore Hershey and the Ladies' Home Journal

Years after Curtis Publishing had sold the *Ladies' Home Journal*, a later editor, Lenore Hershey, displayed striking monarchic tendencies. Like Helen Gurley Brown at *Cosmopolitan* and Katherine Graham at the *Washington Post*, Lenore Hershey managed to gain professional prominence in an era when women usually worked only at home. Hershey was proud of becoming a leading editor in women's magazines, as well as having married and raised a family. An only child and sole girl in an all-boy camp managed by her father in upstate New York, Hershey decided as a young girl that she wanted two things in life: to own a leopard coat and to be editor of the *Ladies' Home Journal*. These two desires so clearly expressed by the young girl are hallmarks of the woman's later managerial style, a style that combined tenacity with femininity and an ability to succeed and survive in a male world.

Although Hershey "rode the wave made by the pioneers of the women's movement," she was well prepared to take advantage of the moment. At the age of six Hershey moved with her mother for the school year to New York City and entered P.S. 26. In the city, Hershey came under the influence of her mother's sister, Aunt Grace, "a rebel, a free thinker, and above all, a *writer*." Her aunt, Helen Grace Carlisle, was Hershey's most significant role model in her childhood, and it was through her that Hershey sat on the periphery of the literary world in her teenage years.

After graduating from Hunter College with a major in journalism, Hershey began to work and write. She wrote a short story one summer weekend, sold it to the *Saturday Evening Post,* and later acknowledged how this success captured her imagination. She got a job in the promotion department at the *New York Herald Tribune,* where she helped to run forums, working with such people as Clare Booth Luce. But no one is a hero without overcoming a setback. In the midst of her developing career, Hershey was hit by a taxi and spent the next year in the hospital and at home learning to walk again, with the support of her husband, an anesthesiologist.

George H. Allen, Hershey's former boss at the *Tribune* who was then at *McCall's,* asked the housebound patient, who felt "overweight, despondent and shut off from life," to do some free-lance writing. From this inauspicious beginning, Hershey joined the regular *McCall's* staff when she recovered. Her journey led from *McCall's,* where she advanced from senior editor to special projects editor, to the top of the masthead at the *Ladies' Home Journal* as its editor-in-chief.

Hershey's description of her move from *McCall's* to the *Journal* well illustrates her internal drive to achieve her goal and outmaneuver any roadblocks that threatened to stop her. In the fall of 1968, it seemed as if *McCall's* was headed for a turnover of editors. Hershey went to Herb Mayes, then president of the company, and asked if she could be considered for the position of editor:

> He patted me on the head and said that despite my many talents, as far as he was concerned no woman could ever edit a mass woman's magazine. Couldn't hack it, he felt.

Affronted by this attitude, Hershey, "in a deliberate act of career coquetry," called Helen Meyer at Dell Publishing, who offered Hershey a position:

> As I knew she [Meyer] would, she called John Carter [formerly of *McCall's* and now at the *Ladies' Home Journal*] for a reference and as I knew he would, he reacted with his usual competitiveness. He called me for breakfast the following morning, and in three days I was out of my dead-end [job] and into the leadership of the *Journal.*

Hershey's career soared at the *Journal.* She served as editor-in-chief for eight years, from 1973 to 1981. In her first issue Hershey invited

Truman Capote to write a column called "Blind Items," composed of gossip vignettes about people without identifying them; the *Journal*'s lawyers shuddered, but finally cleared the Capote vignettes for publication. In this same period, Hershey began the *Ladies' Home Journal* "Woman of the Year" awards. In addition, she made innumerable connections with the rich and famous in Hollywood, Washington, D.C., and New York City, bringing important personalities into the pages of the magazine as contributors.

In spite of these accomplishments, the company administration wished to have her leave.

> As an editor I lived through nine presidents and I believe of the nine presidents, at least three decided that they wanted to oust me and one of them did a wonderful thing: he gave me a gorgeous party on the occasion of my fifth anniversary as an editor. Then he met me for breakfast on the following Monday and told me to fire one of my editors. I said, "Well I can't do that, he worked so long, it's Christmas. . . . I had intended to phase him out in a more gentle way." He said, "Give him a party, I always give people a party before I let them know they're out." But I lived to see him go.

The pressure on Hershey continued for two more years. Eight presidents requested that she find a replacement for herself.

> But I did not want to leave. I was still functioning, I was still a major figure in magazines; I had power, I had input, and so I half-heartedly interviewed people. . . . Frankly I could not see anybody who I thought was good enough to train or to replace me. I hired a "beard" as it were, a woman who I knew would never do it. . . . [She] fulfilled the outside qualifications but I knew she would not be a threat.

Faced with these tactics, the company devised its own counterplot:

> I was called in and the man who was head of the corporation said that they were going to give me my own company, which was a wonderful deal for there was more money than I was earning as an editor, and they gave me this iron-clad contract. *And* they took the search [for my successor] out of my hands; they turned it over to a search firm.

Lured by the presidency of a small communications subsidiary that was owned by the same new conglomerate, the Charter Company, that had bought the *Journal*, Hershey moved on. But the fortunes of the Charter Company changed. Four top executives were killed in a helicopter crash. The chief executive of the company, Hershey's mentor, who had given her free reign on the new endeavor, first went out of the communications business and ultimately put the whole company into Chapter 11 bankruptcy.

By holding on so tenaciously to her power and position at the *Journal*, and purposely hiring someone who was as nonthreatening as her successor, Hershey exhibited many of the characteristics of a monarch. She also did not actually retire. Half a decade later, she is still active as a magazine consultant. She has worked for *Esquire* magazine, helped launch *New York Woman,* and has various other clients, including Phillip Moffit, Hearst, and the American Express Publishing Company.[3]

The Merchant Monarchs

Another field that provides an opportunity for the monarch personality to flourish is consumer marketing, which does not have the high barriers to entry of some other fields. Ranging from the producer to the retailer, the chain of activities in this industry includes the world of fashion and its trendsetting accoutrements, where new ideas and strong promotion can successfully sweep through the marketplace. At the same time, it is possible for some strong leaders to become permanent life-long players.

William Black

William Black provides an excellent case study of the innovative founder-monarch of a firm who, resisting all attempts at usurpation, dies in office.

The "Horatio Alger-like" story of Chock Full O' Nuts began in 1922, when Black opened a nut stand in Times Square. With success and expansion, Black initiated what became an admired and widely imitated innovation on the traditional luncheonette/diner concept. His lunch counters offered a standard menu of high-quality items. The firm was also a pioneer in hiring practices. For example, the firm hired baseball player Jackie Robinson over thirty years ago to be one of the first black vice presidents in corporate America.

This large chain began to falter as the chairman became ill. Since Black was unable to go to his office for over a year, his longtime friend and personal physician actually sat in as president of the firm.[4] Meanwhile, Black claimed to control "through memos, every detail of the operations of Chock Full O'Nuts." The firm was generating about $118 million in sales annually through its coffee and restaurant activities at the time Black entered the hospital in 1981 at the age of eighty-three, but its earnings had been mediocre. Given its extensive cash reserves and its valuable mid-city real estate, the firm began to look like an attractive acquisition target. A disenchanted stockholder, sixty-six-year-old Jerry Finkelstein, began a proxy battle to wrest control from Black. Black was not easily ousted and survived a vicious proxy fight in December 1982. While Black won the fight for control over his firm, he lost the fight for his life. On March 8, 1983, Black died. His widow and the various shareholder groups reached a conciliation by separating the restaurants from the real estate.

Victor Potamkin

Super car salesman Victor Potamkin has been a car dealer for over forty years, beginning with his Philadelphia Cadillac dealership. By age seventy-five in 1986, he had thirty dealerships with sales just short of $1 billion. Known for his discounts and heavy advertising—he buys more television time in New York City than Macy's and Bloomingdale's combined—he has no interests outside of selling cars and raising money for research on Alzheimer's disease. This degenerative illness had taken his wife as a victim. One of his sons commented, "My father has no hobbies. He doesn't play golf. He's in the office every day."[5] He was without a successor until his sons recently joined him in the business. Potamkin reflected on this with pride: "Children of very strong, rich men usually end up playing the piano or being a little mixed up. My children want to outdo me."[6] Should the sons truly be groomed to take over, Potamkin may curb his monarchic tendencies.

Paul Kalmanovitz

Another consumer-products monarch, Paul Kalmanovitz of Falstaff Brewing, built a loosely strung holding company of breweries over a thirty-year period. He began with the Los Angeles beer 102 Brewery in 1956 and kept acquiring discarded, but once popular, local labels. Included in his portfolio were Falstaff, Ballantine, Narragansett, Lucky Lager, Jax, Pearl, and finally the *pièce de résistance*, Pabst. He survived against the well-financed advertising campaigns of the large national breweries by paring his advertising costs and administrative expenses to less than half of those companies, thus enabling him to sell his beers for less than the national brands. In fact, Kalmanovitz was criticized for bleeding the life out of venerable old brand names that limped along only because of their prior reputations.[7]

   After the takeover of the Pabst Brewery following a difficult battle with the Heilemann brewing company, there was a large management exodus. Under Kalmanovitz, Pabst's production fell from 17 million barrels in 1976, well before he took control, to 8.9 million in 1985, and to 7.2 million in 1986. Without advertising, it became very hard to compete in an industry increasingly dominated by a few labels. Anheuser Busch controlled about 28 percent of the market; Miller, 21 percent; Strohs, 8 percent; and Heilemann, 2 percent. Most vocal among Kalmanovitz's critics were the distributors, who felt that they no longer received fair margins. Kalmanovitz commented, "I've been a maverick for 40 years protecting the image of the consumer." Kalmanovitz's health had been failing him and he kept heart-monitoring equipment by his bed. With no children, he and his wife planned to leave their entire estate to charity. On January 17, 1987, he passed away at age eighty-one, still in command. Lutz Issleib, an executive of Pearl Brewing in San Antonio, took command in his mid-forties and began to change corporate policies, such as the harsh advertising limits.

As a monarch, Kalmanovitz built a brewery as if it were a bargain basement chain of stores. He did not, however, build one that could easily outlive him. Like other monarchs, he made himself central to the firm's survival. The development of management depth, consulting after retirement, or the complete severing of ties were never likely events. It is intriguing that in his youth, Kalmanovitz had worked on the personal staff of such familiar monarchs as Franklin D. Roosevelt, William Randolph Hearst, and Louis B. Mayer.

Sheldon Coleman

In outdoor recreational goods we can find another example of a devoted late-career consumer marketer. At age eighty-three, Sheldon Coleman was still calling on customers personally so that he could pitch his outdoor recreational equipment in his favorite way. He enjoys jumping and stomping on his water cooler to prove its durability to his customers and finds his antics make the sale most times. He demonstrates his own durability at the same time. He has commented that "this firm is my whole life."[8]

The company he runs was founded by his father in 1900, a year before Coleman was born. He took control from his father in 1931 and planned to remain until he turned ninety. By 1987, he and his family still controlled 30 percent of the company's stock. Several once-likely heirs retired early when it seemed that Coleman's newly entering son would be his eventual successor. As with other monarchs, who the successors to Coleman would be remained unclear even into his ninth decade.

J. P. Morgan and the Wall Street Tycoons

J. P. Morgan, perhaps the greatest financier of the past century, not only led one of the world's most powerful banks until his death at age seventy-six, but also towered above his contemporaries as the leading statesman of the financial community through his later career. For example, at seventy-one, he served as the nation's informal central banker to calm the financial crisis known as the Panic of 1907. The nation's leading bankers, top government officials, and even the secretary of the treasury had turned to Morgan to arrange for the guaranty of endangered deposits in weak trust companies. The very success of this rescue campaign showed the nation just how much power Morgan wielded. This helped to convince Congress and the public of the need to establish the Federal Reserve System, which was formed in 1913, the year of Morgan's death.

Morgan's vast influence was demonstrated by his rescue effort of 1907, as well as his other similar acts of public service in the financial crises of 1893, 1895, and 1911. These efforts also demonstrated his lifelong skill at the organization of fragmented markets and disparate forms into a common plan. He conceived and funded controversial consolidations of railroads, steel, and other industries. His goal was to reduce competition, which he saw as wasteful. His ruthless determination to bring centralized control to industrial credit greatly contributed to financial stability and helped to build the major U.S. corporations that came into being with the twentieth century.

Morgan's great power through his bank and its array of syndicates worried the public, which was already suspicious of the high profits his bank garnered from government service. As the most powerful financial baron in the country, Morgan became a symbol to the public of an alleged supreme financial conspiracy. In contrast to his nefarious reputation, in reality he stood for loyalty and integrity to clients. In an era of reckless and unscrupulous financial promoters, Morgan maintained his principles of trustworthiness.

Morgan had the physique and personality to go with his monarchical power. He had a large frame and head, with strong facial features and piercing eyes. Known for his aloof style, aristocratic manners, and ferocious wit, he could withdraw from important parties, even those which he himself had hosted, to play solitaire.

This elder statesman of the financial industry was the prime target in 1912 of the famed House of Representatives Pujo Committee, which studied the infamous and mysterious "money trust." Throughout the investigation, Morgan denied the existence of such a system of secret financial control and even denied that he himself possessed great financial power. He was courteous and was treated with dignity in return. Morgan emerged from these hearings with his prestige intact. A few months later he died, leaving his forty-five-year-old son and namesake in charge of the business. Thus in this case the monarch passed his crown to his son and heir. The generosity in his will, similar to his philanthropy while alive, favored such personal interests as art museums and hospitals.

J. P. Morgan's long career is intriguing, for he had once contemplated an early retirement. He had been born into a family wealthy for three generations and could have retired to a life of ease. His grandfather Joseph had amassed a fortune from business in stagecoaches, hotels, and fire insurance. Joseph later put Junius Spencer, J. P.'s father, in business by buying him a partnership in a dry goods firm. Later Junius formed a partnership with George Peabody, an American merchant who had become an established London banker. J. P. first worked for his father's firm and later became the New York representative of this London firm. The firm was initially called George Peabody & Co., but later became J. S. Morgan after Peabody's death. J. P.'s own firm served as the U.S. correspondent for his father's firm, but under varying names. J. P.'s partnerships included ones with Charles Dabney, and then after Dabney's retirement with the Drexels of Philadelphia. After Anthony J. Drexel's death in 1895, the name of his firm, Drexel Morgan & Co. was changed to J. P. Morgan. Despite great success in his thirties, J. P. did not become a major public figure until he entered his forties, when he used his strong European connections to bring a large amount of capital to the U.S. railroad industry.

J. P.'s only son, J. P., Jr. (Jack), was also a leading financier, but not as dominant as his father. He died at seventy-five, still at the helm of the commercial bank formed in 1933 after J. P. Morgan & Co. was forced, along with other banking firms, to leave the securities business under the Glass-Steagall Act. The investment firm of Morgan Stanley was founded by partners who left the commercial bank.

In the case of a more recent financier, the long reign of Robert Lehman and his style of exit were thought to have been far more damaging to the firm than the long reigns of the Morgans had been to their firm.[9] Three Bavarian brothers, Henry, Emmanuel, and Meyer Lehman, founded a commodities business in 1850 in Montgomery, Alabama, which they later moved to Fulton Street in New York City. A second generation of Lehmans led the firm into investment banking through underwriting securities. One of these early public offerings was for Sears, Roebuck & Co. in 1906.

By 1925, Robert Lehman had become the principal partner of the firm, taking it into the financing of what at the time were risky businesses such as petroleum companies, electronics, and airlines. Robert Lehman's forty-year rule deteriorated by the late 1960s, as he insisted on being involved in key decisions, often with little knowledge of the major participants in the critical events. Partners became increasingly distressed over inequities in the patriarch's allocation of the profits. After his death in 1969, long-smouldering resentments erupted into open power struggles. Finally, under Peter Peterson, who had been the secretary of commerce in the Nixon administration, resentment among the warring factions briefly calmed. But Peterson came to be seen as an arrogant figure by some in the firm. By 1983, warfare broke out again as the traders, led by fifty-seven-year-old Lewis Glucksman, overthrew Peterson, who was the same age. A year later, the continued dissension led to the sale of Lehman Brothers Kuhn Loeb to Shearson Loeb Rhodes, which had already become part of American Express. A 130-year tradition had come to an end.[10]

Today, we can still find octogenarians actively running their financial service firms. George M. Ferris, at ninety-two, continues to run his ten-office Washington brokerage firm, Ferris and Company, which he founded in 1932. He arrives at work by 8:30 each morning and rarely takes more than two weeks' vacation a year. Ferris feels that good health has been an essential ingredient in his success. He has noted that his memory has also served him well; he does not remember ever having made any investment blunders.[11]

Arnold Bernhard, at eighty-five, was still chairman of Value Line, a service firm that ranks stocks and advises subscribers on whether they should buy or sell.[12] He worked each day in his firm, which he founded in 1936. It is now the largest investment advisory service in the United States, with 100,000 subscribers. Bernhard himself managed $1.6 billion in assets in Value Line's nine mutual funds. When he took the firm public in 1983, he earned $32 million for his stake in the ownership. The initial price per share was $17. Two years later, it was $27 a share. General health was important to Bernhard, and he was proud that he played tennis regularly until age seventy-seven. His daughter Jean Bernhard Buttner took over as chief executive in January of 1988 upon Bernhard's death, despite her lack of knowledge about stock analysis.

J. Paul Getty, Armand Hammer, and the Oil Barons

The oil empires and the aristocracy they sponsored have long produced sensational family dramas in such "royal" dynasties as the Rockefellers of Standard Oil, the Gettys of Getty Oil, and the Hunts of Placid Oil. Among these, the most colorful succession story is perhaps that of J. Paul Getty, the son of a multimillionaire oil entrepreneur. Getty's father, repulsed by his son's playboy lifestyle, left him a mere $500,000 upon his death in 1930. Nonetheless, Getty, through the assistance of his mother, managed to take over his father's firm and build it into one of the largest independent oil companies. His legacy was just as dramatic. Bought by Texaco in 1984 through a last-minute change of heart by his son after Getty's death, the firm could not survive a full decade with Getty gone. A bitter $12 billion lawsuit raged until 1988 between two claimants to the oil company, as Pennzoil charged that Texaco had broken up a previous binding agreement of sale between Getty and Penzoil. Meanwhile, tales of the founder continue to appear that emphasize how he maintained his baronial style of life and multitude of girlfriends well into his eighties.[13]

A very different sort of oil baron, Unocal's Fred L. Hartley, did not begin as a wealthy man, as Getty did. He joined the Union Oil company with $25 in his pocket and worked his way up from a refinery mainte-nance worker to become chief executive. He triumphed in a bitter take-over battle in the spring of 1985 when corporate raider T. Boone Pick-ens of Mesa Oil attacked. He fended off this hostile takeover by assuming a debt of $4.2 billion.[14] Hartley has avoided the troublesome diversifi-cation programs that have plagued many larger oil companies in the early 1980s. Nonetheless, several on the Unocal board have grown weary of his costly and unsuccessful shale-oil programs intended to produce geothermal power. Hartley has been committed to the business poten-tial of synfuels since he wrote a paper on it in college.[15] On approach-ing seventy, when asked about his retirement plans, Hartley snapped, "None of your damn business."[16]

Perhaps the most charismatic of all modern oil barons is the tireless ninety-year-old Armand Hammer, who has run Occidental Petroleum for thirty years as a second career after political events forced him out of the first one. Hammer may be the only reigning U.S. chief executive with a life-sized bronze bust of himself in the corporate lobby. He also has a four-foot oil portrait of himself hanging in the Occidental board-room.[17] Hammer is further renowned for his close relationships with top Soviet leaders.

Hammer's father, Julius, was a physician who owned his own phar-maceutical company and was also a dedicated socialist. He met with Lenin in Europe in 1907. Ten years later, during the Russian Revolu-tion, Julius Hammer's company broke the Western nations' blockade of Russia to sell the Bolsheviks vital medical supplies. In 1920, when his father was jailed in the United States for allegedly performing an illegal abortion, Armand Hammer was put in control of the family business. On a trip to the Soviet Union, Hammer met with Lenin.[18] Although his autobiography presented this trip as being prompted largely by his idealism, the one-hour meeting led to Hammer's becoming the first for-eign concessionaire under the New Economic Policy (NEP), an export–import venture with the Soviets, and a concession to manufacture pen-cils there. Hammer also intended to collect $150,000 owed to his fa-ther's company, the Allied Drug and Chemical Co.[19] Hammer formed the Allied American Corporation, the business agent for almost forty firms doing business in the Soviet Union. During the late 1920s, Stalin's change of the NEP led to the departure of the Hammers from Mos-cow.[20]

Armand Hammer then sold Russian art with his brother and en-gaged in the distilling business until he bought control of an unprofit-able oil company, Occidental Petroleum, in the mid-1950s. Hammer was able to build up the company in the 1960s and 1970s by negotiat-ing several large energy and real-estate deals, including a fertilizer ex-port–import deal with the Soviets. He was also able to build the company by being an astute and diplomatic oil man. In the 1960s, when oil was discovered in Libya, he convinced King Idris to deal with him instead of any of the larger "exploitative" oil companies. After Muamar el-Qaddafi deposed Idris in 1970, Hammer agreed to give up 51 percent of his Libyan holdings for $136 million in order to avoid outright expropriation. This had far-reaching consequences for the oil industry, as Arab nations, following Libya's lead, demanded greater control of the foreign-based companies drawing oil out of their lands. In 1984, Hammer echoed his legendary relationship with the Soviets by negotiating a plan with Chinese leader Deng Xiao Ping to invest $600 million (Occidental itself has a 25 percent interest and its partner is the Bank of China) in a Chinese mining operation. At the time the deal was made, it represented the largest foreign investment ever made in China.[21]

This oil baron is also renowned for his ability to direct his $20-billion public company as if it were a private firm. He owns 1 percent of Oxy stock himself, but in 1984 persuaded his board to repurchase 5 percent of the company's stock from a threatening dissenting director, David Murdock, who had entered the firm through a recently acquired beef-processing company.[22] A year later, the firm was again in the headlines as a merger with Diamond Shamrock fell through only hours after both boards had agreed to work out a deal. Diamond Shamrock was reportedly suspicious of the management depth below Hammer.[23] At the same time, Oxy's price dropped so much on the announcement of this planned merger that Diamond Shamrock directors felt it was no longer worth the price. They turned out to be mistaken when Oxy's price rose to double that of Diamond Shamrock.[24]

The issue of management depth continued to haunt Oxy, noted by several spurned heirs apparent (Zoltan Merszei and Robert Abboud), until the current president, Ray Irani, was elected three years ago. Nonetheless, Hammer is not overly concerned about succession.[25] He claims to feel "no reason to retire," with his excellent health demonstrated by his daily half-hour swims. He is further known to enjoy fully other moments in life and is the last to leave a dinner party. His friends have commented that "he seems to thrive on age."[26] Some believe that his high-level negotiating has kept him vital and alert. He has concluded multibillion-dollar merger deals roughly each year over the past decade. Hammer has stated, in reference to his retirement:

> I'm going to leave it to the Board. I have no intentions of retiring. I'm in great health. I have a great appetite and I sleep well. All my activities—running an oil company to running conferences on peace—are a reason for my longevity. It takes off the tensions and the edge. I like to tell funny stories and I like to laugh. I think that every time I do it adds years to my life.[27]

Hammer is nearly as famous for his personal acts of diplomacy and humanitarianism, particularly in relation to the Soviet Union, as he is for his business acumen. He has pursued an immodest blend of these endeavors since 1921. As his autobiography shows, he continues his strong interest in improving U.S.–Soviet relations, sometimes expressed through acts astoundingly generous for a private individual.[28] Hammer's eighty-five-year-old wife accompanies him regularly on his globe-trotting missions.

Olive Beech, Juan Trippe, and the Transportation Titans

Since the days of the charismatic and truculent railroad magnates Cornelius and William Vanderbilt of the New York Central, and Edward H. Harriman of the Union Pacific, feisty late-career monarchs have served as great reshapers of the nation's transportation industry. As air travel grew in the 1920s, the nation was introduced to yet another generation of industrial pioneers with monarchic tendencies. Many of the founders of the nation's leading airlines and aircraft makers remained active in their firms for the next half century.

Olive Ann Beech, for example, founded Beech Aircraft with her husband, Walter H. Beech, in 1932. The firm prospered soon after its founding and dominated the market for small private and commercial planes. Olive Beech was a top officer of the company. After her husband's death in 1950, she forcefully put down an attempted coup and dismissed the conspirators, taking sole control. She served as chairman of the board for the next thirty years, but relinquished the presidency to her nephew, who was eight years younger, in 1968. However, she remained in the firm as a powerful chairman. Noted for her close supervision of all aspects of aircraft manufacturing and sales, she stepped aside only when Raytheon purchased the firm in 1980. Then, at age seventy-seven, she served on the Raytheon board of directors until 1983 and still serves as honorary chairman emeritus of Beech Aircraft.

The founders of many of the trunk carriers and regional airlines parted from their creations reluctantly in the last decade, often leaving poor management depth. An example of this was Juan Trippe of Pan American World Airways, one of the greatest visionaries in commercial aviation history, a genius of transoceanic travel, and a leader in the development of new aviation equipment. He was not, however, a genius of organizational vitality. The Pan Am succession nightmare began with his dream of American aviation supremacy sixty years ago.

Trippe's entrepreneurial tale was not one of triumphing over humble origins. He was the descendant of seventeenth-century English settlers in the United States. Trippe's Yale education was interrupted by service as a Navy pilot in World War I. His father was an investment banker and Trippe tried banking right out of college. He later returned to a career in aviation when he helped found the carrier that became Pan Am, the first international air carrier. In 1935, his famed China Clipper opened the Pacific Ocean to air travel. Pan Am, through Trippe, developed its own airplanes: the Sikorsky Martin, the Boeing 707, and the Boeing 747. He introduced notions of route structure and such cultural trappings as the use of nautical terminology in commercial aviation that have remained in the industry.

Despite his imagination, the organization's survival was more a testimonial to the emotional fervor Trippe could stir up than to the viability of the organization based upon his management acumen. Many knowledgeable in the industry assert that a significant portion of Pan Am's past decade of painful deterioration can be traced back to the days when Trippe sculpted the three core dimensions of his management style: he wrote policy with his right hand, implemented it with his left hand, and saw to it that neither hand knew fully what the other was doing.[29] He so thoroughly dominated the firm that generally no system of checks and balances existed to restrain his bursting enthusiasm or correct his misguided policies.

Juan Trippe set many of the standards of the airline industry, from its romance to its arrogance. He was one of those rare individuals whom one must admire for their courageous determination to challenge prevailing practice and stir the world into new adventure. Trippe conceived and implemented a revolutionary network of international and intercontinental air travel. He was also the genius and energy behind many technological advances, pushing Boeing into providing larger, more efficient jets. Trippe also had a supersalesman's charm with senior level government officials that garnered him both senior officials' support and junior officials' resentment.

Often described as arrogant and secretive, Trippe demonstrated a drive that allowed him to demand the impossible—and usually obtain it. His single-minded dedication enabled him to win an astounding amount of support and political favor for his company, but it also alienated many in power. His board of directors, for instance, became so disenchanted with this autocratic president and his penchant for ignoring sound business advice that as early as 1939 they pushed Trippe out of the chief executive post. As one historical account noted:

> The coup d'état took place on March 14, and it was done swiftly and coldly, as gentlemen arrange these matters in their board rooms. According to the minutes, the board voted to amend the bylaws to make the chairman of the board the chief executive officer and to have Juan Trippe continue as president and general manager.[30]

Trippe was infuriated and began a plan to take vengeance by undermining the board's decision. His intimidation tactics in the boardroom so distressed Trippe's successor, Cornelius Vanderbilt Whitney, that

Whitney was forced to appeal to outside board member Thomas Morgan for help. Morgan soon discovered Whitney's difficulty. The company records, such as previous commitments and future obligations, were all locked safely in Trippe's head. Without Trippe's cooperation, even the most trivial problems could not be solved.[31] At meetings, Trippe maintained a chilly, eerie silence. He would sit in his office and spin a globe through the day, commenting from time to time on which subordinates supported the new chief and hence were disloyal to Trippe. His comments were long remembered. Finally, after almost a year of continual obstruction and frustration, the board acquiesced. Trippe was reinstated with full executive power; Whitney would continue as chairman.

Back in the pilot's seat and smug in his victory over the board, Trippe directed his attention to ensuring that Pan Am had a monopoly as America's international carrier. After World War II, talk of an open market in the airways became more pronounced. This worried Trippe; easy access to international routes would weaken the economic advantages he had obtained for Pan Am through personal diplomacy.[32] He not only wanted Pan Am to be the biggest and the best international carrier, but also wanted an exclusive franchise. He saw an erosion of market dominance as a personal threat.

But even Juan Trippe's perseverance was proving inadequate for this mission. While he was absorbed by challenges from Washington, a resurgence of discontent was brewing among the board of directors. For the second time in less than a decade, two members of the executive committee who had eased Trippe's return to power in 1940 "watched as he reverted to his secretive, freewheeling habits, reneging on his promises to name an operating officer and to keep the directors informed."[33] Their attempts to spark a revolt, however, proved more difficult than in 1939 due to Trippe's more skillful stacking of the board with loyalists. Having failed in their attempts, the two directors resigned from the Pan Am board.

Trippe ruled like a king, with his nobles grouped tightly around him. A large number of Pan Am managers were former World War II pilots who had "grown up" with the industry. Vice presidents studied the rosters each time a company report was published or a memorandum circulated to learn of their current standing in the firm. Trippe moved his ten or more vice presidents around rather capriciously. Those closest to his name at the top of a list of names were those currently in his favor. Seating order at dinner banquets conveyed this same message in an embarrassingly public fashion.

Trippe continued his obsessive efforts to make Pan Am the "chosen instrument" of U.S. international flight, but to no avail. Congress voted on the side of the free market, and Pan Am was forced to share its international routes with other U.S. carriers. Refusing to acknowledge defeat, Trippe became obsessed with restoring Pan Am's monopoly, often to the exclusion of more pressing company concerns. According to his friends, Trippe was immune to the seductions of money, but he was not immune to the lure of ambition and power. He had an imperial vision of the world that ultimately clouded his financial judgment.[34] Pan Am's financial progress through the 1950s and into the 1960s is more a tribute to Trippe's ability to attract competent subordinates than to his skill as a manager.

For example, in the mid-1960s air travel was booming, traffic was up 15 percent annually, and profits were rolling in with no end in sight. Trippe was certainly pleased with aviation's emerging place in American travel, but he was not content. In an effort to solidify Pan Am's place as the premier U.S. airline, Trippe began negotiations with Boeing to build a bigger, faster, classier plane. Thus the Boeing 747 was born. His insistence on making the 747 a reality was a spectacular gamble for Trippe, then sixty-six years old. Backing the construction and development of this aircraft would place the company, its employees, and its shareholders at enormous risk. According to one former board member, "If he judged correctly and was lucky to boot, Pan Am's leadership would be maintained. If he was wrong or fate was cruel, the airlines might go bankrupt."[35] Cost overruns and technical problems plagued the 747 from the start. Initially, Trippe refused to be thwarted, but by 1968, at age sixty-eight, he yielded to pressure from his board to step down.

In late 1967, Trippe's longtime colleague, Harold Gray, one of Pan Am's senior pilots, confided to Trippe that he was dying of cancer. Trippe thought Gray was a wonderful man; he felt Gray had the ability to do anything because he was such a fine and courageous flyer.[36] In May 1968, Trippe telephoned his directors to tell them he was going to retire and nominate Harold Gray as chairman and CEO and Najeeb Halaby, a relative newcomer to Pan Am, as president. It is not certain what was in Trippe's mind when he selected Harold Gray as his successor. It may have been sympathy for a respected friend. It may also have been a monarchic trick to pick a successor who could last for only a short period and therefore would be unable to overshadow Trippe's accomplishments and notoriety.

Whatever the true motivation, the board unanimously voted Gray into the chairman's post. Halaby's appointment was also approved, despite board skepticism regarding Halaby's knowledge of airline operations. They assumed that the sixty-two-year-old Gray had five years or so to train Halaby. Unfortunately, an antipathy between Gray and Halaby did not make for effective management, particularly at a time when Pan Am was beginning to flounder. Gray had inherited a messy 747 contract, there was increased competition on all of Pan Am's international routes, and the company had been unable to secure domestic routes to improve its profitability. Company profits declined, along with Harold Gray's health. Behind the scenes, Halaby pushed for Gray's removal. Trippe, horrified at the erosion of Pan Am, kept involved from the sidelines, but did not return to office. In 1974 he left the board.

Gray lasted for eighteen months and then retired. He was replaced by Najeeb Halaby. Even though he had originally come from the outside and knew little of the airline business, Halaby did recognize that Pan Am was woefully lacking in management depth as a result of decades of one-man rule.[37] His solution was a bloodbath that removed seventeen of the company's top twenty-three officers. Not surprisingly, this did little to aid the airline, which was already teetering on the edge of bankruptcy. In April 1972, after twenty-seven months as CEO, Halaby, having failed to right the Pan Am ship, which was sinking under the weight of a declining passenger load and enormous interest payments on the catastrophic Boeing 747 debacle, was replaced by William Seawell.

Seawell, brought in from the military, enjoyed a longer and more successful tenure. Through various cost-cutting measures and drastic route reductions, Seawell managed to stem Pan Am losses. In fact, he was ultimately able to produce three years of back-to-back profits.[38] Seawell had, to some extent, refashioned a "shadow government" that functioned out of his office and which paralleled corporate staff functions. Some suggest he was simply overpowered by market events and internal politics. The board finally pushed Seawell out and announced William Waltrip as the new acting CEO reporting to the board. Seawell continued to hover in the background until August 1981, when Edward Acker was offered the chairmanship. Trippe himself had passed away four months earlier.

In 1988, roughly sixty-five years after its inception and twenty years after Trippe's retirement, the carrier still limps along. Its days of glory lie in the past, however, following a decade that saw the sale of its luxury international hotel chain, its prominent headquarters towering over New York's Grand Central Terminal, its flamboyant terminal at J.F.K. International Airport, and even its historic and profitable routes to the Pacific. In the spring of 1987, four unions representing 20,000 pilots, engineers, and clerical workers who had survived a decade of severe layoffs asked the firm to reorganize or merge with a stronger carrier.[39] Little of the pride or grand purpose of the past remained in the enterprise.

The Kings of Conglomerates

The dramatic exit of leaders of conglomerates is a reminder of how pivotal their role is to the coherence of the firm. Frequently the energy

of these leaders is the only glue that binds unrelated businesses together. A successor must master a confusing swirl of activities that he
or she inherits as the conglomerator's legacy. Often, successors feel
compelled to turn to consolidations and divestitures to get control of a
far-flung enterprise. The conglomerators reviewed here ranged in age
from their mid-fifties to their mid-nineties. Regardless of their age at
exit, their agendas were not yet complete, and their boards were left
with succession crises.

Bluhdorn and Gulf & Western

Charles Bluhdorn, the founder of Gulf & Western, died of a heart attack at age fifty-six while returning from a business trip to the Caribbean in February 1983. As he died while still in full control of his company, there can be no doubt that he left like a monarch, whether he
meant to or not. Bluhdorn's tragic end left the firm in the lurch. Some
may wonder if a succession plan was necessary given such an untimely
tragedy. But it was revealed years later that even had there not been
this fatal heart attack, Bluhdorn's life expectancy was tenous. Bluhdorn
had been suffering from cancer for three years. Several board members, as well as his eventual successor, never knew Bluhdorn was as ill
as he was.[40]

Bluhdorn's life was his work, and he was known for his tireless dedication to the company. He had few, if any, outside interests beyond his
family. His diligence was noteworthy even as a youth. Bluhdorn was
born in Austria, but his family fled the Holocaust and escaped to England. In 1942, upon his arrival in New York as a young man, he began
working as a cotton broker and attending City College at night. He
fought in the U.S. Army in World War II and returned to continue his
studies and to work in an import–export firm. In 1949, he began to
purchase makers and distributors of auto parts. By 1970, his firm was
the sixty-fourth largest industrial corporation in the nation. He had begun diversifying in 1965, buying a zinc company, Paramount Pictures,
Brown Paper Company, Consolidated Cigars, Simon & Schuster publishing, sugar refineries, theater chains, a missile components manufacturer, cable television firms, steel mills, and industrial equipment and
instrument makers. Perhaps he never named a successor because he
felt one would consolidate this range of enterprises and take the company in a totally new direction.

The selection of a successor in the time of crisis following Bluhdorn's
death was not easy. After a six-and-a-half-hour emergency board meeting, President David N. Judelson was bypassed by the board in favor of
Senior Vice President Martin Davis. A board member explained:

Charlie left no written legacy as to who would succeed him, but Davis is clearly the man he would have wanted. No one knows this company better than Martin Davis.[41]

Judelson and Davis had been regarded as fierce rivals. Judelson, the expert on the company's original industrial and manufacturing operations, promptly resigned. Davis, more the expert on the service businesses in the Gulf & Western portfolio, won only after an intense power struggle with John H. Duncan, the chairman of the executive committee. Several board members at first favored Duncan for the position. Thus virtually all top positions in the firm were destabilized following the exit of the leader.

Within three years, Davis had sold off $2.6 billion in assets, divesting the company of sugar operations in the Caribbean and Florida, building products, consumer products, industrial products, and Bluhdorn's prized portfolio of diversified stocks. Davis, a former film industry executive, retained the entertainment and communications units and the financial services units. The board eventually gave Davis the title of chairman as well. During the year of his death, Bluhdorn's title as chairman was left vacant, and his office was preserved in tribute. His wife was named to his board seat.

Harry Gray and United Technologies

As with that of other monarchs, Harry Gray's contentious exit was characterized by hostile feelings toward allegedly disloyal heirs apparent and board members. Amidst unproven—but thoroughly investigated—allegations against him of wiretapping, bugging rooms, and other unsupported charges of cloak-and-dagger-like surveillance between a monarch and various heirs apparent, a brilliant and tenacious conglomerator began the humiliating and painful task of piecing his reputation and sense of mission back together. The sense of attack is not new for this monarch. Harry Gray, a resilient fighter since early childhood, was forced to keep fighting even into his retirement, but he has still not given up.

Financial analyst John W. Adams, of the respected Boston investment firm of Adams, Harkness, & Hill, aptly pinpointed the challenge Gray faced in late career in a September 25, 1985, report on Gray's retirement that year from United Technologies. The report began:

We have long differed with the predominant view of Harry Gray. The world has seen him as an undisciplined acquirer of companies. We have come to know him for the paradox that he is, an entrepreneur in a corporate setting. A born risk-taker, Mr. Gray is also a born leader: initially a rank outsider in the parochial Connecticut Valley, he now commands the virtually unanimous loyalty and affection of those who work with him.

> The supreme irony is that the world is misreading Harry Gray's departure as completely as it misread his career.

What is this "misreading" to which Adams referred? It is the imputation of evil motives to Gray regarding his succession. When Gray was forced to leave the company at the age of sixty-six, his reluctance to do so was not due to a selfish desire to hang onto his power for as long as possible; instead, suspecting lack of preparation of his successor, and recognizing that the company faced perilous economic times ahead, he felt that he could still make valuable contributions to the firm.

The reason for Gray's retirement was the question of succession. Gray's problems with this issue stemmed from two main factors—very bad luck and very poor public relations. Another problem was that in many ways Gray had become the indispensable man, a fact noted, not without admiration, by outside watchers. For example, Adams, the financial analyst, commented in a United Technologies report of December 27, 1979, "Harry Gray has achieved the corporate equivalent of building Rome in a day. However, it may prove to be that the builder—*and only the builder*—knows how to operate the city once built." This may have been an endorsement for allowing a monarch to continue to build an empire, but such a dependence on a single charismatic leader could trouble even a broad-minded board. When this report was published, the board reacted negatively, feeling that Gray was attempting to make himself a permanent leader and not train any successor. Gray countered these charges, saying that both the board and the public were misled. He felt that a lot of the bad publicity stemmed from one particular board member who was especially vocal to the press. This board member alledgedly harbored a personal grudge against Gray, who had refused to involve United Technologies in a business transaction in which that board member was an interested party. As to charges that he delayed developing a succession plan for the board, Gray explained:

> Actually, the story is different. I started building a replacement program in 1975. My problem is that I'm a lousy picker. That's what I'll plead guilty to. I started the program with the consent of the board. The first guy who looked like he was a reasonable candidate was Ed Hennessey, who is running Allied now, but he was fired. It was suggested by a three-member group on the board, two of whom are still alive, that he look elsewhere for opportunities.

Gray had recruited Edward Hennessey as a top financial executive for United Technologies, but he believed that before Hennessey could be named as successor he needed operations experience. So Gray created a business unit out of the Hamilton Standard division of Norton, and the solid rocket division for Hennessey to lead. Gray later said, "If he'd have kept his nose clean and done that it would have been all right, but he made two serious mistakes." One mistake had to do with

Hennessey allegedly demeaning the character of a fellow United Technologies executive. Gray claimed that, when pushed for evidence for the comment in question, Hennessey

> elected to withdraw his statement. That was symptomatic of it. The second mistake made was that he started lobbying the board to become president behind my back. You just don't do that. With the exception of two guys who weren't on the board [at that time], everybody around there [who was sitting on the board when all this occurred] who will tell the truth will tell you that Hennessey lobbied them and told them that I was afraid to let go of the company, that I was afraid to make him president because I was jealous . . . and a whole bunch of garbage.

The next possible candidate for successor was General Alexander Haig, whom Gray had gotten to know socially several years earlier. In June of 1979, when he heard that Haig was going to retire from the military, he asked him to call and talk about career moves whenever it would be appropriate. He contacted Haig in November and gave this account of how he managed to talk Haig into accepting the position:

> Haig said, "Why do you want me there?" I said, "Number one, you're a good administrator. Number two, you're a quick learner. If I can learn the electronics business as I did at Litton Industries, you can learn it at United Technologies. You've got five years to learn. I'm not yet sixty, so I'm being generous when I say you've got five years to learn. I'll tell you within two years whether you're going to make it. Your stock options will still be good. . . . And if you don't make it, you'll make your own choice."

The board was pleased, Gray reported, but a year later, President Reagan appointed Haig as secretary of state. Gray commented:

> When Haig left, the board got panicky: "Where's your successor?" There's only one year difference now, I'm sixty-one instead of sixty. We still have three guys and have time to look at the talent out there. I said, "Let's not jump." They said, "No, we've got to move ahead."

One of the three candidates from within the company, Peter Scott, resigned, giving Gray the reason that he wanted a change of lifestyle. Scott had gotten tired of the wear and tear of travel. Gray said that he and Scott remained good friends after Scott's departure, but that the board panicked further at the loss of another potential successor and pressured Gray to name Robert Carlson, the head of their Pratt and Whitney division, as president. Carlson had come from the equipment making firm of John Deere, where he had lost out in a contest for the chief executive job.

With Gray's serious concerns over Carlson's business judgment, Gray dismissed him.[42] This dismissal, however, was followed by the widely read *Wall Street Journal* article which reported that Carlson and Hennessey suspected that Gray's security staff had spied on them.[43] One board member commented that the firm could not survive without a leader: "The fate of the company is at stake. We could be watching a $15 billion firm sailing off without a rudder."[44] William Simon, a company director and former U.S. treasury secretary, stated, "The intrigue up there is unreal. It is like a James Bond novel. Some of the goings on are just bizarre."[45] Several directors complained that Gray was attempting to perpetuate his own tenure indefinitely, while others felt that Gray had fired Carlson because Gray was genuinely worried about Carlson's ability to lead the firm. As the news of wiretapping and bugging broke, the company's stock dropped two points. At Gray's request, the board immediately began an investigation into these charges. He wanted to clear his name.

A month after Carlson's dismissal, Gray named Robert Daniell, then age fifty, as president.[46] Daniell had had little exposure to the wide-ranging United Technologies businesses, given that his twenty-eight-year career had all been within the Sikorsky division. Thus some speculated that Gray had again managed to undercut the succession process and outmaneuver the board.[47] He inadvertently fueled such cynicism by publicly retorting about his succession, "Who the blazes cares if it takes three months, thirteen months, or two years?"[48] The next board report, insisting that Gray step down in favor of Daniell, was prepared by four outside directors, with outside legal counsel.

Gray resisted the board's decision. He saw the danger of recent external threats to certain parts of the company and felt that, once again, an intended successor might not be up to the task. In a 1987 interview he told me, "I built the damn thing. I really would like to have somebody who I really could say with pride, 'he can run it.' " Gray complained that his forced exit had cut Daniell off from needed advice and grooming. "It's the board, not him. I'm not picking on him. I'm the guy that recommended him. The board is just ruining the environment for him to operate in. . . . Boards have a tendency to create mediocrity."

A year after the board's decision, Gray passed on the chief executive's post to Daniell, with a plan to remain on the board until his seventieth birthday.[49] Several insiders commented that they were pleased with Daniell's mild temperament, finding it a relief from the reportedly abrasive styles of Gray, Hennessey, and Carlson. Daniell was credited with being a quick learner and was able to pare back on those troubled parts of the United Technologies portfolio of businesses still remaining, such as Mostek, the floundering chip-making company.[50] Daniell completed his first year as chief executive with a $592 million write-off and the elimination of 11,000 jobs, or 6 percent of the work force.[51]

Eventually, reports of complaints about Carlson's performance surfaced which lent credibility to Gray's decision to fire him. For example, the chief executives of Boeing and Delta complained about Carlson's relations with them, while insiders complained that Carlson's efforts to circumvent Gray nearly led to the introduction of financially precarious sweeping engine guarantees. Finally, no investigations by either the board, Carlson's own detective firm, or even the FBI could support the charges of wiretapping.[52]

This vindication was hardly sufficient for the damage done to Gray's pride and reputation. Lingering suspicions no doubt lived on in quarters where Gray's side of the story had not been sent or among those who remain unconvinced. Given the long hard route Gray had had to reach the chief executive's post at United Technologies, the assault on his reputation must have hit him hard.

My interview was the first he had allowed since the retirement crisis broke. Gray, born in 1919 as Harry Grusin in rural Milledgeville Crossroads, Georgia, ten miles from Augusta, was the son of a struggling small farmer and merchant who was a German immigrant. His mother died after he turned six. He commented:

> You don't have a hell of a lot of recall at five or six, but I can remember what the farm looked like and the farm animals, but I don't know anything about wider family relationships. . . . All I remember about my early childhood is watching them bury my mother, which I think was a very serious mistake. I didn't know she was sick. The next thing I know, I'm watching them lower her into the ground. Not a very smart thing to do to a six-year-old. I don't know who thought of that one. I've never tried to find it out, because I probably don't want to find it out. . . . I was angry at the world. First of all, my mother goes away for a period of time. The next thing I know she's stone-cold in a casket. Dumb thing to do to a child. The next thing I know, my father is busy doing something and I never see him. Obviously he was busy selling his farm and trying to invest his money. The only person I'm exposed to is a sister who is unhappy because she couldn't finish her premed study. An older sister has already left the family and gone north to get a job.

Harry's father moved his son and two remaining daughters to Chicago. He invested the proceeds from the farm in real estate bought on margin, only to lose everything in the crash of 1929.

Gray said that at this point he virtually never saw his father, and he lived with his sisters, who worked and supported him. His father, Gray claimed, didn't even have a suit in the home and only slept there, on a sofa, on rare occasions. He said that he didn't think he saw his father until he was in college.

> I never had a father around. I had to take care of myself. I was fighting on streets while going to grade school. I was a southerner and was moved into northern schools at age eight in short pants and thick southern accent. I can tell you that's a tough thing to do on the west side of Chicago. Not that it wasn't a decent neighborhood at the time, but they weren't

very sympathetic. . . . I can remember being thrown into a group that was teasing me about being funny looking.

Even though he appreciated his sisters' support, he still felt alone:

When they were at work, they were gone at 7:00 in the morning. . . . One worked downtown at an office that opened at 8:00 and another was going to the University of Chicago to finish her education and left very early. So who was going to send me off in the morning? Nobody. Did I eat breakfast every morning? Sometimes. What about lunch? What do you do with a kid like that? And what do you do with him when he gets home? What time did they get home at night? Where's the kid been all day? School is out at three. Not a very friendly environment. You learn to take care of yourself in that environment. You do learn how to be a survivor.

When he was nine, Gray was sent to the Dakota School for Boys, a modest private residential school where he could be supervised by adults and get away from life on the streets. A schoolmaster and the minister of the local Presbyterian church became role models. Three years later he returned to public schools. He graduated from the University of Illinois with a degree in journalism and marketing in 1941, just before entering the army. In World War II he received a Silver Star and a Bronze Star for gallantry in combat. After the war, he was advertising manager for Esserman Motor Sales in Chicago and became a very successful truck salesman at this leading truck dealer. Gray later sold buses for a bus distributor until he left to join a division of Greyhound called Grey Van Lines. By age thirty-three, he was general manager of this division and the youngest general manager in Greyhound. In 1954 he joined Consolidated Electro Dynamics, a new California company later renamed Litton Industries. By 1971, Gray was senior executive vice president of this firm, which had now grown into a $3-billion enterprise. He was also a member of its board of directors and heir apparent to Roy Ash, the president. Gray was disappointed, however, with chairman Tex Thornton's continued deferral of plans for an early retirement.

Gray joined United Technologies, then called United Aircraft, in 1971. He became chief executive in 1972 and led this aerospace firm into a bold and controversial diversification strategy, acquiring such firms as Essex, Otis, and Carrier. In 1975 he changed the firm's name to United Technologies. Decades earlier, he had changed his own name from Grusin to Gray in order to get a fresh start after paying off the enormous debt his first wife ran up during divorce proceedings, following a brief postwar marriage.

The personal profile on Harry Gray accompanying his Horatio Alger Award begins with the aphorism, "Forget about your problems: look to the future." Harry Gray was angry early on in life, and his anger helped him battle to make a name for himself, against difficult setbacks, and even against retirement. Gray has proven resilient. After retiring, he served on the president's Blue Ribbon Panel on the Strategic Defense Initiative and the president's Export Council. Furthermore, he chairs the Defense Policy Advisory Committee on Trade and the National Science Center Foundation, a nonpartisan organization that brings modern technology into the high-school classroom.

In his well-appointed, large office in a suburban office park, almost in the shadows of the Hartford headquarters of United Technologies, one still feels the aura of great power. A state flag with a Revolutionary War emblem hangs in that office. The flag shows a coiled snake with the motto, "Don't tread on me." A close associate of Gray for many years commented to me, "As tough as he is, he is really surprisingly trusting of people, in fact almost naïve in his belief in other people."

J. Peter Grace and W. R. Grace

Some conglomerate monarchs can get the extended reign they seek. With forty-three years on the throne, seventy-five-year-old J. Peter Grace has commanded his empire for longer than any other leader of a major U.S. firm. He took charge of the family business, W. R. Grace & Co., at age thirty-two, following his father's stroke in 1945. The firm was then family owned. Today the Grace family controls less than 1 percent of the stock. Grace's grandfather, William Russell Grace, had drifted around the world as an adventurer after leaving his prominent family in Ireland. With his brother Michael he started Grace Brothers, a Peruvian trading firm, in 1855. A decade later Grace's grandfather founded W. R. Grace & Co., a New York–based operation that initially served as a correspondent for Grace Brothers.[53] Grace Brothers and W. R. Grace & Co. were heavily involved in such services to Latin American regimes and businesses as armament supplies, shipping, building railroads, exploiting natural resources, and constructing utilities, cotton mills, and sugar mills. Although labeled the "Pirate of Peru" by critics, William Russell Grace served two terms as a reform mayor of New York City.[54]

W. R. Grace, meanwhile, passed control of the business to his son Joseph Peter Grace. That business was good was attested to by the fact that Peter had been raised amid extraordinary affluence, his father having maintained a household staff of sixty-two servants and a 156-foot yacht with a twenty-eight-man crew. When Joseph Peter's son J. Peter took charge of the firm, through major acquisitions and internal development, Grace transformed the firm he had inherited into a major chemical manufacturer in the 1950s. But the expansion policy cut the company's profits in half despite the larger revenue brought in through the acquisitions. Grace avoided removal by his board by a single vote in 1952. He continually took the company in new directions. For example, he greatly expanded the shipping business, in part through his Grace Line fleet, and became a prominent operator of cruise ships to the Caribbean. The Grace Line was sold, however, in 1969. With less emphasis on what was the historic base of the company, the Latin American operations went from being 60 percent of sales in 1950 to less than 3 percent in 1977. At the same time, Grace moved into many new businesses in the 1960s and 1970s, including manufacturing auto parts and operating restaurants and retail businesses.

Following his controversial 1984 appointment as chairman of the president's Private Sector Survey on Cost Control, Grace worked on a study that, through 2,478 recommendations, sought to cut $424 billion from the federal budget.[55] But in Grace's own enterprise, financial performance did not make an outstandingly strong showing; Grace was attacked for waste and inefficiency within his own organization.[56] Despite its growth in revenues, the firm had not attracted very much investor enthusiasm. Since 1950, W. R. Grace & Co. had grown from $200 million in sales to $7 billion. But its stock has rarely beaten the general performance of the market. In December 1985 when a German investor, industrialist Karl Flick, was forced to sell the 26 percent of the Grace firm's stock that he owned in order to resolve some problems with his own firm, the Flick Group, W. R. Grace became a potential takeover candidate and scrambled to repurchase its stock.

With an estimated stock breakup value of up to $25 per share more than its market price, Grace became a takeover target of GAF's chairman Samuel J. Heyman. Grace's defensive stock repurchase forced the firm into a highly leveraged position, resulting in a lowered credit rating. Several business groups prized by Grace were identified as problem areas by top executives and outside critics, but he resisted their divestiture. For example, the retail group's operating return was 4.5 percent, and the restaurants' was 6.1 percent, in both cases only half the industry average. Grace's response to criticism of his refusal to sell was, "I'm not a liquidator; I'm a builder."[57] Nonetheless, by 1987, he divested his firm of $3 billion worth of businesses that represented almost half the firm's revenues and included the retail, restaurant, and specialty chemical operations.

According to former associates, Grace was drawn into heavy industry, such as chemicals, to acquire size and stability in the 1950s, but by the 1960s he did not find these businesses personally satisfying and so attempted to move into consumer products.[58] The firm sold many of these consumer-products concerns at a loss. While W. R. Grace & Co.'s move into retailing in the 1970s showed an effort to bring in the coherence lacking in the early diversification program, the added bureaucratic control necessitated by this move was thought to have smothered the entrepreneurial spirit behind these acquisitions. Grace delegated much of his responsibility for overseeing the heavy industrial operations in order to focus on the retail group. Given his personal involvement in these dramatic strategy shifts, it is not surprising that Grace should feel somewhat defensive about the firm's retreat from these activities and unready to retire.

Perhaps Grace is anxious to return the firm, now half its former size, to a renewed period of building. With time running out, he is preoccupied with the clock. Grace wears two watches, one set at New York time and the other at the local time as he travels. He works hundred-hour weeks with fifteen-minute lunches, no movies, no television, and no recreation. He keeps a battery-powered lamp in his limousine so that should the reading light in the car burn out he can keep on working. He even shaves while on the toilet in morning. "Why not?" Grace bragged to two recent journals; "I'm out of bed and downstairs in five minutes."[59]

This time pressure is displayed not only through his tireless schedule crisscrossing the country, but also in his lack of interest in specifying a successor. In 1982, he named his fifty-seven-year-old cousin and confidant the chief administrative officer and Carl Graf, the same age, his chief operating officer. At that time he commented that these men were the only two in a position to succeed him. By late fall of 1986, however, neither of the two were still candidates. Instead, he had promoted Paul Paganucci, age fifty-nine, and J. P. Bolduc and Terrence Daniels, both age forty-seven, into key positions to stage a three-way succession race. As a director on the Citibank board, he had been impressed with the three-way race used by retiring banker Walter Wriston and decided to copy it, stating, "I saw enough to know that it is a good way to work at it. . . . You get a chance to see how these people run an operation and who's the best."[60] The presumed front runner, Daniels, commented:

> The difference between us and Citibank is that no one knows when Peter will retire. . . . Peter is not going to give this place to us without a fight. He's been through the good times and the bad, and the times now are bad. He's got faults—but he's a competitor and doesn't intend to go out a loser.[61]

Grace himself commented in 1986:

> Why should I retire? . . . I know a lot of people who are bored to death with their life. After about two months of playing golf in Florida, they start to drink. It's not a good scene. We're not built to sit around and enjoy life. That's not why we were created.[62]

In 1987 he added, "I work as hard as anybody here. . . . I would never stay if I wasn't able to contribute."[63] Although his story hasn't ended, J. Peter Grace gives every indication of leaving like a monarch.

William Norris and the Wizards of Technology

Old monarchs can be detected even in the new worlds of technology. Control Data founder William Norris, for example, was a pioneer in the computer industry as well as a widely admired leader in corporate social responsibility. The son of a Nebraska farmer, he trained as an electrical engineer and worked with the emerging digital computer technology during World War II in the navy. After the war he formed a firm in this field. It was later sold to Remington Rand, which merged with Sperry. Frustrated by the corporate bureaucracy, he left Sperry in 1957 to help found Control Data. Norris led the company for twenty-nine years, taking Control Data into such ventures as the manufacture of mainframe computers, disk drives, floppy disks, and Plato educational software, and such services as Ticketron electronic betting and ticketing. He also got his company involved in alternative energy development and economic revitalization for troubled urban and rural communities by building plants in depressed areas.[64] He set up consulting firms to work on contracts, for municipal governments and provided support to small businesses, all in the interest of both social contribution and corporate profits.

Accustomed to thinking in ten- to twenty-year time frames, Norris was criticized for his inattention to the mounting financial crises in 1984 and 1985. After the Securities and Exchange Commission forced Control Data to restate its financial reports for 1984, the firm's income was a mere $5.1 million on revenues of $5 billion.[65] Norris continued to support his investment in imaginative longer-range projects, which averaged 5 percent of the company's assets, but such foresight did not help the stumbling computer giant regain its footing. The firm defaulted on bank loans in the summer of 1985 as sales dropped to $3.7 billion, and Control Data's accumulated year-end losses were $567.5 million. Norris later explained these losses as resulting from profit problems in the areas of greatest revenues: data storage and overseas computer services.[66]

At this point, the board named Robert M. Price to replace the seventy-four-year-old Norris as chief executive. Price, a twenty-five-year employee of Control Data, had served as president under Norris.[67] Unlike many monarchs, Norris had developed a strong successor. But his board did, in fact, eventually challenge Norris's succession plan, which would have given the chairmanship to a longtime associate of Norris, Norbert R. Berg. The vice chairman of the board insisted that Price be named chairman as well as president and chief executive.[68] Thus the divestiture of some of Norris's legacy was facilitated by his exit from the executive office building entirely.

Norris agrees in retrospect that the firm did not keep its production costs low enough to match Japanese competition, but he is proud of his imaginative linking of important social needs with profitable business opportunities. Referring to the mistaken view of the press in thinking his exit was due to misplaced priorities, he explained:

> They never understood it. If they'd wanted to understand it, it wouldn't have made interesting copy. When I announced my retirement at the press conference, I took the opportunity to point out that the problems in the company were primarily of an operational nature. They didn't really have anything to do with strategy. Our strategy is very solid—particularly the part that calls for addressing social needs as business opportunities.[69]

Like many deposed monarchs, he feels his heroic mission was neither completed nor understood.

George Eastman and Kodak

A more mature technological field, photography, has continued to be marked by revolutionary product improvements as well as examples of traditional patterns of monarchic succession. George Eastman, the founder of Eastman Kodak, ran the firm for fifty-two years, until his death in 1932 at the age of seventy-eight.

Eastman was born in New York of immigrant parents. His father established the first commercial college in Rochester. At age twenty-three, Eastman had begun to tinker with photographic equipment. Three years later, he began to manufacture dry photographic plates. The firm was reorganized in 1884, producing the first commercial film and a box camera called the Kodak. In 1890, he reorganized yet again and called the firm Eastman Kodak. He began a profit-sharing plan for his workers at the turn of the century, but fought unionization. Eastman was rebuffed in an attempt to form an international cartel for film and cameras, but he had captured 80 percent of the U.S. market. A leading philanthropist, he gave away fully half of his fortune by 1924. He retired as president at age sixty-nine, but remained chairman until his suicide in 1932. With his work finished, Eastman, who had no family, saw no more value in life.

Edwin Land and Polaroid

Despite his outward modesty, Edwin Land's inner determination and imagination have received unsolicited recognition. He has proved that individuals, however rare they may be, can still fuel the engines of large enterprises to improve the quality of life. Born in Bridgeport, Connecticut, in 1909, the son of a prosperous scrap-metal dealer, Land attended public schools and Norwich Academy. He dropped out of Harvard College to pursue his research interests in 1932, creating what eventually became the Polaroid Corporation.

Although he dropped out of college, Land obtained astounding recognition as a scientist. A Visiting Institute Professor at the Massachusetts Institute of Technology, he has received honorary degrees from Harvard, Yale, Columbia, Carnegie-Mellon, New York University, Williams College, Tufts, Washington University, Polytechnical Institute of Brooklyn, Brandeis, the University of Massachusetts, and others. A fellow of the National Academy of Sciences and of the National Academy of Engineering, he was awarded medals by such scientific groups as the British Physical Society, the Royal Microscopic Society, the American Academy of Arts and Sciences, the Franklin Institute, the Society of Photographic Scientists and Engineers, and many more. In 1963, he received the Presidential Medal of Freedom and has served as a science adviser for several U.S. presidents. He was awarded the National Medal of Science in 1967. In 1986 he was made a foreign member of the prestigious Royal Society of London. He holds 533 patents, second only to Thomas Edison's 1,093 patents. In 1977, Land was inducted into the National Inventors Hall of Fame.

Such accolades, however, are nowhere apparent in an examination of Land's office. Beyond tasteful artwork in this attractive, moderate-sized room, Land proudly displayed an unframed timeline across several sheets of paper, drawn by a Polaroid employee, which highlights noteworthy events in Polaroid's history.

Anyone visiting Edwin Land the entrepreneur is also visiting Edwin Land the scientist. My interviews, accordingly, began with an unexpected and thorough tour of the Rowland Institute for Science, the nonprofit research institute he founded. As with the company he founded fifty years earlier, he did not affix his name to the institution; the name selected was a tribute to an admired physicist. Nestled alongside the Charles River, in Cambridge, this understated but beautiful three-story modern brick building is replete with a large library, a dozen or so spacious and well-equipped laboratories, an inspiring atrium where the labs meet, a delicate Japanese garden in the center of the atrium, metal shops, wood shops, and a coffee area. Designed by the noted architect Hugh Stubbins, the building overlooks the adjacent river and downtown Boston skyline.

With little introduction, we wandered through the institute's library. After weaving through the aisles separating shelves filled with current publications, bound back issues of scientific journals, and core research volumes across scientific disciplines, we came to an abrupt stop. By a desk, Land thumbed through several stacks of reprints from academic research journals. He wanted me to see that these recent pieces had all been written by researchers at the institute. In looking through the piles, I saw many of Land's own solo-authored research articles included within this impressive collection. He then looked back at me and said in halting tones, "This is what I do. . . . It's hard to explain my career, let alone my retirement to you; you and I operate in such different worlds." Edwin Land's role as a manager and role as a scientist had been intertwined throughout his career. From its inception, he served as the Polaroid Corporation's president, chairman of the board, and director of research.

Thus Land is as proud of his renowned scientific contributions to the fields of polarized light, photography, and color vision as he is of his role as the founder of Polaroid over fifty-five years ago. He invented the first polarizers of light and introduced the revolutionary scientific and commercial applications of this process. He led the research behind the films and cameras that produced instant photographs. This resulted in the replacement of the fourteen steps of film development outside the camera with one step within the camera. Land made an important contribution to basic scientific knowledge regarding color vision in his "retinex" theory of color vision. This challenged the prevailing concepts of color vision, which postulated that the varying wavelengths of light that come to the eye are responsible for color vision. Instead, he hypothesized that it was retinal–cerebral connections that determine color experience.

In his executive role, Land was the entrepreneur behind one of the nation's most admired high-technology companies. He fashioned a collegial, knowledge-seeking organization with a highly committed work force. Status distinctions were minimized and career development and job enrichment were emphasized. Long a leader in socially responsible business practices, the firm has acted far in advance of legislation regarding employment opportunities for women and minorities and employee benefits. Land considered the social system at Polaroid to be a "noble prototype in industry."

Some of the most convincing testimony of this success came from the frequent interruptions during the day. The interruptions were from enthusiastic well-wishers of all statures who approached with the eagerness of old friends. Whether custodians, security guards, current research colleagues, middle managers from Polaroid, or top Polaroid executives, Land warmly and promptly greeted them by name, introduced me, and then asked one or two personal questions about their families or their own careers. Following one such greeting, Land grabbed my arm and said gently, "See, they liked me there."

As we left a restaurant, a fellow patron bolted from his table and rushed up, breathlessly thanking Land for some sage advice given years earlier when this person was founding his own technology firm. Land looked at this young admirer with slight embarrassment. While he had not forgotten any other surprise well-wishers regardless of status, he did not immediately recognize this latest one. Land turned to introduce me, and then the admirer interrupted apologetically, "Oh, I'm sorry, I'm Steve Jobs and I came by when we were setting up Apple Computer." Land laughed and greeted Jobs with recognition. Then Jobs, without prompting, quoted from a 1944 presentation given by Land on scientific manufacturing companies.

Some outsiders, however, became less reverential toward the close of Land's reign at Polaroid. As the enthusiast behind Polaroid's innovative, but ultimately commercially unsuccessful, instant motion-picture system called Polavision, Land was frustrated by the financial community. He felt that some financial analysts and journalists did not have the proper technical background to appreciate some of his late-career priorities. Land unveiled Polavision at the April 26, 1977, shareholders' meeting. Analysts questioned the project's costs and projected profitability, while Land addressed the leaps in engineering and technological advancement illustrated by this product. Finally, one exasperated analyst cried out, "But Dr. Land, what about the bottom line?" Land halted in his tracks and then fired back, "The bottom line? The bottom line is in heaven."[70] Land is pleased that this response has since been enshrined in *Bartlett's Familiar Quotations.*

Around this time, popular journals that used to celebrate Polaroid's scientific, commercial, and social accomplishments began to carry critical pieces. Some even suggested that Land's emphasis on innovative job design, worker participation, and cutting-edge research were not sufficient to prepare for marketplace changes. Some began to report the appearance of disillusionment as the firm's glamour and glory faded.[71] Some thought that Land, subtly pressed by the Polaroid board to begin thinking about a successor, was dragging his feet. In Land's mind, however, the timing for an executive change was not right.

Polaroid's long-standing rival, Eastman Kodak, entered the instant photography field in the late 1970s. Kodak so dominated the photography industry that this intrusion into Polaroid's bread-and-butter business could have been disastrous. Furthermore, Land was convinced that he needed to be active and on-site to effectively launch the historic and successful patent infringement lawsuit that followed. Land believed that he alone had sufficient knowledge and credibility to explain fifty years of technological advances to the lay audience in court.

Furthermore, he was never convinced that late-career leaders are necessarily a problem. He felt that it depended on the management style of the leaders. As he explained:

> Polaroid was always beautifully organized. We set out to build a prototype of a corporation where we could have thousands of workers both in school and producing. We were relating the building of profits and growth to advances in science and technology. The leadership becomes a problem only when it atrophies. Leaders must make their jobs grow and not just climb a hierarchy. I never really *led* a big company. The glory of manage-

ment is a myth of the business world. This firm was not a hierarchical command structure, but rather was like multiple suns and research satellites. The whole concept is not to dominate but to govern more like a U.S. president. There you have a central federal government with individual states with their own governors.

True to his words, Land was rarely consumed by the ceremonial functions of high office. He spent much of his time in research labs and in meetings with employees instead of making speeches and chairing committees. Eventually three board members met with Land over dinner and reluctantly brought up the issue of succession. They admired Land's genius and dedication, but felt a change was needed. As two of them related the conversation to me, one director said, "Land, if you get killed tonight, who should we pick to succeed you?" Without a moment's hesitation, Land replied, "William McCune."[72] That was all they needed to hear. At the 1979 stockholder's meeting, Land indicated that he was "considering a lesser association" with the company following a 70 percent decline in profits due to the board's decision to write off Polavision. He added, "I didn't use the word 'retirement,'" and said that he eventually would devote himself to "full-time scientific activity."[73]

This is just what he has done. Following his retirement, he still owned 8.3 percent of the firm's stock. In May of 1983, he skipped the annual shareholders' meeting for the first time in forty-six years. The newspapers then noticed that his enthusiastic presence was missed at the firm.[74] In his "retirement" he has been working as much as twelve hours a day, six days a week, in his laboratory at the Rowland Institute. Instead of becoming embittered, as have many deposed monarchs, Land is in touch with many of his old colleagues at Polaroid and is immersed in his new career as a full-time researcher. He stated, "I am now living out the dream I have had since I was seventeen years old!"

Conclusions

These monarchs led their enterprises for lengthy reigns that ranged from twenty to sixty years. They were often in office until the last day they breathed. Their age when they left the firm ranged from the mid-fifties to the mid-nineties. Their names are familiar to us not because of their monarchic reigns, but because of their magnificent accomplishments. By reviewing these profiles of business leaders in late career, we can dispel at least five myths, discussed below, surrounding monarch departure style. We can also appreciate strikingly similar truths regarding features that do characterize their exits. Finally, by noting parallel heroic barriers to exit in all these very different leaders, we can understand what produces this departure style. These business heroes have chosen to deny an ultimate ceiling on career length.

Turning to the myths, the first we might consider is that aging monarchs are evil or selfish figures. Many scholarly discussions of aging leaders refer to Shakespeare's King Lear, who cannot give up his throne until he is convinced of his daughter's love for him. Later, once he has abdicated, he suffers for his vanities. Reviews of monarchs' departures often assume the perspective of the impatient heirs apparent. Thus monarchs are presented as barriers to the careers of others, not to mention dangerous martinets who severely punish those who dare to challenge the leader's presumably antiquated world view. Unfortunately, we generally miss the monarch's own perspective.

While the monarchs do hold their office longer than others, they are quite a varied group. Some are constructive later career figures; others are not. The public resents the imperial manners of some monarchs. The monarchs often protect their reign through the terrorizing campaigns of self-serving loyalists. Sometimes open warfare erupts between aging monarchs and younger aspirants. The careers of Cuba's Fidel Castro, Romania's Nicolae Ceausescu, Yugoslavia's Josep Broz Tito, China's Mao Tse-tung and Deng Xiao Ping, and the Soviet Union's Joseph Stalin and Leonid Brezhnev each represented two to three decades of repressive communist rule over their respective nations. Nonetheless, as monarchs there were differences among them, beyond their attention to domestic versus foreign affairs. Some, such as Tito and Mao, were revered, while others, such as Stalin, were reviled, but all were fearful of a close to their career and tried to immortalize themselves rather than groom successors.

We can step beyond these communist leaders to other modern world leaders and see the same struggle. The almost forty-year rule of Mohammed Reza Pahlevi, the Shah of Iran, and the twenty-year rule of Philippine president Ferdinand Marcos again represent self-styled heroes who encouraged corruption and ruthlessness to remain in office. Both began their reigns as saviors attempting to introduce economic reforms, stabilize national defense against outside threats, and to symbolize national unity. While they saw themselves as heroic, late-career villainy set in when they began to go to war with their own constituents. In some cases, their inability to acknowledge their own mortal limits led to insulation from attack and the defense of their withered agendas. Successors were to be undermined as dangerous threats to the national cause.

Even in democratic settings, we can see equally desperate monarchic behavior in top rulers. J. Edgar Hoover's fifty-year reign at the Federal Bureau of Investigation was marked by a turning away from his early crusade against law-breaking gangsters toward counterintelligence activities against law-abiding politicians and social activists. Even U.S.

presidents were intimidated by this public bureaucrat. Admiral Hyman Rickover's thirty-year reign as head of the nuclear navy was made possible through his maneuver to create a special act of Congress. The multi-decade rule of such city mayors as Richard J. Daley of Chicago, James Michael Curley of Boston, Teddy Kollek of Jerusalem, and Erastus Corning of Albany, New York, remind us that democratically elected figures can also undermine serious succession challenges and indefinitely lengthen their reign. Four-term president Franklin Delano Roosevelt was so consumed by his mission to lead the nation out of the Great Depression and World War II that he refused to acknowledge his own ill health. Roosevelt skillfully selected nonthreatening running mates and kept subordinates at odds with each other through overlapping agency assignments. Two months after negotiating with Churchill and Stalin at Yalta, the enfeebled president died, leaving in charge Harry S Truman, who was largely ignorant of the issues discussed and the terms agreed upon.

Looking at these varied leaders, we must appreciate that the monarch style is not a product of a given corporate culture or certain rules. Boards of directors cannot simply pass mandatory retirement rules for top leaders and then relax. Furthermore, it is clear that the monarchs are not thoroughly evil creatures guided solely by their thirst for power. These leaders rose not only on the basis of their superior muscle, but also on their ability to sell their constituents their sense of heroic mission. They later became captives of their own legends.

These corporate monarchs also developed romanticized visions of themselves in history. Juan Trippe launched the nation's first transoceanic air carrier with his skills of global diplomacy and his Phileas Fogg–like enthusiasm for the glamour of travel around the world. Trippe's vision defined the industry, from its development of aviation technology to its use of nautical terminology in the air. Nonetheless, the airline's greatness ended with his rule. Each of his four successors had an unsuccessful and aborted tenure. Because of Trippe's unwillingness to groom a next generation of leaders, Pan Am was notorious for its weak but arrogant management.

The corporate monarchs are not evil figures in that they are not willfully destructive figures. They correctly saw themselves as leaders who revolutionized the way we live and work. At the same time, like self-styled revolutionary leaders of government, they began to cling ever more tightly to the ownership of their role when they saw the end approaching. In an effort to secure more firmly their imprint upon their creation, they inadvertently tarnished their reputations and harmed the vitality of their own creations. Monarchs are neither totally destructive nor totally constructive, but a mixture of both.

A second myth is that the monarchs tend to be clustered in certain industries, such as the media and consumer marketing, but we have also found ready examples in such fields as transportation, heavy industry, financial services, and high technology. It would be naïve, indeed, to write off monarchic behavior as "show business nonsense," as some management advisers do.

Furthermore, this is not a departure pattern characteristic of all entrepreneurs nor is it limited only to such figures. We will see in later chapters that entrepreneurs can be found across all departure styles. In this chapter, we have discussed such founding entrepreneurs as Cyrus Curtis, Bruce Henderson, Victor Potamkin, Olive Beech, William Norris, Louis B. Mayer, Edwin Land, Charles Bluhdorn, George Eastman, and Juan Trippe. We have also seen powerful heirs such as J. Peter Grace, J. Paul Getty, and Robert Lehman. We have also seen the successors of established operations such as Leonard Goldenson, Fred Hartley, Harry Gray, Lenore Hershey, and Lewis Wasserman.

The qualities of the monarch's empire had less to do with the specific industry type and more to do with the conditions at a given period. In each case, these monarchs were courageous, independent leaders who guided their firms through times of turbulence. These great leaders launched their careers at times when their industries were so unsettled that they had to project a definition of the industry as well as articulate a strategy for the firm. Railroads at the time of the Vanderbilts, air travel in the days of Beech and Trippe, banking in the days of Morgan, automobiles in the days of Ford, management consulting in the days of Henderson, movies in the days of Mayer, and computers in the days of Norris represented largely uncharted waters. The proper rules of navigation had to be drawn out and the destinations had to be selected. These monarchs had to invent their own concept of the destiny of the firm and the industry. In doing so, they became inseparable from that sense of destiny. They wanted to see the elusive promised land.

A third myth dispelled is that a monarch's departure style in late career is indistinguishable from an autocratic managerial style in evidence throughout his or her career. Again in later chapters, we can recognize some who left office more gracefully, but were nonetheless autocrats. It is true that none of the leaders reviewed in this chapter were of weak temperament. They were successful because they had forceful personalities as well as transforming insight. While some such as Trippe and Hammer were notorious for their insistence on the strict obedience of subordinates, others such as Norris, Land, and Morgan were far less hierarchic and in fact showed an impressive facility for developing top partnership teams of creative and challenging lieutenants.

A fourth myth is that the monarchic leader surrounds him- or herself with the luxurious trappings befitting the role. Some cultivated imperial auras and opulent surroundings, such as Morgan, Trippe, Getty, Grace, and Wasserman, while others such as Kalmanovitz functioned in spartan conditions with spare decorations and few luxuries. Auto mogul Potamkin still commutes between car dealerships on Amtrak. Equipment maker Coleman still enjoys making entertaining and arduous customer calls.

Still further on this style theme, it would be wrong to expect these monarchs to embrace common political or social ideologies. While some such as Peter Grace, were adamantly anticommunist, others, such as Armand Hammer, favored closer ties with communist nations. Some, such as Norris and Land, fought the monopolistic control of industries; others, such as Morgan, Trippe, and Eastman, tried to reduce competition and overtake their industries. Trippe tried to shape regulation; Morgan and Grace fought it. In terms of social contribution, Norris and Land favored charitable causes and government programs that assist the underprivileged in society; Morgan, Eastman, Vanderbilt, Hammer, and Getty generously supported cultural institutions such as art museums.

A final myth is that these figures are merely all hopelessly locked in classic oedipal battles against the still-haunting specter of an intimidatingly successful father. While Morgan's and Grace's fathers were prominent and successful business leaders, neither they nor their fathers were fully self-made. Henderson's father did rise from poverty to great affluence selling books and seemed to have presented tough standards to reach. Hammer's father was a successful drug merchant and an associate of Lenin before his son began to build his own business empire and establish Soviet connections. It is also true that Lehman was born into the burdensome existence of a prominent family dynasty. It seems that several of these men were, in fact, motivated to exceed the dizzying career heights of their fathers. Some, such as Hammer, would even seek to diminish their fathers' role in an effort to persuade themselves and us of their triumph. Some such as Getty openly fought with their fathers.

The formulation of these oedipal illusions in a simplistic form fails to account for the standards of attainment set by those whose fathers were not business successes. Gray, the son of an indigent immigrant, changed his name from Grusin, denying his heritage and re-creating his own identity. Many, such as Mayer, Kalmanovitz, and Bluhdorn, were immigrants themselves. They did not work as hard as they did, or as long as they did, merely to demonstrate that they were self-made. Several of these men raised the funds for their own education, cracked unfamiliar industries, and made their own networks of associates and backers without the assistance or challenge of direct parental models.

In this discussion of what these monarchs are not, we have also revealed some truths about who they indeed are. First, they did not follow anyone's model on how to run their firms. Instead, they relied on their own judgment and imagination to fundamentally challenge prevailing practices in their industries. Second, the domain of these monarchs was one of constant turmoil. They thrived on creating order out of turbulence. When conditions calmed, they would in fact stir the pot and search for new challenging industries to move into. Third, there was an unhealthy focus upon the individual leader as critical to the life of the firm. Rules were flexible in terms of dealing with their own mortality despite the nagging reminder of the inevitable. This was evident especially through their fixation on time, evidenced by the wearing of multiple watches, and through feverish assignment schedules, as well as through an acute awareness of their health as shown through their bravado over work endurance, continued athletic talent, regular exercise routines, and continued use of health monitoring equipment. Several pointed to the special longevity of a parent as proof of unusual genes. They felt that through continued good health, they could justify their extended reign. Finally, they tended to avoid naming a realistic successor, preferring instead to (1) name none, (2) nominate an obviously flawed or unhealthy successor, or (3) set up a destructive contest with ill-defined criteria to let contestants battle each other.

The conclusions drawn from these profiles are consistent with the findings of my survey of one hundred recently retired *Fortune* 500 chief executives. Some of the statistically significant results were that the monarchs in the study were most likely to report "no preparation for retirement" (40 percent of monarchs versus 20 percent of other CEOs). They were most likely to report a desire to always remain in the mainstream (50 percent of monarchs versus 30 percent of other CEOs), and they were most likely to report a sense of frustration over a still "uncompleted mission" (50 percent of the monarchs versus 12 percent of the other CEOs). Also, they were most likely to admit that they should have groomed a successor earlier (75 percent of the monarchs versus 34 percent of the other CEOs).

As a result, the monarchs surveyed did not feel confident that their organizations would adapt well to a new leader until the actual time of their retirement. They did not identify their successors until six months to a year before their retirement. Most of the non-monarch chief executives announced their succession decisions far earlier. In fact, the ambassador and general chief executives generally identified their successors two years earlier. These monarch chief executives still tended to lack confidence in their successor fully a year after their retirement. Perhaps saddest of all in these reports was that fully 80 percent felt that they were forced out of office.

This unfortunate career end for the monarchs overshadowed the fact that they had been impressive organization builders. Looking at the Compustat financial performance figures for the monarchs' firms, we find that they led their firms to annual growth in assets during their reigns of an outstanding average of 43 percent per year, versus 19 percent for the other chief executives. It should be noted that the monarchs' firms had an asset base half the size of the other *Fortune* 500 firms. They also led firms that had the greatest growth in sales each year of their reign (38 percent for monarchs versus 24 percent for others). Finally, they enjoyed the greatest average annual growth in employment (16 percent for monarchs versus no change for other CEOs). Their profitability was not as exceptional as their firm growth. By the end of their reign, their performance had faltered. Asset growth from the two years before leaving until their retirement was not any different from the other chief executives. Meanwhile, sales growth was actually lower than the others over that two-year period (25 percent for monarchs versus 33 percent for other CEOs). Even more tragic was that their growth in earnings per share was paltry compared with that of the non-monarchs over this two-year period (8 percent versus 72 percent). Despite this sagging performance, they tended to maintain a higher growth in employment (12 percent for monarchs versus 3 percent for other CEOs). Two years after they left office, sales growth again led the group (35 percent from when the monarch CEO retired versus 20 percent for the others) and income was up quite a bit (43 percent following the monarchs versus no increase following the exit of the other CEOs). This situation two years after they left office may reflect a delayed payout of their strategy or else the corrective actions of their successors. This may depend upon whom one questions.

Emotions regarding their ouster from their firms ranged from wistfulness to grief. One prominent retired conglomerator reflected:

> I frequently regret the timing. I could have served well for another few years, but the younger men were too eager for advancement.

It is intriguing to note that this man's initially designated heir apparent died of cancer six months before he was to be publicly named.

A prominent retired airline chief executive elaborated on his feeling of emptiness:

> After being deeply involved in a company that has had frequent troubles, it is hard to step aside and not be active in management. There was a succession conflict when I joined and when I left. I had hoped to avoid its repetition.

The long-reigning monarch of a major retail chain also regretted the timing of his retirement, but offered a different twist:

> I set the policy. I could not arrange for succession earlier. In retrospect it would have been better to retire earlier and develop a second career.

Thus it seems that these monarchs had become caught in a career trap. They had become imprisoned by their own heroic barriers to exit. Furthermore, the monarchs had far fewer outside directors on their boards to challenge them.

Their sense of heroic mission led them to a series of never-ending goals or unattainable standards of success. The mission may have been set by the model of a parent or another industry leader. It may also have been of an internal origin independent of any outside reference figure. Its purpose, however, was to show that these leaders had left a permanent legacy in their institution. Grace allegedly clung to his retail stores as long as he could. Hartley allegedly ignored critics of his shale-oil project. The longer they tried to cement this sense of permanence and uniqueness, the more they in fact jeopardized their reputations and perhaps their firms. They had reshaped their firms and often their industries, but did not know when to quit. Unlike the governors, whom we will look at last, they defined their accomplishments largely within the firm. They tended to have few involvements in outside organizations, whether charitable, civic, or corporate. They identified with the heroic stature they held in the firm. The monarch's arena of accomplishment was within the firm. As George Eastman said in his suicide note, "My work is done, why wait?"

7

THE GENERAL'S DEPARTURE

Always the outward evangelist remained,
transparently sincere in his call to duty . . .
What emerges was increasingly an overwrought,
lonely tyrant without family or real friends,
unable to share, as once he had shared, the
fellowship of the desert warriors.

> *Monty: The Final Years of the*
> *Field Marshal, 1944–1976,*
> **Nigel Hamilton**

In an address to Congress upon his retirement in 1951, General Douglas MacArthur proclaimed that "old soldiers never die, they just fade away."[1] Many top corporate warriors do not quietly recede. Before their light is extinguished, it flares up in a final flash of glory. The corporate general leaves office reluctantly, often because of poor health associated with advancing age or the pleading of an emotionally conflicted board. The corporate generals' desire to continue to direct their firms' activities makes it difficult for them to depart quietly.

Although as with monarchs, the leader's heroic mission is important to generals, it is not as important as are their needs for a heroic identity. The generals' greatest barrier to exit is their identification with heroic stature. They treasure the respect and recognition they have earned, and in leaving high office, they leave behind a great deal of their self-worth. The military general's identity is intertwined with the trappings of office such as the uniform, the medals, and the power to direct the battle. In this chapter, three well-known military generals—

Douglas MacArthur, George S. Patton, and Charles de Gaulle—will serve as models for the corporate general.

General Douglas MacArthur and the Military Model

As commander of all Allied forces in the Pacific, and after directing many successful battles against the Japanese, General Douglas MacArthur accepted their surrender on September 2, 1945, on the battleship *Missouri,* marking the end of World War II. After the war, MacArthur, as supreme commander of Allied Occupational Forces in Japan, guided the nation's demilitarization and transition to democracy and domestic recovery. When ordered by President Harry Truman to lead troops in Korea in 1950, he eagerly accepted this new adventure, perhaps too eagerly. In 1951, against orders, he led an offensive campaign into North Korea and called for an invasion of mainland China, whereupon Truman relieved MacArthur of his command. In retirement, MacArthur served as chairman of Remington-Rand from 1952 to 1964 and remained active in Republican party politics until his death in 1964 at age eighty-four.[2]

Throughout his career, MacArthur was alternately portrayed as brilliant, charismatic, arrogant, aloof, egotistical, and pretentious. He was very proud of a distinguished family military heritage and was driven to maintain the inherited mantle. He was born in 1880 to Arthur, Jr., and Pinky MacArthur. His father, General Arthur MacArthur, Jr., had led a courageous assault during the Civil War and later fought in the Spanish-American War. By the end of his career, he had become the military governor of the Philippines. The elder MacArthur, like his son Douglas, was relieved of command by a U.S. president—in this case William Howard Taft—for insubordination. MacArthur had previously clashed with Taft when the latter was the secretary of war in President Theodore Roosevelt's administration. After Taft relieved him of command, Arthur MacArthur spent the last years of his life drifting through a series of positions considered beneath his talents. He was passed over for appointment as army chief of staff despite being the most senior general in service. He died in 1912 while addressing a group of fellow Civil War veterans.

His son Douglas was inspired by this model of bluntness, pride, courage, and arrogance. The elder MacArthur had advised his adoring son, "There are times when a truly remarkable soldier must resort to unorthodox behavior, disobeying his superiors to gain greater glory." Douglas was later provided the opportunity to follow this soldier's formula for greatness. He attended West Point and graduated first in his class in 1903. His mother moved so as to live near him as he went through the military academy. She later interceded on his behalf to secure a promotion she felt was overdue. MacArthur was decorated nine times for heroism in World War I and, by age thirty-eight, had been promoted to general. Following a clash with General Pershing, he was banished to the Philippines in 1927, in keeping with his father's example.

Unlike his father, however, he returned in 1930 as army chief of staff, an assignment marred by his brutal charge upon the beleaguered Bonus Army marchers, a group of 25,000 penniless veterans and their families who marched on Washington to ask Hoover to pay them their army bonus. MacArthur was granted leave by President Roosevelt in 1933 to assist the Philippine Commonwealth and was named field marshall of the Philippine army under Philippine President Manuel Quezon y Molina in 1936. He retired from the U.S. Army in 1937. In 1941 he was recalled to active service as commander of U.S. Army forces in the Far East. He was awarded the Congressional Medal of Honor in 1942. In 1945 he became a five-star general. Like his father, he challenged his superiors, first the joint chiefs of staff during World War II and then President Truman during the Korean War. In 1951 Truman stripped him of all command, but MacArthur returned home as a symbol of national glory. He faded away with great reluctance. He commented to the 1962 graduating class of West Point, "Today marks my final roll call with you. But I want you to know that when I cross the river, my last conscious thought will be of the corps."[3]

Like the other generals in this chapter, he left with great reluctance, with a feeling that he still had great things ahead of him to accomplish, and dreaming wistfully and with nostalgia of his days of greatest glory.

Another military hero with a similar retirement profile is George S. Patton. Patton was born in 1885 just outside Los Angeles to a family with a heritage of prominent Virginia military men.[4] He graduated from West Point in 1909 and served under the famous General John Pershing as chief of tank service of the First Army in World War I. Patton was frustrated during the interwar years and worried about his future. But in 1940 he was delighted by the extended tour of duty that took him out of near retirement. He became a brigadier general, training troops, until, once the United States entered World War II, he racked up his legendary triumphs commanding forces in North Africa and Europe. Patton, like MacArthur, was noted for his egomania, rigid discipline, emotional impulsiveness, and charismatic style of leadership. He was also famous for his mastery of the symbolic accoutrements of power, from wearing ivory-handled pistols and an impeccable, well-decorated uniform, to his use of majestic and historic imagery in speech. Following a brief period of postwar anomie, he died in a freak car accident. Once he had returned to a life of action, readjustment to sedentary civilian life would have been unendurable.

A third example provides an even more dramatic example of the general's departure style. France's General Charles de Gaulle was born in 1890 to intensely conservative and patriotic parents who were slightly impoverished members of the minor nobility. His father was a stern educator who inspired Charles with a love of tradition, a sense of public responsibility, and an all-consuming love for France. A distinguished military career was interrupted by two humiliating years in German captivity. As had happened with MacArthur and Patton, a military career that seemed to be stalled was taken out of mothballs by the advent of World War II. In 1940 de Gaulle became leader of the Free French Forces and a symbol of resistance to the Nazis. After the war, he was elected president of France. But exasperated by the political party bickering in civilian postwar life, he resigned after a short term in office.[5]

He did not, however, leave public life. He organized the Rassemblement du Peuple Français (RPF) to serve as a grand unifying party. But when this party failed to attract enough votes to return him to office in 1953, he retreated to private life again. In 1958, amid national dissension over the Algerian war, de Gaulle made his famous return from exile, and with fervor and gratitude the people elected him president of the Fifth Republic. De Gaulle seized on conditions of national distress with a "characteristic glee [seeing them] as [a means] to reenact his mission and to renew his charm."[6] He served as a rallying figure for national pride until the late 1960s. Then the great national strikes of 1968 over constitutional reform led him to stake his presidency on a reform referendum that was defeated. In 1969 de Gaulle went into permanent retirement, and he died a year later at age seventy-two. Like other generals, he demonstrated the desire of some retired leaders to return to command. They are not always saddened by, and in fact may even appreciate, the crises that necessitate their triumphant return to office. Sometimes it is even suspected that some corporate generals exacerbate the crises that precede their return.

Harold Geneen and the ITT Battlefield

Harold Geneen, one of America's greatest corporate "generals," fought battles at American Can, Bell & Howell, Jones & Laughlin, and Raytheon before moving on to the battlefield of ITT. There, as the combative leader of a sprawling conglomerate, Geneen commanded armies of accountants and efficiency experts in a crusade to create and lead one of the world's largest industrial empires. Undeniably dedicated to his heroic mission, he was a turnaround wizard in his various top executive positions as he moved from firm to firm. Nevertheless, his shifts were, in part, motivated by his desire for greater successes. As he confessed to a subordinate, his ambition was to be "president of a corporation larger than General Motors," the largest industrial concern in the world.[7] This goal was not achieved.

Geneen was born in England in 1910, a year before his family emigrated to the United States. His parents later divorced but managed to put their son through a Connecticut preparatory school from age seven until his graduation. His father had been a real-estate developer, music promoter, and record company founder, and his mother an actress and singer.[8] Instead of attending college full time, as his classmates did, Geneen went to work as a page at the New York Stock Exchange and enrolled in night school at New York University. After graduation in 1933, he began his career as an accountant for Lybrand, Ross and Montgomery, a CPA firm that later merged into Coopers & Lybrand.

In 1942, Geneen left Lybrand before being promoted to partner and joined the staff of a client firm, becoming the chief accountant of American Can's wartime torpedo division. Here he helped develop the internal cost-control methods that would later anchor his reputation. After the war, Geneen moved to the corporate headquarters of American Can, but when no vice presidency materialized, he switched employers again, becoming, in 1945, controller for Bell & Howell under a monarchic chief executive who had run the company for twenty-six years.[9] Geneen's predecessor as controller had been in office at Bell & Howell for thirty years, but budgeting and forecasting were virtually nonexistent until Geneen's arrival.

When the chief executive died in 1949, his heir apparent, Charles Percy, was made chief executive at age twenty-nine. Geneen had already come to see that he was not in the line of succession, but he felt he could work with the young Percy, which he did for fifteen months. Frictions with other company executives, however, intensified. In particular, engineers resisted Geneen's emphasis on immediate financial goals over longer term product development that could have built upon Bell & Howell's strategic technical advantages. Any friction between Geneen and his friend Percy had more to do with style. Geneen was disdainful of Percy's insufficient concentration on pressing company matters. The two also differed sharply on human relations approaches to management, with Geneen insisting on more demanding standards and longer hours.[10]

Geneen left Bell & Howell in 1950 to join Jones & Laughlin Steel as chief controller, where he again found little awareness of the value of inventory and the cost of materials, and no realistic assessment of rates of return on capital investments. The firm was run by two Mellon bankers who had joined the Jones & Laughlin company board as officers. Admiral Ben Moreell served as the formal chief executive. One of the bankers, Charles Lee Austin, served as president. Initially, Austin stood behind Geneen's challenges to the chiefs of production and industrial engineering, and many top executives were dismissed following these confrontations. But the relationship between Austin and Geneen soured when some of Geneen's financial innovations and production ideas fell on deaf ears. When Austin and Geneen clashed in 1955, Moreell suggested to Geneen that Harvard's Advanced Management Program would provide a nice, thirteen-week cooling-off period, according to Geneen's biographer Robert J. Schoenberg.[11]

At Harvard, Geneen made contact with executives from Raytheon, an electronics firm in nearby Lexington, Massachusetts, and soon joined its top management team.[12] When Geneen started with the firm, Raytheon's sales were $175,490,000, down 4 percent from the prior year with profits of $1.255 million. But by the end of Geneen's four-year tenure at Raytheon, sales were $375,156,000, with earnings of $19 million.[13] Geneen was given great liberty to decentralize the system. He pushed profit-center responsibility to lower business unit levels, set ambitious targets for profitability, and reduced delinquent receivables and huge inventories. But his intimidating style was seen as abusive by some. Raytheon's president, Charles F. Adams, did not approve of tactics that humiliated subordinates, and he publicly insisted that Geneen "stop that" on occasion and reprimanded him in private.[14] Disappointed with Geneen's abrasive style, Adams refused to name Geneen his successor as president, despite Geneen's expectations.

Geneen moved to ITT in 1959 as chief executive. The firm had most recently been run by a board committee and a caretaker president, General Edmond H. Leavey. Leavey took charge at age sixty-two and served until his own retirement at age sixty-five in 1959. He had stepped in following the death of his predecessor, William Henry Harrison. ITT's founder, Sosthenes Behn, had led the company since its founding in 1914 until his ouster by the board in 1956, when he was seventy-four years old.

Sosthenes Behn and his brother had founded the company when they acquired control of the Puerto Rican Telephone Company as collateral on loans they had made as agricultural brokers. The Behn brothers continued to expand into Caribbean telecommunications. In 1925 they purchased the International Western Electric subsidiary of AT&T, which was divested by court order, as well as other cable and radio firms in South America, Europe, and Asia. Sosthenes ran the company alone following the death of his brother in 1933. He was replaced after a series of proxy fights over the firm's sagging performance in the 1950s and died soon after.

Geneen, a serious financial executive with solid operating experience, took charge. Under his command, ITT grew over a period of twenty years from a loose, worldwide communications network with sales of $765 million to a multinational conglomerate with sales exceeding $22 billion.[15] At last Geneen had his own army. He directed the controllers of all subsidiaries to report directly to his corporate controller. All unit heads were required to design detailed five-year operating plans, and to participate in marathon monthly meetings in New York and Brussels. In an effort to make his firm the nation's largest and most profitable, Geneen searched out acquisitions regardless of what they produced, as long as it appeared that they would contribute to the corporation's earnings. His purchases took ITT into cable, radio, pumps, publishing (Bobbs-Merrill), electrical appliances (Cannon), home building (Levitt), hotels (Sheraton), car rentals (Avis), industrial food services (Canteen), baking (Continental), lawn supplies (O. M. Scott), insurance (Hartford), and paper (Rayonier) businesses around the world. He maintained control over his empire by close oversight of its operating and financial data, through his imaginative strategic vision (for example, "The Wizard Avis" computerized reservation system), and through the stressful interrogations called "general management meetings" where, in a room with dozens of peers, managers were forced to present and defend their divisions' showings.[16]

Geneen experienced a great deal of public scrutiny over various acquisitions, including ITT's friendly but aborted purchase of the American Broadcasting Company in 1966. After stockholders from both companies approved the merger and the Federal Communications Commission seemed to concur, resistance to the merger grew within Congress, the FCC, and the Justice Department. One reason for the resistance centered on the independence of ABC News, given ITT's close involvement with foreign governments. Geneen withdrew his offer and a year later canceled the deal, as allowed by the agreement, while the court appeals process dragged on.[17] In 1971, the conglomerate survived a difficult antitrust suit against its purchase of The Hartford Insurance Company, but it was forced to divest itself of several other firms.[18]

Early in 1972, ITT was back in the headlines because of Sheraton's donations to the San Diego Convention and Visitor's Bureau, which was lobbying the Republican party to hold its 1972 convention in San Diego (where Sheraton was opening a new hotel).[19] ITT was found not guilty of any wrongdoing. Later, the firm allegedly attempted to undermine the presidency of Chile's Salvador Allende Gossens in a venture involving the Central Intelligence Agency.[20] The charges of concealment, deceptive practices, and perjury surrounding these highly publicized proceedings, not to mention the public distaste for the conglomerate's attempts to meddle in the affairs of foreign governments, damaged ITT's relations with other nations as well as within the United States. When Chile expropriated ITT property, the U.S. government refused to compensate ITT from insurance funds available for this purpose because of the company's provocative foreign activities. The stock dropped by half. In 1976 the firm acknowledged bribery charges filed by the Securities and Exchange Commission; it signed a consent decree in 1979.[21]

This was clarified by Phil Gilbert, an attorney for Geneen, in correspondence with me in December 1987:

> When the Overseas Private Investment Corporation, a U.S. government agency, failed to pay ITT compensation from insurance policies subscribed and paid for by ITT, covering, to the extent of $92,000,000, losses resulting from the Communist expropriation of ITT's Chilean telephone system, the matter was submitted to arbitration. ITT was completely victorious in the arbitration, and Chile thereafter paid ITT $125,200,000. In 1976, the firm was faced with claims of allegedly "improper," but totally lawful, foreign payments, filed by the Securities and Exchange Commission, and, after completing its own internal investigation, ITT signed a consent decree in 1979 without admitting any violation of any laws.

The board of directors had begun to pressure Geneen to formulate succession plans as early as 1972. That year, he had his longtime friend, Tim Dunleavy, named president, but as one board member commented, "Dunleavy couldn't possibly have succeeded Geneen, not possibly. . . . It was really a gesture of cooperation with Geneen that we stuck him in there as president."[22] Dunleavy was seen as Geneen's puppet. Consequently, the board rejected Geneen's effort to have Dunleavy named as his successor. Geneen gained an extension from ITT of its general retirement age in 1975. But the unraveling scandals and series of falling annual profits, during years when two-thirds of the *Fortune* 500 companies had experienced profit gains, added to the board's dismay.

Finally, the board selected treasurer Lyman Hamilton as Geneen's successor. Geneen had switched his support to executive vice president Rand Araskog, who was seen as a Geneen loyalist and an executive with greater operating experience. Hamilton's mentor had shielded him from Geneen, but by the time this mentor was fired by Geneen, Hamilton had already had great exposure before the board and had gained their respect. As the newly appointed chief executive, Hamilton at first acted deferentially to Geneen between his being named president on March 1, 1977, and his assumption of the title CEO in January 1978. He assumed that his tutorship under Geneen would end when he officially took charge. Geneen, meanwhile, was not making the transition an easy one. Reportedly, former protégé Dunleavy observed, "Hamilton was just being so nice to him and Geneen was being a pain in the ass."[23]

Once Hamilton took official command, he immediately began to reverse the fundamental Geneen philosophy of continual growth. Instead of attempting to turn around losing units, Hamilton decided to dispose of them. In 1978 he mapped out fifty businesses that he deemed inadequate performers out of an overall 250 businesses. Hamilton ended the general management meeting and other such practices. He organized the firm into five distinct business clusters, each with its own chief executive. Geneen attempted to intervene several times as board chairman, but was continually rebuffed, and in July 1978, by board decree, he was actually barred from attending management meetings without Hamilton's explicit invitation.[24]

Geneen began to make preparations for a comeback. Hamilton responded with what some considered to be a sense of continued insecurity over his role instead of projecting an aura of confidence. He attempted to diminish Geneen's voice further by relying on an inner circle of trusted advisers. A continual flow of press reports denigrated Geneen and heaped praise upon Hamilton. Meanwhile, the stock continued to drop. Hamilton missed the firm's annual picnic in Brussels when he chose to go on a three-week trip to visit key Asian customers in June 1979. Geneen, however, not only attended but delivered an address which was followed by an enthusiastic seven-minute ovation.[25]

That July, the board voted to dismiss Hamilton and replace him with Araskog, Geneen's previous choice as successor. To Geneen's disappointment, Araskog announced that he would continue Hamilton's strategy of dismantling the Geneen empire. When Geneen objected, Araskog requested that the board remove Geneen, his former mentor, from the chairmanship.[26] Geneen's attorney explained this by saying that Geneen left "because he became an investor in a computer company that might ultimately become a competitor of one of ITT's divisions." Araskog sold all or part of one hundred companies between 1979 and 1987. After a $4.3 billion sale of telecommunications businesses to France's Compagnie Générale d'Electricité, ITT's stock almost doubled. By 1987, ITT was largely out of the telecommunications business, and its $17.4 billion in sales came largely from insurance and financial services, with hotels, auto parts, defense electronics, and paper representing the remaining business. The closure of the Brussels headquarters marked the final demise of the heyday of Geneen's multinational empire. The number of employees dropped from 348,000 in 1980 to 123,000 in 1987.[27]

To gain the needed room to maneuver, Araskog had to neutralize Geneen loyalists. When ITT's System 12 telephone switch was losing money, Araskog fought off a threatened takeover.[28] But always the most dangerous threat was the haunting image of Geneen. One board member described how difficult it was to remove this industrial giant from an active role. "It was a very distasteful job for me, a very difficult and sad job for I always liked Geneen very much. He did not want to hear what I had to say; he did not want to step down."[29] Geneen continued on the board until March 1983, by which time he was seventy-three years old.

During Geneen's nineteen-year reign, ITT revenues grew from $765 million to $22 billion. He revolutionized the role of management controls, and he defined an ultimate standard of personal absorption in office work. His dedication was so complete that it could not have been easy for him to contemplate retirement. Although he had wide-ranging interests in music, science, literature, and government, relative to other top leaders, he was consumed by his office. He had few ongoing outside organizational involvements beyond a single bank board directorship, which he vacated as he attended to his defense in Washington during the ITT political scandals. He now chairs several corporate boards. Geneen was married twice, but had no children. His first marriage ended in divorce in 1946. He was reported to be thoroughly devoted to his second wife, June, his former Bell & Howell secretary, despite his penchant for sixteen-hour work days and holiday work schedules. Geneen was totally absorbed in his work. Maintaining his heroic reputation was central, and he mounted strong defenses of his administration against later criticism. In 1984 Geneen published his own pithy management maxims in a book entitled *Managing*. After leaving ITT, he formed investor groups, but his image of greatness was as the reigning commander of ITT. His tenure was, for many former employees, a time of greatness, followed by an unpleasant era of layoffs and strategic retrenchments.

Unlike the monarchs, Geneen left office on his own, yet as a general, he strove to recapture lost stature. This led to battle with his own successors. While the monarchs cannot leave until they exit feet first, through death or a palace revolt, the generals leave reluctantly and then stage a return effort.

William Paley and the CBS Saga

The drama of the executive moves made by the prestigious broadcast executive William S. Paley is so compelling that it has been captured in various published accounts. After several efforts to retire from CBS, the network he began in 1928, Paley made yet another triumphant return to high office in September 1986, at age eighty-five.[30] Following a climactic nine-hour board meeting, board members Franklin Thomas and Henry Schacht had to repeat the grim task of removing yet another CBS top executive, this time fifty-six-year-old Thomas Wyman, to accommodate Paley.[31] Like Geneen's return to the stage, Paley's return boosted the morale of a traumatized organization that cherished the grand memories of lost glory. As news correspondent Mike Wallace commented, "To have the man who built the thing in the first place back in charge, everyone will welcome that."[32]

Paley had led a revolution in the media since his graduation from the Wharton School of the University of Pennsylvania. Paley's grandfather,

Isaac, had been a wealthy businessman in Russia who came to the United States in 1890 to escape the specter of Russian anti-Semitism.[33] The family money was soon lost through poor investments and through Isaac's genteel, semiretired lifestyle. In contrast, Isaac's son Samuel was an ambitious entrepreneur. He built one of the nation's leading cigar companies. William, his son, worked for a short time in his father's business but radio soon attracted his attention. In 1928 he purchased a fledgling radio network, United Independent Broadcasters. Paley soon changed the name to Columbia Broadcasting System and boldly developed its commercial, entertainment, and public-service opportunities in an industry that had previously been dominated by David Sarnoff's NBC. The rival company was two years older than CBS, was far larger, and had signed up most of the leading performers of the day. But Sarnoff was more conservative in terms of promotion and programming, emphasizing technology over entertainment.[34]

In 1929, Paley's first full year of ownership, CBS earnings were approximately $474,000. Toward the end of the first decade, the network had earned roughly $30 million. Paley was noted for his blend of talents including superb salesmanship, market prescience, exquisite personal tastes, gracious manners, and bold business moves. He got CBS off to a solid footing by bringing top-flight entertainers to the network, but he also quickly realized that radio could increase its popularity and importance by reporting the news. In 1930 he hired a respected journalist from the *New York Times,* Edward Klauber, who soon helped the network become a respected and popular force in a medium characterized by flamboyance and hype. Klauber introduced the standards of thoroughness and balance found in respected American print journalism to radio news reporting.

In 1935, CBS made one of the most important moves in its history. Edward R. Murrow was hired to arrange for personalities to give informative talks over the radio network. Two years later, Murrow was sent to London to take care of CBS's interests in Europe. It was not until the outbreak of World War II that Murrow's talents as a broadcaster became apparent. A brilliant commentator himself, Murrow attracted such energetic reporters and insightful commentators to CBS as William L. Shirer, John Gunther, Eric Sevareid, Howard K. Smith, Charles Collingwood, and Richard C. Hottelet. Throughout the late 1930s, the nation relied on CBS's fresh, riveting European reports.

The success of CBS News brought increased recognition to Paley. In the meantime he was becoming a member of high society. His marriage to prominent socialite Dorothy Hart Hearst in 1932 had widened his social horizons and gave him entrée to the New York literary and political scene. In 1945 Paley joined the U.S. Army to serve as deputy chief of staff to General Dwight D. Eisenhower's Psychological Warfare Division. In 1951 he became chairman of President Truman's Materials

Policy Commission. Paley and Dorothy Hart Hearst were divorced in 1947. His marriage to Barbara (Babe) Cushing Mortimer that year brought Paley even closer to conservative New York aristocracy.

As television gained in popular appeal after 1949, Paley conducted a stunning raid on NBC, hiring away top talent with remunerative contracts. Despite the success of Murrow's hard-hitting "See It Now" news program, Paley's relations with Murrow, while friendly, were not without strain. CBS president Frank Stanton, with a doctorate in psychology from Ohio State, increasingly became the public spokesman for the company. When producer Fred Friendly created "CBS Reports" and "Face the Nation," which diverted viewers' attention from "See It Now," Murrow left to run the U.S. Information Agency. Stanton, Friendly, and Walter Cronkite overcame alleged differences to build upon the integrity of the Murrow legacy.[35]

Stanton, the designated heir to Paley, lost out on his chance to become the chief executive—just moments before it was assumed he would succeed Paley—when the company founder decided to waive the mandatory CBS retirement rule. Stanton learned of Paley's change of heart only five minutes before his promotion was to have taken place in February 1966. Though bitterly disappointed, Stanton remained a loyal CBS spokesman and mediator until his retirement in 1973 at age sixty-five.[36]

Meanwhile, Stanton's successor, Charles T. Ireland, Jr., died after less than a year on the job. Next, Arthur Taylor attempted to stamp his imprint as CBS president. Taylor, also a Ph.D., had been a well-respected fast-moving executive at International Paper. Though Taylor was seen as Paley's heir, his brief tenure, begun in 1973, ended abruptly with his surprise firing in 1976. Taylor was accused of allowing television programming to deteriorate and of pressuring Paley to retire. In the merry-go-round of succession, Taylor was followed by John Backe, head of the CBS Publishing Group. This time, Paley actually yielded the chief executive's title, which he had kept for himself for thirty years. However, after a mere twenty-three months in office, Backe was also dismissed by Paley in May 1980, despite CBS's improved ratings and financial performance.[37]

This third fatal strike at a successor from a "retired" or retiring Paley led the board to ensure his complete removal from power. Thus in September 1980, three months after it named Thomas Wyman president and chief executive, the board painfully managed to separate Paley from the title of chairman. One insider commented on Paley's reluctant exit, "He believed quite sincerely that Wyman could be effective even though Mr. Paley was still there as chairman."[38] Wyman, formerly Green Giant's chief executive, had left that company after it was acquired by Pillsbury.

Wyman's reign lasted a record six years, until in September 1986 he, too, was dismissed. During his tenure, he had beaten back vicious attacks from a series of hostile raiders. The firm was saddled with high debts and lower profits due to these raids and also to a general slump in advertising revenues. Moreover, several Wyman projects had failed. Major disappointments included the toy business, the theatrical film unit, the software group, and the general publishing group. Profits in 1985 were $27.5 million on sales of $4.8 billion. This faltering performance led Paley, who still controlled 8 percent of CBS stock and who resented Wyman for having pushed him out of office, to begin to discuss change. Paley was further annoyed that his advice from the sidelines was continually rejected.[39]

On top of this, Laurence Tisch, a recent investor, now controlled 25 percent of CBS stock and had become sympathetic to Paley's agitation against Wyman. He was influenced by the failed efforts to prop up ratings, weak stock prices, fallen morale and prestige, and unrealistically optimistic forecasts from Wyman.[40] The Tisch–Paley alliance was strengthened following a revealing *Newsweek* report in September 1986 on the "civil war" inside CBS, which indicated that Wyman had been secretly developing a deal to sell the network to a "white knight," such as Coca-Cola, before discussing this strategy with the full board.[41] When these revelations came out, the board again reinstated Paley as chairman and Tisch was named chief executive. Several commented on Paley's renewed physical vitality at this time.[42] For CBS, the returning general was a reminder of past glory. Although the general had reluctantly left command, his spirit had still haunted the firm. And when the opportunity to return came, he seized it.

Paley was given a hero's welcome by CBS employees who remembered the days of past glory. Reporter Morley Safer commented, "The signal to us in the trenches is that we're going to do business as we once did it in a very classy and thoughtful way. Even if it's only symbolic, it's a very important symbol." Paley was hailed as keeper of the firm's tradition of public service. A pattern has been repeated over the last few decades at CBS. A former, Paley-appointed board member commented, "You have to recognize Paley had not wanted to retire . . . he regards it as his company. There have been five presidents since I've been on the board. It keeps you alert because it's always Paley versus the President."[43] The pattern may continue, but the current president has three times as much stock as Paley. Nearly two years into the relationship, each executive seems deferential toward the financial or programming expertise of the other.

Robert Woodruff's Lingering Taste for Coca-Cola

Robert Woodruff was as closely identified with Coca-Cola as Paley with his network and Geneen with his conglomerate. Woodruff did not invent Coca-Cola, nor was he its original promoter. Nevertheless, from 1923 until his death in 1985, he was known as "Mr. Coke."[44] His father was a successful financier and chairman of the Trust Company of Georgia. John S. Pemberton, an Atlanta druggist, had created the initial product which was sold as a thirst quenching "brain elixir" in 1886. Asa Candler bought the rights to the syrup and formed the Coca-Cola Company in 1891. Candler repositioned Coke from a medicine to a beverage, took the company nationwide, and franchised bottling. Candler's election as mayor of Atlanta in 1916 and his wife's death diverted his interest in the company.

The Woodruff group, primarily Robert's father, bought control of Coca-Cola in 1919. Robert Woodruff was named president in 1923. A college dropout with a difficult relationship with his successful father, Robert Woodruff had struck out on his own and had become vice president and general manager of White Motors, a Cleveland trucking concern. He left it when his family asked him to return to Atlanta to help out at Coca-Cola. Robert's sales genius is credited with major packaging innovations, remarkable sales force training, and path-breaking international expansion. Coke became a worldwide symbol of America.[45]

Woodruff served another twenty years, retiring as chief executive in 1942, but his influence hardly ended there. He remained active in management, challenging his successors as the chairman of the executive committee until 1944. In 1955, he again retired from active responsibilities, but managed to remain a director and serve as chairman of the finance committee. This provided him with ample opportunity to interfere in the decisions of the new Coca-Cola chief executive, William Robinson. Even though Robinson had the bylaws changed to have the chief executive responsibility formally rest with the president, the organization continued to respond to Woodruff's initiatives.[46]

Robinson's successor as chief executive threw the same long shadow as had Woodruff. J. Paul Austin joined the company in 1949 and by 1962, at the age of forty-seven, had become president. He was named chief executive in 1966 and chairman in 1970. In 1971 Austin made Charles Duncan, whose own firm, Duncan Foods, had recently been purchased by Coke, president, while he continued as chairman. Three years later Duncan resigned, frustrated at having to live in Austin's shadow. Duncan's successor as president was J. Lucian Smith. Widely thought to be Austin's successor, Smith resigned suddenly in August 1979 for "personal reasons," throwing the executive suite into confusion. Many believe that he had been forced out by Austin, who was now sixty-four.[47] Austin announced that he would stay on for an extra year, although he was scheduled to retire in a few months under the firm's retirement rules. A six-man team was promoted to the vice chairmanship to battle with one another while Austin preserved his position.

At this point, Woodruff returned to active service and overruled Austin on many key company matters, including the choice of a new chairman.[48] Woodruff was unhappy with the apparent forced exit of Smith and exercised his 17 percent control of the company stock to correct things. Austin's selection of Ian Wilson was overruled when Woodruff named company president Robert Goizueta chief executive.

Goizueta, the son of a wealthy Cuban architect turned businessman, had earned a degree in chemical engineering from Yale.[49] He worked for Coke in Cuba until 1961, when he and his family fled the Castro regime and Coke transferred him to Nassau. In 1966, at the age of thirty-five, he was Coke's youngest vice president, with responsibility for research and quality. In 1975, Goizueta became an executive vice president in charge of the chemical division, and in 1978, he took over administration, legal affairs, and external relations as well. In 1981, he became chief executive at the age of forty-nine. He entered office suggesting that his predecessor, Austin, had been too preoccupied with protecting past successes and had failed to develop new markets.

Unlike his fellow contestants, Goizueta had maintained a close relationship with Woodruff, occasionally stopping by the aged patriarch's south Georgia plantation homestead.[50] Many had felt that Austin's fears of Woodruff's lurking in the shadows had worn him down and led him to run an increasingly one-man show. During Austin's reign, Coke had lost market share to Pepsi. Meanwhile, Austin had become increasingly estranged from his own board, especially after he allowed his wife to decorate Coke's new headquarters and banned eating in the park across from the headquarters, fearing that food would attract pigeons. Eventually, as his grip on his command deteriorated, Austin prompted precisely the intervention he most feared—Woodruff exerted his influence again.

Woodruff's renewed activity in his nineties at Coca-Cola seemed to correspond with a noted improvement in his health.[51] Woodruff was named the company's first and only director emeritus in 1984, just before his death at age ninety-five. Only a month after Woodruff's death, Coke changed its secret formula after ninety-nine years and introduced the so-called new Coca-Cola. This destruction of an American icon was met with a public outcry that shocked top management into returning the product that the late Woodruff had so carefully guarded and imaginatively promoted. It is unlikely that such a change would have occurred while Woodruff was alive. Although he had left the chief executive's office with his retirement in 1942, Woodruff, a classic example of a "general," frequently found the "crises" that necessitated his reengagement at Coke for the next forty-two years.[52]

Family Responsibility at Amerada Hess and Winnebago

At age seventy-two, company founder Leon Hess returned to take control of Amerada Hess in 1986 as chairman, replacing his successor, sixty-five-year-old chief executive Philip Kramer.[53] The prior year, Hess had demonstrated that he was still in charge by announcing stringent antitakeover measures and the need to protect the firm from hostile attacks.[54] Hess returned to command to protect the company and to groom his thirty-one-year-old son, John B. Hess, as his potential successor.

Hess's career began in 1933 with a single delivery truck and an enormous ambition to turn his father's coal yard and gas station, in Asbury Park, N.J., into a major enterprise. As his venture grew to be the thirteenth largest oil firm and the 173rd largest firm in the country, he appeared to have been successful. But Hess's triumph began to fade with the collapse of the oil market in 1986. The firm's sales fell from $10 billion in 1981 to $4 billion in 1986. Earnings over these five years fell from $213 million to a loss of $2 million. The stock price was half of its high for the year when Hess returned.[55]

With a 17 percent stake in the ownership of this troubled enterprise, Hess is not interested in retirement. When asked at age seventy-three about his future plans, he recalled taking checks to his ninety-two-year-old father for signing until his death in 1965. He said, "As long as I live, have my health and can justify my existence, I expect to stay."[56] His son will have to wait for his turn at the helm.

Unlike a monarch, Hess had left voluntarily and named a successor, but when the company he founded was in danger, like a true general he came back to rally the forces.

The relationship between father and son is more strained at Winnebago, although John Hanson, another "general," may yet relinquish control to a family member. In 1958, Hanson, the owner of a Forest City, Iowa, farm-equipment dealership, a furniture store, and a funeral home, persuaded local investors to join him in reopening a recently closed recreational-vehicle factory.[57] Through innovative cost-saving production processes, he was able to offer a mobile home for half the price of his competitors.

In 1971, at age fifty-six, he made his twenty-nine-year-old son, John V. Hanson, president, and his thirty-five-year-old son-in-law chief executive, and he retired. However, with the 1973 Arab oil embargo, vehicle demand plummeted and earnings tumbled from $17.3 million to a loss of $6.7 million. Hanson ended his retirement and climbed back into control, exercising his 40 percent ownership and stripping the titles away from his son-in-law and his son. Hanson commented, "My son was hurt. Some people rise too fast. It was the Peter Principle at work."[58]

Next, Hanson installed J. Harold Bragg, then a fifty-five-year-old vice president of manufacturing at Lenox Industries, as chief executive. With stock prices having fallen from $50 a share to $4 a share, Bragg was under enormous pressure, but profits continued to slip and the stock price remained at $4 a share. Disenchanted Winnebago veteran employees contacted Hanson, but found him depressed, in part because of poor eyesight. His vision returned through new cataract surgery and at a twelve-hour board meeting in March 1979, Hanson ousted the chief executive and returned from retirement. At this point, John Hanson resigned in protest of his father's latest move. He stated, "My father's entire motive was to regain control of Winnebago. Bragg was really turning the company around."[59]

Hanson pared the work force back to a mere 800 from its former 4,000-person level. Sales dropped another 60 percent from 1979, and the company lost $135 million. Three years later, however, it offered a new fuel-efficient line, and the firm began to recover. By 1984 sales hit a record $411 million, with healthy profits. Hanson promoted Ronald E. Haugen, the developer of this new line, to chief executive, but Winnebago overproduced in the midst of an overall decline in the industry that year, and sales dropped another 5 percent and earnings 35 percent. Yet again, a Winnebago chief executive was stripped of his title as Haugen was demoted to president. In 1985 Gerald W. Gilbert, a fifty-two-year-old Control Data executive, was brought in as the fourth chief executive in a decade. Hanson challenges those critics who would call him an egomaniac: "My pride and joy, my baby wasn't doing well. That's why I came back."[60] As with Paley and Woodruff, a dramatic change in health was associated with a renewed interest in active leadership. A crisis continually brought Hanson out of retirement, to offer his skills to the company that needed him.

The Call of the Board at Bank of America, MGIC, and Beatrice

A. P. Giannini led the banking empire he founded in 1904 until he retired in 1931 at age sixty-one. When he returned from a European vacation to find that his successor, Wall Street investment banker Elisha Walker, had repudiated his policies, Giannini led a furious crusade to recapture the enterprise that he had created out of the Bank of Italy as the Bank of America. Once again at the helm, he led the firm until his death in 1949 at age seventy-nine and was succeeded by his son Mario.

In 1986, another Bank of America chief executive, A. W. "Tom"

Clausen, was asked to return from retirement to take control of the bank he headed during the dramatic expansion days of the 1970s. Clausen had left the Bank of America to run the World Bank, following the thirteen-year reign of Robert S. McNamara. After five years of mixed success, Clausen retired from the World Bank in July 1986 at age sixty-three. Criticism of Clausen while at the World Bank ranged from prolonged internal staffing battles and White House frictions to uncertain guidance in dealing with the global debt crisis.[61] Three months after he resigned, his old board at the Bank of America, under pressure to remove Samuel Armacost, invited Clausen to return. The bank had begun to deteriorate, in part because of troubled loans made during Clausen's first term, and in part because of $6 billion in loan losses during Armacost's reign. Falling investor confidence, unrealistic projections from Armacost, and very real takeover threats led the board to act. Clausen was given the mandate to stop the slide toward further deterioration while fending off future acquisition attempts.[62] Some industry sources criticized this action by the board and indicated that Clausen had been a major contributor to the bank's difficulties. By late 1986, his difficulties seemed to have only grown, with further loan losses reported.[63]

Max H. Karl was another financier who returned to active service after retirement. At age seventy-five, this founder of the Mortgage Guaranty Insurance Corporation (MGIC) took charge of the firm he had sold to Baldwin-United in 1979. Although he had shifted his work pace to a slower gear and spent more weekends at his home in Florida, he had, after selling it, retained chairmanship of the troubled Milwaukee-based company. After it was spun off from the bankrupt Baldwin-United, Karl jumped at the chance to revive MGIC. With the industry's image tarnished by scandals and defaults in the early 1980s, his peers welcomed Karl's return to active management in the hopes that he could restore faith in providing mortgage insurance.[64]

In telecommunications, Theodore Vail, the visionary leader of AT&T, provides another example of a top executive's return to office at the pleading of a board. Vail was born on a farm in 1845 and worked with his father until 1868, when he became a telegraph operator for the Union Pacific Railroad. He later went into the mail service, and by 1876, at age thirty-one, he was the general supervisor of the Railway Mail Service, reporting to the postmaster general.[65] In 1878 Vail met several of the founding backers of the Bell Telephone Association and was offered the job of general manager. He accepted, and he served until 1887, creating the long distance network, acquiring local operating companies, and establishing its manufacturing arm, Western Electric. Following fights with his backers, he retired to a Vermont farm.

In the early 1900s, he was involved in several South American utility development projects. With the 1905 death of his wife and the 1906 death of his only child, he returned to the United States. In 1907 he was asked to return to AT&T as president, twenty years after he had retired. The board had come to accept Vail's original strategic visions and had secured further capitalization. Vail set up a central administration to coordinate all Bell and AT&T companies and established a structure for the firm that lasted until 1984. He continued as president until 1919 and then served as chairman until his death a year later.

Finally, another example of a board inviting a retired chief executive to return comes from Beatrice. Following the removal in 1985 of controversial Beatrice chief executive James L. Dutt by his board, the consumer-products concern brought back William W. Granger, Jr., a retired vice chairman, and William G. Karnes, a retired chief executive, to serve as chief executive and as chairman of the executive committee, respectively. Their return to power was greeted with an instant jump in the stock prices of 2⅞.[66] When Karnes had initially retired in 1976 at age sixty-five, he had left two co-equals in charge at Beatrice, William G. Rasmussen and James L. Dutt. Rasmussen took control for three turbulent years until his retirement in 1979, and Dutt took over for the next six stormy years until his dismissal in 1985. During his command, Dutt introduced a highly centralized management of the diverse businesses, encouraged disruptive turnover, and spent lavishly on corporate image projects while profits faltered. Dutt's staffers reportedly criticized formerly autonomous units on such trivial items as stationery design, and required his picture to be hung in each office.[67] More than forty of the fifty-eight corporate officers left during Dutt's six-year reign. Returning heroes Granger and Karnes ran the company until it was sold to private investors a year later.

The experiences of MGIC and Beatrice suggest an important caveat: not all returning executives are vain or villainous. There are many occasions when a former chief executive reluctantly steps back into office from a very pleasant retirement because of a sense of obligation to his old firm. He may have been asked to assist in a time of crisis. Instead of acting as a conspiratorial general, in fact, he may be acting as a statesman. Whether a returning CEO is a corporate general or an ambassador depends on whether he has plotted his own triumphant return to office and plans to stay, or whether he has come back to offer his services and has a quick exit in mind once things stabilize. Generals are back in office for complex reasons. They do not necessarily return merely to stabilize a troubled company. Often they use their return as an opportunity to lead their organization to even greater glory.

Conclusions

The leaders reviewed in this chapter are generals, because like the great warriors MacArthur, Patton, and de Gaulle, they came to rely upon the corporate battlefield for their primary adult identity. Chief executives who leave office in the generals' departure style have a strong ongoing need to establish a lasting legacy. Unlike the monarchs, their need for successful heroic mission is not as motivating as their need to retain their heroic stature. Their position in the firm is symbolic of a lifetime pursuit of greatness. After a reluctant retreat to other activities, whether a phased or a full retirement, they charge back to regain their lost command as soon as they see an opportunity to stake a claim.

In my survey of one hundred retired chief executives, 78 percent of the generals, versus 23 percent of the other chief executives, suggested that one of the most invigorating aspects of their retirement was the reduction in stress. Thirty percent said that they did not prepare at all for their retirement. Unlike the ambassadors and governors, very few left for new corporate positions (10 percent versus 38 percent of the governors), and only some became active in civic associations (20 percent of the generals versus 56 percent of the ambassadors). A third of the generals suggested that one of the most difficult aspects of their retirement was "being on the sidelines of decision making" (33 percent versus 13 percent of the other chief executives). They were also more likely to have found their retirement difficult because of a loss of faith in their successors (17 percent of the generals versus 3 percent of the others). Astoundingly, a majority stated that one of their biggest regrets in the timing of their exit was the loss of power they felt (83 percent of the generals versus only 18 percent of all others). This may be a key feature that distinguishes the generals from the others. Fully three-fourths felt that their absence from the center of attention was one of the most traumatic aspects of their departures (75 percent of the generals versus 15 percent of the others).

In terms of their post-retirement connection to the firm, 90 percent held onto a position, and this was far greater than any of the monarchs, ambassadors, or governors (60 percent, 62 percent, and 16 percent, respectively). Like the monarchs and the ambassadors, virtually all continued on the board for over two years (90 percent versus 33 percent of the governors). In this way the generals got their foot in the door to stage a return to power. They continued to advise their successors without waiting for an invitation to do so, and 44 percent maintained formal consulting relationships. They remained very attached to their company affiliation. Fully half used their predecessors' retirement as a model, versus only a third of all others.

Overall, the generals were highly committed leaders whose identities were anchored in their positions. They had fewer outside interests than the ambassadors or the governors, but they had more breadth of interests than the monarchs. Those who gingerly moved toward developing influential roles in their outside activities quickly returned to their old corporate affinities if these outlets seemed unfulfilling, wasteful, or without the promise of leadership.

Leaders like Geneen, Paley, and Woodruff did not eagerly embrace their retirements as a release from the wearying strains of high office. Instead, they thirsted for the obligations of high office that others may resent. Nor did these men behave like monarchs, for all had made the effort to leave office. (Monarchs, it will be recalled, do not believe in relinquishing their office until death or overthrow.) As for their outside activities, none seemed to be as alluring or as gratifying for the generals as they were for the ambassadors and the governors. Even Paley, who was a president of the Museum of Modern Art and is involved in various cultural organizations, does not seem to find in art a substitute for CBS.

The mere return to office alone is not evidence of a general's mentality. It is the entire situation that must be considered. A. W. Clausen returned to office at the request of the board to provide institutional stability to the besieged Bank of America. At AT&T, Beatrice, and MGIC, we saw other examples of noble service from retired executives. Once in office, they face great temptation to remain. The more active Woodruff and Paley became in their positions, the healthier associates found them. As symbols of past days of glory, Paley, Geneen, and Woodruff were able to inspire strong emotions of loyalty and past pride from their troops, much the way MacArthur, Patton, and de Gaulle had. And the generals' return to active service instilled in them a sense of pride and security.

With agreement uncharacteristic of most of the other chief executives, all of the generals in my survey acknowledged regret over the timing of their exit, and yet they also found the most rejuvenating aspects of their retirement to be the removal of stress and pressure. This implies a paradox: if the job was so stressful and wearing, why did they mourn its loss? We must consider how the generals articulated their sense of loss in response to questions. One banker commented, "I still go to the office and am reminded of the loss of power. I'm trapped. I need it, but my advice to others is to make a clean break." The head of a major chemical company commented, "I was tired upon retirement. After a year or so, however, I felt I would have been able to continue to serve, but then it was, of course, too late." Another banker commented, "I wanted my successor designated CEO two years before my mandatory retirement date in order to observe his performance while I was still active." An ambassador would have begun such trial periods before the transfer of power in order to act as mentor and guide rather than to oust a troubled successor.

A co-founder of a leading computer hardware manufacturing firm said, "I didn't feel any planning was necessary, since I remained in a full-time office at first and a half-time position later. Now, several years later, I realize I failed to appreciate the blow to the ego. There was a loss of ego and identity to me that I could not fill." The former chief executive of a leading forest-products firm stated:

> I had to retire because of a company tradition. I don't believe in lame-duck business leaders with regard to succession. A president or a state governor has power formally granted and taken away, but a corporate chief executive has many informal devices to maintain power. Despite this, what really hurt was the realization that they don't need you. They pretended I was needed, but I could be dead and all would go on. I could actually be dead. I wish this were not so.

These leaders left office in pain. The stress they experienced was not necessarily the pressure of the office, but rather the tension surrounding their exit. Retirement stripped them of an identity and left them few alternative means of maintaining their self-esteem. They turned down few outside opportunities, because, as one forest-products executive put it, "I haven't been deluged with offers." Outside activities are not fulfilling to these people. Trusteeship and board directorships do not provide the lost title of "leader." The ambassadors and governors, discussed in the next two chapters, will present some striking contrasts.

8

THE AMBASSADOR'S DEPARTURE

Toward the end of the meeting, Kennedy asked Eisenhower whether he would be prepared to serve the country "in such areas and in such a manner as may seen appropriate." Eisenhower replied that of course, "the answer was obvious," but he added that he hoped it would be in the area of serious conferences and consultations on subjects that Eisenhower knew something about, "rather than errands which might necessitate frequent and lengthy travel."

From *Eisenhower: The President*, Stephen E. Ambrose

Ambassadors, like generals, also remain within their firms after retirement. Unlike the generals, however, the ambassadors do not seek to return to top office positions. They work to support rather than to subvert their successors. Guided by an inner sense of accomplishment and fulfillment, the ambassadors are not searching for more battles to further prove their heroic valor.

President Dwight D. Eisenhower followed the ambassador model. When his successor John F. Kennedy publicly thanked him for his assistance during the transition period and asked if he would be available later for serious consultations and conferences, as opposed to symbolic but exhausting global errands, Eisenhower was delighted. He wanted to play a serious, but not a taxing role. Following the Bay of Pigs crisis and through the Cuban missile crisis, the former president served as a wise mentor to Kennedy and on other occasions acted as a diplomat in his service.[1]

In the private sector, leaders who make an ambassadorial exit often express their eagerness to serve as a post-retirement mentor to a new leader, frequently one who is much younger. The retiree may or may not care about having an office or a title, but he or she does crave to be consulted. They want to assist, but no longer lead.

Thomas J. Watson, Jr., and IBM

IBM has long set wide-ranging industry standards for information technology, product marketing, financial soundness, human-resource management, and social responsibility. Nonetheless, as a firm, it has been reluctant to boast of its achievements. Perhaps this stems from fear of resentment, a concern over antitrust prosecution, and protection of proprietary practices and product knowledge. The standard IBM executive contract drafted by top management in 1968, under the reign of Thomas Watson, Jr., includes a provision requiring managers to pledge not to divulge information regarding a wide range of company data. This policy of a low profile but responsible public image has continued.

Tom Watson, Jr., succeeded his "monarch" father, who ran IBM from 1914, the year of Tom, Jr.'s birth, until some six weeks before his own death at the age of eighty-two in 1956. The son of an upstate New York farmer and lumber dealer, Tom, Sr., sold organs and sewing machines from a buggy for a couple of years after he got out of high school. He eventually took a job with the National Cash Register Company. Watson rose in the National Cash Register Company from salesman until he was vice president and a director in 1913. Then he and John H. Patterson, the company's owner, clashed and Watson was fired.

After moving from Dayton, Ohio, to New York, Watson got a position with a prominent business reorganizer, Charles R. Flint. In 1911, Flint had consolidated a number of fledgling business product firms that made punch cards, scales, and time clocks into the Computing-Tabulating-Recording Company. Tom Watson, Sr., became president of this operation in 1914 and changed its name to International Business Machines in 1923. Through technological breakthroughs made in its engineering laboratories and a well-trained sales force, IBM, introduced a large number of advanced products, and the enterprise, now worldwide, flourished. By 1945 IBM had become so successful that it had to be shocked out of its complacency. The firm did not enter electronic computing until 1948, after Sperry Rand's Univac computer cut into IBM's business with the U.S. Census Bureau. IBM had initially turned down this machine when its independent developers first brought its design to IBM's attention for what Thomas J. Watson, Jr., explained were antitrust reasons. Despite its late start, IBM secured almost 80 percent of the U.S. computer market in the 1960s and 1970s and became virtually the generic label for automated data processing.

As with many sons of successful men, the younger Watson was at first intimidated by and rebellious toward his high-powered father. He remembered as an eleven-year-old child crying to his mother that he did not want to join IBM, even though his parents had not told him to plan on such employment. When he joined the firm in 1937 after his graduation from Brown University, he led the life of a happy bachelor and found his way embarrassingly well-paved. Watson told me during an interview in the spring of 1986:

> I had an embarrassing three years here as a salesman before the War. People were tossing me easy territories and business that would inflate my sales quota and make me a member of the honored One Hundred Percent Club. I was young enough not to have had the presence to say, "I won't have this."

Serving in the Army Air Force gave Watson a chance to mature. During the war, he became associated with General Follet Bradley, who built up Watson's self-esteem. In July 1945, the two men discussed young Watson's postwar career:

> This conversation is so clear in my mind, it could have been held last night. He said, "Tom, what are you going to do when the war is over?" I said I had a job as a pilot with United Airlines. He said, "But I always thought that you would go back and run the IBM company." I told him that I didn't own that company, so I never even considered that. He said again, "I just thought you would go back and run IBM." That last thing raced around in my head for about three minutes and I said, "General Bradley, do you think I could actually run the IBM company?" He said, "Of course." I couldn't think of anything else, and within two weeks I called my old man and I said, "I would like to come up on a work day and just meet the people that are around you up there, because, to be honest with you, I may be coming back to IBM if you will have me." Of course, he always wanted me to do that, so this was great news to him.

This authority figure who knew Watson and whom Watson greatly respected felt that he was worthy of succeeding his father.

Soon after his return to IBM, Watson reported directly to his father as an executive vice president until his father's death in 1956. The pressure was great because now Watson, as the new president, had to prove his own worth without his father for protection. He could ruin the whole enterprise. He recalled during our interview:

> I was terribly shaken by his death, but he had a great life. I was now going to get the firm by myself. This was an awesome kind of responsibility, but also something I really wanted and wanted badly. I ran scared for the first ten years.

The younger Watson adopted and expanded many of his father's policies, including the emphasis on promotion and training from within, a strong emphasis on fairness to employees, and corporate and personal self-improvement programs. His book, *A Business and Its Beliefs*, is a testimonial to the genius of his father, and in it he quotes the elder Watson's beliefs on the importance of employee morale, education, management development, and sales integrity. Tom, Jr., continued his father's practices and placed all workers on salary, eliminating the distinction between blue-collar and white-collar workers. Where promotions were not likely, jobs were enlarged. Not only was the formal chain of command used to address employee questions, grievances, and other problems, but several lines of communication were available between workers and supervisors.

Watson proved himself to be a worthy son and a strong leader. By the end of the first five years of his tenure, computers and peripheral products and services represented 75 percent of IBM's revenues. The System 360, the first mainframe computer compatible with smaller machines, was introduced in 1965. IBM introduced the System 3 in 1969 to meet the emerging minicomputer market.

During his tenure, Tom, Jr., tackled a series of threatening antitrust suits, continued the company's tradition of social responsibility, pioneered several new areas of employee welfare, and saw the company's profits increase more than ten times and the number of employees quintuple. He received several awards for being an outstanding businessman and served on many civic and educational boards.

Watson was thus able to feel fulfilled when he retired early, for his heroic mission was accomplished, and his leave-taking of the company provides a classic example of the ambassador's departure. By all measures, he was entitled to feel satisfied with his record and generously shared the credit with his father and fellow IBMers. When arranging our interview, Watson stated his pride in the ease with which the transition was accomplished:

> I'd be very glad to chat with you about succession and retirement of CEOs. In my particular case, my time frame was foreclosed because of a heart attack. Nevertheless, I suppose I take as much pride in the success of my successors, the lack of intramural fights and politics, and the progress of the Company since my departure, as I do in the fact that the Company grew ten times during the fifteen years I was CEO.

Thus he had institutionalized his father's heroic stature and championed his own at the same time. Always more modest than his father, he rejected the trappings of high office, preferring "conspicuous economy" in executive style.

Perhaps Watson represented the epitome of the ambassador type of departure style because he found it easier than other corporate heroes to overcome the barriers to exit that many face. He explained:

Generally, I think it's wrong to allow the fellow who had been chief executive officer up until sixty to remain as a full-time employee and chairman of the board, but not [also remain] as the chief executive officer. This is trouble because it dilutes the ability of the new guy to get started. My father died, so there was nobody around here to dilute me in any way. I think that the less they have of these former CEOs hanging around the better.

I began thinking of a rule requiring age sixty retirement after spending time in Bermuda with a Shell vice president. He told me he was retiring at sixty. I then met their exploration guy and he retired at sixty. I began to ask around and people said that on the whole, you get more energy out of a man younger than sixty than one older than sixty. I asked, "Well, doesn't the older guy have wisdom?" People replied, "Yes, but he doesn't always have the energy to use it. It's better that the top people step aside."

IBM quietly adopted the age sixty retirement rule in 1966. Within the next few years, plans for an orderly succession had been completed. In 1974, when I reached sixty, I would hand the top job over to Frank Cary, who everyone agreed would make a brilliant and worthy successor.

But in 1970, at age fifty-seven, I had a heart attack. (This is the part of my experience that I do not recommend.) Rather than bring Cary in ahead of schedule, I asked the board if I could turn it over to Vin Learson. He still had eighteen months before his sixtieth birthday, and I thought he had done enough for the business that he ought to have the opportunity if he wanted it.

Learson served from June 1971 to December 1972. He stepped aside just after he turned sixty and the job went to Cary, as we had planned years before. I remained on the board of directors throughout, to help maintain stability and continuity.

On the other hand, he stated:

If a man has done very well, there is always a feeling of friction [between the old and the new CEO]. Furthermore, I guess maybe I'm speaking from the other side of the fence, I think it is much better for the individual involved. For your own peace of mind, you have to walk away.

I asked him if he believes that it is a mistake for other retired chief executives to follow his model. He replied that there is a difficult trade-off between the valuable post-retirement advice a CEO can give and the danger of his interfering in his successor's plans.

I am of two minds: You want the guy to be around so you can say, look, I know you built that plant down in Louisiana, but we really have a labor problem down there now, and how do you think we are going to get around the labor problem? You would like to be able to ask the fellow that kind of question. That is what is best for the business. What's best for the person is probably to chop everything at the time he retires. I think you should support him with an office and whatever secretarial help he needs and carry on as long as is appropriate with the kind of things he has generated outside the business.

Watson was unwilling to discuss his relationships with his four successors for this book, but informed students of IBM have suggested that Watson was closest to Frank Cary and John Akers and personally more distant from T. Vincent Learson and John Opel because of prior clashes. This may have made his position as an internal IBM ambassador less pleasant during two of the successions. Harry Levinson and Stuart Rosenthal suggest in their book, *CEO,* that resentment grew between Watson and Opel when Opel was an assistant to Watson.[2]

As for the Learson situation, Watson was again unwilling to comment for this book. He did not wish to revisit what he regarded as a private or sensitive matter. But several accounts suggest that the introduction of the System 360 was the event that triggered tenser relations between Watson and Learson. Watson's younger brother Arthur, known as Dick, and Learson were both contenders as successors to Tom Watson. They were both assigned to the 360 project, with Vincent Learson responsible for marketing and Dick Watson responsible for development and manufacturing operations. Both were senior vice presidents with wide company recognition. The project was a complicated engineering and manufacturing effort, which revolutionized IBM's approach through its notion of compatibility across machines and peripherals. Dick Watson's prior responsibilities as head of IBM World Trade had been very well handled but did not involve product development and the coordination of distant laboratories. Learson supposedly made excessive and forceful requests for changes in product specifications to which Dick Watson faithfully acquiesced. Since these commitments were not met on schedule, Dick Watson's credibility was damaged. In an internal postmortem memo regarding this project, Tom Watson is said to have acknowledged that "we somehow have an organization that destroys more men than it produces at the upper end of the scale."[3]

In hindsight, Watson is still pleased with his early retirement from the office, which opened up for him an entirely new life that he would never have experienced otherwise. In addition to his prominent role as an outspoken U.S. ambassador to the Soviet Union during the invasion of Afghanistan, he has served on several government policy commissions regarding arms control, the war on poverty, technological development, labor, and international affairs, as well as on the boards of directors of such firms as Time, Inc., Pan American World Airways, Bankers Trust, and Mutual Life, and on fourteen civic boards and university boards of trustees, such as those of Brown University, California Institute of Technology, MIT, the John F. Kennedy Library, and the Institute for Advanced Study at Princeton.

At the end of the interview, Tom Watson reflected on the feelings of release and exhilaration when he finally stepped out:

The board made every noise in the world to keep me here, every possible noise. They individually came to me and they collectively came to me and so forth, but I wanted to live more than I wanted to run IBM. After my heart attack, I told the doctor [when I was in the hospital] I was going back to IBM. He looked at me right in the eye, and he said you would be a lot better off and you will have a lot better chance for a longer life if you did not go back to IBM. That was about the end of the conversation. He left. I didn't want to eat any lunch, it was such a shock. By dinner time I felt a little better. The next morning I got up and by that time I was walking down the corridor of that hospital, when I saw the sun coming in the window, I felt better than I had felt in decades, absolute decades. The next morning I felt even better and I said what the hell is making me feel even better. I felt like somebody had taken a pack off my back.

Tom Watson still holds a passionate attachment for, and identification with, the people and the institution of IBM. Although he returned to the board and took an office in the education center near corporate headquarters, he did not feel the need to place his personal imprint on the firm after he had left office. He was content to have performed well and to have left a lasting legacy. He had met his heroic challenge and was now able to enjoy a life of pursuing his personal interests.

Albert H. Gordon and Kidder Peabody

In 1931 Kidder Peabody, a prestigious investment firm with a genteel Yankee tradition, faced insolvency until thirty-year-old Albert H. Gordon stepped in to lead the firm back to health. After taking charge of its turnaround, he would remain for the next fifty-five years. In 1971 Gordon retired as chief executive with a sense of accomplishment, but he stayed on to assist Kidder Peabody in many non-policy-making ways. By the time he transferred power to his protégé Ralph DeNunzio in the late 1970s, the once-insolvent Kidder had roughly $90 million of capitalization. Seven years after he retired, the closely held firm decided to sell itself to General Electric for $600 million in order to secure access to the substantial pools of capital required by the changing nature of major securities operations.

The firm had developed from an earlier one, J. E. Thayer and Brother, a private bank founded in 1824.[4] In 1865 Henry P. Kidder, Francis H. Peabody, and Oliver W. Peabody reorganized the company and, after the Thayers departed, renamed it. Henry Kidder, forty-two years old at that time, ran the firm until his death in 1886. Then the Peabodys ran it, developing a close relationship with the nation's major railroads in the post–Civil War years. By the turn of the century, Kidder Peabody was a leader in pioneering the first public offerings of many emerging industrial companies, such as AT&T, Lorillard, and Procter & Gamble.

With the death of the last of the original partners in 1905, official control passed to sixty-three-year-old partner Frank W. Webster. In actuality, a younger partner, Robert Winsor, was making the key decisions. Winsor officially became the senior partner in 1919 at age sixty-one. While the leadership of many of Kidder's investment company peers had passed on to a new generation of financiers, Winsor retained tight control until his death in 1930. Kidder's decline was attributed, in part, to Winsor's autocratic and antiquated management practices.[5] The firm was still provincially centered in New England despite the growth of New York City as the nation's financial center. Aggressive prospecting for new clients was viewed as unseemly. The firm was expected to draw business based strictly on its good name. Through the 1920s, Winsor discouraged the firm's promotion of common stock, as he was wary of its quality, except for that of AT&T. Furthermore, Kidder's underwriting performance had dropped off dramatically. Meanwhile, Winsor retained tight control, even though he could no longer keep up with a good deal of day-to-day information-gathering because of his preoccupation with the illness of his wife and a major lawsuit he faced for misrepresentation. After the stock market collapsed, many New England firms fell victim to the economic downturn. Additionally, between the years 1926 and 1930, a large number of depositors withdrew their funds as aging partners died or retired. By November 1931, the firm faced insolvency.

Albert H. Gordon, then a commercial paper salesman at Goldman Sachs, helped to devise a plan to save the venerable company. He saw the Kidder demise as a great opportunity for himself and convinced Edwin S. Webster, Sr., the son of deceased senior Kidder partner Frank Webster, to put up much of the capital needed to save the firm. Webster was running his own engineering firm, Stone & Webster, and was not free to join, but wanted his son, Edwin, Jr., an older Harvard classmate of Gordon's, and Chandler Hovey, another relative, to join Gordon. Further backing came from J. P. Morgan, Jr., Mortimer L. Schiff of Kuhn Loeb, and Frank Dumaine of Waltham Watch, among others. The younger Webster was incapacitated for a long while following a horseback riding accident. To Gordon's surprise, the deal still went through. New York City was set up as the headquarters, with Gordon in charge and Hovey in charge of the Boston office. Later, the younger Webster joined Gordon in New York.

Gordon's plans included shifting the firm more into the securities business and out of private banking and foreign exchange. He emphasized the underwriting and distribution of high-grade securities to rebuild the firm's reputation, and through the purchase of several smaller houses around the country, built up Kidder as a leading national distributor. In rebuilding the firm's underwriting capability, Gordon also served as the chief policy maker and principal recruiter.

Another Gordon priority was to rehabilitate Kidder's antiquated accounting procedures and internal operations. By the late 1940s, the firm had rebounded as one of the top underwriters in the nation, and by 1957, Gordon was in sole command. In 1965, the firm was incorporated, with Gordon as chairman and his two fellow managing partners becoming president and vice president. By the end of the 1960s, Kidder had clearly surpassed even its pre-World War I relative strength.

In 1969, Gordon elevated Ralph DeNunzio, age thirty-eight, to the management committee and began to think about retiring. DeNunzio had joined Kidder in 1953 just after graduating from Princeton and had been groomed by Gordon for fifteen years through several internal assignments. Eventually, in 1971, through Gordon's sponsorship, DeNunzio served as the youngest chairman of the board of governors of the New York Stock Exchange. The time Gordon invested in developing a successor was noteworthy, especially for the brokerage industry. Instead of seizing the opportunity to retain a controlling interest in the firm as well as to stay in command until his death, as had his predecessors, Gordon believed it was important to move young managers into the positions of older ones, with while leaving the older ones with the opportunity to remain on as staff rather than as managers. He pointed with pride to the strong productive members in the firm who were in their seventies, eighties, and even nineties. Those willing to accept new roles and learn new professional skills in late career were invited to stay in the firm, although they had to yield administrative roles. Gordon explained:

> In Kidder, anybody that has an ounce of productive capacity, as measured by the bottom line, does not have to retire. We have had people ninety-two still active and productive. We have had some whose production declined, but if it was still sufficient to justify the expenses of the organization, they remained. It is necessary, however, to give responsibility to other people so that they can learn. In our game, there are more decisions per minute than any business you can think of. If you take off more than two or three weeks you begin to get rusty.

Gordon described his selection and grooming of DeNunzio as a process of trial assignments:

> He was a great salesman in New York. When we needed him in the Chicago office to beef that up, he went and it worked out very well. When the syndicate manager there retired, we replaced him with DeNunzio and worked him hard. In doing the other fellow's job, DeNunzio became very good at pricing, selling, and activating people. He was excited by the business and did not really like vacations. No one else was willing to work as hard, learn as much, and be as loyal to Kidder as DeNunzio.

DeNunzio was also praised for his work at the New York Stock Exchange during a difficult period. He aided in introducing new technology, opening the Exchange to the general public, and strengthening the Crisis Committee, which helps merge endangered firms. According to Gordon, DeNunzio's rivals

> blew themselves out of the running. One person, Dudley Cates, certainly would have been chief executive if he'd wanted it, but he was more of an entrepreneur and did not want the routine. He was very inventive and loyal but left to create new products. If he had it to do over, I believe he would do just as he has done.

Another possible contender, Amyas Ames, left to run Lincoln Center. Gordon did not believe that Ames was out to be chief executive:

> Ames was a great go-between. He was great at pouring oil on troubled waters. Ed Webster was the official head of the institution until his death in 1958 and I was the actual head. We had differences of opinion and personality differences. I often suggested that he was being buttered up by other people. Some of the business was too much for him. It got to the point where there were too many conflicts. I suggested Ames as an intermediary and the conflicts stopped. Ames, however, never wanted to learn the details of the business and wanted to leave by 5:00 P.M.

As for those differences with Webster, Gordon believed that Webster made short-term decisions that did not always allow for such longer term goals as customer loyalty. On the other hand, Webster believed that Gordon was bypassing him. Finally, Webster had begun to listen to some Kidder associates who tried to ingratiate themselves with Webster by attacking Gordon. Gordon gave an example:

> After important conferences with clients, I would give them a dinner at home. These antagonists told Ed, "Gordon's just building himself up, not the firm." Therefore, I announced that I would not give another dinner and invited him to assume the responsibility of taking these groups of twenty people to dinner. After three of these dinners, Webster asked me to take them back.

On a staffing issue, Webster and Gordon disagreed over who should serve on the executive committee when a space became available. At first, rather than select Ames, Webster insisted on someone from Chicago who would be more susceptible to his influence. Gordon admitted that he has not always agreed with DeNunzio's style of delegating or his decisions:

> There were a couple of things over which I did not draw the line and I got my way, but as you get older, you have got to recognize that you are going to get your way less and less.

Gordon was eager to continue to serve Kidder as an institutional symbol, general goodwill ambassador, and even still negotiate deals. He worked a full day and a full week well into his mid-eighties. Equally anxious that his presence never be resented by younger people, he sold back much of his ownership to the firm, retaining only 6 percent by the time of the sale to General Electric. He said that he never wanted anyone to think of him as "that old greedy bastard."

Gordon's father, a Boston leather merchant, was a major influence on him as a model of late-career activity. His father never retired and died at age eighty-seven. As a young man, Gordon was counseled by his father to pick an industry where he would have the most control over his life. He also advised Gordon to go to New York, "where the pot boils faster."

In addition to his long hours at Kidder, Gordon was very active in outside affairs. He served as New York State Republican Finance Committee chairman, served on four major corporate boards as well as on the boards of such nonprofit institutions as the Chapin School, the Memorial Sloan-Kettering Hospital, the YMCA, and the Roxbury Latin School. He has also been a major organizer and generous benefactor to Harvard University development campaigns and has served as a Harvard overseer.

With Gordon, we see an ambassador-style departure, as the leader eases into retirement from the chief executive position without giving up his attachment to the organization. Like Watson, Gordon was able to build a relationship of trust with a much younger successor, in this case one almost three decades younger. Gordon supported DeNunzio and was dedicated to Kidder's strength, even if it meant sacrificing its independence to gain the large amounts of capital needed in the competitive environment of securities firms in the mid-1980s.

Marvin Bower and McKinsey & Company

A graduate of both the Harvard Business School and Harvard Law School, Marvin Bower left the field of law in 1933 for consulting. Many would not be surprised at this today. Given the times, however, it was a striking move, as management consulting then was only an emerging occupation, while law, of course, was a well-established profession. And on top of that, Bower left the nationally respected Cleveland law firm of Jones, Day, Reavis & Pogue to join a firm founded only seven years earlier by Professor James O. McKinsey of the University of Chicago.

As an attorney, Bower had served as secretary for a number of bondholder committees where Jones, Day had acted as counsel. Much of this work involved the reorganization of companies following their default as they fell victim to the Depression. Bower became convinced that there was a need for a business with the professional standards of a law firm that could provide independent advice to executives on managing. He joined McKinsey's "management engineering" firm despite the shock of his attorney colleagues.

In 1935 McKinsey left the firm to serve as chief executive of Marshall Field. The McKinsey consulting company had advised this leading retailer on its reorganization and divestiture of manufacturing operations. Following McKinsey's exit, his business merged with the consulting group of another larger accounting and consulting firm called Scovell, Wellington to form McKinsey, Wellington & Company. Both the consulting and accounting firms were headed by C. Oliver Wellington.

Bower, as manager of the New York office of McKinsey, was principally involved in merging the McKinsey & Scovell consulting staffs, as H. G. Crockett, head of the Scovell consulting staff, was also in New York.

When McKinsey died three years later, the two firms decided to separate, but Bower was unwilling to return to his original firm as the other partners intended. He felt that the management-consulting company should become a national one with multiple offices and should hire directly from graduate schools, as did the top law firms. His former partners did not want to do either.

So Bower suggested to Crockett that they form a new firm made up of the eastern part of the merged firm. Bower was able to retain the McKinsey name. The former McKinsey firm retreated to Chicago and became A. T. Kearney and Company, named for its senior partner. Asked why he did not put his own name on the firm at that time, Bower said:

> I felt our firm would have a better chance of opportunity if my name were not on the door. Our people would be better team players. Also, some clients would demand that they be served by the one whose name is on the door, and we would lose flexibility.

Bower insists that this "was not modesty but rational thinking." He may have been correct, because the firm has since grown into a network of thirty-eight offices worldwide with more than one thousand consultants of forty-four nationalities.

Bower's pride in the firm's growth has as much to do with its nature as its magnitude.

> We have grown organically from within right from the start. We did not make acquisitions nor have affiliations. Each expansion of the firm was led by a partner and a small group of people who were willing to move to a new location, and employ and train high-talent nationals from that country.

Bower retired as managing director in 1967 and gave up all ownership a few years after that. But a full twenty years later, at age eighty-four, Bower continues to consult actively and to participate in training, research, and other company affairs in a non-decision-making capacity.

In addition to yielding his management positions, Bower began many years earlier to sell his share ownership gradually to younger partners. He says, "You cannot have a smooth succession if older partners do not gradually turn over the firm to the younger partners." Bower groomed several potential successors, but did not anoint one. Instead, the actual selection was through a collegial decision-making process with a secret ballot and a three-year term of office. The ease of transition and the productive, yet noninterfering, method of keeping a connection with the company mark Bower's exit as that of an ambassador.

The firm avoids conflicts of interest with a policy that prohibits service on boards of directors of private corporations. However, it permits service on boards of nonprofit organizations, and Bower has served as a trustee of Brown University, Case Western Reserve University, the Committee for Economic Development, and the Joint Council on Economic Education. He is currently active in Religion in American Life, an interfaith group promoting religion, and the board of directors of the associates of Harvard Business School.

Winthrop Knowlton and Harper & Row

From 1982 through 1987, as the Luce Professor of Ethics, Business, and Public Policy and Director of the Center for Business and Government at Harvard's Kennedy School of Government, Win Knowlton pooled the accumulated wisdom from the several distinct careers he had entered and used it to develop a novel educational program at Harvard that brings business and government leaders together to discuss important social, political, and economic issues.

In 1965, Win Knowlton left the prestigious investment firm of White, Weld and Company (since acquired by Merrill Lynch), where he had established a respected reputation, to work in the federal government. He served in the Johnson administration as an assistant secretary of the treasury. He recalled the reaction of his father to this move: "Every time I would go to see my father, who would have stayed at Kuhn Loeb until he was eighty-five, he just thought I was absolutely out of my mind."

In 1968, Knowlton returned to the private sector as the executive vice president of Harper & Row Publishers. By 1970, he was president and chief executive, and from 1978 to 1981 he was chairman and chief executive. After eleven years as chief executive, he decided to retire and move into something new. He was fifty-one. Commenting on the unconventional timing of yet another maverick career move, he stated:

> Most people do not know when to leave. I felt, in my case, that I just had used up all my good ideas and that I was emotionally out to lunch. I felt

> that I was giving less of myself than I had given previously. My signals came from inside me. I just knew I did not want to do it anymore. A lot of people do not let themselves face up to it. They just can't admit it; it's scary to them.

Perhaps he felt more confident in addressing this feeling than others did, as he knew that when he needed "recharging," only moving on would help.

Although he relinquished the chief executive position in 1981, Knowlton retained the chairman's title for four more years. He commented in 1985, while still chairman, on the difficulties of the ambassador style of departure, as well as on its advantages:

> On one board where I sit as a director, the chief executive did not want to retire. It was very difficult for him. He finally did so and stayed on the board. The successor has been very candid with the board about some of his weaknesses. It has, however, sometimes been embarrassing to have the CEO there when we've reappraised the company, revealing that some of the things that the CEO had taken pride in were not as effective as he had led us to believe, or perhaps even believed himself. You have to question the extent to which somebody who retires should stick around.
>
> On the other hand, I think the General Electric approach, where you have to get off the board completely, has its limitations, too. The issue illustrates the difficulty for somebody who is leaving the scene and who is still vigorous and interested and committed, and who wants to have something to hang on to. In my case, I left Harper & Row as the CEO but stayed on as the chairman. It has required an enormous amount of tact on my part to do that without getting in the hair of my successor and appearing to be looking over his shoulder all the time. Things seem to have worked out all right. For example, I suggested to him the other day at dinner that perhaps I should give up the chairmanship, so that he could move up and I could be part of picking his successor. He responded that he was in no hurry to do that, so I'm staying on.

Knowlton left Harper & Row's chief executive post for two reasons:

> First, I was tired of doing it, I was stale, I didn't have any new ideas; but second, I also wanted to write a novel. Writing a novel is a very demanding full-time task, but I felt this sense of emptiness and sense of loss and lack of identity, in part because the writing of a novel is something that doesn't give you any identity or any output until it's completed and it takes a while to do. So, I hung on to my presidency of the New York City Ballet during that period. It was very nice to have a place to go to, to have people to work with and to continue to solve problems. It was very reassuring in midstream to engage in the negotiation that led to my taking this job here at the Kennedy School. So, we all condition ourselves as chief executive officers to solve problems, to be identified with an institution which gives us a uniform and a number, and to work closely every day with other people. My sense is that the transition probably shouldn't be too abrupt for the good of the person, or for the good of the institu-

tion, or in terms of finding ways for the person to make a contribution to other institutions, nonprofit or public sector. Perhaps we should learn how to stage the process.

Knowlton cautioned that the chief executive's natural tendency to close his or her administration in a "blaze of glory often leads them to become increasingly drawn inward . . . to work harder on corporate problems in the last year or two." He suggested that chief executives should instead be encouraged to join other boards for exposure to other exit patterns and to broaden their interests and identities.

Because he left top office younger than most, Knowlton believes that he had an easier time creating new options for himself. He also suggested that retiring chief executives may eventually be used more as members of the executive team who act as liaisons between the public sector and industry associations and their own firms. He has served on six major corporate boards and has been the president of the New York City Ballet, a vice chairman of the board of Teachers College, and a director of the Helsinki Watch Committee, the International League for Human Rights, and several publishing industry associations. He has also written four books.

Roughly a year after Knowlton relinquished his post as chairman, Harper & Row was sold to Rupert Murdoch's News Corporation of America for $300 million. The board turned to Knowlton to negotiate the deal.

Parting Promoters David Ogilvy and Estée Lauder

So far, this chapter has described leaders with an unusual degree of personal humility, but this is not necessarily a characteristic trait of ambassadors. We will now consider several outstanding self-promoters who were able to handle their ambassadorial exits with a great deal of style and fanfare. For example, the advertising giant David Ogilvy, the founder of Ogilvy & Mather, referred to his image in an interview when he was seventy-five:

> I am a sort of symbol of creativity. A lot of younger creative people don't think so, but the fact is that in the great world at large, I am that.[6]

But he commented more modestly on the frequent description of himself as a living legend:

> The only reason I am a legend is because I've outlived all the others. Rubicam is dead. Leo Burnett is dead. Stanley Resor of J. Walter Thompson is dead. I'm not only alive, I'm still going strong.[7]

Perhaps the only thing he has missed since coming to America is the granting of his lifelong desire to be made a knight. Born in England in

1911, he failed out of Oxford University in 1931 and became a chef at the Hotel Majestic in Paris. He began in advertising in 1935 when he joined the London firm of Mather and Crowther. From 1939 to 1942, he was associate director of George Gallup's Audience Research Institute. For the rest of the war years, he served as a British diplomat in the United States. In 1948, he founded the New York agency with $10,000. Ogilvy retired as chairman in 1975 and served as worldwide creative head until 1983. At seventy-five, Ogilvy moved to France, where he currently lives in a chateau in baronial luxury.

Nonetheless, he has stayed active in the firm, albeit with some distance. He has said with pride, "One of the reasons we're not an old and tired agency is that I am not running things any longer."[8] He owns less than 1 percent of Ogilvy stock, although he once owned 30 percent. He spends six months out of the year visiting the company's 220 offices around the world.

When asked to define his role in 1986, Ogilvy commented:

> I am a director of the company. My advice is asked. And when it's asked, I give it. . . . I don't like my present role as much as I liked my active role. . . . There's some advantage to the company in having the last surviving symbolic figure around.[9]

He added that William Phillips, the current chief executive, agrees: "He thinks I have some value to the company and that he can make good use of me—Which he does—and I love being made use of."[10] Later he added, "I've made a lot of speeches and written a lot of talks to different audiences and I'm always selling Ogilvy & Mather. I hope I conceal that sometimes, but I am."[11] He has written several practical books on advertising. Ogilvy has also served on the board of directors of the New York Philharmonic, was a trustee of Colby College, served as chairman of the United Negro College Fund, and has served as a trustee of the World Wildlife Fund International.

The queen of cosmetics, Estée Lauder, is most fairly categorized as an ambassador, and not a monarch or general. In her late seventies, she turned over the chief executive's position to her son Leonard, who is now in charge of decision-making at the $1 billion cosmetics empire.

Born Josephine Esther Menzer in 1908 into a middle-class New York family, Estée Lauder founded the firm that bears her name in 1947. It was initially based on the commercialization of a skin formula developed by a Hungarian immigrant uncle of hers.[12] Her late husband and devoted partner, Joseph Lauder, functioned in the organization as a loyal assistant rather than as the dominant party, as in so many traditional husband-and-wife teams. Among her most popular product lines are Youth Dew, Estée Lauder, Clinique, Aramis, and Prescriptives, which have been marketplace leaders in a very competitive industry.

Lauder's drive and imagination not only built a cosmetics empire, but also helped her forge a completely new identity for herself, one which she now claims as her own.[13] Her social skills and wealth have allowed her to mingle with the world's aristocracy and leading celebrities, generally on a basis of equality. Although very self-made, she has been unusually hostile to the presentation of her career as a rags-to-riches tale. The identity of being *nouveau riche* would erode the aura of long-established nobility she has worked so hard to cultivate for herself and her firm. It is especially noteworthy that the publicity of an unauthorized biography was the catalyst for Lauder to prepare her own autobiography in an effort to preserve her glorious image.[14]

Jerome Gore and Hartmarx

At Hartmarx, the success of the last leadership transition was interrupted only briefly when, in 1987, Jerry Gore had to return, reluctantly, for two months to calm a crisis. Hartmarx (formerly Hart, Schaffner & Marx) grew out of a small tailoring shop founded in 1872 by twenty-one-year-old Harry Marx and his eighteen-year-old brother Marcus. In 1889, they were joined by Joseph Schaffner, another relative. Since its origins, the company emphasized both the manufacturing and the retailing of top-quality men's clothing. The company's balanced strength in retail and wholesale over its history is one of the most successful examples of dual distribution in the clothing industry. It led the industry in such major achievements as progressive labor relations, early magazine advertising, standard pricing, and scientifically proportional fit and sizing. Through a dynamic acquisitions program in the 1960s and 1970s, it became the largest manufacturer and retailer of men's tailored clothing. New licensing agreements with prominent designers allowed the firm to extend beyond its traditional image into high-style items.

Jerome Gore had been chief executive and president since 1975, but the retirement of the forceful and imaginative John D. Gray in 1981 allowed Gore a freer hand in stabilizing the business and coordinating the far-flung network of autonomous manufacturing and retail operations. The return on assets increased roughly three times its initial 5 percent during the course of Gore's tenure.

Gore first began to work for Hart, Schaffner & Marx (renamed Hartmarx in 1983) in 1941. He had been an honors student and an accounting major at the University of Illinois when in the fall of 1940 he casually signed up for an interview for an auditing position. HSM interviewed Gore twice and hired him. He was "tickled pink to get the job at Hart, Schaffner & Marx," a small but prestigious company. Gore was getting married, and his salary paid $25 to $40 per month more than most graduates earned. In an era when jobs were difficult to find, he felt himself a lucky man.

Gore's rise to power at HSM was steady and, in retrospect, carefully managed. In the early 1950s, Gore adroitly chose not to become the controller of the company, recognizing that he was not interested in concentrating on the financial end of the business. At the time, he was backed in this decision by a senior vice president of finance, the man who had hired him and who was a lifelong friend and supporter. By 1955, Gore was an officer of the company. In 1960 Gore became a vice president and was elected to the board. This rise in the organization assured Gore that he had a good future with the company, but according to him there was no suggestion that he might become its chief executive officer. However, Gore did become chief executive officer and president of Hart, Schaffner & Marx in 1975 and chairman in 1981.

Gore's qualities of gentleness and quiet dignity commanded attention and respect. These characteristics enabled him both to lead his management team at Hartmarx and to plan and implement a smooth transition in leadership. On January 1, 1985, Jerome Gore stepped down as CEO, and Richard Hamilton assumed the chair. This transition of power had been planned to accommodate anticipated conditions for eight years, for Gore had a clear sense of the need to groom a successor and how to go about it.

In Gore's opinion, one of the primary responsibilities of a CEO and the board is the preparation of capable people to take over the organization. It is the board's responsibility, he maintains, "to get exposed to the top three or four people in the company," by bringing "them in to make presentations, or to sit in on discussions of problems that are in their area of expertise." In this way, the board can see how its candidates operate. If it looks as if there is not a capable person to take over as CEO, the board can start to consider bringing one or two people in from the outside. "We came to this conclusion about eight years ago," says Gore.

This tough decision eventually led to the hiring of Richard Hamilton from Florsheim Shoes in 1978. By 1981, Hamilton was made president and chief operating officer of Hartmarx, and in January 1984 it was publicly announced that Hamilton would succeed Gore the next year. Gore's care in planning the succession process seems consistent with his belief in a mandatory retirement policy and the reasons behind such a policy.

It is essential to have a policy about retiring, according to Gore. Retirement policies for the CEO, other top executives, and board members bring certainty and predictability to the organization and to its members. "If you don't have a policy, then you run into all kinds of problems. The board is uncertain. The executives are uncertain as to what is going to happen." Although a mandatory retirement policy may force a good CEO out, over the years the lack of a policy will create many more problems and disadvantages for the company, according to Gore.

Why else should organizations install a mandatory retirement policy? Gore feels that a range of personal problems begins at around the age of sixty-five:

> Problems do start to crop up—problems associated with the amount of vigor that the man has, the amount of innovativeness, his willingness to take risks, and his tendency to maintain the status quo and to start to try to protect his position. It's like the guy who says, "I'll know when I start to get senile. I'll resign then." Of course, he starts to get senile and he is the last one to know that he is getting senile.

Gore also believes that in an organization where there is a pattern of consistent retirement among the top managers, there is also a greater retention of good younger employees. If younger executives stay around and wait five years for the CEO to reach sixty-five, and it is then announced that he is going to stay on for another two or three years, the younger people are going to start to leave. "A firm policy with no exceptions helps attract and keep younger managers," says Gore.

The clarity of Gore's position on retirement matches his clearly articulated views on the roles and responsibilities of each group in the governing coalition of the organization. For example, it is the board's responsibility "to keep pushing" the current CEO to talk about his succession, his successor, and how to give his successor the needed experiences to become a future CEO. The board should ask the CEO every time they meet: "Who is going to succeed you?" On the other hand, the CEO must lead the board, for most boards meet four to six times per year. "The CEO really has to be the one that will lead them down the path."

Gore's articulate vision of how best to organize a company and manage succession leaves the impression that he is a man who understands the differences between personal and organization issues and how to balance them. Nevertheless, he obviously feels the pain of letting go of his position and power:

> I had dinner with a retired CEO a couple of months ago. He has been retired from one of the major advertising agencies in this country for two years. He knew I was retiring, and he said, "Jerry, there is only one thing. For two years, the new CEO (who was his fair-haired boy) has *never* called me up. He's *never* said: 'I have this problem; what do you think I ought to do?'" The next morning I went in to see Dick Hamilton, and I told him the story. I said, "Look, I don't want you to be calling me more than two, three, or four times. But please, call me at least once!"

And finally, Gore expressed his understanding of the price the succession process exacts and how he managed it, using one last story to illustrate his point:

Somebody said to me, "Aren't you a dead duck?" I said, "Wait a minute! The right image is lame duck." [pause] But I think that is part of the transition.

Gore's initial retirement plan collapsed in 1987 when his chosen successor, Richard Hamilton, resigned, not quite a full two years after Gore's retirement. My interviews with Gore were held in the fall of 1984; therefore, only the point up to the selection of Hamilton was discussed. My analysis of later events is based on discussions with five current top insiders. Hamilton's tenure as CEO had begun in a tough period for retailing. Furthermore, he had had the mixed blessing of following in the wake of Gore's extraordinarily successful tenure. Toward the end of 1986, his second year, sales were flat and earnings were down substantially due to corporate reorganization and restructuring. Frequent clashes in style with his top lieutenants—Harvey Weinberg, the retail head, and Bert Hand, the manufacturing head—hastened Hamilton's exit. Both Weinberg and Hand were longtime Hartmarx employees with common values and strategic approaches, but there was no conspiracy between them to oust Hamilton. The disagreements came about because Weinberg and Hand, more direct and candid, had basic personality differences with the more reserved and distant Hamilton. Several insiders have suggested that Hamilton, a dignified leader, became less trusting and more autocratic as chief executive.

Gore, still on the board, came out of retirement for two months until a new succession plan was stabilized, creating a triumvirate. Former chief financial officer John Meinert became chairman; vice chairman Weinberg was named chief executive; and Hand, who had been president, became chief operating officer. Gore was able to escape again to his privacy and freedom.

Irving Shapiro and Du Pont

When Irving Shapiro was designated to the top post at Du Pont, shock waves rippled through the business community. Not only was Shapiro Jewish, a Democrat, and an attorney in a company traditionally run by Republicans with chemical backgrounds, but he wasn't even perceived as the heir apparent. Shapiro's appointment to the chairmanship left "the logical candidate" in the chief operating officer slot while Shapiro vaulted into the top seat. In retrospect, Shapiro's predecessor, Charles McCoy, seems to have made a very shrewd move.

Given the circumstances of his ascendancy, it is interesting that Shapiro is adamant about the importance of a well-planned process to ensure a smooth executive transition. According to Shapiro, the first function of a new CEO is to provide for his succession. This means designing and establishing the programs necessary to guarantee that there is a proper successor "when the time comes." Shapiro also stresses the importance of strong communications:

> About the last thing any sensible CEO should do is to walk into a board meeting cold and say, "I want to tell you today who I want to nominate to be my successor." The board would be offended by that kind of procedure. You must first evolve some lines of communication with key directors—so they are privy to your thinking both for emergency purposes and in terms of being able to evaluate the development of people as things go along.

Additionally, Shapiro speaks of "little fictions" that one must arrange in order to send signals to the organization. In his mind, the challenge of the whole process is to avoid surprises. Large organizations function best when they understand what is happening and what direction the CEO is taking, says Shapiro.

How then does Shapiro explain his "surprise" elevation to the CEO title?

> [My appointment] was an unusual situation in the sense that the logical candidate was somebody else. All the signals had gone out that way, and then McCoy changed his mind, so he had to start building some fast bridges. And it worked in my case; although it took some time. But I would regard my appointment as the exception to the rule.

In the summer of 1973, McCoy decided to change horses. On July 16, he designated Shapiro vice chairman and Edward Kane, then considered the heir apparent, as president and CEO. But according to Shapiro, McCoy kept his options open until December, when he formally announced his retirement and his chosen successor. Despite the last-minute change, McCoy used that five-month period to get Shapiro into harness and to familiarize the organization with its soon-to-be leader.

Irving Shapiro ran Du Pont for seven years. In that time, he came to be regarded as a model chief executive. He chaired the prestigious Business Roundtable, and he was selected as *Industry Week's* "CEO of the Year" in 1980. He also spent time preparing for his successor. In January 1980, Edward Jefferson became president of Du Pont under Shapiro. And so the signaling began:

> Once Jefferson became president of the company, I had him preside at our executive committee meetings, which shocked the organization because he wasn't the CEO. But it got them used to the idea that they were working with him, and it gave him an informal measure of authority that his position otherwise wouldn't have given him. And so it wasn't much of a shock to the organization when one day I retired and he had the formal title.

Nor were outsiders surprised. Industry analysts had regarded Jefferson as the probable successor to the top spot at Du Pont for some time.

And as Edward Jefferson settled into his new role, Irving Shapiro began his life as a retired chief executive. But as it turns out, Shapiro is as busy now as when he was heading Du Pont. In addition to six board memberships and involvement in numerous nonprofit organizations, he practices law with Skadden, Arps, Slate, Meagher and Flom in Wilmington. Furthermore, Du Pont is still on his calendar. In fact, if it were not for his continued attachment to Du Pont, Shapiro would be termed as a governor.

At Du Pont, the policy has been for a retired CEO to remain on the board for life, first as chairman of the finance committee, which oversees company operations and financial policy, and then as a regular member of this important committee. Thus Richard Heckert, the current chief executive, at one time came under the active scrutiny of five former Du Pont chief executives. However, a recent change in the company's retirement policy has reversed this custom. Starting in 1989, no prior chief executives will sit on the board except for Richard Heckert. The new policy, introduced in late 1986, perhaps reflects the will of the Bronfman family, owners of the Seagram's Company, which owns roughly a quarter of Du Pont stock. They are said to have requested proportionate board representation.

The retired Shapiro is still chairman of the financial policy committee, responsibilities that consume approximately two hours per day, and the rest of the day belongs to Du Pont, too, if need be. He stated:

> I really needed an organization like this [law firm] to retire to, a place where they could function whether I'm here or not. They understood when I came here that first call was at Du Pont. Free time is available here.

In explaining his advisory role at Du Pont, Shapiro admitted that the company's practice of retaining the former chief executive as chairman of the finance committee is unusual. He attributed it to Du Pont's history as a family company and to the wise recognition that much can be gained from the collective wisdom and experience of former chief executives.

Of course, the negative side is that retired CEOs may "get in the hair" of the existing chief executive. Shapiro felt this aspect is mitigated if the company's people are "civilized." Corporate culture also plays a significant role:

> Part of what makes it work is the culture of the institution. There are fairly well-established norms for behavior, and it's the rare situation where people who have left office depart from those norms. Occasionally it will happen, but not often. And when it does, it corrects itself very quickly because the system simply won't tolerate it.

It is this cultural system that Shapiro believes heavily determines a CEO's retirement style. Therefore, what works at one company will not necessarily work at another. He is convinced that Du Pont's practices are appropriate for its culture and cites the high level of stability retired CEOs impart to the company, when they remain on the board, as a positive result of their presence. According to Shapiro, the Conoco acquisition would have been a difficult transaction for the newly appointed Jefferson to pull off if he had not had former CEOs on the finance committee supporting his position. Just as their support may propel a new venture, so their reluctance may give pause for reflection. Shapiro recalls that if he could not sell McCoy, Greenwalt, and Copeland on a proposition, it was a warning signal to go back and rethink the issue. "I might come back a second time and replay it, because I was persuaded I was right. But the second reflection was a valuable mechanism."

Shapiro feels that chief executives who keep busy after retiring have an easier time of it than those whose lives start to revolve around the golf course. But busy or not, all retired CEOs must eventually deal with the loss of what Shapiro calls the "psychological perks" of the office.

> All the perks of office, not the material perks but all the psychological perks of office that you don't realize have really taken hold of you, become a very important part of your mind-set, and the day they're gone, you recognize that you've got to learn to live in a different way.

Irving Shapiro seems to have adjusted quite well. In his retirement, he has played very much the role of an "ambassador," which is slightly different from being an ambassador-type CEO. In many respects, the Du Pont system rather than the individual himself encourages the ambassador role for the retired CEO. Because of this system at Du Pont, age gaps between CEOs are compressed, as is the average tenure in office. The organizational dynamics stress the perception of a retiring CEO as a valuable asset and the importance of having a well-established heir apparent who is guided into the new role before his or her predecessor retires. Thus Du Pont has a history of stability within the organization as a result of smooth CEO succession.

Roger Damon, Richard Hill, and the Bank of Boston

The impact of corporate culture on chief executive succession is perhaps nowhere more clearly evident than at the Bank of Boston. What one discovers in digging behind the seemingly unmomentous CEO successions of the past two decades is a fascinating series of well-planned transitions inspired by a corporate culture that stresses gentlemanly decorum and mutual respect among colleagues. Roger Damon, chief executive of First National Bank of Boston from 1966 to 1971, describes the Bank of Boston philosophy behind the ambassador model as "Always conduct your affairs so as to command the respect of your neighbors and fellow citizens."

Lloyd Brace demonstrated this philosophy in 1966 when he decided to step down from the office of the chief executive a year-and-a-half early in order that his successor-to-be, Roger Damon, would have a full five years as chairman. The bank's mandatory retirement age required that Brace resign in 1968. Damon, being only three-and-a-half years younger than Brace and the heir apparent, would be expected to assume the CEO title at that time. Out of respect for his friend Damon and in keeping with the best interests of the organization, Brace believed that a three-and-a-half-year tenure as chief executive would be difficult at best and potentially destructive to the organization. He therefore handed over the reins to Damon early and moved into a newly created post, chairman of the executive committee. From this position, Brace made himself available to Damon and to the newly appointed president, Richard Hill. Brace continued as a board director for two years following his retirement.

From Roger Damon's perspective, Brace deserves great credit for having the strength to step aside early: "I think it was very tough on him to give up his authority; it was a tough role for him to play," Damon asserts. "But he did it and he did it well." Damon is a strong supporter of retired chief executives remaining in some unintrusive capacity immediately following the CEO transition, particularly in the banking industry, which depends so heavily on personal relationships. In addition to the continued confidence he believes people derive from this type of transition, Damon feels the successor is likely to be better prepared, knowing his precedessor is there watching. "After all," Damon says, "you're trying to make his job better, not easier."

Damon followed his own advice when preparing for his retirement in 1971. Having earlier worked out an agreement with his heir apparent, Richard Hill, regarding Hill's successor, Damon offered his resignation to the board, nominating Hill as the new CEO and William Brown as president. As is customary at the Bank of Boston, Damon remained on the bank board following his retirement and steeled himself to assume his new, powerless role. "I made up my mind I wasn't going to interfere. I knew Dick wanted to do some things that I didn't think he ought to do. He knew it. And I knew that as soon as I lost my chief executive power, he would do it." As a testimony to Damon's resolve, Hill describes Damon's behavior as director as "scrupulous, absolutely scrupulous. He would never open his mouth. Never. Lloyd was the same way with him." This pattern has served the Bank of Boston well. Because its objective puts the firm's interest first, it has allowed the organization to make a smooth transition between CEOs whose visions for the bank were often quite different.

Given the fourteen-year age difference between Damon and Hill,

Richard Hill had a long tenure in office to look forward to. But Hill is a firm believer that one of the principal responsibilities of the chief executive is to develop an organization that can succeed him. Therefore, as early as 1976 he developed, with Brown's help, a detailed succession plan involving approximately twenty executives in the bank's upper echelons. The plan, which Hill proudly calls his "archives," laid out career movements for these managers with the intent of helping himself and Brown identify Brown's replacement as president at the appropriate time. But perhaps most revealing about Hill's plan was that it called for him to step down as CEO in 1983, two years early, and the year of our interview, and become chairman of the executive committee, just as Brace had done with Damon. Hill explained his logic to Brown this way:

> Look Bill, you're only two years younger than I am. I cannot have a bureaucracy like this run by somebody for only two years. It just isn't right. You have been gradually taking over more and more direct responsibilities and it's not fair for you to only have two years. So that's why I think I ought to step down two years in advance and you'll have the full four years.

Having seen the process work with Brace strengthened Hill's resolve to go ahead with the plan. Ironically, Hill claims that having this plan, the existence of which had been well known to the Bank of Boston board since 1976, made it easier for him to approve of the long-range planning effort currently under way at the bank. While reluctant to assert his own vision on the bank once he was out of office, Hill was able to support long-range planning knowing that someone else would be making the difficult, strategic decisions that resulted. To have had to make some of these decisions himself would have been difficult given his background perspective and long tenure at the bank. Now they are in the hands of those who will take the bank into a new decade, with Hill in an advisory capacity:

> The principal decisions that are going to be made with respect to this bank's future are going to be made within the next two years. They have to be. We haven't got much time so they'll be made when I'm here. They will probably ask my advice; I'll grumble about a few things. But I know these people well enough to know they're going to make the right decision.

The difficulty of dealing with significant strategic changes instituted by a successor is often cited as a major problem for a retired CEO who remains engaged as an ambassador. Hill's attitude is that recognizing that the world changes helped him to deal with the major alterations at the Bank of Boston: "I'm not going to kick myself around and say, 'Gee, why didn't I think of this and do it three or four years ago?' I'm going to say that I think I did what was right for the times and now my successors are doing what's right for their times. You've got to do that."

In addition to feeling comfortable with past decisions, Hill is confident and excited about his new role at the bank. His participation in the chairman's office will supplement his work in customer relations for the company as well as his five outside board directorships.

Even so, Hill is quick to point out that he hasn't completely retired yet and still faces the "decompression chamber." Like many of his peers, Hill believes it is difficult to give up the "psychological perks" of the office and sink back into the relative anonymity of the non-chief executive, but he anticipates that he will have plenty to do when the time comes.

Charles F. Adams and Raytheon

Raytheon Company represents an interesting comparison of succession styles between its first two leaders. The stormy exit of the firm's founder, a monarch, is in marked contrast to the graceful, ambassador-style succession that occurred twenty years later. As the driving force behind the creation of Raytheon, Laurence Marshall took untested but promising inventions in radar and microwave technology and created a multimillion-dollar company. A tireless man who radiated confidence, Marshall's ability to sell—in terms of acquiring both financial backing and later, large government contracts—catapulted the growing company through its first quarter-century of operation.[15] But even in the wartime-related boom years, trouble brewed just beneath the surface.

An unhealthy dependence on government contracts left Raytheon weak and shaken after World War II, when government buying came to a sharp halt. The termination of work for the government drained money and resources from the weakened company at a time when it desperately needed every dime. In fact, it was about two weeks from receivership. As the organization struggled with its financial problems, organizational turmoil, long camouflaged in the chaotic environment of a wartime boom, was beginning to surface. Marshall, a man of great creative genius, had little sense of organization or order. Raytheon was in a shambles, and the board groped wildly for a solution.

An investment banker with the rather traditional firm of Paine Webber Jackson & Curtis, Charles Francis Adams was a most unlikely candidate for savior of a large electronics firm. After military service as a naval officer in World War II, Adams returned home with a new interest in general industrial management. But he knew little about electronics, had no experience in industry, already held a comfortable job with a recognized institution, and knew Marshall well enough to know he was going to have some differences of opinion with him. Despite such barriers, Adams could not resist the challenge. Thinking Raytheon's troubles were mostly financial in nature, the board initially offered Adams the post of chairman of the finance committee. But Adams wouldn't hear of it:

> I said the problems are organizational and operational, not financial. The financial problems are the result of the other problems. If you want me as chairman of the finance committee, forget it, because it will just keep getting worse. You really have to get into the total structure.

The board looked around, but no one wanted the number-two job at Raytheon. So they came back to Adams with an offer of the executive vice president post under Marshall. Adams fully understood the mess into which he would be stepping. Before delivering his answer to the board, he consulted many close associates. One of these, Harvard Business School professor Phillip Cabot, advised that "the first step in a mess like this is to reduce chaos to disorder."

Adams decided to accept the executive vice president slot, but anticipating opposition from Marshall, obtained an agreement in writing that said that he could carry any deadlock between himself and Marshall directly to a board vote. The agreement proved fortunate. From the beginning, Adams and Marshall clashed repeatedly and the board always sided with Adams:

> I was very fond of Marshall, even though we differed. We knew each other well. Then came the embarrassing period, when I had to raise issues [on which we disagreed]. So we had a very unhappy relationship as it developed. On every one of these issues the board solidly backed me. Marshall got more and more unhappy and uncomfortable. I felt badly. It was his company. He created it. Under the circumstances I was in, I could do nothing else. Eventually, he said he wanted to retire. He became chairman for a while. I became president and within that year he left completely.

Adams became president in 1948 and then in the same year chief executive. With Marshall's departure, it appeared that the company had turned a corner. Adams, after succeeding a deposed monarch, was bringing structure and organization to Raytheon. The company's fortunes were picking up.

Personally, Charles Adams was quite different from his predecessor. Quiet and aloof, Adams was a private person who led a balanced life and did not intrude into the private lives of others. He was unaffected by rank and given to orderliness and logic. His lack of concern with rank and the trappings of power would prove risky when Harold Geneen entered the Raytheon fold. Geneen started with Raytheon in 1956 as executive vice president and almost immediately began instituting drastic changes in the company culture, such as his infamous executive group interrogations and central controls. The firm had recently lost some top financial talent and needed outside assistance. Sales had fallen 4 percent from the previous year. Sales stood at $175 million and profits at $1.255 million. By 1958, sales were $375 million with profits of $19 million.[16] Though much of Geneen's style was in marked contrast to his own, Adams tried to give his new executive vice president all of the discretion he needed to push profit center responsibility to lower levels. On occasion, Adams intervened during unusually humiliating executive interrogations and said quietly and firmly, "Stop that!" to Geneen.

Meanwhile, Geneen widely publicized what he interpreted as his positive effects on Raytheon's improving bottom line. He even changed the design of the 1957 annual report to make it seem that his position in the company was on a par with Adams's. Adams was not a man to care about such things, but he made up his mind not to anoint Geneen as his heir. When Geneen departed for ITT in 1959, the price of Raytheon stock shot downward. Adams was shocked. "I had not realized," he said later, "that Geneen had created a constituency among security analysts."

With Geneen gone, Adams discussed appointing a Geneen recruit from Ford, Richard E. Krafve, as executive vice president. The board approved, and Adams, "mindful that the world had accused him of holding back Harold Geneen, promised Krafve that he would, in a reasonable period, make him president of Raytheon if all worked well." But like Geneen, Krafve would prove impatient. Within a year, Adams made Krafve president but he retained the chairmanship for himself, transferring the authority and responsibility of the chief executive office to the chairman's office, so that except for titles, the power structure remained unchanged. Unfortunately Adams chose not to make this fact public. Perhaps he took it for granted that people understood what he had done, which would have been typical of his low-key, nonconfrontational style of leadership. Perhaps it was an attempt to give Krafve added prestige without turning over the reins of power until he felt confident that Krafve could manage.

Whatever his reasons, by not making it clear that he remained chief executive, Adams created a misunderstanding both inside and outside the firm that was deepened when Krafve began acting as though he possessed complete control. The final Krafve–Adams showdown took place two days before Christmas in 1961. Differences had arisen over executive appointments, with Adams favoring technical competence as the criterion for promotion. At this point, Krafve asked the board to make him chief executive. When that request was turned down, he resigned.

With the two executive vice president disasters of Geneen and Krafve behind him, it is not surprising that Adams turned to an insider for his next executive vice president. Tom Phillips was more in the Adams mold, and from 1962 on, Adams encouraged Phillips to take an overall view of the company with an eye to becoming chief executive. Adams was pleased with Phillips; they conferred often and easily, with none of the subtle tension that had been present with the former executive vice presidents. In 1964 Adams had Phillips elevated to president; four years later he recommended to the board that the chief executive officer be transferred from his own office (of chairman) to that of the president. Phillips would be the CEO. In typical Adams fashion, he also recommended that their salaries be reversed, so that Phillips's was higher than his own.

According to Adams, his action in stepping aside as chief executive was motivated by the realization that he had reduced the chaos to disorder once more. The fine-tuning was best left for someone else. Another Raytheon manager, Brainerd Holmes, was elected executive vice president in early 1969. One Raytheon observer commented:

> News that Holmes had moved up occasioned no surprise. The troika of Adams, Phillips, and Holmes had been well-established for years. But a subtle shift took place. Phillips had become chief executive, Holmes was now executive vice president, and Adams moved back. The chairman became the elder statesman to whom both the younger could turn. An ideal situation. Adams was very pleased.

In 1975, at the age of sixty-five, Charles Adams retired as chairman of Raytheon. But his retirement meant little physical change. Situated in an office close to Phillips's, Adams remains to this day chairman of the finance committee, but he is quick to point out:

> I am here in this office because Tom Phillips wanted to keep me as a consultant and for no other damn reason. I am here in a role of no authority but to keep up with certain kinds of things, to offer useful advice when it is asked for and to plunge in but only on a very, very rare occasion—when I think they might have missed something.

He added:

> This could happen because I am fourteen years older than Tom Phillips and because I proved to him that the roles could be reversed and that he could emerge as chief executive without being under the shadow of somebody who had been around there; do his own thing in his own way. He had enough exposure to that so that he could have me here in the back office and not be thinking, "It is my sole desire to get rid of the old SOB so that I can do my own thing." That happens to be unusual. It [was] made possible by the reversal of the chief executive role before my retirement.

While scrupulously avoiding temptations to intervene, Adams has been on hand for top management consultation and external representation. He conveyed institutional stability even through troubled periods. For example, many Raytheon watchers were surprised when Holmes left in anger in 1986 when he was not named Phillips's successor. At that time Adams helped calm the waters. Holmes expected Phillips to retire early and yield command, but the board refused to name Holmes, already sixty-five, as chief executive and asked Phillips to remain in office.[17] With Adams still present, employees and outsiders were assured of leadership continuity and stability at an awkward time. Through the ambassador style of departure, the firm gained by the internal transfer of accumulated wisdom and the external appearance of continuity of command.

Conclusions

Unlike the monarchs and the generals, the ambassador type of retiring leaders never wage war with their own organizations. They leave their positions feeling accomplished and appreciated. In return, their firms gain internally through the transfer of accumulated wisdom within the organization and externally through the appearance of continuity of command. The leaders profiled in this chapter were not necessarily humble figures, but their self-esteem was enhanced, rather than threatened, by a firm that would easily survive their departure.

Five direct benefits resulted from these leaders' continued engagement with their firms into old age. First, as wise elder statesmen, they provided a safe haven to which other officers could turn for advice and counsel without fearing public embarrassment or a loss of power. Just as Kennedy could consult with Eisenhower over Cuba, Tom Phillips of Raytheon could turn to Charles Adams for advice. Ron Daniels at McKinsey could turn to Marvin Bower, and Ralph DeNunzio of Kidder Peabody could turn to Albert Gordon. There was one person on earth who truly understood their unique position and constraints. Regardless of whether or not the advice was correct or followed, just to know it was available must have been of some comfort. The chief executive's job can be a lonely one.

Second, an informed former chief executive with no further ambitions for office can be a valuable stabilizing force. The chemistry between people and positions is not a perfect science, and some problems cannot be foreseen with clarity. Thus the gradual process of exit allows the retiring chief executives to guide the organization through unplanned difficulties in the succession process. Tom Watson, Jr., of IBM, Jerry Gore of Hartmarx, and Charles Adams of Raytheon each played such a role.

Third, the retiring chief executives benefited from their own phased withdrawal from their firms. Marvin Bower of McKinsey, Albert Gordon of Kidder Peabody, Charles Adams of Raytheon, and Thomas Watson of IBM spent over five combined decades in dedicated service as leaders of their firms. It would have been unappreciative, unjust, and wasteful to terminate abruptly their contact with the firm. Through their post-retirement in-house activities, these executives had time and opportunity to anchor their personal identities more securely outside of their firms.

Fourth, as Winthrop Knowlton of Harper & Row suggested, retiring chief executives can contribute still further to the company by sharing their external professional networks. They can shield new chief executives when needed, provide them with further contact and exposure at other times, and substitute for them as representatives on especially busy occasions. The work of former top leaders in outside institutions can be important to their old firms.

Fifth, the ambassador style of exit can be reassuring to customers, workers, and suppliers concerned about the continuity of command. As Irving Shapiro of Du Pont and Richard Hill of the Bank of Boston suggested, a new chief executive can implement fairly revolutionary changes in ways that seem less threatening to key stockholders when the presence of the former leader is in the picture. Retired leaders thus serve as symbolic guardians of the company's goals when capricious or impatient acts of new leaders in a hurry to assert themselves may disturb those associated with the company. The support of retired leaders is very reassuring to other parties that there is a rational plan behind the change.

For these benefits to materialize, the ambassadors had to begin planning years in advance for their retirement and the succession process. Unlike the monarchs and generals, Gordon of Kidder Peabody, Adams of Raytheon, and Watson of IBM planned their successions as much as a decade in advance of their exit. Ambassadors' greater involvement in outside organizations allowed them to develop greater self-awareness and identity beyond their firms. They were more civic-minded and community-oriented than the other types of retiring leaders, including the governors, as we will see in Chapter 9. Monarchs and generals were least involved of the four in any activities outside of their businesses, while the governors were more involved in those activities that could lead to meaningful new careers. The ambassadors' outside activities were of the type readily integrated with their careers.

In order to choose qualified successors, ambassadors observed potential candidates over many years in a variety of settings and assignments. Such data would be superior to that coming from outside executive search firms. As a result, there was a greater age difference, often about ten years more, between the outgoing and incoming leaders among ambassadors than I found with the other exit patterns. This had the additional advantage of reducing intergenerational conflict between historic rivals. Such mentor–protégé relationships are more effective when there is such an age gap. This provides for both grooming and reasonable overlap of shared experience without competition.

The survey data of the one hundred retired chief executives show that, in characterizing the most rejuvenating aspects of their retirement, ambassadors were far more likely to suggest greater time for themselves and more privacy (50 percent for ambassadors versus 25 percent for the other types of retired CEOs), they were more likely to suggest that they were able to devote more time to civic interests (40 percent versus 20 percent), and they were more likely to suggest they could now spend more time with their families (30 percent versus 14 percent). They felt the most important preparation for their own retirement was through their involvement in civic activities (56 percent of ambassadors versus 24 percent of the others). Similarly, they were the most likely to report that the transition was easy (52 percent versus 35 percent). Their timing was most often influenced by the availability of capable younger executives (60 percent versus 50 percent) and followed a process suggested by company tradition (35 percent versus 8 percent). As would be expected, they tended to identify their successors earlier. While 62 percent continued to hold a position in the firm and 90 percent remained on the board for over two years, they were the most cautious group in waiting for their advice to be solicited from their successors before offering it (80 percent versus 50 percent).

Overall, the conditions and personal qualities conducive to ambassador-like exits are stable organizations and contented individuals. The leaders who exited in the ambassador style were the most satisfied with the contributions they had made in their careers. They might yearn for continued heroic adventures, but their mission was largely fulfilled. They believed that they had left a lasting legacy in the organization, but they also had managed to anchor their identities outside the firm so that their stature was secure. Finally, unlike the situations facing the monarchs, their firms were not in the throes of life-threatening crises at the time of their departure. Their legacy seemed safe.

This is not to suggest that there are no problems with this departure style. There are several.[18] First the mentor–protégé relationship may become unproductive, with the successor never growing into the new job. Second, as Watson suggested, it is easy to offend the retiring chief executive and bore the new CEO. Third, as Knowlton pointed out, it is sometimes embarrassing to challenge the veracity and robustness of the previous CEO's actions when he or she is present. Fourth, as Gordon found, it is possible for the lines of authority to get blurred and for the retired chief executive to be lured back into action. Fifth, as demonstrated by Gore and Watson, the board can become very reliant upon the retired chief executive.

9

THE GOVERNOR'S DEPARTURE

It is as indefensible for a man, who has
capital, not to apply himself to apply it
in a way that will be of most benefit for
the country as it is for a laborer to refuse
to work. It is the duty of everyone, rich or
poor to work. I love to work—I cannot see
how anyone can prefer to remain idle.

W. Averell Harriman,
former chief executive of Union Pacific,
Brown Brothers Harriman, and United
American Shipping, U.S. ambassador,
governor of New York,
presidential adviser

Chief Dan George led his tribe of Canadian Indians for twelve years
before retiring at age sixty-two for a new career, acting. Within a decade, he had acted in such productions as the television series "Caribo
County" and the films *Little Big Man* and *Harry and Tonto*, where his
strong-featured, weatherbeaten face became familiar to millions. After
retirement from tribal leadership, he was determined to "do something
that would give a good name to the Indian people."[1] He achieved this
goal, winning widespread public recognition for Indian culture and tra-
ditions. His dignified portrayal of Indians instilled a sense of pride in
young people unacquainted with their heritage. He won an award in
human relations from the Canadian Council of Christians and Jews and
a 1971 Oscar nomination. He stated that he was "proud to see young
Indians, after viewing *Little Big Man*, walk out of the theater and walk
up to a white man and shake him by the hand." The joy over his new
career was mixed with ironic tragedy. The night he prepared to attend
the 1971 Oscar ceremonies, his wife died. He survived her by another

decade. When he died, he had fulfilled his mission as both tribal leader and cultural emissary.

We can find many late-career leaders who follow a pattern similar to that of Chief Dan George. In essence, this is the model of a career switch. In politics, another example of career change is that of state governors, who frequently serve a term of office and then move on to a different calling. In contrast to the open-ended reign of the monarch, the general's eager return to office, or the ambassador's maintaining of advisory status, the retiring governor-like business leader usually leaves office for a completely new activity. The governors have long had extensive interests outside their firms. Retirement for them is often merely a career change as they turn to pursue outside interests. After they disengage from their firms, their careers do not fade into the sunset. Any new activities tend to be leadership roles and not solely board memberships. Meanwhile, the firms they depart are led by successors with a clear hold on their reign. Two examples of the governor style of leader actually became governors. Both Chester Bowles and W. Averell Harriman started as successful young entrepreneurs, then left their companies, went into politics and were elected state governors, and still later became influential international diplomats and policy-makers. In this chapter, we will first look at three common routes taken by departing governors: (1) public service; (2) the starting of new enterprises; and (3) turnaround challenges.

From Private Sector to Public Service

Many diplomats, philanthropists, legislators, and other public servants have previously been successful business executives. Benjamin Franklin was such a multifaceted figure that few biographers have even reviewed the entirety of this renaissance man. Some feature his scientific, philosophical, or diplomatic accomplishments. Others feature his personal life, from his flamboyant social life and gregariousness abroad, to his strained family ties. We rarely learn much of his first calling as entrepreneur, printer, and modest publisher. A success in his early business career, Franklin was able to retire at the early age of forty-two into these less remunerative pursuits. His crucial diplomatic roles, as well as his influential service as a delegate to the First Continental Congress of 1775 and the federal Constitutional Convention of 1787, carried him into his eighties, nearly twice the age at which he retired.

President Herbert Hoover was a mining executive before he entered politics. Wall Street's Securities and Exchange Commissioner John Shad was a retired vice chairman of E. F. Hutton. Former defense secretary and World Bank president Robert McNamara was a past president of Ford Motor Company. Bernard Baruch, a prominent benefactor of the

Democratic party, the chairman of the War Industries Board, and U.S. representative on atomic energy to the United Nations, had been a leading securities and commodities trader. Ambassador Sol Linowitz, a prominent negotiator, was former chairman of Xerox. Philanthropists George T. Delacorte and Albert Lasker are so renowned for their civic involvements that few remember their earlier careers as successful businessmen. In fact, the second careers of many business executives who enter public life overshadow impressive accomplishments in their first careers, as the cases of chief-executives-turned-public-servants Ellsworth Bunker, Chester Bowles, and W. Averell Harriman illustrate.

After thirty-five years with the National Sugar Refining Company, a firm founded by his father, Ellsworth Bunker entered a second career as a diplomatic troubleshooter for several U.S. presidents. He started this career almost by accident. As president and chief executive of National Sugar, Bunker had had close business dealings with Argentina. When he was nearly sixty, he was asked by President Harry Truman to serve as ambassador to Argentina, a post Bunker accepted, assuming it to be a one-shot fling at diplomatic work before a complete retirement.[2] By the time he died at age ninety, he had spent three decades in service to four U.S. presidents, with assignments as ambassador to India, Nepal, Italy, South Vietnam, and the Organization of American States. He also served for three years as president of the American Red Cross.

Chester Bowles co-founded the advertising agency Benton & Bowles in 1929.[3] Despite the stock market crash that year and the subsequent depression, his pioneering use of customer surveys and other innovative advertising practices made him a millionaire. By World War II, he had already retired from business and entered into public service. He ran the Office of Price Administration during the war, was elected governor of Connecticut in 1948, served as ambassador to India in the 1950s, and won election to the U.S. Congress. During the Kennedy administration, he was a policy adviser, known for his staunch criticism of American military involvement in Cuba and Vietnam.

W. Averell Harriman's business career began in 1917 at age twenty-six, when he left his father's employment at the Union Pacific Railroad and struck out on his own. He purchased a run-down shipyard in Chester, Pennsylvania, and built it into the United American Lines, the nation's largest commercial fleet with sixty-three ships. After heading this firm from 1917 until 1925, he founded the investment bank W. A. Harriman, where he was a managing partner until 1931, when it merged with Brown Brothers. Then he became chairman of the board of the Union Pacific Railroad, ran his father's railroad for a decade, and by age fifty-one was ready for a new career.

Harriman's father, Edward H. Harriman, had built this railroad into a major system, but got little support from his own father, a wandering Episcopal clergyman, who disapproved of the business career chosen by his son Edward. Edward worked as a messenger on Wall Street, married a wealthy woman, and won several lucrative battles with such fierce, rich rivals as James J. Hill and J. P. Morgan before building his own railroad empire with 23,000 miles of track and $1.5 billion in assets.[4]

Averell Harriman, raised with great wealth and left with an estate of $100 million, was instilled with a strong sense of social obligation, perhaps a legacy from his clergyman grandfather. To repay society, he believed, was the burden of the privileged. On a voyage to Alaska sponsored by Harriman's father, the family friend and environmentalist John Muir interrupted someone praising the elder Harriman for his benevolence, stating, "I don't think Mr. Harriman is very rich. He has not as much money as I have. I have all I want. Mr. Harriman has not." Later Harriman responded, "I have never cared for money except as a power to put to work . . . making everybody and everything a little happier."[5] Averell was impressed by his father's statement, and later in his career would show how much influence that pronouncement had made.

After his successful business career, Harriman spent the next forty years in government service. From the state chairmanship of the National Recovery Administration in 1934, Harriman went on to serve as chairman of the Business Advisory Council of the department of commerce, and during World War II as President Roosevelt's ambassador to the Soviet Union. After the war, he was ambassador to the United Kingdom, coordinator of the Marshall Plan to rebuild postwar Europe, secretary of commerce from 1946 to 1948 during the Truman administration, and governor of New York in 1952. In the 1960s, while in his mid-seventies, he assisted presidents Kennedy and Johnson by leading sensitive international negotiations involving Southeast Asia and nuclear testing.[6]

Starting Over with a Start-Up

Walter Mack, as president of the Pepsi-Cola Company in 1939, led it back to independence after a bankruptcy had allowed it to be taken over by Lofts Candies in 1931. Under Mack, Pepsi entered the supermarket revolution of the 1940s and 1950s and became a serious number-two competitor to Coca-Cola. In 1950, a vicious proxy battle stripped Mack of power. Nonetheless, he left Pepsi with a sense of accomplishment and went on to run Nedick's restaurants and to found two other beverage companies, C & C in 1978, and King Kola, founded when Mack was eighty-two. The average age of members of his executive team on this latest project was sixty-two, and it included his chief chemist from Pepsi, sixty-three-year-old Thomas Elmezzi, who supervised production.[7]

Forrest Mars of M&M/Mars was another consumer-products executive in the governor mold. Renowned for his fanatical dedication to the company he had founded with his father in the 1920s, he was unable to get along with his co-founder and was ousted in 1932. He was given $50,000 and the foreign rights to Mars products. He then devised a recipe for sweeter candies and successfully set up shop in Britain. His father died in 1934, but Mars did not return home until World War II, when he introduced M&Ms, his new candy, into the United States. In 1964 he bought the remaining control of the original company and merged the two firms. A decade later, in 1973, he retired, turning the business over to his two sons to manage. After a short while, he concluded that "retirement is the beginning of death" and returned to candy making with a boxed chocolate called "Ethel M" (after his mother). He lives upstairs over the factory that makes this product.[8]

Another example among governors of a successful start-up is the model provided by James W. Rouse. This prominent developer retired after building extravagant marketplaces in Boston, Philadelphia, and Baltimore, as well as large housing complexes, including the entire planned city of Columbia, Maryland. Like Mack and Mars, Rouse returned to work but not to enrich himself further. Instead, in 1981, two years after he retired, Rouse formed the Enterprise Development firm, which funds the Enterprise Foundation, an institution devoted to upgrading rundown inner-city dwellings and to creating decent, affordable low-income housing.[9]

We can also find examples of governors who remain in the same industry but start up new firms. James A. Ryder, after retirement, moved from one truck-leasing firm to another. On June 8, 1978, the *New York Times* announced the "retirement" of Ryder, age sixty-seven, who had founded the $1-billion-a-year Ryder Systems. He had entered the trucking business at age twenty with only one Model A Ford truck. The report stated that he was leaving only to "pursue personal business and financial affairs."[10] Significantly, however, he had refused the $200,000 offer from his old firm not to set up a competitor. Some industry observers see Ryder as a monarch who lost control over his board and then launched a new business as a vendetta. A year later, while James Ryder was still Ryder Systems' largest shareholder, he founded a rival leasing firm called Jartran (for James A. Ryder Transportation):

> I had become bored with such a big company [as Ryder Systems] and the way it was structured. I was ready to fly my own thing and no longer had that latitude. I didn't start Jartran to compete with Ryder, I just wanted to have some interesting things to do.[11]

One year later, Ryder dipped back into his old firm to hire away a former subordinate to serve as president of Jartran, and four years after its founding, Jartran had a fleet of 32,000 vehicles.[12] "I got over a personal identification with Ryder Systems long ago," Ryder said. "Now I get a thrill when I see the word 'Jartran.' "[13]

Despite its impressive sales, Jartran lost $31.9 million on sales of $79.6 million in 1980, as it struggled through logo battles with Ryder Systems and pricing disputes with U Haul. Lacking sufficient equity to cover its losses, it filed for reorganization under Chapter 11.[14]

These examples show that entrepreneurial personalities did not necessarily become monarchs when they left. Instead, they parted from their firms and tackled new challenges. Rather than protecting their old castles, they went out to build new ones.

Turning to Turnarounds

The third route taken by many governors after they leave is the challenge of using their skills to assist an enterprise in difficulty. W. Graham Clayton, Jr., Amtrak's chairman and president, led passenger rail service through a critical rebuilding period while he was in his mid-seventies.[15] He had previously served as chairman and president of the well-regarded Southern Railway and as secretary of the navy under President Jimmy Carter. One of his successors at Southern, L. Stanley Crane, also retired as chairman and president and performed a turnaround. Crane had worked at Southern since 1937, except for a two-year hitch at the Pennsylvania Railroad in 1960, and left it to help save the loss-plagued remains of Penn Central's bankrupt freight and commuter operations. They had been merged with several smaller northeast lines to form Conrail, a nationalized railroad with 39,000 workers and 14,000 miles of track across fifteen states.[16]

Working twelve-hour days, Crane eventually succeeded in rescuing the service. An adroit lobbyist and an insightful administrator, Crane devised new route plans, cut unprofitable lines, negotiated difficult wage settlements, and introduced revolutionary technical changes to automate the repair garages and to utilize high-speed rails. By the end of 1981, his first year, the firm was already profitable. A manager who had predated Crane at Conrail commented:

> When he came here, the people had lost confidence in themselves. They had been through bankruptcy. They'd been depending on the government for all their funds. They had been through 10 years of being kicked around. He had to make them believe in themselves again.[17]

Each year the picture so improved that Conrail became an attractive acquisition for other railroads. In particular, his old railroad, now called the Norfolk and Southern, fought hard to purchase the line, but Crane resisted until the time was right. In 1987 Conrail went public in one of the largest public offerings in U.S. history.

A dramatic turnaround by a governor going from one industry to another was led by retired oilman John Swearingen, who had forcefully guided Standard Oil of Indiana for twenty-three years. When he retired in 1983, the firm had moved from its position as a second-tier oil producer to the fourth largest in the industry, with sales of about $29 billion and with the second highest profits in the industry. Swearingen had joined the firm in 1939 as a chemical engineer and had long been identified with it in the public's mind. Although he carefully groomed seventy-one-year-old former president Richard Morrow, once the head of Standard's Amoco production company, to take the CEO position, some speculated that Swearingen's haunting presence would overpower his lower-keyed successor.[18]

Swearingen, however, promised to make a clean break and in fact did just that. A year later, however, the Federal Deposit Insurance Corporation poured $4.5 billion into the unstable Continental Illinois Corporation of Chicago and brought Swearingen in as head of the bank. Continental's assets had dropped from $30.4 billion to $12 billion that year. Swearingen developed a deferential and smooth relationship with a fellow newcomer to the bank, former Chase vice president William Ogden, who was brought in to head the Continental Bank and Trust subsidiary.[19]

One of Swearingen's first moves was to remove eleven of the fourteen outside directors, including many prominent leaders of Chicago's business community.[20] He next began to fill twenty-five top-level positions, and within a year the firm had stabilized and begun to rebuild its image and operations. The public was quite comforted by the moves. By July 1987, Swearingen made plans to retire again as he announced that Citicorp's Thomas C. Theobald would succeed him at Continental Illinois.

Another example of a CEO who went to another career is Philip Caldwell, former head of Ford. But the turnaround he is most proud of is the one he effected at the company he left, not the one he went to. Philip Caldwell told me that one of his greatest career accomplishments was to bring stability to the management-development process at Ford Motor Company. Brushing aside speculation over his battles with Lee Iacocca, or his relationship with his successor, Donald Peterson, Caldwell prefers instead to speak of the cars developed under his reign at Ford—cars that have taken hold of the market with their novel design and efficiency.

Yet he describes this and his other accomplishments as joint efforts of management teams at Ford Motor Company. He does not deny the unpleasant heritage of executive succession at Ford (to be discussed further in Chapter 11), but as he sits now in his New York office at Shearson Lehman Hutton, he is content that he helped to change the history of Ford Motor Company and that the monarchic empire of Henry Ford I and the succession battles of Henry Ford II are now colorful features of Ford Motor Company's past. The company's future is no longer a prisoner of its history. When this was accomplished, it was time for Caldwell to leave.

Royal Little—Twenty-Five Years After Textron

Royal Little is often called the father of the diversified conglomerate. Having started Special Yarns Corp. on a shoestring in 1923, Little transformed it into Textron, one of the first American conglomerates.[21] Few major U.S. industrial corporations were so closely identified with a single person as Textron was with Royal Little for close to forty years. He described to me how he had conceived of Textron:

> After thirty years in textiles, I thought that there must certainly be some way to make a better return. Textiles were . . . at the bottom with 5 to 6 percent. I bought all kinds of unrelated, diversified businesses. Textron was the first to get away from the cycles in the economy and from the antitrust prosecution that came with size.

In spite of this intense involvement with the company, Little wanted to leave like a true governor. In 1951, when he was only fifty-five years old, Little decided that all chief executives should be compelled to retire at sixty-five and therefore began to plan his own succession. He stated: "I had a hell of a problem; everyone thought I was crazy. No one could run 30 different businesses. So I brought in Rupert Thompson who was recognized for his management talent."

Little was born in Wakefield, Massachusetts, in 1896. His father died of typhoid four years later. In 1902 his mother remarried, wedding the "black sheep" of a prominent Boston family.[22] His stepfather tried unsuccessfully to establish a printing business, in the process moving the family six times, eventually ending up in California. In 1910 Little's uncle, Arthur D. Little, founder of the prominent Cambridge consulting firm, offered to sponsor his education. His schooling at Harvard was interrupted by his service in World War I. After graduation, he resisted his uncle's pressure to become a chemical engineer and instead moved into the synthetic fibers business by purchasing and rejuvenating a struggling manufacturer. An early printer, pilot, ski expert, and former white-water enthusiast, he went on an African safari at age eighty-seven.

In speculating on Little's motivation regarding retirement, we may find a combination of several factors:

- his modest lifestyle and personal tastes do not require a large income;
- his strong physical condition;
- his recognition of his own strengths and weaknesses and their applicability to the changing needs of his corporation;
- his lifelong playful outlook on business, and;
- his observation of the painful experiences of Ford Motor Company and Montgomery Ward when their founders resisted releasing the reins.

Not wanting to subject Textron to the same succession turmoil he inferred from watching other companies, Little was particularly sensitive to the organizational concerns and future requirements of the company. As he surveyed Textron in the early 1950s, he saw that it was in no shape for the departure of its chief executive. Among other things, Textron had always been a one-man show, and it lacked a management team capable of succeeding Little and running the conglomerate by 1961, his sixty-fifth birthday. So in 1956 Little hired his banker, Rupert Thompson, to become chairman of the executive committee and then chief administrative officer for all nontextile divisions. Thompson, ten years younger than Little, became president in 1957 and began the transition to the office of chief executive. Little meticulously developed his successor by increasing Thompson's responsibilities month by month. He also brought George Miller, a Wall Street lawyer familiar with acquisitions, into the Textron fold.

Little kept close tabs on Thompson and Miller until he was convinced they were ready to succeed him. Then, in mid-1960 Little suggested to the board that he relinquish the chairmanship and CEO post, only not on his sixty-fifth birthday, but eight months earlier. According to Little, the company needed a new image distinct from the one he had given it. Also, Textron's era of constant acquisition and mergers was coming to a close. Little had no real interest in operations and felt the Thompson-Miller team was ideally suited to take the corporation through its next phases of growth. He commented on his choice of Thompson to succeed him:

> The major task we had was to reconceive of the corporate role as managers of capital rather than operators of individual businesses. That was the main reason that I wanted Rupert Thompson to replace me. He had been a banker all his life, and therefore knew how to judge people and manage capital. I wanted the corporate level to judge men on their use of capital, not to operate individual businesses.

Little's efforts to disassociate himself completely from Textron were resisted by Thompson and the board, as Little was still perceived as a valuable asset. As a compromise, Little agreed to stay for eighteen months as chairman of the executive committee. During this transition period, he continued to work on acquisitions and to advise his successor when requested.[23] He found this to be one of the more unpleasant times in his life. In his book, *How to Lose $100,000,000*, Little comments:

> You may be doing your retiring chief executive officer a disservice by asking him to remain on the board. If he's in good shape mentally and physically, he'll be much happier getting involved with new, exciting projects rather than remaining a eunuch, so to speak, on the board of a company where he had formerly been the decision maker.[24]

Little is not saying that relinquishing power is easy, but that it is more painful to sit around and watch someone else call the shots. And so, effective January 1, 1962, Royal Little resigned from the Textron board. In fine health at age sixty-five, this founder gave up a CEO's pay, power, and prestige for the good of the company and himself. After retirement, he continued his many outside charitable and business activities, and he founded a venture capital firm called Narragansett Capital, which his son recently took over. At age eighty-eight, Little offered the following view of retirement:

> I don't believe in retiring. I have had friends who ran big corporations. They quit and went off to Florida or somewhere and in four or five years they were dead. Their minds died first, then their bodies. That's not for me. I think I have stayed at it as long as I have because I find business interesting in itself, not just for the money you make. I have everything I need and then some, but I am not extravagant. I take the bus to work and my car is eight years old and has 12,000 miles on it. I use it mostly to drive to the airport.

Thus Little demonstrates a continued need governors have for an active mission in life. However, like other governor-type chief executives, the need for heroic status did not guide his involvements. Institutional trappings of office probably mean far less to Little than an ongoing purpose in life. This deemphasis on heroic stature and continued emphasis on a heroic mission keeps governors from staying on in their old firm, but drives them still further in search of adventure.

Douglas Fraser—From the United Auto Workers to Academia

After forty-seven years in the United Auto Workers, Douglas Fraser's retirement as its president in 1983 marked the end of an era. As an assistant to founder Walter Reuther in the 1930s and 1940s, he had worked from an era of bloody organizing battles, to adversarial negotiations and power plays, and at last to union management and partnerships. Douglas Fraser's career path was in the service of a passionate cause rather than guided by the lure of power. Ideological conviction, not personal ambition, drew Fraser into the trade union movement at age twenty-seven, and often throughout his career he has placed the welfare of the group above personal considerations. "Even before I started to work," he says, "I had views on politics and what was equitable in our society."

Born in Glasgow in 1916, the son of a trade unionist, he attributes his political sensitivity to his upbringing:

> First of all I went through the Depression. That is a humbling experi-
> ence, I will tell you. You get evicted from a house as we did, when I was
> a kid. Then we were in a working-class neighborhood. There was nobody
> on our block that had a job, nobody. We were all auto workers. That was
> helpful in a way, because misery loves company. Everyone was in the
> same boat and suffered together. I think probably that did more to mold
> my point of view.

When Fraser got out of the army, he turned down an offer to be a supervisor at the De Soto auto plant:

> The offer was very attractive, because I was married and had a couple of
> kids and was trying to get some sort of economic security. I think my wife
> might have silently wished I would take the job for the sake of the finan-
> cial security and kids, etc., but never said anything. My sisters thought I
> was crazy. My mother had some doubts about my sanity, I think. But I
> had made up my mind what I wanted to do with my life.

Just before entering the army in 1943, Fraser had become president of UAW Local 227 in Detroit, which had brought him tremendous gratification:

> I can recall in the early days of the union, when I got on the staff, you
> take an umpire case and you get a discharged worker back to work. Dis-
> charge is a damn death penalty in an industrial setting and you get an
> enormous amount of these. You get enormous satisfaction out of that,
> which lasts for a long time.

In 1951 Fraser became administrative assistant to Walter Reuther, the legendary labor leader credited with turning the auto workers' union into one of the most powerful and progressive labor organizations in the nation. Fraser worked for Reuther until Fraser was elected regional director in 1958 to replace Ed Coke, who had died suddenly. In 1962 Fraser was elected to the executive board of the UAW; in 1970 he be-came vice president; and finally in 1977 he became president.

Fraser describes his rise to power with characteristic modesty, repeat-edly pointing to the role of good fortune in his success: "I never dreamt I would become president of the UAW. . . . In politics so much de-pends upon being at the right place at the right time. So much of it is luck."

Fraser served as UAW president until 1983, when he resigned in compliance with the UAW's compulsory retirement rule, which prohibits anyone on the executive council from running for office after age sixty-five. Though Fraser would have preferred to have remained at the UAW, he defends the rule on the grounds that it is best for the organization, if not always for the individual: "I am philosophically opposed to leaders staying on into their seventies. We learned as young union leaders to avoid the stodgy A.F. of L. executive council, which was filled with people in their high eighties."

Fraser was a member of the group that introduced the retirement rule in 1964. According to him, the rule was Walter Reuther's suggestion:

> "Let's do it now," Fraser recounts Reuther saying, "when we are all far removed from that age, because if we wait until we are approaching that age, we will never make the decision." I know when I was going, people said, "Let's make an exception." I said, "I will have nothing to do with that." There were seven of us who retired. We all started together as kids and we ended up in the union lines together, and there wasn't a single person that did not want to stay on, not a single one was really ready. We had some very, very good people, and we had some people that it was good for the union that they left, a couple, not too many. We lost some good regional directors, and we lost a good vice president. But I think of other conventions and I think of the 1980 conventions, when two directors left who would not have left had it not been for the rule and who should have left.

Fraser felt he left office with "a lot of energy" still to contribute and speculates that Walter Reuther, too,

> would have had a lot of energy had he lived to retirement age. I think you get into a philosophical question. I would say that each individual should make his or her own decision. The difficulty comes when the individual isn't objective concerning himself. If someone is an individual entrepreneur, let them go until they are ninety-five, but when you affect an organization, you can't decide in isolation. You can't decide in a vacuum. You have to take it to the organization for which you work.

Since his retirement from the UAW, Fraser has remained very active in political affairs. He has, for instance, been a member of the U.S.–Japan Commission, the Chrysler board, the Kaiser board, the Villars Foundation for the Aging, and the East-West Accord. He has also served as president of the Committee for National Health Insurance and has taught at Harvard, the University of Michigan, Wayne State, and Columbia. Although Fraser enjoys teaching, he would not like to do it exclusively. "I want a little more activity than that," he says; "I want a greater variety." Hence he remains active in these other involvements. Fraser believes that his continued involvement in the labor movement has made his retirement easier than it would have been had he slipped into a life of golfing, hunting, and fishing.

At the same time, Fraser has found it difficult to remove himself entirely from UAW activities:

> People say, "Well, boy, aren't you glad to be away from that pressure?" The answer is no, I am not glad to be away from the pressure. There is nothing like being at the negotiating table at the UAW. There is nothing to compare with it!

Fraser at first had some quiet concerns regarding some of his successor's approaches, but has come to applaud his recent triumphs.

In his retirement, as in his early days in the union, it is Fraser's sense of fairness and obligation to the group that dictates his behavior. And because Fraser has spent his retirement doing the type of work he did at the UAW, he has been fulfilled:

> I think that is where we have an advantage over auto industry leaders because the things that we do are so satisfying, because we are doing things for other people. That is the whole business about the labor movement—particularly if you are elected officers—the membership gives you the power to right some wrong; and from my early days in the labor movement, you get an enormous amount of satisfaction doing something or correcting an injustice that couldn't be corrected.

David Rockefeller—Overcoming the Lure of the Chase

Despite having what *Fortune* magazine estimated as a billion-dollar fortune, David Rockefeller has avoided a carefree life of leisure in his retirement, just as he did in his career. The grandson of John D. Rockefeller, the brilliant and forceful founder of the Standard Oil empire, and the son of John D. Rockefeller, Jr., the prominent philanthropist, David Rockefeller began life with enormous resources, but also with a mission—he was determined to be as personally influential as the name he had inherited.[25] His life has been marked by complex feelings regarding his identity as a Rockefeller. Although he serves as the standard-bearer of the dynasty, both through civic leadership and the stewardship of the family fortune, he has struggled to show that he is capable and hardworking despite his wealth and reputation. For one thing, he chose not to glide through his career on the basis of his family's name. Instead of immediately entering a family business concern, he elected to earn a bachelor's degree at Harvard, then study at the London School of Economics, and finally earn a doctorate in economics from the University of Chicago. Only then did he accept an offer in 1946 from his uncle, Winthrop Aldrich, to join the Chase National Bank. There, he worked his way up from assistant secretary through second vice president rather than short-circuit the path through family connections. One reason he accepted his uncle's offer was his interest in making a civic contribution. The bank offered him the authority, social position, and opportunity for the community service he sought to perform without necessitating a campaign for public office.

Unlike his politically active brother Nelson, David continued to select private-sector leadership as his avenue of public contribution. He was offered cabinet posts in three U.S. presidential administrations, but declined to interrupt his rise at the bank. He eventually was appointed president of the bank in 1960, but his family heritage may actually have worked against him. He felt that the chief executive post was almost a decade overdue, in part so that it did not appear he was appointed through nepotism.

In essence, he shared the chief executive title with chairman George Champion. This was a very difficult period for the ambitious David Rockefeller, because the conservative Champion restrained many of his initiatives. While Rockefeller worked to introduce wider international financial awareness at the bank and modern management methods, Champion focused on domestic banking. Nevertheless, they managed to achieve jointly a series of important firsts for the bank. For instance, Chase became the first bank to fully automate check-handling operations and one of the first to provide computer-based services such as tax-return processing, airline-ticket handling, and rent collection.[26] In 1969 Rockefeller took sole command of the international bank, making great headway in that sphere.

Despite his successful rise to the top, Rockefeller's tenure at the helm of the Chase was not without a series of prominent setbacks. Three years after appointing Herbert Patterson as his successor as president and chief operating officer, Rockefeller fired him, responding to pressure from the board's disappointment in the new executive. Challenges in the early 1970s, including competitor Citicorp's impressive 15 percent annual growth in earnings, led Chase into aggressive domestic real-estate lending, which led to a problematic exposure to real-estate investment trusts, which in turn led to an embarrassing investigation by federal bank examiners.[27] Continued lackluster performance generated widespread alarm, and Chase's "gentleman culture" was seen as a core source of the problem.[28] Rockefeller, determined to show that his aura of gentility was not an obstacle, instituted a dramatic change. He reorganized the bank, bringing in several outside senior managers from industry to key posts in retail banking, planning, human resources, and communication, and promoted twenty-five-year Chase veteran Willard Butcher to the presidency.

The turnaround began in 1976 with an ambitious three-year plan to triple earnings by 1979. By the end, however, Rockefeller's success surpassed even his most ambitious goals. In 1979 Chase showed a 45 percent annual growth rate. Some had doubted Rockefeller's ability to accomplish a turnaround, but a turnaround is exactly what he delivered. His secret weapon in the battle was his new president, Willard Butcher. In many ways, Butcher is very different from Rockefeller. Eleven years Rockefeller's junior, Butcher rose through the Chase organization under the same gentlemanly rules as most, but when put in charge of Chase's operating problems in the early 1970s, Butcher spearheaded nothing less than a total overhaul of the Chase corporate culture.

The partnership that Rockefeller and Butcher formed in this crisis period seemed ideal on a number of fronts. Rockefeller, the policymaker, had more interest in implementation, and Butcher, the operating head, was more interested in strategic planning. Their natural talents were a perfect complement to each other.[29] Additionally, the crisis gave Rockefeller a golden opportunity to test Butcher's worthiness to be his successor. Based on the results achieved, one can surmise that Rockefeller had every confidence in Butcher as his replacement. The financial community, including Chase's own board, also gained confidence in Butcher as potential heir to the bank's top post.[30] Having earned such wide respect, Butcher was regarded as a probable successor for Rockefeller's job long before the announcement of such action was actually made.

But even as the rumors of Butcher's ascension flew, observers wondered what Rockefeller's role at Chase would be, even when he officially stepped down. As one bank analyst remarked:

> You know damn well Rockefeller will want to keep his fingers in the stew, and there's bound to be a transition period that could be as little as a year or up to five years. It's very hard to really understand how a guy who is a major stockholder, who has had total access to everything as chairman of the bank—well, if he wanders into meetings, are you going to tell him to leave?[31]

Whether Rockefeller wanted to "keep his fingers in the stew" is questionable. What *is* clear is that both Butcher and the Chase board wanted to keep him in the kitchen in some capacity. A full month before the announcement, one board member stated, "I would not be surprised if there was a little arrangement to sustain David's involvement for a bit more time. He is certainly young for his years, and it's a shame to lose an asset like that."[32]

And so when the announcement was made in December 1979 that Rockefeller was stepping down as CEO, it was not too surprising to hear that he would remain chairman of the board until Chase's annual meeting in April 1981. Any time a man as powerful as Rockefeller maintains ties with his organization, questions of who is really running the show naturally arise. Such was the case with Chase, but signs indicated that Rockefeller really wanted to turn over the reins to Butcher.

As the final phase of a well-planned, orderly transition began, Rockefeller, the business statesman, began preparing his successor for his new role. And Willard Butcher, having spent over thirty years in Rockefeller's shadow, finally emerged as one of the world's leading bank figures.

Although Rockefeller initially maintained contact with the bank, he actually remained as chairman of the board for only nine months. He served as the chairman of the Bank's International Advisory Committee during this period as well, but ultimate power rested unequivocally with Butcher. Rockefeller maintained no executive responsibilities. As he explained:

> I thought it was easier for Butcher and better for him to be completely his own boss. I'd been on the board twenty-three years and it's awfully hard, with the best will in the world, not to be called upon by others and then interfere.

He added that his role in other family enterprises could have further complicated matters, with possible conflicts of interest between the Rockefeller family's investment advisory service and the bank.

Rockefeller's responsibilities in family investment concerns further contributed to his ease in exiting from Chase. As the Rockefeller of his generation most interested in holding the family together, he has worked to maintain its economic and social vitality. By the time of his retirement, his brother Nelson, a former New York governor and U.S. vice president, had passed away, as had John D. III, another older brother. David oversaw the Rockefeller Brothers Fund and various Rockefeller family interests. Furthermore, in mid-1981 Richardson Dilworth, the longtime chairman of Rockefeller Center, Inc., retired, leaving David Rockefeller as his successor.

David Rockefeller had always been extraordinarily involved in activities beyond these family concerns and the bank. *Fortune* magazine labeled him the "consummate business statesman" for his intertwined interests in domestic social problems, international diplomacy, cultural institutions, economic development, and international finance.[33]

He felt that it was his "duty to be a guardian of sound economy not only at home but in many countries abroad as well." He has worked with well over three hundred heads of state, including Nikita Khrushchev, Golda Meir, King Juan Carlos, Pope John Paul II, Margaret Thatcher, and Anwar el Sadat.[34] Responding to frequent attacks that he should have been at home minding the store instead of traveling, Rockefeller argued that the development of contacts was an important part of his job. In fact, his peer, Citibank's chief executive Walter Wriston, reported that he traveled as much but with less fanfare and publicity.

After retiring, Rockefeller continued his work with international organizations. He was, for example, very active in the Council on Foreign

Relations, the Trilateral Commission, and the International Executive Service Corps, which he had established in the 1960s to encourage other executives, who were either on leave of absence or retired, to serve in developing countries. In addition, he has devoted a great deal of time to the newly formed Americas Society, which coordinates the Council on the Americas, the Center for Inter-American Relations, and the Pan American Society.

Beyond his involvements with those internationalist organizations, Rockefeller serves as a major force in fields as diverse as the arts, urban revitalization, and education. Currently he belongs to more than fifty organizations, including the board of Rockefeller University, the Trustees of the Museum of Modern Art, which he chairs, and various Harvard University visiting committees. He knows roughly 50,000 people on a first-name basis through these many activities. In fact, Rockefeller is involved in so many activities that once a year he meets with his wife, his children, and selected advisers to decide which organizations he must let go.

In sum, Rockefeller was able to leave office gracefully because he was never pushed out of his job but rather lured out by other activities. Despite the early suspicions of industry critics, he left office as a success. He brought in modern management practices, introduced the bank to a wider network of international activities, helped clean up the portfolio of domestic loan problems, and built up strong internal management development. Prior to his retirement, there was speculation about his future role at Chase. "No one," concluded *Institutional Investor*, "not Chase directors, not Chase executives, not even Butcher wanted Rockefeller to completely sever his ties to Chase." Satisfied that the bank was stable and in good hands, he felt there was no need for him to cling stubbornly to power. He could turn to other activities.

When contacted in April 1986, a year after our initial interview, he commented that his outlook has lasted:

> For my own part, I seem to continue to be as busy as ever. Indeed, I have just returned from a three-week visit through the Far East in which I was able to combine some pleasure with business. Other than limited ongoing Chase commitments, I find myself deeply involved with the Rockefeller Group, our family office, the Rockefeller Brothers Fund, Rockefeller University, the New York City Partnership, and the Americas Society, not to mention working on an art catalogue, contemplating writing some memoirs, and taking on a number of more ad hoc assignments. Perhaps I have been more fortunate than some others in having these opportunities, but my retirement has been a very rich and rewarding experience. Certainly any fears of sitting at an empty desk waiting for only the phone to ring have proved unfounded![35]

Thus David Rockefeller has mastered the heroic barriers to exit by looking beyond the bank. He was driven to prove that he was greater than merely the holder of a dynastic family name equated with international wealth and power. Recognizing the privileges he was born into, he nonetheless wanted to earn the recognition that was handed to him. His doctorate in economics was earned rather than honorary. His position at the bank followed a steady climb up through the ranks. His final performance in office was judged favorably. Though he was no longer in command of a prominent international institution, his stature was secure because of what he had accomplished.

Thomas Carroll—From Lever Brothers to the International Executive Service Corps

Thomas Carroll sat at the helm of Lever Brothers for thirteen years before retiring in 1980. His life and work style since that time have not changed much; Carroll planned it that way. Reflecting on his retirement, Carroll states:

> One thing seemed quite clear to me, and that was, I was not going to pull my oars back in the boat and coast downstream. *That* I knew had to be avoided. . . . The goal was to try and have a somewhat similar life and work style, perhaps not at the exact same pace, but still connected to a lot of activity. I wanted to remain happily connected to the business community, in an environment which I would like. I have grown accustomed to and have friends in it. I understand the customs and mores.

Carroll first remained on the Unilever (parent company of Lever Brothers) board as a director, but held no office and devoted only a small portion of his time to that activity. He also maintained his directorships on boards where he had been involved before his retirement, but the lion's share of his time and energy since retirement has been channeled in a much different direction. As CEO of the International Executive Service Corps (IESC), Carroll heads a nonprofit organization started twenty-three years ago by David Rockefeller. Every year it sends eight hundred retired executives as volunteers to assist enterprises in less developed countries. IESC's business is to improve the lives of residents building those countries' economies. And according to Thomas Carroll, the retired executives get enormous psychic rewards from their activities as well.

It would be an exaggeration to say that Carroll planned his "retirement" to IESC far in advance. Although he began thinking about retirement two or three years before he actually stepped down, Carroll claims he never really came to grips with the issue until a couple of weeks before his actual retirement. Unilever, the British parent company, had an unwritten policy of retirement at age sixty for its chief executives. Carroll had served as chief executive for thirteen years, and he was approaching that age. He raised the issue of his succession and became locked in disagreement with Unilever, who wanted him to appoint one of their directors as heir apparent. He therefore offered his resignation as a director on their board.

Some of the options he loosely considered after retirement were teaching at a business school in the Sunbelt, starting his own venture with several old friends, or going on his "Super-Senior" tennis tour. Early on, he rejected the tennis option as a "coasting downstream" alternative. "You can be a kid again," he said, "but how many cups can you win and how much can you care?" He also rejected the idea of starting a new business, for he felt this would require more work than he wanted to dedicate to his "new vocation." The academic alternative remained open until he discovered the IESC option.

Just prior to his retirement from Lever Brothers, Carroll called the chairmen of all of the boards he served on to inform them of his plans to retire, as he expected that some of the boards might prefer to have only current CEOs who still led institutions on their boards rather than retired executives. He assumed his loss of institutional identity would lessen their interest in him. None of the chairmen, whether of boards of private corporations (e.g., American Airlines or Mays department stores) or cultural institutions (e.g., the Museum of Modern Art), accepted his offer. Frank Pace of the IESC in particular was excited by Carroll's disclosure that he was retiring from Lever Brothers.

> I called Frank Pace who was running this [IESC] show and offered to resign. Frank said, "No, this is a wonderful opportunity! Let's get together, fast. Before any of those other SOBs get you, I want you." He urged me to come down here. He told me of his own plans to retire [from IESC] and felt it would be wonderful overlap . . . if I were to become chief operating officer [of the International Executive Service Corps] and when he retires I would be chief executive. And that is what happened.

As rewarding as Carroll finds his new position, he admits that giving up the CEO's perquisites of office and the aura of power can be tough:

> You have to read Bob Lear's article, "How to Retire Without Quitting Work." He became executive in residence at Columbia [after retiring from Schaefer Brewing]. He wrote a very funny thing about getting up and going down the hall to the coffee machine and getting his own coffee in a paper cup. What a comedown that was! The thing I missed most was the limousine.

Despite the lost limousine, Thomas Carroll seems to have managed his transition from Lever Brothers with much grace, perhaps because in his mind retirement was never a subject to be feared. In fact, he describes with enthusiasm how his new career has helped bring adventure and meaning to other older executives, while at the same time helping the "poorest of the poor" in developing nations and improving the image of America abroad.

Jack Nash—From Oppenheimer to Odyssey

Jack Nash is an example of an entrepreneur who did not need to cling to his creation to know he had been successful. He had joined Max Oppenheimer, a European currency trader, in the early 1950s to help him build the brokerage house Oppenheimer had just founded. The business grew, but by the early 1970s Nash and his partners needed to orchestrate a turnaround, creating a more retail-oriented firm:

> from a primarily institutional research firm that was threatened by the advent of [several deregulatory actions]—at first, negotiated commission [1972] and then May Day [1975] when commissions became fully negotiable. We built our small retail brokerage base and expanded our institutional franchise into high net worth individuals through new products and expanded sales effort, including opening of branch offices—which in the past we had not done.

Nash and his partners had built Oppenheimer into a 2,000-person firm, with a gross of $300 million and a profit of $20 million after taxes the year of his retirement. He stated:

> I came in with nothing and built this firm with my partners into one of the most profitable firms this size in the business. My drive was probably the product of an inner anger. I was born in Europe. I was unhappy with school and it took six or seven years until I found myself. This business did it for me.

It is perhaps this feeling of accomplishment that helped to ease Nash's exit. With the growing realization that he was immersed in unsatisfying office management rather than in deal making, he decided to leave the chief executive post in search of new adventure.

As the man credited with building Oppenheimer & Company from a tiny investment firm to one of the top securities companies in the country, one might expect to see Nash among the monarchs or generals. But at the early age of fifty-three, Nash stepped down in 1982 as chairman of Oppenheimer and since then has completely removed himself from the firm's operations. In fact, Jack Nash began his exodus as early as 1979, when he physically moved his office up two floors to signify his deemphasized role within the firm.

Gradually, Nash began transferring large pieces of control to his heir apparent, Stephen Robert, later president, and to executive vice president Nate Gantcher. In 1982 he relinquished further control by selling the Oppenheimer firm to Mercantile House Holdings of London. Because all these changes had been occurring slowly and consistently in the executive suite, there were no dramatics on the day of Nash's departure. At the request of the new acquiring company, Nash agreed to return to the Oppenheimer office one or two days per week for a year to help make the transition work. The ease with which Nash distanced himself from the firm puzzles many. To Nash, it was very logical:

> Initially I had gone down twice a week and I found I had nothing to do. Nobody was interested in what I was doing, and nobody was interested in my opinion. So I began going down once a week, and saw there was really no reason even for that. I then said, "What the hell do I need this for?" I went to Steve and Nate and I said, "There is really no point in my coming down. I think what you ought to do is this: if you want me, call on the phone, and if you have a problem with something, call me. But I am not going to sit there and review all your various problems. It makes no sense."

Nash did not need to stay for either financial or personal reasons. Financially, he was set for life. Personally, he was confident his mission had been successful. He did not need a title to prove his worth. This sense of accomplishment enabled Nash to leave Oppenheimer gracefully. Because Nash did not attribute his success to a fortunate break at Oppenheimer, he did not feel that his destiny depended on that firm. His identity as a businessman is firm; his trust in his abilities is secure. Describing himself as a childhood failure with no focus, Nash stated it took him six to seven years to "find himself" within the business. Suddenly, though, he realized he was good at something:

> I think business really became the first time I truly focused. I found out I was very good, I would get things done. I understood complicated things. I could motivate people.

Nash had no reason to believe that he could not repeat his success at Oppenheimer elsewhere. His confidence meant that potential successors within the firm posed no personal threat:

> I owned a large part of the business, I had a large part of my equity in there. If I hadn't built up the other people, some new buyer would come and say, "Nash does this, Nash does this, Nash does that. What happens if Nash one day says goodbye, good luck. What if he gets run over by a truck, what have I got?" . . . No [I never felt threatened by potential successors], I thought it was first of all making the firm better and second of all, giving me the alternative to do something else. I was getting as much as I was giving.

Nash's new challenge is running his own firm, Odyssey Partners, with his longtime partner from Oppenheimer, Leon Levy. They maintain a small but profitable closed investment firm that retains entrepreneurial energy. Soon after the transition was complete, he began a regular exercise routine for the first time in his life. Like many governors, Nash demonstrates a model for late-career change that draws upon past skills and aptitudes often buried by the responsibilities of office.

Thornton Bradshaw—From ARCO to RCA

Soon after RCA overcame decades of poor leadership succession, it ironically lost its independent identity. A smooth management succession preceded the December 12, 1985, announcement that the General Electric corporation would merge RCA operations into its own. General Electric, along with Westinghouse, had originally helped launch this company. RCA had been plagued by troubled top leadership for a long while as a result of the management vacuum left in the wake of a hero's exit. The hero, David Sarnoff, was born in Russia and emigrated to the United States in 1900 at the age of nine. Six years later he began working for the Marconi Wireless Telegraph Company as a messenger. By 1917, he was commercial manager of Marconi and held that position at RCA when it absorbed Marconi in 1919. Sarnoff was made general manager in 1921 and RCA president in 1930. He died in December 1971.

Sarnoff, a brilliant and tenacious innovator, had built the Radio Corporation of America and the National Broadcasting Company out of a consortium of electrical equipment companies. He ran it as a monarch, leaving no prepared successors. Sarnoff's legacy was built upon technological advancement, not organizational strength.

When Thornton F. Bradshaw, then age sixty-four, was hired by RCA in July 1981 as chairman and chief executive officer, he announced that orderly succession would be one of his top priorities. RCA had, in the preceding six years, undergone considerable leadership stress. Robert Sarnoff, son of RCA's first leader, was forced to resign in 1975 when the core businesses had not achieved satisfactory results despite large research costs. His successor, Anthony Conrad, was fired after ten months when it was discovered that he had neglected to file income tax returns for five years. Conrad's replacement, Edgar Griffith, lasted five years as chairman, but he too was eased out by the RCA board because of his contentious personality and his failure to develop a cohesive management team. In particular, he had failed to plan for a successor. For example, Griffith's firing of ITT veteran Maurice Valente, whom he had picked as president six months before, created an embarrassing uproar in the press and precipitated the board's actions.

Searching for the next chairman of RCA, the committee of outside board members wanted someone who could bring harmony to the turbulent and demoralized ranks of management, and above all, find and train a management group to succeed him. Bradshaw, an outside director on RCA's board for nine years, spoke in the terms they longed to hear and had a record that matched. He stated upon his hiring:

> I'm a team man interested in team building. I've never seen a situation where one man runs an organization, although he may think so. A team runs an organization and that means people must respect each other and have pride in themselves. That starts at the top. When I leave, I want the transition reported on the business pages, not on the front page.[36]

Before taking over at RCA, Bradshaw had been the president of the Atlantic Richfield Company for sixteen years. He had come to ARCO after having taught at the Harvard Graduate School of Business and worked as a consultant with the firm of Cresap, McCormack and Paget. (Interestingly, Bradshaw's partner at ARCO, chairman Robert Anderson, also turned out to be a governor in departure. He bought oil fields from ARCO in 1986, a year after retiring, and merged his new enterprise with a small refinery to form one of the nation's leading independent oil companies in 1987.)

Bradshaw gained experience at ARCO in designing a smooth exit. When he felt that his administrative skills were no longer what the company needed most, he simply left. As he explained it later:

> The oil industry today [1985] is a very different one from what it was three years ago. The time had come for ARCO to use its cash flow of several billion a year to strengthen its oil business. This is largely an engineering matter, and I was not able to do it. I am not an engineer. The people who are there are very good indeed at that sort of thing. I think for the good of the company the new management is better than the old.

Describing his relationship with Robert Anderson, the chief executive of ARCO at the time that Bradshaw was president, he said:

> We have a marvelous partnership and we both enjoyed it very much. We respected each other's role and strengths. Bob is a great entrepreneur. He had a great sense of smell and was always thinking in terms of the breezes that were blowing from the future. He doesn't like administration, in the sense of running a large organization, seeing that good people stick together, seeing that people don't step on each other's toes, etc. I like to think that I was pretty good at the administrative side, that I was a builder in terms of building people, also a tempering influence.

At RCA, too, Bradshaw worked well with other people, never assuming unwarranted power for himself. Indeed, NBC president Grant Tinker credited Bradshaw's hands-off approach with allowing NBC to stick to a programming strategy that was uncommercial in the short run but eventually proved to be shrewd.

Critics of Bradshaw faulted his laissez-faire style and claimed he was an inactive chief executive. A colleague at RCA complained that he was not demanding enough, and someone who had worked with him at

ARCO in years past said he had run that company like a "gentlemen's club."[37] The truth is more complicated.

Bradshaw did not see the role of chief executive officer as being strictly one of internal operations. Except in times of corporate crisis, a leader, Bradshaw believed, has an obligation to involve his organization in the world: "No business can run in a vacuum. Every business is part of the whole commonweal. Any chief executive officer that does not realize that is shortchanging his company."

Bradshaw's thirty-three-month term as RCA's chief executive was largely successful, although some said the atmosphere at RCA became so serene under him that lower-level managers found it "boring."[38] Bradshaw recruited highly talented men, such as Grant Tinker at NBC and Richard W. Miller in finance, to lead RCA out of businesses that were inappropriate to its portfolio, notably the C.I.T. Financial Corporation, and to strengthen the corporation's traditional businesses. RCA's strength had been badly eroded over the previous two decades by too much diversification, but Bradshaw led the company back to profitability and restored its original emphasis on electronics, communications, and entertainment.

The net income of RCA increased eight times, to $341 million during his tenure, and its stock price more than doubled to $40 a share.[39] RCA subsidiary NBC moved from *Fortune*'s "Ten Least Admired" list to the "Ten Most Improved" list. Nonetheless, the $341 million RCA earned was on sales of $10.1 billion in 1984, the year before it was taken over by General Electric.

RCA was not without problems—consumer electronics and semiconductors in particular remained areas of weakness. But in 1985, Thornton Bradshaw bequeathed a vastly improved RCA to Robert Frederick, a former General Electric top executive, in what the *New York Times* observed was the firm's "first orderly transition in two decades."[40] On schedule and without great ado, ultimate power passed to Frederick, with Bradshaw remaining as chairman. The succession was as Bradshaw anticipated. Speaking of it in 1985, he predicted:

> I think that by the time the succession occurs next March, the day after will be like the day before. He will be the chief executive. He will be doing the things that he would be expected to do as chief executive, and there will be one major change that will occur on that day. That is, he will have the last word. . . . As soon as he is chief executive officer he will make the decisions and I will not contest them unless I think the company is going down in flames.

But in spite of the turnaround at RCA, General Electric's strong offer could not be ignored by the board, and nine months later RCA was sold. Frederick resigned from the firm, while his key subordinates were retained.

Bradshaw's departure from RCA was planned well in advance. He had entered the firm with no expectations to stay forever. From the outset, he saw his role as transitional; he was there to steer a turnaround, a task he felt he had accomplished when he left. Bradshaw conceived of his job as one that emphasized working with others, finding talent, preparing a succession team, and delegating power, and he was comfortable with this.

In retirement, Bradshaw has served as president of the Los Angeles Philharmonic Association, as vice chairman of the board of directors of the Aspen Institute of Humanistic Studies, on the Los Angeles World Affairs Council, and as chairman of the Claremont Colleges. In a book he co-edited on corporate social responsibility, Bradshaw calls himself a humanist: "Those who believe, as I do, in the intrinsic value of the decentralized market system must act now to develop a more humanistic, responsible and innovative form of capitalism to meet society's demands as well as satisfying its needs."

Bradshaw has wider interests than those of many other business leaders, and a broader world view. Perhaps this is what has allowed him to make two governor-like exits in his career. He can readily imagine life outside the business world, and perhaps it is that vision that enabled him to relinquish power in RCA so smoothly.

John deButts—AT&T to Tranquility

Theodore Vail, the first president of the American Telephone & Telegraph Company, was a "general." Subsequent AT&T chief executives have departed from this model. When John deButts retired on February 1, 1979, he ended forty-two years of service with AT&T, yet made no attempt to hang on to power, stage a coup, or sabotage a successor. During this period of service, he had held twenty-two separate positions, many of the later ones specifically designed to test and strengthen his ability to run the largest private corporation in America.

After a successful staff assignment in headquarters early in his career, deButts attracted a number of high-level supporters who gave him timely boosts up the corporate ladder. In particular, Frederick Kappel, AT&T chairman from 1956 to 1967, developed a liking for deButts. After a tour of duty as president of Illinois Bell, deButts returned to New York headquarters as an executive vice president of AT&T. This put him just two rungs below Chairman Kappel and one rung under the president and heir apparent, Haakon Romnes. When Kappel retired ten months later in 1967, having reached the Bell System's mandatory retirement age of sixty-five, he promoted deButts to vice chairman. This position, which had been left vacant for a time, made it virtually certain that deButts would succeed the newly appointed chairman Romnes when Romnes turned sixty-five in 1972.

As Kappel had intended, deButts became chairman and CEO in 1972 after Romnes's five-year tenure was up. Upon his elevation, deButts faced three major problems: (1) corporate earnings had been flat since 1968, and large unforeseen demand left the company scrambling to make significant capital investments at a time when they were financially weak; (2) service problems, particularly in New York, Boston, Miami, Denver, and Houston, plagued the corporation; and (3) competition within the industry was just beginning to heat up. A staunch believer in the efficiency of the monopoly position within the telephone industry, deButts became more embroiled in this provocative issue as his time in office progressed. By the end of his term, it seemed to consume him.

When deButts retired in 1979, it was two years before the established retirement age, making him the first AT&T chairman to retire before his sixty-fifth birthday. His successor, Charles L. Brown, thus served seven years until he retired at age sixty-five. In announcing his retirement, deButts said he chose to do so at a time when he could "confidently leave a business that is strong financially, strong in its service quality, strong organizationally, strong technologically and especially strong in its management capability." Like Jack Nash, it would appear that deButts had achieved a degree of success with which he was pleased. He was therefore "free" to leave AT&T, mentally as well as physically. Or so he thought. In an interview three years after his retirement, deButts admitted that the adjustment of giving up control wasn't as easy as he had originally anticipated:

> It didn't turn out the way I thought it would. I'll be honest. Obviously, when you are up to your ears in the nitty-gritty of day-to-day problems of the company and constantly thinking about what organizational changes you should make, if any, what kind of long-range planning you should do, what business you should get into, what business you should get out of . . . you can't just pull down a shade on it. It doesn't go away.

In retirement, deButts felt a need to restrain the nearly uncontrollable impulse to jump back into the fray every time he saw an issue that affected AT&T. Some skeptics have suggested that deButts's early retirement was prompted not by a feeling of accomplishment but instead by a realization that the history of the Bell System as a monopoly in the telephone industry was over. Having so rigorously defended the monopolistic position all through his career, deButts was ill-disposed to allow this evolution to occur. His post-retirement reflexes may have, in part, reflected displeasure at the company's new willingness to compromise this once-sacred tenet. Whatever the reason, deButts's membership on the AT&T board for two years after his retirement gave him some justification for maintaining his high level of interest in the affairs of the organization. But even this, deButts later contended, should pass, and the retiree must instead draw comfort from the fact that he was the one who picked his successor and had confidence in his ability to handle things: "After all, I am the one who recommended Charlie Brown to take my job."

AT&T corporate policy allows a retired CEO to remain on the board for three years after his departure from the chairman's post. DeButts stayed for two, and even that, he felt, was too much: "I have a very strong feeling that when a CEO retires, he ought to get out and leave it to his successor." Despite his successor's urging to stay, deButts declined. Staying active with outside interests, deButts contended, significantly aids the difficult, but necessary, transition. Despite poor health, after retirement deButts became involved in horse breeding and hunting. On December 16, 1986, he died on his ranch in Upperville, Virginia, far from the new Madison Avenue AT&T headquarters building he had helped plan.

As at Du Pont, the AT&T corporate culture seems to play an influential role in encouraging smooth and orderly transitions, in which the good of the company is placed over personal ego. Mandatory retirement ages and limited tenure on the board after retirement have helped establish a system within AT&T that encourages governor-type exits. James E. Olson, the chief operating officer under Brown, became chief executive on June 1, 1986, as most anticipated, with four executives promoted to top executive positions. One of them, Robert Allen, was named president and chief operating officer in September 1986. When Olson succumbed to cancer in April 1988, at age sixty-two, Allen, aged fifty-three, was named chairman and chief executive. Like Olson, Brown, and deButts, Allen is a former president at Illinois Bell.[41]

Robert Lear—From Schaefer Brewing to Academia

Robert Lear maintains that his unique career was due to his lateral mobility, and he warns aspiring managers not to use him as a model for upward success. From U.S. Steel to Duff-Norton to American Standard to Carborundum to Indian Head and finally to the F. & M. Schaefer Corporation as chairman and chief executive officer, Robert Lear's career has exemplified the "mobile manager."

Consistent with the career of an adventurer, Lear accepted his last position as CEO of Schaefer Corporation with the expressed intent of staying for only five years. Given the troubled state of the company upon his appointment, Lear's task was gargantuan. Nonetheless, he accomplished his mission by 1977. At the age of sixty, Lear took early retirement and begin a new life as a professional corporate director and executive-in-residence at Columbia Business School. Although his work at Columbia is without salary, Lear takes this job as seriously as his board responsibilities.

> When I took the job as chairman at Schaefer I said there's nothing in the world that can keep me here after October 1, 1977. I'm going to leave at that time. By then I'll have my successor trained and will have the company cleaned up enough, so that he will be able to run it or somebody will be willing to buy it. I am going to leave the vested interest to do something in the way of a contribution to society.

Given this determination and his five-year planning horizon, it is not surprising that Lear found the transition from corporate America into "retirement" at Columbia Business School enjoyable. His departure style was almost aggressively governor-like. But, Lear warns, no amount of planning can truly prepare a retiring chief executive for the loss of trappings and ceremony. Simple tasks like planning a meeting, once handled by the CEO's administrative staff, now fall squarely in the retired CEO's own lap. In calling a meeting, Lear noted, he now has to phone people himself. Once called, these people may not appear. If they do arrive, they may not feel compelled to stay. If paper for notes was needed, he had to take care of that. He had to arrange for coffee. He had to mail out an agenda and keep the minutes himself.

According to Lear, several harsh realities await the CEO upon retirement. First is the discovery that people are not going to be inundating them with "thousands of fabulous opportunities when they retire from their fabulously successful careers." Second, those executives attracted to the world of not-for-profit institutions may find that fund-raising is a much more difficult and less interesting task when they no longer have the power of the CEO's office. Lear also sees fewer chief executives going into government service upon retirement, which becomes unappealing to the corporate head who has had enough harassment from the public sector to last a lifetime. Why should a former CEO set himself up as a target of criticism in a high-profile political appointment over the same types of haunting issues? From Lear's perspective, this borders on self-abuse.

One other factor that Lear perceives as making the retirement transition more difficult for the CEO is his or her lack of specific skills. He states, "After a few years, the only thing the chief executive knows how to do is how to be a chief executive. That's his only trade and he's out of touch with what the other trades are doing." Lear is quick to distinguish between the entrepreneurial CEO, who may never have left the day-to-day operations of his business, and the administrative CEO, who is usually found running the larger U.S. corporations. Many top executives in corporate life have become isolated from the professional skills of their industry. Lear felt that the way to continue to utilize the skills he had cultivated as an institutional decision maker was to become included in other board directorships. Upon assuming the chairmanship at Schaefer, Lear received a commitment from the company that allowed him to go on one new outside board each year, so that he could have five directorships when he retired. "This," Lear says, "is where I [got] my income to support me in my outside endeavors."

As with other aspects of his succession plan, Lear did a commendable job in preparing vocational activities for himself for his life after Schaefer. As the first executive-in-residence at Columbia and later visiting professor, Lear not only had to define the position, but then had to convince stubborn faculty and administrators to support his program. Though few would expect Robert Lear to fail, hardly anyone anticipated the overwhelming success he would have at Columbia. Lear was honored in 1982 by the Columbia MBAs, who presented him with a plaque. The award, called the Robert Lear Award for Outstanding Service to Business School Students, is now given annually.

As for his board responsibilities, which currently number thirteen, Lear's sense of mission is clear. His directorships have included Cambrex, Church & Dwight, Champion International, Clevepak, Crane Company, Korea Fund, Scudder Capital, Growth, Development and International Funds, St. Regis, Turner Construction, and Welch, Carson, Anderson, and Stowe. Since most of his boards meet within a small radius in New York City, Lear can often be seen "patrolling" from company to company, speaking with numerous executives in the firms to keep on top of events that may not be discussed in formal board meetings. The ever-present "cop on the beat," Lear is dedicated to an activist role as a prepared board member. He has seen too many retired executives, who remain as directors, spend more board time discussing their golf game than keeping current on important and subtle areas of business. Lear feels his association with Columbia Business School has enhanced his ability as a director, as has his retired status:

> The boards were happy I was going to be at Columbia because I'm available to serve on the Audit and Compensation committees, and do extra work for the board. I have the time and freedom. I'm also in the milieu of the intellectual, the young, new, fresh. I can make a contribution from education as well as a contribution from having run a business.

Despite his urging CEOs to actively pursue corporate directorships on retirement, Lear opposes the practice of chief executives remaining on their own boards. He admits that this belief is partly due to his having worked for a family business where the founding father stayed on the board after Lear had assumed the chairmanship. Lear described the situation as "very difficult." In his own case, Lear remained on the Schaefer board for a short period, primarily to assist in the sale of the company to an outside party. Having finally strengthened a company so recently close to bankruptcy, Lear was anxious to show lenders, whose confidence he had gained, that he approved of the policies that were continuing under his successor. He feels it was in the company's best interest for him to do so. Lear represented the outside directors in negotiating the sale of Schaefer to the Stroh Brewing Company. Once the sale was completed, Lear resigned.

In Lear's mind, retirement need not be the dreaded climax to a long career. "The whole idea," he claims "is to get executives planning earlier for the time they're going to retire."

Reginald Jones—From General Electric to General Industry

Over the years, General Electric has developed a routine succession process that emphasizes internal development and smooth transitions. The visionary salesman Gerald Swope, who had propelled the company to start merchandising electrical appliances, retired in 1939 at age sixty-seven after eighteen years as president, returning to office in 1942 for two years when president Charles E. Wilson was serving with the War Production Board. Chief executives Ralph Cordiner and Fred Borch both retired at age sixty-two. Reginald Jones retired at age sixty-three on April 1, 1981. As of mid-1979 the press had identified six potential candidates to replace Reginald Jones upon his retirement. One candidate, Thomas Vanderslice, was highlighted in the media as a particularly strong contender for the CEO post. Less than a month later, three of these men were promoted to vice chairman. Despite outside speculation, Vanderslice was not among them.

Reginald Jones had become chief executive at age fifty-five in 1972, after thirty-three years of service. By 1974, he had already begun to prepare a slate of possible contenders to succeed him. In a company renowned for its management depth, Jones had a great deal of talent from which to choose a successor. His initial pool of ninety-six was pared down to seven candidates by 1977, and in 1978, Jones began his so-called airplane interviews.[42] Without notice, Jones invited each of the seven contenders into his office for a private audience and asked, "Suppose you and I were on a plane later this week, the plane crashes, and we're both killed immediately. Who should be the next chairman of GE?"

According to Jones, the ensuing two-hour conversation usually revealed some rather insightful observations. Jones kept detailed mental notes on what each executive had to say about every one of his competitors. In this way, he learned not only about each individual from a variety of sources, including themselves, but also about the chemistry of the group—who could work with whom.

Two months later, each of the executives was called in for a second interview. In this scenario, the plane crashed, but only Jones died. Now the individual had the option of proposing himself as the best candidate for the CEO slot. If that was their choice, Jones then asked them to identify who the other member of the executive office should be. The process went through two sessions with each candidate. All information from the two sessions was shared with the five members of the Management Development and Compensation Board. Based on their deliberations, the board decided to promote three of the seven candidates to vice chairmanships, where they could be watched more closely for fourteen months. The passed-over candidates resigned for top jobs at other major corporations.

The tactic of using vice chairmanships to review potential successors seems to be gaining popularity in many U.S. corporations. For one thing, it serves the important role of signaling to the organization and the outside business community that succession plans are under way and receiving appropriate management attention. The role of the vice chairman slot was not new to GE; Jones himself had been named a vice chairman six months before his appointment as CEO.

In December 1980, Jones announced his plan to retire on April 1, 1981, after a forty-one-year career with GE. His successor, Jack Welch, was one of GE's three vice chairmen.

Upon his retirement, Jones severed all management ties with General Electric, a result of both company policy and personal preference. He currently works out of an office at a GE subsidiary in Stamford, Connecticut, but is far removed from corporate headquarters in Fairfield. In Fairfield, Jones says, he might be tempted to "look over the shoulder" of his successor, Welch. Despite his lack of involvement with GE, Jones has not been bored. A director of nine corporate boards and associated with several nonprofit organizations, Jones's schedule seems as busy as when he ran GE. And Jones does not seem to miss his old role at all:

> The big difference between what I do now and my former assignment is the level of pressure. I don't miss my former job at all. I found it was easy to move from "who's who" to "who's he?"[43]

While one might be hard pressed to picture the legendary Reg Jones in the "who's he?" category, his seemingly tranquil transition into retirement is still admirable. And in this case, as in others, the corporate culture seems to encourage the governor type of departure.

The next CEO succession at GE appears to be a long way off. Jack Welch was forty-five years old upon assuming the chairmanship of General Electric and thus will probably retain the title well into the 1990s. This may very well have hastened the departure of four of the original seven contenders for the CEO post.

Conclusions

The governors have generally worked hard and long toward a goal. Once they reach this goal, they may be either satisfied or depressed, but they do not fight for more time to change anything within their institution. They have had the impact they desired and now look elsewhere for meaning in their lives. In many cases, successors have led their organization in far different directions from those mapped out by the governor. Thus governors may anticipate the pain of watching their work dismantled, but they do not want to be tempted to engage in the destructive act of protecting their old programs.

In reality, their legacies cannot be destroyed by a change in strategy. Much of the legacy was not a given business plan, but rather a robust organization. Governors have frequently built strong teams of successors and look with pride on the continuity of command, as was the case with Philip Caldwell.

In general, governors, like ambassadors, are delighted to see their child grow up and live its own life. Unlike ambassadors, however, the entrepreneurial governors know they can re-create their old successes in a new situation. Those of the non-entrepreneurial mold, organization stabilizers such as Swearingen, Bradshaw, and Lear, enjoy the challenge of turnaround, of reducing chaos to disorder and sometimes even tranquility. Thus, unlike the ambassadors, the governors' heroic statures are not organization-bound; their accomplishments and reputation are portable. They refuse to stand in anyone's shadow, but carry their heroic statures in their briefcases from office to office.

In my own surveys, several consistent factors stand out. First, the governors' firms were somewhat more mature, in that they were a third larger than the average of the other firms in terms of assets, and usually about a decade older. As for the individual chief executives, they were certainly far more prepared for their exit personally and had done more to prepare the organization than the other types of departing leaders. For example, over half said that they had spent time on personal financial planning, while none of the monarchs and only 20 percent of the generals did this. Over half had established prior links to new business activities, while only a quarter of the ambassadors, 10 percent of the generals, and none of the monarchs had. Fully 47 percent said that early preparation was the most helpful part of their retirement, while only 26 percent of the ambassadors, 14 percent of the generals, and none of the monarchs mentioned this. Almost half reported no difficult time in retirement. This group was the happiest with their exit.

As for preparing the organizations for their exits, they were most likely to initiate discussions over this with their board and other top executives (58 percent for the governors versus 47 percent of the ambassadors, 20 percent of the generals, and 25 percent of the monarchs). They were the only group to emphasize that they had helped their successor establish relations with outside constituents of the firm (customers, industry executives, government figures). Both governors and ambassadors suggested that the outgoing chief executive work to help the successor establish a strong relationship with his or her board of directors. Governors felt confident in their successors' abilities earlier than the other chief executives did—on average a year before their retirement. They tended to have identified their successors almost as early as did the ambassadors, roughly two years before leaving the company.

Their continuing involvement with the firm was quite minimal, the trait that most distinguishes them from ambassadors. While 60 to 90 percent of the other executives continued to hold a formal position in the firm, only 16 percent of the governors did so. And while 90 percent of the other chief executives remained on the board for over two years, only a third of the governors did so. A third left the board immediately, and the other third remained on the board for only two years or less. Fewer than a third (31 percent) continued to keep an office at the firm. In contrast, almost two-thirds of the ambassadors maintained an office, as did 80 percent of the monarchs and 90 percent of the generals. Finally, they were least likely to have retained even a consulting relationship with the firm (21 percent versus roughly 40 percent for each of the other groups). They were most likely to cite either their predecessors or another specific leader from an outside corporation as having served as a negative exit model for comparison. In terms of their own renewal, the governors were most likely to start their own businesses, join more corporate boards, begin a new executive position, or obtain a teaching position after retiring as chief executive. After monarchs, governors were the least likely to turn to recreational pursuits after retirement. Thus, they are similar to ambassadors in that they leave office gracefully, and similar to monarchs in their need for continued contribution.

The governors we have heard from in these chapters are fundamentally different from the other three types of retiring chief executives in one particular way. They, unlike the others, combine two seemingly opposite qualities—a strong attachment to a sense of duty to accomplish, and an almost serene disregard for the trappings of authority. Like the monarchs, they retained an ongoing sense of a heroic mission. They felt the need to make a lasting imprint upon the world. They, like the monarchs, were quick to equate traditional retirement with a lack of productive activity, and a lack of productive activity with death. They kept on working with a determined and, in fact, impassioned commitment to make a unique contribution to the world. Whether working in hospitals, museums, government offices, new start-ups, or challenging turnarounds, they believed in putting their portfolios of executive and personal resources to continued good use. As exercise keeps muscles free from atrophy, the governors believe that they and society gain from their continued involvement.

Unlike the monarchs, these governors had a lesser sense of heroic identification with the status provided by their firms. If they were entrepreneurs, such as Jack Nash, Forrest Mars, Royal Little, or Averell Harriman, they were not worried about "losing the baby" to someone else, as some psychologists regularly insist is the case with top leaders. In fact, quite the contrary is true. Perhaps a guiding sentiment for these leaders is the closing phrase in Henrik Ibsen's *Enemy of the People:* "The strongest man in the world is the man who can stand alone."

10

THE SMALL BUSINESS
LEADER FACES DEPARTURE

I'm not sure he has the ability to sit down and resolve. There's a big question mark: Is he going to be an executive? Does he have the ability to analyze ways and consider action? I may have made a mistake.

> Hal Walton, a founder, reconsidering his successor as he prepares for his own retirement

Family businesses, whether the corner grocery store or Corning Glass Works, present further complications beyond the departure styles examined thus far. The detailed case history we now turn to can provide us with more insight into the drama and the complexity of roles involved in family business leadership succession. Although the names of the firm and the people involved have been disguised, the basic facts of succession are true. The case concerns a metal-parts manufacturer whose founder was struggling to make a new retirement plan following the untimely death of his eldest son. I became involved with the company when a member of the board of directors told me that the firm had received one thousand résumés in response to an advertisement for a chief executive that appeared in a national newspaper. I researched and wrote up the case with a Harvard research associate, Alice Morgan, in the spring of 1984.

Company History

Hal Walton had invented the Flowseal valve after founding his own firm, Walton Engineering Company, in 1962. Walton already held more than twenty patents for design that he licensed to various manufacturing companies. He planned to produce the Flowseal valve himself, however, and began to investigate appropriate technology. His design called for four electron-beam welds, and he knew that Weston Standard, a division of Universal Equipment, manufactured and sold electron-beam welders. Walton took his pilot model to Weston Standard and asked that the required welds be made. If this could be done successfully, he intended to buy the necessary machinery from Weston Standard for his own firm. Recalling the events that followed, Hal Walton explained:

> They said they'd be happy to weld the parts to demonstrate that their machines could do it. When I went back to pick up the parts, I was told the vice president would like to see me, so I went directly from the lobby to the vice president's office. He said, "Well, there's no beating around the bush; we'll get right to the point. We're greatly impressed with your product line and we'd like to have an exclusive license."

Shortly thereafter, Hal Walton signed a favorable licensing agreement with Universal Equipment, joined the firm as program manager for his valve, and closed his one-person Walton Engineering firm. Over the following three years, the product line was established and thoroughly tested both in the laboratory and on-site at a steam-power plant. By 1964, an advertising campaign had begun, and representative organizations had been established all over the country. Then, in 1965, Universal Equipment drastically revised its corporate strategy and divested much of its industrial-products business. The company sought a sublicensee for the valve product line, but after two years had still not found one. In 1968 Hal Walton bought all the relevant tools, jigs, dies, fixtures, and inventory and founded Flowtrol to produce his valve as he had planned to do six years previously.

Profile of Harold M. Walton

Hal Walton is versatile, self-reliant, and creative. "In 1930," he recalled, "my parents sent me $75 so I could come home from college for Christmas. That was the last money I had from them. From then on, I was on my own." Walton attended the University of Wisconsin for a year before entering the U.S. Naval Academy, graduating in 1934. He proceeded to MIT for a master's degree in mechanical engineering, after which he became a development engineer with Linde Air Products, a division of Union Carbide. In 1940 the U.S. Navy recalled him to active duty as commanding officer of a small patrol ship. He was transferred to the Brooklyn Navy Yard in 1941 and then to the staff of the commander of special forces in the Pacific in June 1945. Three months later Walton was able to leave active service, and he enrolled in Harvard's Advanced Management Program. After graduating from the program, Walton worked for several manufacturing concerns in engineering, marketing, and general management positions. These included Union Carbide, Rockwell International, and Black, Sivalls & Bryson, as well as Chapman Valve, his last employer before going into business for himself and developing the Flowseal valve. During the years between 1965, when he had ceased working for Universal Equipment, and 1968, when production started at Flowtrol, Walton supported himself by playing the stock market. He comments:

> When I started this business, I had a lot of soul-searching to do, because I had generated enough funds so that I didn't have to work. With the gamble on Flowtrol, I was putting everything on the line. But I thought it would be much better to be doing something for industry and society instead of just living off the stock market. And I had these patents which were no good if they weren't working, so I decided to start the company. I was fortunate in that I was able to handle the financing myself, so that I didn't have to give up much of the business.

Ever since its founding, Flowtrol has prospered. Growth was financed conservatively, and by 1982 Flowtrol had no long-term debt. Sales in 1980 were 44 percent higher than those of 1979, and 1981 sales were up 47 percent over those of 1980. In 1982, sales were essentially flat (see Figure 10.1). Flowtrol's profitability had been notable throughout its history, and the early 1980s brought no change in this regard.

In 1982, Walton was Flowtrol's president and CEO. All department heads reported to him, and his long familiarity with every aspect of the business made him capable of, and interested in, every type of activity from metal cutting on the shop floor to nationwide marketing. He routinely examined reports on every level. Walton's familiarity with the product line made him an expert salesman; he was often able to see potential applications that were obscure both to the representative and to the plant manager or parts purchaser. Similarly, new product ideas, versions of the valve that might have additional applications, had been developed by Walton as a result of discussions with users of current products.

Company Leadership

Walton had thus been Flowtrol's central figure since he had established the company in 1968. He owned the land and buildings used by Flowtrol, as well as all but 14 percent of the stock. (That portion had been

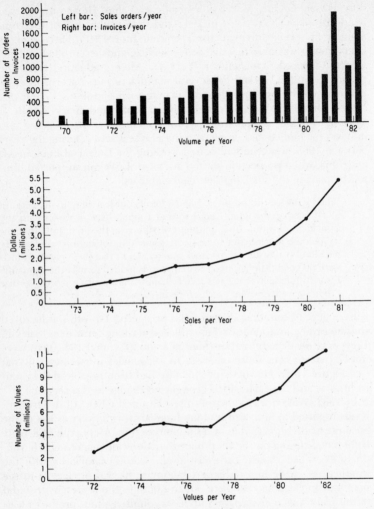

Figure 10.1 Flowtrol Performance.

bought by the firm's original vice president of sales.) He had designed the product line and had overseen every phase of production and sales from the beginning.

Flowtrol manufactured and sold globe and check valves for use in utilities plants (both fossil fuel and nuclear), chemical plants, oil and gas wellheads, and in other applications where a tight seal under high

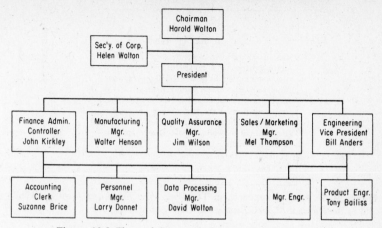

Figure 10.2 Flowtrol Corporate Organizational Structure.

pressure was critical. The patented Flowseal mechanism, developed by Hal Walton in 1962, provided a valve with very few components that was fairly light for its capabilities, and that could be serviced without removal from its place of installation. Flowtrol produced the valve in various sizes and configurations and marketed it via manufacturers' representatives throughout the United States and in several foreign nations as well. The company's headquarters and manufacturing facility were in Williams, Rhode Island. A partial organization chart appears in Figure 10.2. In 1982 the company had seventy employees and sales of just over $5 million.

Walton had originally hoped that his oldest son would become Flowtrol's chief officer, but the son had died in an airplane accident in 1974. Walton had looked hard for people who might be capable of growing into the job, and he had carefully considered applicants generated by search firms, as well as individuals who were already serving Flowtrol in various managerial capacities. He had hired a manager of operations who seemed promising, only to find that the man "just seemed to be retired. He came in late and left early, and he had no programs at all, so I terminated him in a hurry." A subsequent manager became ill with a fatal disease.

Within Flowtrol there were three especially promising candidates for executive responsibility. Mel Thompson, the sales manager, had worked as an engineer at nuclear power plants, and before that he had been a manufacturer's representative in a firm partly owned by his father. He had served in the navy and had an MBA from the University of Connecticut. His experience in sales was still somewhat limited, and he had

PRESIDENT

Outstanding Opportunity

Our privately held company, well capitalized and highly profitable, requires C.E.O. to assume the operating duties of retirement aged Owner-Chairman. This metal cutting manufacturer of proprietary product lines has experienced significant growth over the past several years under the direction of the Chairman-President, and is located in an appealing rural Southern New England community.

Forward your qualifications, in confidence, to:
Box ES-593, *The Wall Street Journal*

Figure 10.3 This ad appeared in The *Wall Street Journal* of April 27, 1982, and in the *National Business Employment Weekly* of May 2, 1982.

done no general management. Walton believed Thompson was a good decision-maker, but was not yet ready to take on wider responsibilities.

Walter Henson, the company's manager of operations, had good experience in manufacturing control, but lacked exposure to the financial and sales functions. Walton believed Henson's personality led to conflict; he had lost two previous jobs. He would have to demonstrate that he could hold a job successfully before Walton was willing to consider him a candidate for advancement.

The third internal possibility was John Kirkley, the controller. An MBA from the Harvard Business School, he had served Rhode Island Bank and Trust as vice president, and before that had been controller at Fallon Brothers Investments. But he had no background in manufacturing, sales, or engineering. Walton believed Kirkley needed more time before he could advance into broader responsibilities. All three of these men were in their early forties.

Even younger and more specialized in his training and experience was Walton's second son, David. David, a soft-spoken, technically oriented thirty-three year old, was Flowtrol's director of data processing. David had majored in computer science at Purdue University and had spent the next six years in Indianapolis working first for the city and then as a systems programmer for a specialty retailer. David believed it was important for him to have business experience in settings other than Flowtrol to prove his worth both to himself and to his father. David knew that he would have to choose within a few years whether he wanted to continue on a strictly technical path or to make the switch into general management. His current project, introducing materials requirements planning to Flowtrol, currently absorbed all his time, but once this had been implemented, he would have the opportunity to gain exposure in other areas. Both he and his parents hoped, therefore, that a new executive at Flowtrol would be capable of and interested in providing appropriate guidance for David's development.

Walton, now seventy years old, was determined to develop a viable plan of succession. He sought to turn over some of the day-to-day operating responsibilities to someone who might eventually step into the full executive responsibilities. His wife, Helen, had retired not long before as Flowtrol's controller after ten years in that position, and the couple enjoyed sales trips in Flowtrol's recently purchased mobile home. Walton believed such trips were especially important now, because Flowtrol had resolved some production bottlenecks and could meet greater demand thus. Walton's profound knowledge of the product line made him the company's most effective salesman, and he had some ideas about how to generate increased purchases and new customers that he was eager to try out.

He had often discussed with Flowtrol's board of directors his efforts to find a new chief operating officer (COO) and president, and he did so again in early 1982. Joel Bannon, a Harvard Business School professor and member of the board, suggested to Walton that he run an ad. With the assistance of Bannon and Alvin Perold, Flowtrol's auditor, Hal drafted one that appeared in the *Wall Street Journal* in late April. Perold agreed to place the ad and to receive the replies, thus helping to keep the process confidential. Perold was screening the résumés in accordance with several criteria that Walton had developed—a slow process, since there were over a thousand responses (see Figure 10.3).

Selecting a Successor

In seeking to share the responsibility of managing Flowtrol, Hal Walton was not looking for an immediate replacement. He had no desire to stop working, or even to work fewer hours per day, or for only part of the year. He planned to retain his post as chairman of the board and to continue as Flowtrol's CEO. The new employee would function as president and chief operating officer. All department heads would report to the president, who would also implement new strategies, as well as maintain present operating levels. Walton had no wish to sell his business, despite numerous offers from individuals and from other firms. Under the circumstances, an equity position was not available unless the new president could convince the man who owned 14 percent of Flowtrol to sell some or all of his holdings.

When asked about the criteria he and Alvin Perold had used to evaluate the résumés they received, Hal noted, "It was more a set of negatives than of positives—more a matter of ways in which people didn't qualify."

Given the nature of Flowtrol's business, Walton hoped to find good candidates with strong engineering backgrounds who were involved in manufacturing operations. The right candidate, he believed, would have to have functioned in a decision-making capacity, so anyone who did not appear interested in being a "number one man" was eliminated. Walton looked for a career progression from narrow areas of responsibility to larger ones, and for a present position of considerable supervisory stature. He also looked at the candidates' current job settings. He believed that someone who had spent all his or her working life in a large corporation would not function effectively in a firm like Flowtrol:

> I had to have the impression this person could operate in a small business. So many were used to having such large staffs that I felt they'd be lost here. At Flowtrol they'd have to be able to treat everything on a very detailed level, which doesn't happen in a big firm.

In addition, Walton was looking for someone who would fit in well with his present managerial staff:

> I've got a number of excellent people here, department heads. I've got a sales manager, a controller, an operations manager, a senior engineer. These are very able individuals, and somebody coming in as chief operating officer has to be acceptable to the department heads.

Walton reserved for himself the final decision, and an important element in his decision was age. Flowtrol's department heads were all in their early forties. Walton wanted a president in his mid-fifties, because he believed an older candidate would be less threatening to his current managers and would leave open the possibility that one of them might ultimately move up in the executive hierarchy, when he (the new president) retired.

Alvin Perold read through the résumés and sent the most promising forty to Walton. Walton reviewed them, and in late May he got in touch with Janet Wolff, a professional recruiter based in Boston who had been recommended by one of the members of Flowtrol's board. Wolff and Walton reviewed the forty best résumés together, and Wolff was given the task of following them up by telephone.

Walton was determined to choose Flowtrol's new president before the summer was too far advanced. By July, Janet Wolff had followed up the most promising leads and had interviewed roughly twenty-five people. Walton was ready to make his decision. He eventually interviewed about eight of these final candidates, and after review and discussions with his wife and with Jan Wolff, he made his choice. He decided to offer the job to Brooks Carswell, who had recently resigned his post as president of Cranston Equipment Corporation, a company that made plastics and packaging machinery. He had been passed over for CEO in favor of a family member. Walton commented:

Brooks [Carlswell] not only had an engineering background, he had a master's degree in manufacturing engineering—machine design. He was a navy man, had been through Harvard's A.M.P. [Advanced Management Program], and had held responsible managerial positions. He was in the right age bracket. He had no ambition to acquire equity—so many of the candidates were understandably ambitious for aggressive control and that was not what I wanted. And there he was in Ames. I didn't want the responsibility of taking someone away from a job and moving him here and having him not turn out. There were also plenty of candidates who were unemployed but would have required moving, although I didn't talk to any that seemed to fit. I opted for the easy way out.

Before making Carlswell an official offer, Walton arranged for him to meet with Phil Denton, an industrial psychologist whom Walton had previously consulted on another matter. Carlswell and Denton spent about three hours together, and Carswell came away feeling that if the interview and the few written tests he had been given had gone well, the job was his. His intuition on this point was correct, and in mid-July Walton asked Carswell if he would become Flowtrol's president. Walton had recently sent Jan Wolff a note:

Brooks has checked out amazingly well. I think I should settle on him. He has a good technical background, sales experience, is a good administrator, has handled acquisitions and has been stable in employment and life-style.

Preparing the Successor

Carlswell had left Cranston Equipment with generous severance pay and was in no hurry to find a job. On the other hand, the more he learned about Flowtrol, the more he liked the sound of it. He wanted a position that entailed responsibility; he was interested in running operations. He liked the fact that the firm was nearby. He had dealt with divisions of Cranston which, like Flowtrol, were in the $6-million range; in fact, Carlswell had planned and carried out several acquisitions of firms that were very much like Flowtrol's size, which had then become divisions of Cranston Equipment. As a result, he did not think the transition from a $60-million company like Cranston to one about a tenth as large would be too difficult. And he and Walton seemed to get along well, which was clearly a critical factor.

Carlswell found the idea of working with Hal Walton appealing, although he realized that it might be difficult at times. Walton had, after all, been not only chief executive but a major contributor to all facets of the business and might have trouble relaxing his control over the firm's operations. But he was impressed with Walton's willingness to allow Flowtrol to change. And Carlswell felt the selection process, particularly the final interview with Phil Denton, the industrial psychologist, had been extremely well handled:

> I think it was a pretty enlightened thing for Hal to do. I would recommend it to any one-man-dominated company. Hal had a lot of faith in Phil, and really it's obvious that if you come to work at Flowtrol, and you aren't going to get along with Hal Walton, you may as well save your time and energy and do something else. So in this way Hal was able to get an objective reading.

Brooks Carswell became president and COO of Flowtrol on August 18, 1982.

Walton had discussed the addition of Carlswell with each of the department heads privately before Carlswell started work. Walton wanted to be sure that the move would not alienate members of a smoothly working team. The rest of the organization learned about the change only when Carswell arrived on the scene. Reactions in the company were strongly supportive: a second in command was clearly desirable, and Carlswell's age (fifty-six) meant that the younger department heads still had opportunities for advancement within Flowtrol.

In early October, Walton and his wife left on a selling trip. Carswell commented:

> I felt very good about that, because Hal was willing to leave when I had only been here about two months. I thought it was a vote of confidence, based on very little evidence.

While he was away, Walton called in regularly two or three times a week, and Carlswell was able to reach him if any pressing questions arose. Carlswell was able to guide Flowtrol during his absence without undue difficulty.

To ease the process of transition, Walton and Carlswell both consulted Phil Denton, the industrial psychologist. Carswell explained:

> There are certain things, I'm sure, that displease Hal about me, and there are certain things that he does that sort of bother me. Each of us talked to Phil, and then Phil in turn got back to us. It did help. For example, Hal has a habit of starting to talk, then pausing. I've always been in what you might call a verbally combative situation, so when he'd pause, I would interrupt. He told Phil, "It really bothers me to have Brooks do that." Great. Phil told me about it, and now I'm careful to be sure Hal is finished before I start to respond. I found it very valuable to have this kind of assistance.

Taking Charge

When Carlswell began his tenure as Flowtrol's president and COO, he knew he had a lot to learn: "At first I wondered what the devil I could contribute—I was sure I would never know as much as Hal about valves and about the company."

But Carlswell did have marketing and strategic planning experience that he believed would be useful to Flowtrol, and he soon realized that his background in general management was also of value in his new position. He found that Walton had been Flowtrol's major force for so long that many of his subordinates were essentially task-oriented, accustomed to moving from task to task under Walton's close supervision. Carlswell planned to try to make the staff more self-actuating. At the same time, Carlswell himself often shared the tendency toward task orientation:

> I have to admit even I am doing a fair amount of it, partly because I am new and don't want to go off in some direction that makes no sense. I am also still trying to determine exactly what Hal wants me to do, and what he would like to do for himself.

Clarifying Leadership Roles

Carlswell was Flowtrol's chief operating officer. He reported to Walton, and nearly everyone else reported to him. There were only two exceptions to this rule. Helen Walton, the corporation's secretary, also reported to her husband. In addition, one man, the first Walton Hal had hired for Flowtrol, still reported to him. This individual had been a designer and technical consultant for Flowtrol since its founding and was responsible, with Walton, for the development and production of all company products. He had little formal training, and although he held the title vice president of engineering, in fact he did no supervision. Although Walton viewed him as temperamentally unsuited for management, he felt a strong sense of loyalty toward him for his many years of devotion to Flowtrol. As a result, this vice president served as a kind of roving consultant and reported only nominally to Carlswell.

Decisions on policy were made by Walton, Carlswell, and the manager whose function was involved. Thus, although Carlswell had made only two sales calls by early December, he and the sales manager and Walton worked together to develop Flowtrol's first marketing plan.

Walton's role as president had been mostly that of checking to see that operations or engineering was running smoothly, rather than actively participating in those functions. Carlswell was surprised to learn Walton's monitoring was often at a very detailed level. He might want to know why a particular man was chosen to work the first shift, and another the second. "Hal looked at every invoice; he had his hands on everything." Carlswell did not plan to emulate Walton's management style, although he intended to utilize some parts of it. He found, for example, that he enjoyed dealing with problems directly rather than through those reporting to him. Instead of talking about manufacturing issues in an office, he reviewed them on the shop floor. Implementation could be easily monitored, and Carlswell could check out new policies in action by walking only a short distance from his office. Carlswell found Flowtrol's intimacy exhilarating:

> At Cranston, I used to wake up at 4:00 in the morning and wonder if I really had any impact on the larger company. I didn't see much of it— maybe 2 percent—but through policy and strategy decisions I hoped I was having an effect. But I really wondered. Here there is no question: you can see everything. I probably work more hours here, but there is not as much anxiety, because I am more in control of what is going on. As long as you can see what is going wrong, you can do something to make it right. When you are dealing through three layers of people, everything is much more remote, and there is really a lot of anxiety.

At the same time, Carlswell sometimes experienced a sense of claustrophobia. He missed his frequent travel. He was dealing with a few products that came in a few sizes, rather than with several diverse product lines. He could easily identify the company's market, which was nearly all domestic or Canadian. In these respects, the world of Flowtrol differed greatly from that of Cranston Equipment.

Business Development at Flowtrol

In order to assess the potential for Flowtrol, Carlswell had familiarized himself with its market position and that of its competitors. He estimated that the company's market segment was about $25 million a year, and that it might be shrinking because construction of new utility plants had slowed. The MROs, or maintenance and repair orders, were still strong, however. Flowtrol currently held about 20 percent of the market. As Carlswell noted:

> You can go from 1 percent to 2 percent of a market a lot easier than you can go from 10 percent to 20 percent. If we grow much more, we are suddenly going to become visible, especially as the overall market is probably shrinking a little. In my experience, nothing arouses the interest of your competitors as much as loss of market share.

Carlswell believed that if Flowtrol began to invade its competitors' shares of the market, there would be an immediate response. Some firms would decide to get out without challenging Flowtrol. Others, however, would stay and fight, probably by reducing prices. In Carlswell's view, it would be difficult to compete with Flowtrol on price:

> Flowtrol is a very low-cost producer. I come from a company where at the end of ten years you had three weeks' vacation, and after twenty years you had six. There were fourteen paid holidays, sick leaves, and so on. This company has three weeks' vacation at the end of fifteen years—and so far there is only one person eligible! There are eight paid holidays,

and none of the fringes you get in the larger metalworking operations. Our biggest competitor is Rockwell International. I have known other divisions of big companies, and I can't believe that Rockwell is a low-cost producer. But Flowtrol is, and that will help.

Of course, Carlswell realized that Rockwell, with its huge capitalization, might attack Flowtrol's position by accepting very low margins on its valves. But on the whole, he had faith that Flowtrol could increase its sales and its market share.

Moreover, there were other strategies for growth Carlswell considered appropriate for Flowtrol. He would have to determine, with Walton, how these strategies fit into Walton's vision of the company's future, and what level of risk Walton was willing to contemplate in order to implement them. Carlswell noted, "If, say, the absolute goal is to quadruple the company in five years, you have to take all sorts of huge risks." Flowtrol had been financed very conservatively, and Carlswell was not sure what financing alternatives Walton would be willing to consider.

One means of increasing Flowtrol's size was through acquisition, a route with which Carlswells was quite familiar. Flowtrol could double right away by acquiring another company of about the same size:

> With our balance sheet that would be easily accomplished. We have to decide about that. And we need to consider other types of development as well. Do we want to get into a completely new product that takes a new kind of sales force and new manufacturing? All these things are possible, but we have not yet addressed the issues specifically.

Carlswell believed that because Flowtrol had been so successful, there had not been much motivation to consider alternative strategies. Now, however, he expected that some strategic decisions would need to be made. Expansion or growth seemed easy to attain:

> Hal has built an organization, frankly, that is capable of doing a lot more. If we grew, everyone would just move up. Hal has managed to develop or hire people within the last couple of years who have the potential to run a much larger operation, keeping up with Flowtrol as it grows.

Seven Months After Carlswell's Arrival

By March 1983, Carlswell had settled into his new job. Some major strategic decisions had been made, and Flowtrol was gearing up to expand its sales, leaving such matters as new products or acquisitions for the future. Mel Thompson, the sales manager, planned a sales conference for March 10–11, at which Flowtrol's representatives would meet with one another and discuss how best to sell the product. Walton had taken another trip of several weeks' duration and was convinced that the additional sales effort would increase the company's current backlog, enabling Flowtrol to use all the new capacity it had recently added and to continue to grow.

Carlswell accepted this strategic decision, and he was doing his best to become familiar with Flowtrol's product line and with the details of running the company. He had not encountered any unexpected difficulties, but he did feel that it was taking longer than he had anticipated to master these details, since they required attention to matters that were not part of a COO's concerns in a large organization. The management style he had used previously had to be modified for his new position:

> As president of another company, I had management techniques where I did not have to know a great deal about the intimate details of the company. Here I must know not just that we sell valves or what kinds of valves, but what particular materials go into every piece of each valve.

Carlswell believed he was making good progress in this area, and he praised Walton's capacity as a trainer. He also expressed gratitude that he had been given considerable freedom to make important decisions on marketing, personnel, and manufacturing policies. Carlswell accepted the idea that one of his roles was to give David Walton the training and support he would need if he was eventually to step into an executive position at Flowtrol. He remarked:

> One of the considerations, I think, in my being hired at the age I am, is that this company has some very good people for its size. They still have plenty of time to develop over the coming years. I always consider it part of my job to develop a successor, and while I haven't yet had much time to work on this, I certainly view it as a priority. Both the sales manager and the controller have great potential, but they need multidisciplinary experience. I hope to help them get it. Both men were captains in the navy, so they both know how to take command.

Planning for David's materials requirements planning and shop-scheduling system was well under way. A DEC PDP-11 computer and IMS software package had been acquired, and Dave and the controller were working on a simple management information system to help Flowtrol keep track of its business.

When asked about personal goals, Carlswell expressed a desire to go into the field to sell Flowtrol's products:

> There are two reasons for that. One is that we have a very "thin" sales force and I could provide backup where needed. The second is that it's very difficult to determine a complete policy for a company if you don't understand the sales and marketing aspect. This is something, of course, that you'd never do in a larger company.

In summary, Carlswell believed that he was already in a position to make a contribution to Flowtrol, although he was not yet in full control of all the details he needed to know. He agreed with Walton about the company's direction, and he had some ideas about how to achieve the greater sales that were essential for growth. He had encountered only cooperation from the people who reported to him, and he had a very high opinion of their capabilities. Carlswell's agenda included extensive training of key personnel, including David Walton, and implementation of control systems to keep Flowtrol a low-cost producer.

> I feel that where the company is today, I can make a substantial contribution. That might not have been true when the company was starting—I'm just not an entrepreneur. I view myself more as a business manager, and the company has grown to the point where it needs some fairly sophisticated things to happen.

The Anxiety of Facing Departure

Walton's goal in seeking a president for Flowtrol was to remove himself from day-to-day responsibility so that he could "look over the shoulders of others and see what needs strengthening." He wanted to spend more time in the field, making clearer to the manufacturers' representatives the advantages Flowtrol's products provided and how best to sell them. Walton had intended no immediate retirement from active functioning as Flowtrol's CEO; he wanted a president and COO with whom he could work harmoniously, but who would be able to take over should it become necessary. By March 1983, Walton was beginning to have some doubts about his choice of Carlswell: "At this point, I don't know if Carlswell is going to satisfy the requirements of the job or not. He has not sold me completely yet."

One problem Walton encountered in working with Carlswell centered on communication. Walton worried that Carlswell did not always listen to what he was being told; he interpreted an incident that occurred during the selection process as possibly characteristic. The Waltons had arranged to meet Carlswell at a restaurant whose name was very similar to that of another local eating place. Because of the possibility of confusion, Walton had been particularly explicit in making the appointment. Nonetheless, Carlswell had gone to the wrong restaurant:

> We've talked about the need for good communication. That's one of the reasons I asked Phil Denton to meet with Brooks. And I'm still not sure he really hears what I'm saying. And he himself has a tendency to verbalize the obvious, rather than getting to a more profound level of discussion.

Walton, like Carlswell, was conscious that Flowtrol required a different managerial style from the one Carlswells had used at Cranston Equipment:

Brooks had not been involved in detail. At Cranston, he relied on others to give him reports, and he did not have the hands-on type of experience which I feel is necessary at Flowtrol. It's been a case of his having to learn to do the job.

Walton wondered if Carlswell would be able to pay attention to all the details essential to running the company.

But a more important drawback, in Walton's view, was that Carlswell too often acted merely as a conduit, transmitting material from others without giving it added value. Walton recalled in particular the analysis Carlswell had sent him concerning a new machine that Flowtrol was considering buying. The machine costs were outlined in detail, but no information on the labor costs associated with it were included. When Walton realized this and asked Carlswell about it, he was told that the report was only preliminary. In Walton's view, this made very little sense. He was not prepared to act on a preliminary report, and he naturally assumed that the material he received was based on a complete analysis. Carlswell, Walton believed, had merely passed along the information he had been given, without doing any further exploration and without reaching any decision. "I'm afraid he may be too much of a pass-through individual—not resolute and decisive enough."

There were occasions when Carlswell did take action; for example, he had taken out a substantial business insurance policy without consulting Walton. Walton felt, however, that this decision actually came from Flowtrol's controller, and that Carlswell had simply accepted it:

> I think Brooks is dedicated, hard-working, interested and animated. . . . But I'm not sure he has the ability to sit down and resolve. There's a big question mark: is he going to be an executive? Does he have the ability to analyze ways and consider action? I may have made a mistake.

What Went Wrong?

It is important to take a detached view of the growing problem of Walton's successor and look at the dynamics of the situation. Flowtrol was a small entrepreneurial firm facing many transitions simultaneously. Its external market, internal organization, and company leadership had all matured and required alert responses. The firm had experienced rapid growth in the past few years, but now had to contend with new marketplace pressures as the various competitors struggled to grow in a crowded slow-growth market. Some of the competitors were comparably sized, while some were much larger. Flowtrol seemed to have survived largely because of its strongly personalized sales effort and low-cost production. The basic technology of the product had not been dramatically altered in almost twenty years, but custom-tailored refinements were common. What innovation did occur was largely the result of Hal Walton's insights gleaned from sales trips. Thus the engineering and sales functions were almost completely reliant upon Hal Walton. Similarly, the operations and finance function relied heavily upon Hal's decision-making. Although the firm was roughly fifteen years old, it was still organized as it had been at its creation—a system that was highly controlled by the core entrepreneur. The firm was guided by Walton's vision. He owned over 86 percent of the company, he had created the initial mission, and he had yet to relinquish substantial control of any part of the business. The firm was fueled by the energies of the chief executive. He carefully scrutinized even detailed travel reports and trivial purchase decisions.

This reliance upon Walton's watchful eye, creative energy, and determined spirit had been critical for Flowtrol's early survival. He had had to put together a production and marketing operation with very little capital and an unorganized marketplace. It was important to prove the value of his product by applying it to a large variety of industries. Many industries did not initially appreciate the usefulness of the Flowseal. He was unable to support a large payroll and thus did not delegate to others the more subtle tasks of getting his new business off the ground.

As the business matured and became a more significant player in the marketplace, it became a serious competitor in a stable, nongrowing market. Its magnitude of activities had expanded so much that it stretched Walton's span and depth of control near to the point of snapping. Walton had to develop carefully a strategic plan dealing with such realities as flattened sales, competitive retaliation, and an unclear operating mission (for example, what should be given priority among cost, quality, volume, and flexibility for customer-specific job-shop designs). Among the key customer groups, the energy industry had certainly explored challenging new technological frontiers through the 1970s. Flowtrol needed to fundamentally appraise the continued vitality of the Flowseal, as the product life cycle pressures would dictate strategic product development. Keeping up with the swelling number of small, day-to-day activities served to distract Walton from dealing with the difficult longer-range issues.

In addition to the maturation of the business, there were many individual life-stage issues to consider. For example, the three key department heads were squarely lodged in their early to mid-forties. The classic mid-career/mid-life danger is characterized by concerns over diminished feelings of new opportunities in life and nagging doubts about the appreciation of one's contribution. A failure to achieve career expectations, coupled with a history of career disappointments, can heighten these feelings. Because of Walton's intense involvement in their functions, the three department heads had never really had complete control of their functions, nor had they had the opportunity to learn what the others' responsibilities entailed. Thus, they were unlikely to gain the needed breadth for general management competence, let alone a sense of professional fulfillment.

Walton's younger son had just completed some early career adjustments while he had tried to find an identity in the work world. His occupational interests and general disposition did not suggest a predilection for management, however it may have been wished by his parents. Walton's wife, who had essentially been his business partner, confidante, and adviser, had recently relinquished her executive responsibilities only to see her former job slot filled at lightning speed. She was startled about the suddenness of the firm's replacement of her role and felt a bit disenfranchised.

Finally, Walton had to grapple with his own life-stage transitions. At seventy he had to account for his own record of accomplishment. He had held management posts with a half-dozen employers and yet had never achieved a top executive post until forming his own firm. The survival of a product line he had nurtured for almost twenty years— from Universal Equipment to Flowtrol—was now endangered. Thus, soon after the death of his older son, and as he sensed his own mortality, the mortality of his business contributions also seemed very real. Should something happen to him, he could not trust the survival of the firm to any of his current management team. The recent tragic death of his eldest son and intended heir had left him stunned and empty. Flowtrol, as a surrogate child, had become an intensified last hope as a vehicle for immortality.

Since the board of directors was thoroughly controlled by Walton, the selection of a successor was entirely in his hands. His criteria were ambitious, but in many ways realistic. It was true that he probably did need to develop his internal talent further before appointing a successor from within. His emphasis on functional expertise in areas such as metal parts production, as well as an appreciation of the work culture and pressures of a small, scrappy enterprise can easily be defended.

At the same time, Walton's criteria revealed his ambivalence about letting go. He was searching for a hard-driving, independent, operational leader who would eagerly acquiesce to Walton's changing wishes. Walton was looking for a person with initiative and imagination, but also a person who would not question Hal's own visions for the business. Hal wanted someone who would assume a sense of ownership as president but who would not actually share equity in the business, despite the career risk implied by stepping into this situation. Walton expected his successor to have a good feel for the intricacies involved in the many different functions; however, Walton had not attempted to develop his department heads for any general management breadth.

Beyond the contradictions revealed in his explicit search criteria, the overall search process and the eventual selection revealed more of this ambivalence. For example, the newspaper advertisement dangled the CEO's position, but Walton was seeking only a chief operating officer. The use of a more detached vehicle such as the newspaper advertisement and post office box provided him with maximum anonymity and minimal commitment. Walton could reconsider and withdraw the position at any time without anyone on the outside sensing his vulnerability or reluctance. Additionally, in this process we can see Walton's unexpressed desire to re-create his successor in his own image, given the apparent importance of naval officer experience and local community attachments.

At the end, we see that Walton's ambivalence about retiring and his effort to re-create a figure resembling himself in Flowtrol had failed. Instead of introducing and then orienting Carlswell, the newcomer, Walton fled the scene. By going on the lengthy sales trip as a way of easing the transition, he may have given unclear signals to all parties. Uncertain expectations were not confronted. Walton and Carlswell were unclear over such things as the degree of delegation of responsibility between them, the degree of attention to be directed toward management development, and the degree of openness for adjusting corporate strategies.

It is a tribute to Carlswell's own competence and charm, as well as to the good faith of Flowtrol's managers, that there was no insurrection within the ranks. It seemed that Carlswell's greatest problems were with Walton rather than with the organization.

When Walton began to feel that, despite all his efforts, he had made a serious mistake, he had essentially five options:

1. Say nothing—give Carlswell more time to get settled.
2. Confront Carlswell and try to work out the problems, perhaps with a third party.
3. Release Carlswell and begin a new outside search.
4. Confront Carlswell and begin to develop internal backup strength intensively.
5. Release Carlswell and abandon the entire succession and retirement question.

At this time, three points can be deduced from this situation. First, there are no villains involved. The problems are not due to treacherous acts and schemes of deception. We see hardworking, anxious people badly conveying unclear expectations. Second, the key characters are probably not fully aware of their own career goals. For example, Walton has a strong set of unexpressed ideas about the threatening nature of any successor through power grasps, ownership struggles, strategic shifts, and a reduced involvement for him in his primary life activity. Carlswell, meanwhile, along with others in the case, seems to have a passive dependence on a strong leader. He acquiesces, instead of persuading. Third, when the characters do talk, they tend to talk past each other.

At this crossroads, what could they have done to save the deteriorating situation? Through the use of a skillful, impartial third party, Carlswell and Walton could have been coached to recognize the source of their tensions. They could have discussed whether it was possible to reach common ground on each issue and clarify expectations. They could have then set mutual checkpoints to see if things were improving. At the same time, they could have jointly planned possible contingency plans for Flowtrol and for Carlswell's career should the relationship fail. If Carlswell still didn't work out, the department heads could eventually have wound up working for a peer and should have been prepared for this possibility. Realistic anticipation can reduce suspicion and later hostility. Good internal succession plans and a thoughtful outplacement program can reduce the trauma of having to replace a possible successor and keep all players on the same side regardless of the flow of events.

It was not to be, however, and Walton announced the termination of Carlswell at the next board meeting. Walton further announced that he had no intention of retiring. Finally, it may be of interest to note that at this meeting, Walton's ninety-seven-year-old mother served her own homemade cookies.

Walton's departure style was that of a monarch. He was in no hurry to leave. He flirted with the idea of succession, but withdrew his plan as time for a possible transfer of power neared. This type of departure is common in small businesses. Generally run by an entrepreneurial founder who has built the company from the ground up, the small business tends to be the focus of the owner's life. In the founder's view, no one can know as much about the firm as he does and no one can run it as well. Thus transferring authority, whether to someone inside or outside the company, is enormously difficult. Even when the successor is a handpicked family member, as Walton had planned, the same succession tension may be manifest. In Chapter 11, we will look at a variety of family business succession challenges. We will also review the implications for the management of family enterprises through succeeding generations.

11

PARTING PATRIARCHS OF THE FAMILY FIRMS

I know it sounds funny, but I like President John Kennedy's crack to the press about the appointment of his brother Robert as attorney general, "Nepotism isn't too bad, as long as you keep it in the family." But there was no question in either of our minds. Jamie was the man for the top job.

Amory Houghton, Jr., on the transfer of power to his brother James upon his retirement as chief executive of Corning Glass

As Hal Walton's situation in Chapter 10 suggests, family businesses present special considerations that complicate the departure categories presented in each of the prior four chapters. For example, a monarch's presumed drives may be tempered by ambassador-like sponsorship of offspring. With the overlap of domestic and occupational roles, conflicting loyalties, sibling rivalries, parent–child authority tensions, spousal commitments, and other such emotions come into play in leadership transition. In addition, emotional forces are further complicated by concerns over the management and inheritance of shared wealth and power.

The leader of a family business can fall into any of the four categories of departure types: monarchs, generals, ambassadors, or governors. Hal Walton was a classic monarch, as were J. Paul Getty and H. L. Hunt, who died in their eighties, leaving power vacuums in the next generation.[1] But the conflict and confusion that follow in the wake of monarchic departures can be found as well following the other leadership departure styles if they occur in a family firm. For example, the graceful ambassador-style departure of Barry Bingham, Sr., of the *Louisville Courier Journal* was followed by ferocious family feuding, resulting in the loss of control of the family enterprise and severed family bonds.

This drama may seem extreme, but the emotions behind these events are quite common. Over 80 percent of America's corporations are owned or controlled by a family.[2] This includes 35 percent of the *Fortune* 500 firms. Among such prominent family firms are Cargill, S. C. Johnson and Sons, Estée Lauder, Bechtel, Levi Strauss, Strohs Brewing, Mars Candy, Dow-Jones, Schwinn, the *Washington Post*, Hyatt Hotels, E. & J. Gallo, and Hallmark Cards. Regardless of size and prominence, only 30 percent of family businesses survive their founders. The average life expectancy of these firms is twenty-four years—a period that usually coincides with the founder's career in the firm.[3]

To gain further insights into the succession tensions that confront family firms, I surveyed a group of chief executives who belong to the Young Presidents' Organization (YPO). Founded in 1950, the YPO has 3,500 members in forty-seven countries. To be eligible for membership, a candidate must have become president of a firm by the age of forty and have managed a company with at least fifty employees and sales of $4 million. About 40 percent of the members run family businesses.

I took the opportunity of sending questionnaires to a group of ninety YPO members who were to attend a week-long seminar at the Harvard Business School in January 1987. At the time of the seminar, most of them were approaching their mid-forties—that is, they were still young executives. Seventy-five percent of the attendees returned the questionnaire before they arrived.

The questionnaire asked about their attitudes toward retirement, and their answers varied according to whether the respondent fell into one of three categories: (1) founders of companies (39 percent of attendants); (2) relatives of founders (41 percent); and (3) those not related to the founding family (20 percent).

Founders said they never intended to retire, did not look forward to retirement, did not think that age should limit their tenure, and would consider retirement only in cases of poor health, boredom, or because one of their children was ready to take over. Relatives of founders were almost as determined not to retire as founders. They did not look forward to retirement. They did not consider age a limiting factor. They would consider retiring only for reasons of health, boredom, or their children's coming along. It seems likely that founders and their families felt a deep emotional commitment to the enterprise.

Nonfamily presidents, however, felt differently. More than half of them looked forward to retirement, felt that retirement should come at no later than seventy (significant numbers suggested even lower ages), and as reasons for retiring cited the attainment of life goals, as well as, interestingly, starting their own businesses.

There were significant differences among the young presidents about what criteria they would use in choosing a successor. Founders and family members espoused drive, integrity, and a facility for understanding people, much the same qualities they saw in themselves. However, only 10 percent of these founders and family members sought assertive leadership qualities (e.g., independence, courage, charisma, innovativeness, etc.). Nonfamily managers, however, were more likely to mention leadership strength and relevant functional and industry skills. There was general agreement that it would take two years to locate such a person, regardless of the desired criteria.

As for the grooming of the successor, founders felt it would take two years; family managers, one year. Nonfamily members felt grooming a successor would require only six months. Only 10 percent of the founders referred to the delegation of responsibility, while over 50 percent of other chief executives claimed that they would gradually hand over their own responsibilities. In discussing retirement, the founders never thought of themselves as mentoring, coaching, counseling, advising, or teaching. Instead, they presented themselves more as judges who would put candidates on trial assignments.

We learn more of founders' leadership mission by asking how they would like to be remembered after retiring. The founders pointed with pride to their creations' success. They also showed concern for their employees. The family managers pointed to having built deeper, more secure foundations for their firms and to having introduced fairness into their firms' cultures. Perhaps this reflects what family members feel that the founder neglected earlier. Finally, the nonfamily members expressed far more impersonal goals, such as the financial stability, the market clarity, and the growth of the business, that they wanted to be remembered by.

This chapter will examine three very different family successions at close range. In the first profile, Dunkin' Donuts, we consider an entrepreneur's ambassador-like departure and transfer of power to his son. In the second profile, Corning Glass Works, we describe the transfer of command of a 130-year-old firm between brothers. In both of these profiles, first names will be used to avoid confusion of family member identities. In the third, we see Henry Ford II stabilize the troubled firm founded by his namesake. Here we observe the passage of top office to nonfamily management.

William Rosenberg—Dunkin' Donuts

William Rosenberg is an example of a founder for whom it was comparatively easy to locate and prepare a successor. His enterprise was a compelling family drama from its origins right through its succession to the next generation of leaders. The business involved family bonds with his father, his brother, his sons, and his brother-in-law, as well as financing from his mother through the insurance on the death of his brother.

Bill Rosenberg left school in the eighth grade to help support his family during the Depression. By age twenty-one, he had already become a branch manager of a leading ice cream distributor. Eight years later, following World War II, he opened the Industrial Luncheon Service, which delivered meals and coffee-break pastries to factory workers. He described his initial financing:

> I had $1,500 in war bonds. My brother was killed in the war, and his insurance gave my mother some money. This was the only time in her life that she ever had any savings, but she loaned me $1,000. My brother-in-law, an accountant, invested $1,250 and loaned me another $1,250.

When he realized that a large portion of his sales volume and profits were derived from his coffee and doughnuts, he came up with the idea of a limited-menu establishment featuring such items—essentially a single-product restaurant that sold high-quality, freshly baked doughnuts with excellent, freshly ground and brewed coffee.

The novel idea was not greeted warmly. Boston bankers and other potential backers scoffed at the concept, as Rosenberg recalled.

> I'd go to the banks and try to get financing for a doughnut store. The average banker would say, "You mean a single-product business like a doughnut?" I'd answer, "What's wrong with that?" They'd say, "You don't understand! That's not enough to attract the public." I'd say, "What about Coca-Cola?" And the banker would say, "Oh, well, that's entirely different!" I would reply, "It sure is! Coke is a refreshment—our product is a refreshment, a dessert, a breakfast food . . ."

But he persevered, convincing his suppliers that if they helped him, it would open a new market for their products. In 1950, the Open Kettle Restaurant, forerunner to Dunkin' Donuts, opened in Quincy, Massachusetts. By this time, Bill's brother-in-law, Harry Winokur, had joined him as a full partner. An extremely bright, honest, and thorough man, he had all the traits necessary to be an asset to the business. In five years, with Harry running the office and Bill managing operations, they expanded from one to five restaurants, and Bill wanted to begin franchising. By the time he became chairman emeritus in 1983, there would be 1,250 Dunkin' Donuts shops worldwide.

This expansion was not without growing pains, however. Clearly the most painful of all was the exit of Harry Winokur. Winokur felt they were expanding too rapidly in the doughnut business and was content with the original industrial catering operation. If this were the under-

lying motive, however, Harry's next move was rather ironic. When Harry
left, he and George Rittenberg, the former Dunkin' Donuts attorney,
founded Rosenberg's major competitor, Mister Donut. Rosenberg offered another explanation:

> Harry was married to my ex-wife's older sister. While Harry and I were
> equal partners, I was the one who got all the publicity because I was the
> most visible. Whenever we went anywhere, people would say, "Have you
> met Bill Rosenberg, Mr. Donut himself?" This caused friction with my
> sister-in-law, and although Harry and I never had an argument, her jeal-
> ousy had to upset him. His family didn't want him, an educated accoun-
> tant, playing second fiddle to an eighth-grade dropout. But Harry wasn't
> a salesman, wasn't a promoter, wasn't an entrepreneur, and he didn't
> excite people. Years later, we offered to reconcile and merge the two
> businesses, but they sold out to a food conglomerate.

Another close family member in the business early on was Bill's father.
This relationship was a more pleasant one. Bill commented, "Pop worked
for me as the purchasing agent for the industrial feeding business, because he had owned a market when he was younger. He was happy in
this job. It was the last and best job he ever had." Bill's father died in
this job at the age of sixty-six. Also helping him get started was his
brother, Leon, who was his first route man and supervisor for the Industrial Luncheon Service and later a branch manager. He also managed a Dunkin' Donuts shop before he died at the age of forty-five.

In time, Bill's imagination, hard work, and determination paid off.
The year he became chairman emeritus, the firm had sales of
$475,840,000 and profits of $7,890,000, with a 19 percent return on
shareholder equity. Of the 1,250 shops established by then, 66 were
outside the United States, including some in such unlikely locations as
Japan and Thailand. The company did not listen when told that
doughnuts would never appeal to the Asian palate. On traveling to Asia,
Bill enjoyed the heroic welcome he received from government figures
and Dunkin' Donuts associates abroad. He was also pleased that the
company's sales growth did not come merely through the increased
number of stores, but was also due to the regular increase in revenues
and profits for the average store.

Bill began to prepare for his own succession twenty years before he
actually became chairman emeritus. In 1963, at the age of forty-seven,
he named his son, Robert, to the presidency. Up to this time, Bill had
served as chairman and president. Many were surprised by this decision
as Robert, a recent graduate of the Harvard Business School, was only
twenty-six years old. Bill was adamant in his belief that his son was the
best qualified candidate for the job. He had decided that his executive
vice president was not the person for the presidency several years earlier and had been waiting for his son to graduate.

The grooming began far earlier. When Robert was fifteen years old,

Bill asked his son where he wanted to go to college. According to Bill, Robert's response was that he wanted to do what was required to do what his father did. They developed a plan then for Robert to begin working in the business until he was old enough to attend the Cornell School of Hotel and Restaurant Administration. Finally, Robert would broaden himself by getting an MBA at Harvard Business School. This is exactly what happened. The next summer, Bill put his son to work in their Quincy commissary of the Industrial Luncheon Service.

> [T]he first year I put him to work in the bakery handling pots and pans in the middle of July when it gets so hot it sometimes hits 110 degrees. People would say to me, "How can you work the poor kid like that?" I'd answer, "It's good for him! Look at what I had to do!"

Bill rotated Robert through different positions through the ranks during his summer vacations, exposing him to such positions as doughnut baker, store manager, and vice president of operations. While in his final year of business school, Robert was attending the meetings of the executive committee. Upon Robert's graduation, Bill informed him that he did not have sufficient confidence in the talents of the executive vice president to make the man president. He explained to his son that he was intending to make him president instead. Robert was reluctant to take command over the experienced executive vice president, so Bill asked him to work as assistant to the executive vice president and let him know when he was ready to move up. After six months, Robert decided he was ready. Bill reassured his son of the wisdom of this decision:

> Look Bobby, I'm still going to be around. We've still got Sam, the vice president of real estate. We've still got Jack as vice president of operations. Norm is going to stay on as vice president of finance. Hopefully, Joe will remain as executive vice president. How wrong can you go? I'll advise you at home, in the car, over the phone, and in the office.

After convincing his son, Bill's next task was to prepare the other top executives. He met with each one alone.

> They said, "What are you, crazy? A twenty-six-year-old kid president?" I said, "Look how he knows this business. He's trained and ready. Are you going to help the kid? Are you sure? If I'm still here, what can he do that's so wrong?" After another six months, I called each one in. Only one had quit, the executive vice president. Everybody said, "Your kid is terrific, he's won the respect of everyone! He's really good!" I told them, "Don't tell me what you think I want to hear! Give me the truth!" They said, "Bill, the kid is great!"

When the firm went public in 1968, Robert was chief executive officer and Bill was chairman of the board. The sale of stock introduced the scrutiny of Wall Street analysts. Overexpansion in certain markets caused the firm to suffer its first drop in profits a few years later, but Bill resisted the subsequent pressure from the investment community to retake control of the company. He explained his reasoning:

> Wouldn't that be a kick in the ass to any guy who I supposedly had enough faith in to put in the job in the first place? I've got to admit that you are going to be more caring about your son than about a total stranger, but the fact still remains that if you have a decent individual in office who has ability and is trying his hardest, you don't pull him out when he's young and makes a mistake. Why would you want to destroy him instead of developing him? There should be opportunities to make mistakes.

He went on to praise his son's brilliance in building the business:

> Dunkin' Donuts wasn't doing tremendously well when I turned it over. It was just getting started. The groundwork was laid. . . . Bobby is the guy in charge of the team that built a big multinational enterprise.

His son sold the original catering business and expanded the doughnut-shop chain into other foods.

Nevertheless, Bill acknowledged that tensions between father and son do exist on various levels, as one would expect. One level is with regard to strategy and business practices. Father and son differ in subtle ways over the core definition of the business and the definition of the appropriate standards of product quality. For example, Bill Rosenberg claims that he has been such a stickler on product quality that he may have become an irritant to his successors. While most restaurateurs may use two ounces of coffee for a ten-cup pot, Bill pushed for three-and-a-quarter ounces to correct for errors in roasting, grinding, and water. Bill referred to a lesson he had learned long ago, when criticized by factory workers and their union leaders. He had cheapened the food in a cafeteria he operated in order to please the treasurer of one of his client companies:

> Poor quality is indefensible. I cannot defend myself. I am in a much better position when someone says, "You know, your product is expensive!" I can say back, "Isn't it the best product you ever bought?" He'll have to agree. If I had to tell him it's lousy, but it's cheap, he may just respond that it isn't worth a nickel. If I had to charge a dollar for a doughnut, to serve the best doughnut in the world, I would! If the business won't support that price, then we're in the wrong business. You can't compromise with quality in products or in the people who work for you.

With such reminders that cheapening quality is a costly strategy, Bill feels that he has successfully served as a conscience to the firm. He believes that top management has come largely to share this enthusiasm for customer satisfaction and for the promise of the franchise system.

The second level of tensions surrounds the personal chemistry of the father–son relationship and their respective life stages. The son is moving into his fifties, while the father has entered his seventies. But Bill still has a lingering aura as the highly charismatic founder of a firm that has been built up by his very professional son. Each feels that the problem in clarifying their respective roles is more the other's fault, but great warmth and affection prevail. The son sees his father as reluctant to let go, while the father sees the son as too sensitive about appearing to be in the shadow of the father. But given their closeness, they can openly discuss such a tender topic. They have further shored up their respective roles by avoiding clashes in the business and maintaining separate social lives.

Why was Rosenberg willing to relinquish power at all? To some extent, he was willing because he sees himself more as the entrepreneur than as the operator:

> There was no question in my mind but that I'm an entrepreneur, and entrepreneurs are much more valuable starting and creating than trying to operate, although you could do it if you wish. Just to be an entrepreneur who hustles and builds a business is one thing, but to be an entrepreneur who knows how to organize a plan in his mind and put it into effect, I think I have the ability. But I don't think you should be wasting your time doing that if you have the ability to start new things, something that most people can't do.

Bill Rosenberg loves to start new businesses, he is good at it, and he knows he is good at it:

> I have a philosophy that if you put me anywhere and I wasn't making a living, I would find a way. I have started enough things in my life. . . . When I was a kid, I delivered orders from my father's grocery store. I sold ice cream at the beach during summer vacations. When I got older, I delivered ice. When I quit school, I went to work for Western Union and became their highest commissioned kid. When I got old enough to drive, I had an ice cream truck route and built it from the lowest sales to next to the highest. During the winter, I sold shoes. I found out that by working your balls off and trying harder, you can succeed. I found out that I had the ability to do well. Some people think you get where I am by being lucky, but I know if I wanted to start another franchise system, I could do it.

In fact, Rosenberg founded the International Franchise Association in 1959. At the time, many scandals had surfaced surrounding the practice of "get rich quick" schemes that defrauded franchisees. Bill pointed out that "I realized right from the beginning that in order for the franchisor to succeed in the long run, the franchisees had to succeed. You had to teach them to run a profitable business through customer satisfaction." In an effort to help clean up the shady business practices of some franchisors, he enlisted the support of the major restaurant, gas-oline, and consumer products franchisors to improve common stan-dards and promote ethical business practices. He feared otherwise, that the prevailing behaviors would inspire restrictive government regula-tion. He takes pride in his indirect role in inspiring such later franchise success stories as Century 21, and today the International Franchise Association is considered the voice of franchising around the world. In 1980, he was the first to be inducted into the I.F.A. Hall of Fame.

More recently, Bill has become very active in the harness-horse in-dustry, another area he considers in need of the organizational skills of entrepreneurs. He is involved in breeding and racing and was instru-mental in getting the various segments to cooperate in forming the North American Harness Racing Marketing Association to promote the sport.

In addition to this self-awareness of the appropriate use of his set of managerial skills, Bill Rosenberg was able to relinquish control because he himself did not live in the shadow of a successful father. He termed his father "a failure in business" whose bad example provided valuable lessons for his son.

> My father was a very bright, intelligent man, but not a successful busi-nessman. He never succeeded. . . . His insight was fantastic, but his abil-ity to follow through was negligible. I learned a lot from his inability to start at the bottom and work his way up. He was always looking to start at the top. In this way, he taught me that you've got to be a hard worker, you can't just have good ideas. You've got to get them started yourself, because nobody believes in a new or a good idea that just hangs out there without a way to make it happen. If you're a visionary, people will be especially suspicious until you can show them that you can do what you're selling them. You have to get in, pitch in, and make it work and knock your brains out to show them it will happen. Then they will all jump on the bandwagon. My father never did that. He never took that first step. He was waiting for it to happen, or for someone else to do it. That's how he taught me a valuable lesson.

Thus Bill was not driven by an oedipal struggle to meet or exceed the accomplishments of his father. He felt that his parents did not enjoy the life that they might have, given their imagination. There was no doubt Bill was accomplished. He knew that he had risen far in life as a result of his own imagination and hard work.

Finally, Bill may enjoy some degree of fulfillment in that he can see the lasting strength of his creation through his son. The business not only lives on, but flourishes under the control of his flesh and blood.

> What the hell could make me happier than to have my son running my business? Everybody is saying, "Your kid is great, he's fantastic!" That makes me great. He's my guy. I fathered him. I taught him. I brought him along. He makes me look good.

This pride in the accomplishment of his son only intensified Bill's sense of completeness in his heroic mission. There is a sense of immortality that comes through:

> What have you accomplished if what you have created dies when you do? The only true accomplishment is having created and organized something so that it will succeed and grow after you are gone.

In putting his own son in charge, he placed an extension of himself in the future. This increased his sense of immortality. Whether he would have left his position so willingly otherwise is an open question. Even so, Bill Rosenberg is not eager to leave the business entirely. While he may be content with the completeness of his heroic mission, he still has a need to be involved. Soon after his full recovery from life-threatening cancer in his early sixties, Bill was recharged with a new vitality. He divorced, remarried (this time to a much younger woman), and returned to a vigorous routine.

Early in 1983, Bill was approached by his son and their executive vice president, Tom Schwarz. Tom was being courted by other companies, and he longed to serve as a president. However, he had strong ties to Dunkin' Donuts and the Rosenbergs and didn't want to leave. Would Bill move up, allowing Robert and Tom to move up also? He would and did, commenting:

> Chairman Emeritus? I never heard the word before. What does it mean? As long as my salary continues, I don't give a damn what I'm called!

It was hardly the income that was important, but rather the continuing membership role as a key player that Bill cared about. He still wanted to feel he was valued as a contributor to a cause in which he believed. Despite the lure to be a monarch, Bill Rosenberg is working toward an ambassador style of exit. Why did this entrepreneur not become a monarch? The answer must lie in the self-restraint brought on by his awareness of his own limitations as well as by his son's preparation and alertness to the potential for his father's slippage into the monarch's departure. Both parties were able to use their knowledge of themselves and each other to draw lines at critical points.

Amory Houghton, Jr.—Corning Glass Works

The career of Amory Houghton, Jr., from Corning to Congress, shows quite a different family business situation from that of Hal Walton or Bill Rosenberg. Generally referred to as Amo by close associates, this leader had to master the types of challenges peculiar to the succeeding family leaders who maintain the dynasty established by the founding generation. Amo displayed skillful handling of both the common inter-generational tensions between himself and his father, also named Amory, and the sibling tensions between himself and his brother, James, generally referred to as Jamie. By the time of his retirement in 1983, Amo was only fifty-six years old, but he had served as chief executive for almost two decades (1964–1983). He had become president of the company by the age of thirty-five.

Amo faced a forbidding heritage upon entering the business. His family had founded Corning Glass Works over 130 years earlier and still controlled 30 percent of the ownership. He represented the fifth generation of the family in the operation. His father and grandfather both led the firm to greatness, while maintaining a dignified position in their communities. After two decades as chief executive, Amo's father left the firm at age fifty-eight to serve as ambassador to France. His grandfather left at about the same age to serve in the U.S. Congress. Amo's fear in joining the firm in 1951 was living up to the patterns set before him. He emphasized his mother's role in providing him with the confidence to assume the mantle:

> My father was a fabulous person. He and my mother were a great team. He was farsighted and astute as an executive, but there was a special family glue that my mother gave to all of us. My folks constantly said that we were stronger together than apart, but there was a more natural, happy, responsiveness in my mother. For example, when I was concerned about going back to Corning, she inspired confidence. Hell, I was the fifth generation of the family in the company and my father was a very impressive individual. I had all the natural hang-ups. "Can I do what he did? What should I do that's different? Why should I do it? Why am I doing this?" But she said in soothing tones something to this effect, "Look at you, you're yourself and you're lucky to be you. You've got a good education. You've got a sense of humor. You've got a nice family. You're with people who love you. You have an opportunity here. You've got to be what you are, not what your father is." Somehow that message came through for me and my brother Jamie.

That sense of responsibility to the family as well as to the community continued to guide him through his career. Amo went on to praise an influence in later life, Thomas Watson, Jr., the retired chairman of IBM. Amo had served as a director on IBM's board after Watson took over from his father, Thomas Watson, Sr.

> I'll tell you another person who has had a tremendous influence on my life, that's Tom Watson. Despite the father-son rivalry, he's always been proud of keeping that "junior" on his name. He always talked about his father or his mother in the most glowing terms. He had no hang-ups, no worries about being a second generation product. It was just natural family pride.

The "junior" always followed Amo's official identification as well. Unlike Watson, however, Amo's father lived to see most of his son's reign. Watson's father saw only a few months.

Amo also credited his mother in calming sibling tensions between him and his younger brother Jamie. He spoke to me about Jamie, who is ten years younger than he.

> In families which have succeeded with a string of internal leaders, it is often due to the influence of the mother. I have a terrific relationship with my brother. He's been around the company a long while and is ready to take charge. He's anxious and highly competent. He's eager to be off and running. We've been best friends for a long time. And you know, we're not without individual ambitions either, but somehow, we've been able to work that out. In some cases, two brothers can be terribly competitive. In other cases, it can turn out the other way. In our case, we have a smooth and respectful relationship. I hope it continues that way.

At this point in the interview, Amo yelled across the hall to Jamie and invited him to join the interview. They both commented on how some press coverage of the succession had nearly threatened to drive a wedge into their relationship. They referred to the emphasis on mutual support and the longer-term view of life that their mother had inculcated in them as fundamental values since childhood.

Nonetheless, 1983 was a rough time in the financial world to pass on control to a sibling. The success of Amo's heroic mission was being challenged by Wall Street analysts and by some in the business press. Such major, historically profitable businesses as the manufacture of light-bulb glass and picture-tube glass were no longer attractive enterprises. Sales of Corning, overall, remained flat for several years, hovering around $1.5 billion, while net income dropped 41 percent over the four years immediately prior to Amo's retirement.

Despite this, Amo thought new management under Jamie was appropriate and the timing was right. Jamie had served as vice chairman and chairman of the executive committee for the past twelve years and had been in the firm for twenty-one years. Amo himself had become president fewer than ten years after entering the firm and chairman after twelve years. Both had graduated from Harvard College and Harvard Business School. Amo began the process of succession by discussing the issue with his fifty-four-year-old president, Thomas MacAvoy.

> I had originally talked to Tom MacAvoy about this three years earlier. I said, "You know, there is a whole group of people coming along here who are damned able and they've got to have a shot at the top. They need time to have impact. Just because we got our jobs early in life, doesn't mean those roles are etched in stone. Somehow we've got to work this thing out so that we can help in the evolving process of the company in new and different ways yet still give others the opportunity to lead." Once we had made our peace on that, then Jamie was clearly the guy. I know

it sounds funny, but I like President John Kennedy's crack to the press about the appointment of his brother Robert as attorney general, "Nepotism isn't too bad, as long as you keep it in the family." But there was no question in either of our minds. Jamie was the man for the top job.

Amo had served as chief executive for two decades, in the pattern set before him. He had lived up to his family calling. Perhaps now it was time to seek an ambassadorship like his father or the U.S. Congress like his grandfather. Tom MacAvoy, the Ph.D. who had worked his way up to the presidency from Corning's research labs, left office with his older partner Amo and became vice chairman.

Despite the delicate considerations surrounding this transition, Amo believed that the spirit of the succession was damaged by a misleading press report. He recalled several months later, "The day it really hurt, was when that *Wall Street Journal* article came out." Amo was long credited with the maintenance of Corning's admirable sense of social responsibility to its community and to its work force. He worked hard for employment stabilization within the firm and the encouragement of extensive investment in their upstate New York region. Amo led Corning, always respected for its technical expertise, into innovative emerging technologies that were adjacent to its core business. Through internal development, joint ventures, and acquisitions, Corning moved into such exciting new fields as fiber optics, biotechnology, and medical diagnostic equipment. On top of this, his last few years in office were marked by an intensified emphasis upon productivity improvement.

The spirit and content of the upsetting *Wall Street Journal* article implied that Jamie had been the sole designer of this new dynamism, while Amo had been the guardian of old-fashioned company paternalism and *noblesse oblige*. This article, "With New Chairman, Corning Tries to Get Tough and Revive Earnings," quoted several financial analysts thought to support the following lead comments:

> Corning Glass Works' management training program, so the joke on Wall Street goes, consists of three weeks of polo, three weeks of squash, and three weeks of platform tennis. Corning has a reputation for laid-back management style. . . . The new boss, who had been vice chairman, has a reputation for toughness and is the chief architect of strategy, including management reorganization.[4]

Amo responded to the personal attack he felt from this piece in an interview several months later.

> When they talked about polo playing, squash, racquetball, and that sort of thing, frankly, it hurt. It set a bad tone, not just for me, but everyone involved. Maybe that's what they felt. Maybe that's what had been fed the press by Wall Street. Maybe that's what they thought we were doing. Excluding me, I don't think it's an understatement to say that this was hardly what we were about.

Amo's adjustment to this disappointing newspaper article was to discard it as the product of a single, misguided journalist. He was content with the knowledge of his own true role in the accomplishments of the firm. He stated that the article was the only truly unhappy incident in the succession.

> Aside from that article, the transition has gone extremely well. There have been some tough things to do and changes to make. There have been different personalities putting their stamp upon Corning's leadership and that's good. But the hardest thing is to be truly joyful in letting go. I have to accomplish things. If I do something and I don't get the credit for it, that's something else. As long as I know inside me that it was something pretty important and I made it happen, I'm happy to let someone else get the credit. I know this sounds Pollyannaish, but the real sense of accomplishment is in the development of the organization. Sharing credit is part of developing others. I really enjoy seeing others develop, whether it's the New York Yankees' farm team or the Harvard freshman hockey team. I enjoy seeing who's coming along, who's next in the flow of talent. . . . The *most* important thing in management is people. The *second* most important thing is people. The 14th and 50th and 139th is still people. One often gets so caught up in the company structure, its process, its history, its precedents that you can forget the key to company survival is really the younger people. Getting them in office and removing stones from their path, that's what is satisfying.

Thus Amo steered clear of the late-career desperation that monarchs and generals have to prove the triumph of their entire heroic mission to all. Amo's resolution of hurt feelings was accomplished through honestly recognizing within himself that performance standards had been satisfied. In addition to his inner-directed values to help him get through the transition, Amo also saw unassailable external signs of the success of the company. It had grown larger and stronger and a new generation of talent had been nurtured to lead the firm into the future.

As for his own future, the entirety of his personal legacy would not be defined by his three decades at Corning. His exit from office opened the door to new opportunities for growth and personal impact.

> If I'm a young guy coming into Corning and I say, "I don't have to wait for these people to die off," this signals opportunity to the newcomer. But, it also creates an opportunity for me. What I do with my time on earth is my most important resource. Whether I do something further with my life or if I just fritter it away will be determined by whether I move on to something new. This is an opportunity to pursue an entirely different course which may be exciting, but may have nothing to do with hierarchies, corporate status, or other such things that surround the trappings of a CEO. Rather than bemoaning the loss of status, there are tremendous opportunities out there. Status is like a passing breeze.

While moving on to something new, Amo was reluctant to cut all ties with Corning.

I need to stay out of the hair of my successors. We don't have an age limit on our board. I know that Walter Wriston will leave Citicorp's board on retirement, but I think that's a mistake. He will argue very eloquently that there is nothing worse than having your old boss sitting around and second-guessing you. Certainly I agree, but the old boss doesn't have to second-guess a successor. I don't know what my future role will be at the company, but I intend to be a counselor. I'm there as a stopgap if anyone needs me. For example, I've offered to represent Corning on trips abroad, to the extent Jamie is interested.

Finally, when asked what new activities he might pursue, Amo described the job specs.

It's important to use your time in office to the best of your abilities and then to let go. I've always been a very structure-upholding person. Now I'd like to try to be more of an individual contributor. I don't know where I'm going, but I did do something which used my primary talents and I guess I've touched the lives of a few individuals. There are a lot of people who make a hell of a lot more money than we do in the glass industry. What we do here is to produce something of value to all. We're people who take materials out of the ground and do something with them. Rather than just go down to Florida or hang on with outside boards, there are other and brand new opportunities to have impact. I'm interested in improving Corning, New York, as a place to live. Corning has always been a symbol to our family. It is not a bedroom community. If we can't attract good people to Corning, the headquarters and research will have to move. If this happens, the whole business begins to unravel. Corning, as a city, must be a vital, adaptive place.

Would his next calling be to public office? When asked in 1983, he responded, "Maybe, but diplomacy and political office are only the means to an end. The world tends to be impressed with status or position or wealth. That's how to get things done. If the public office gives me a better lever to help others, it would be worth it." Following in his father's tradition of late-career public service, Amo was elected to the U.S. Congress in January 1987 as a freshman representative from New York. Before Amo's election to Congress, his adjustment to a new career late in life was not easy on his family or on his personal pride. He persisted nonetheless in his determination for two main reasons. First, he knew it was important to have a new career so that the leadership succession at Corning would not be impaired, and second, his work in government created a new opportunity to be among the shapers of his world. The fact that he was ultimately successful in the transition was due to an inner set of values fortified long before he had taken command at Corning. Unlike many leaders, whether of family firms or national governments, Amo did not confuse his personal identity with the job he held. By the end it was clear that Amo had managed his exit as a governor's departure.

Henry Ford II—Passing the Wheel

While a publicly traded firm for over thirty years, the Ford Motor Company retained a strong family influence. For example, with 13 percent of the ownership, the family had 40 percent control of the firm. Many popular writers and Ford scholars have drawn comparisons between two prominent top auto executives, both named Henry Ford, who each ruled the same firm for roughly four decades apiece.[5] The imperial imagery, personal vulgarity, and legendary autocratic management style common to the two can combine to overshadow profound differences in their departure style. While their exits were highly publicized events due to the vocalized anger of two disappointed aspirants, there is an understandable temptation to overstate the dynastic inferences of almost eighty years of rule by two leaders whose names differed only by a numeral. Henry I was forced into an exit plan, while Henry II crafted his own three years before leaving and lived up to this plan after retirement until his death seven years later. Perhaps inspired by his wider interests in the community, or by his longtime desire to insulate his troubled personal life, or even by his loathing of comparisons with the brutality of the firm's founder, Henry II sought to establish a succession process with the apparent smoothness of the assembly line of top executives at his cross-town rival, General Motors. Henry I was a prototypical monarch and Henry II an imperial ambassador.

The memoirs of family members and various Ford Motor Company top executives provide conflicting interpretations as to the originality of important market and manufacturing innovations attributed to Henry Ford, not to mention the reality of the facts of his own personal life. Henry Ford I's image was that of an appealing popular folk hero and a ruthless tyrant whose imagination and record of accomplishment became symbolic of the American dream of unbounded opportunity. Ford's rise from humble origins, his effective self-promotion, his entrepreneurial genius, and his sweeping social visions catapulted him into heroic status.

Meanwhile, his notorious warfare against his own executives sidetracked the careers of his top production and financial leaders. Threatened by talented lieutenants such as Charles Sorensen, James Couzens, John and Horace Dodge, and William Knudsen, he eventually drove them out of the firm after they had made substantial contributions to the company's success. By the mid-1940s, the elderly and enfeebled Ford had given over his trust to the brutal guardianship of Henry Bennett, a sycophant with gangster connections. Bennett competed with Ford's son Edsel for power in the firm, although he confessed to little knowledge of automobile sales and production.[6] His strength lay in his shadowy underworld connections and his autocratic command. In 1943, following the untimely death of the harassed forty-seven-year-old Edsel, Ford planned to name Bennett president.[7]

A new Henry Ford, however, was about to arrive to rescue the horrified Ford family, with the backing of the War Production Board. Ensign Henry Ford II, Edsel's son, was drawn back from the navy to become executive vice president of the company in 1943, through the efforts of his grandmother Clara and his mother, Eleanor, who worked to outmaneuver the plotting Bennett and who pressured Henry Ford I to name Henry II as his successor two years later. Eleanor Ford was determined that her father-in-law not destroy another family member: "He killed my husband, but he's not going to kill my son."[8] She threatened to sell her 41 percent of the company. Henry I resigned and died a year and a half later, in April 1947. Thus, Henry Ford II took control at age twenty-eight, promptly exorcised the firm of Bennett and his ruffians, and lived up to his family's hopes for the next thirty-five years.

As such a young man, Ford needed experienced senior-level assistance. Among the loyal and competent colleagues Henry II recruited were old loyalists of his deceased father as well as newcomers such as Charles "Tex" Thornton's famed "Whiz Kids" from the U.S. Army Air Force, who included such notable talent as Robert S. McNamara, J. "Ed" Lundy, and Arjay Miller. Ford also enlisted the assistance of highly respected senior talent from elsewhere, such as Ernest Breech, a former top executive of General Motors and Bendix, and a team of GM alumni who joined Breech. Overall, Ford was able to build up a strong management staff, albeit one filled with rival factions. Under Henry Ford II, the firm reorganized its manufacturing, planning, and marketing, markedly improved its labor relations, and introduced a string of successful new automobiles, such as the Thunderbird, the Fairlane, the Falcon, and the Mustang. With much fanfare, this large family firm became a publicly traded corporation in 1956, and people stood in lines outside of brokerages to buy into this record-breaking stock offering.[9]

By 1960, Ford was ready to take over from his mentor Ernest Breech. At age sixty-five, after fifteen years of service, Breech resigned. During the 1960s and 1970s, various top executives served as president, but the still young Henry Ford had no need for a successor as yet. For the most part, the relations between these presidents and their boss were positive. Ford was especially saddened by McNamara's departure for Washington to serve as secretary of defense under President Kennedy.[10] Ford, too, got more and more involved in national concerns. Through the 1960s, Ford became increasingly interested as business and societal issues confronted each other. Ford involved himself and his corporation in several areas of social responsibility, including urban poverty, racial discrimination, and urban decay. President Lyndon Johnson appointed Ford chairman of the National Alliance of Businessmen, a group of U.S. business leaders seeking productive jobs for the hard-core unemployed and meaningful jobs for disadvantaged young people. He also served as chairman of the National Center for Voluntary Action and served on the U.S. delegation to the United Nations. Some thought that he, too, hoped for a later position in government, especially an ambassadorial post.

Meanwhile, back at the firm, Henry Ford II had become concerned over the continued vitality of the remaining "Whiz Kids," given recent triumphs in the marketplace by General Motors. Impressed by his various successes in key roles at GM, Ford recruited Semon E. Knudsen, son of Ford pioneer William Knudsen, who had gone to GM after being dismissed by Henry Ford I. The prior year, 1967, Knudsen had been passed over for the presidency of General Motors and was receptive to Ford's 1968 offer of the presidency. His predecessor at Ford, Arjay Miller, was made vice chairman and head of the finance committee. While the national press applauded this audacious move, various internal factions were disappointed by this outside hiring. In fact, several independent researchers of Ford Motor Company history have concluded that Knudsen's dismissal in 1969 was due more to internal sabotage than to animosity between Ford and Knudsen. In particular, it has been suggested that Knudsen was badly undercut by an ambitious and tough Ford executive named Lee Iacocca.[11] Don Frey, a protégé of Iacocca and his successor at the Ford division of Ford Motor Company and a liaison between Iacocca and Knudsen, recalled:

> It was like being the meat in the sandwich. In Lee's mind, he was at war with Bunkie [Knudsen]. That made me guilty of fraternizing with the enemy. I'd tell Lee that Bunkie wanted some changes and Lee would tell me to tell Bunkie to "shove it up his ass."[12]

With an outside job offer in hand from Chriscraft, Iacocca and a group of top Ford executives threatened a mass defection if Knudsen were not replaced. In his own account, Iacocca, on the other hand, has suggested that Knudsen's failure to display proper deference to Henry Ford II sabotaged Knudsen's chances for the chief executive's position. For example, Knudsen supposedly failed to secure Ford's final clearance for the 1971 planned line of new car models. Whatever the reasons, Knudsen was fired, and in the reorganization that followed, company affairs were directed by three presidents reporting directly to Henry Ford, one of whom was Lee Iacocca.[13]

Ford acknowledged his disappointment with the succession process by this point:

> I'd like my epitaph, but I don't think I've accomplished it yet, [to be] an organizational arrangement that will be stable enough and good enough— I'm not talking about individual people now, I'm talking about an organizational arrangement that anybody can fit into. That is the big thing that General Motors has.[14]

Succession was an important issue, but it wasn't particularly urgent because at the time of Knudsen's departure in 1970, Henry Ford was only fifty-three years old. When Ford experienced an attack of angina pectoris in 1976, all this changed. Initially after Knudsen's departure, Iacocca directed North American Automotive Operations. Later, the three-president structure was superseded by the election of Iacocca as president of the company. By 1976, Ford was not satisfied with many of Iacocca's personal characteristics, and he had growing doubts about Iacocca's record of performance. In June 1978, Ford gave his board an ultimatum: it would be either he or Iacocca that they supported, and Iacocca was fired.[15] Two weeks later, Iacocca went on to become president of Chrysler and then chairman a year later, leading the spectacular Chrysler recovery.[16]

While Iacocca charged that the dismissal was due to ethnic bigotry and the threat he represented to Henry Ford II, many company officials disagreed. Insofar as the interests of the Ford Motor Company and its shareholders were concerned, we must consider an assessment of Iacocca's performance as president. In discussing this matter, Philip Caldwell, who ultimately succeeded Henry Ford II, said:

> Despite the market acceptance of the Mustang and some other car lines, the company had lost market share generally for fifteen years. Customers were dissatisfied with quality. The product strategy and planning process had broken down and some of the other basic control systems had been allowed to atrophy. Costs were out of step with the prices the market would accept. As a result, car profits overall declined to unacceptable levels and in some cases, entire major car lines operated at a loss. Lee put his time and energy in the North American car business and that was the least successful part of the company. The cars brought to market in the late seventies were cold in the marketplace. Profits from the North American truck business, International Automotive Operations, and Ford Motor Credit largely carried the company in the late seventies and early eighties. In talking to me about the situation, Henry Ford told me that he did not trust what Iacocca would do with the company—that he did not think Lee was the right person to run the company.

A Donaldson, Lufkin & Jenrette financial analyst's report written in July 1978, after Iacocca's resignation, provides evidence to support Caldwell's view:

> Once again, the event [Iacocca's resignation] has been dramatized by the press as an essentially "political" or personality-based decision on the part of the Company's chairman and chief executive officer. We suspect that this kind of interpretation is mainly superficial. We think, rather, that the evidence clearly indicates that Lee Iacocca's departure was the logical and probably unavoidable outcome of a *business* development of major importance to Ford during the last several years. In this regard, we surmise that the political maneuvering—along with the ultimate emergence of per-

sonal feelings—and the resultant pressure to resign, which allegedly precipitated the final event, began after the decision was made by Mr. Ford
to respond appropriately (i.e., in terms of altering the managerial structure of the company) to the overriding *business* realities. . . .

It is our conjecture that the basic cause of Mr. Iacocca's departure was
the spectacular growth of Ford's overseas earnings during the last several
years, a development which raised the relative importance of this profit
center within the company's worldwide total to one of superiority vis-à-
vis North American automotive operations. . . . Ford's overseas profits
increased by 379.6% between 1972 and 1977. (During the same period,
incidentally, GM's offshore earnings rose by only 117.7%.) As a result of
that dramatic degree of growth, Ford's profits outside of the U.S. and
Canada last year [1977] represented 42.1% of consolidated net income
versus a corresponding contribution from its North American automotive
operations of 37.5%.

. . . Concurrently, the profit contribution made to the Company's overall
net income by North American automotive operations failed to increase
at all at a time when arch-rival General Motors was able to expand its
earnings within the combined U.S. and Canadian vehicle markets by nearly
50%. Although Mr. Iacocca's responsibilities as President of the Company
were broader than that, his background, interest and principal day-to-day
emphasis were focused on the North American Automotive business.

Comparative Sources of Earnings Growth and Changes
in Profit Composition, 1972–1977

| | General Motors | | | | | Ford | | | | |
| | 1977 | | 1972 | | | 1977 | | 1972 | | |
	Amount (000's)	Total	Amount (000's)	Total	Change	Amount (000's)	Total	Amount (000's)	Total	Change
North American Automotive	$2,647	79.3%	$1,807	83.5%	+46.5%	$627	37.5%	$656	75.4%	−4.4%
U.S.	2,530	75.8	1,720	79.5	+47.1	595	35.6	567	65.2	+4.9
Canada	117	3.5	87	4.0	+34.1	32	1.9	89	10.2	−64.0
Overseas	253	7.6	116	5.4	+117.7	705	42.1	147	16.9	+379.6
Non-Automotive	148	4.4	65	3.0	+128.3	85	5.1	22	2.5	+286.4
Non-Operating	290	8.7	175	8.1	+65.7	256	15.3	45	5.2	+468.9
Consolidated	$3,338	100.0%	$2,163	100.0%	+54.3%	$1,673	100.0%	$870	100.0%	+92.3%
Per share	11.62		7.51			14.16*		6.82*		

*Summary: full-diluted would be $13.06 and $6.66, respectively.

It is clear [from the table] that in every important way, Mr. Caldwell
managed his part of the business brilliantly. The contribution made by
overseas operations to overall profit growth and stockholders' equity during the last five years was huge and dominant. It is equally apparent that
Mr. Iacocca failed to match the corresponding performance of General
Motors in his principal area of responsibility. North American Automotive Operations made no contribution at all to the Company's strong
earnings and the resultant improvement in overall returns on stockholders' investment during the period.[17]

In an interview, Caldwell shared the following chronology of the events of the succession:

> To assist him, Henry Ford brought in McKinsey and Company in 1976 to study the problem of a proper and ongoing organization of the company which would provide the framework within which succession could take place. This led to the recommendation, among others, that an Office of the Chief Executive be established.
>
> On April 14, 1977, Mr. Ford announced a three-member Office of the Chief Executive in which he continued to be chairman and chief executive officer; Iacocca continued as president and for the first time was designated chief operating officer, and I was elected vice chairman of the board of directors and given particular responsibility for strategic planning and policy development.
>
> In his announcement to the company and the public, Henry Ford explained that this was "designed to pave the way for a natural and smooth management transition at an appropriate time." He further stated, "It is my intention, with the approval of the board, to continue to serve as chairman and chief executive for the next three years and afterward as chairman until my sixty-fifth birthday." He was then fifty-nine years old. At a press conference the same day, a reporter asked Mr. Ford who was in charge in his absence, and he replied, "the vice chairman."
>
> On June 8, 1978, Henry Ford announced that I had been designated deputy chief executive officer, and stated, "by delegation, I shall share with Mr. Caldwell all authority delegated to me as chief executive officer by the board of directors." He also announced that Iacocca would continue as president and chief operating officer but would report to the vice chairman, and in the absence of the chairman and vice chairman, would be chief executive officer.
>
> Henry Ford further announced that his brother, William Clay Ford, had become a member of the office of the chief executive and had been elected chairman of the executive committee, succeeding Henry Ford.
>
> Iacocca found this arrangement unsatisfactory to his own ambitions, and after a period of explosive and highly publicized maneuvering, on July 14, 1978, he resigned, effective October 15, 1978, and ceased to play any part in the affairs of the company.
>
> Iacocca's duties were formally assigned to me by the action of the board on September 14, 1978, when I was elected president, effective October 16, 1978. I continued as vice president and deputy chief executive officer.
>
> In his remarks to the stockholders at the annual meeting held on May 10, 1979, Mr. Ford announced that he would resign as chief executive officer effective October 1, 1979. He also announced that at the meeting of the board immediately following on that day, the Organization Review and Nominating Committee would nominate me to be chief executive officer and Mr. Ford to continue to serve as chairman, which he had agreed to do for an indeterminate period. The board accepted these nominations and we were elected chief executive officer and chairman, respectively. He emphasized that after October 1, his role would be "completely nonexecutive." I continued as president. Implementation of the succession plan was completed on March 13, 1980, when Henry Ford

resigned as chairman and as an officer of the company, and I was elected
to succeed him. He was sixty-three. At his request, he remained an employee until his sixty-fifth birthday in September 1982, and a director and
chairman of the finance committee until he died on September 29, 1987,
shortly after his seventieth birthday.

When Henry Ford told me in March 1977 that he wanted me to succeed him, he also laid out the timetable he had in mind and he followed
it thereafter with only one deviation. He accelerated his retirement as
nonexecutive chairman, because he found the concept of being chairman
of the board, but not chief executive officer, an ineffective and unwork-
able arrangement.

The myth is that Henry Ford II did not provide well for his own
succession. The facts are to the contrary. He had a plan and he put it
into effect over a three-year period. It is not unusual that some succession candidates are disappointed with the outcome, and certainly that
was true in Iacocca's case. What was unusual was the fury of the candidate who was not selected.

The smoothness of the transition in which for the first time a non-
Ford headed Ford Motor Company, as well as the process by which the
new top management team was put into place, was the fulfillment of
Henry Ford's dream of more than thirty years. The succession from
Henry Ford in 1979 and the subsequent achievements of the successor
team were the final steps in the conversion of Ford Motor Company to
a public corporation that was completely professionally managed. Despite earlier troubles with potential successors, his actual departure was
truly ambassadorial.

It was during the period from 1977 to 1979 that Caldwell, working
with Ford, defined the precise organizational structure to be put in place
and proposed the occupants for the key positions. Caldwell had brought
to his position hands-on experience in all facets and most functions of
the company, perhaps more than any other senior Ford executive. In
all, he had served successfully on fifteen assignments in his thirty-two
years with the company, including assignments in purchasing, engineering administration, product planning, and manufacturing, as well
as in running and improving large business segments of the company—
North American Trucks, Philco, Ford of Europe, and International Automotive Operations.

Perhaps of even more importance to the establishment of a stable
system of ongoing management succession was that in the process,
Caldwell had developed a personal knowledge not only of the key players, but of the "farm system" that would provide the players for subsequent succession echelons. He had seen the benefits of creating management teams with complementary skills. Having used this concept to
successfully fill the number-one and number-two positions in Europe
on several occasions, it was natural that he followed the same pattern

in filling the chairman and president positions on his own retirement
in 1985. Chairman Donald Peterson, who had followed Caldwell in
heading North American Truck Operations, had spent his earlier years
in product-planning activities; President Harold Poling, in heading Europe and North American Automotive Operations, had been highly effective in cost control and very dedicated to quality improvement.[18]

During the late 1970s, the strategy had been set—get back to the
basics of quality first in everything, building products with integrity and
distinction that would really serve the needs of customers, be the lowest
cost producer, strengthen dealer distribution systems, foster employee
involvement—and firm plans had been developed to carry it out. Caldwell had put potential successors in position and they had proven themselves in the crucible of the company's most difficult five-year period
since the immediate post-World War II era, when Henry Ford II took
over from his grandfather.

Constant dedication to the strategy laid down in 1979 and 1980 has
paid off handsomely. After Ford suffered losses in 1980, 1981, and
1982, the largest turnaround in its industrial corporate history was consummated by all-time record profits in 1983 and again in 1984. Caldwell's successor team has continued the strategy it had helped implement, and that put Ford Motor Company in position to take advantage
of the greatest weakness of General Motors in sixty years.[19] The successful Taurus and Sable models developed by Donald E. Peterson and
his team were noted for their functionality, efficiency, innovative technology, and attractive aerodynamic styling. The company has now gone
on to even greater heights of achievement, with market acceptance and
profits greater than General Motors.

Though restless about the readiness of the company for the future,
as he had always been, Henry Ford II lived to see the fulfillment of his
dream of continuity of the company as the "wheel" passed successfully
from one management team to another, not once, but twice.

Conclusions

The detailed case history of Hal Walton in Chapter 10 described the
difficulty of an unsuccessful leadership transition by the founder of a
family firm. Hal Walton's struggles represent many, but certainly not
all, of the tensions common to succession in a family business. There
was no overt oedipal battle between a controlling father and an ambitious son. Nor was there the classic open warfare across succeeding generations of avaricious and ambitious brothers and sisters. Nevertheless,
the transfer of power in Flowtrol was no easy matter, for Hal's identity
was inseparable from the firm's. The founder's late-career self-concept
led to the sabotage of any immediate successor.

In the Dunkin' Donuts situation presented in this chapter, we saw a more typical set of tensions between a founder reluctant to let go and a son eager to be his own man. Bill Rosenberg's perspective on his transfer of power to his son Robert, however, involved certain atypical features. First, the founder, a self-made success, involved his son as a partner at a very early age. Second, his son became president and chief executive before the age of thirty, just as his father was entering his fifties. The teacher and student roles were well handled, and the son not only managed the father's original idea but built it into a much grander multinational enterprise. Third, the founder saw his immortal contribution succeeding without his personal presence required. Fourth, both were able to discuss candidly the sensitive role tensions that could destroy their relationship as partners, not to mention as father and son. Finally, there was a self-awareness on the part of the founder as to where his strengths lay. While regaining active command of the firm was not a temptation, his recently improved health and continued imagination prompted him to search for other opportunities toward which to contribute his energies.

Similarly, the Corning Glass Works situation demonstrated how brothers in a family-dominated enterprise could work at overcoming destructive tensions between generations and within the same generation. Again, the leader's self-concept was critical. Here Amory Houghton, Jr., managed to take control from his father, lead the company for about two decades, and then pass control on to his younger brother. The childhood relationship of the brothers, and their effort to maintain personal goals and identities outside of their leadership roles, were valuable qualities nurtured by their mother. Even so, the tensions surrounding such a transition can begin to erode core values, as the impact of the *Wall Street Journal* article threatened to do.

At Ford, we saw the passage of control from an aging monarch to a still somewhat imperial ambassador in the transition from Henry Ford I to Henry Ford II. We also saw the difficulties of moving to nonfamily managers in a firm still under strong family influence. Rival factions eventually gave way to a team approach.

The differences among these three situations remind us of the extraordinary range of special challenges that family firms face in planning leadership succession. We can distinguish at least four sets of discrete tensions that must be anticipated in family businesses: first, tensions within the founders that have to do with their mastery of their quests for heroic stature and heroic mission; second, tensions between generations, often between founders and their offspring; third, tensions within the succeeding generations, often between siblings or cousins as they vie for controlling positions for themselves and their own offspring; and fourth, tensions between the leader of a family firm and long-term employees, old customers, and regular suppliers.

The first of these challenges, those within the founder, refer to the particular difficulty that entrepreneurs confront in transcending their personal barriers to exit. Given their ability to shape the business around their own image, entrepreneurs sometimes build themselves a palace with no door to let themselves out. They sculpt their businesses to match their changing interests and thus are often thoroughly absorbed in the enterprise. Most founders reported that they had become aware of their ambition to run their own businesses early in their twenties and many in their late teens. This youthful dream of independence from the authority of others became reality in adult life. The enterprise is both child and companion. To leave the firm is like abandoning a close friend or a member of one's immediate family. Their personal identities have become intertwined with those of their firms. Not only does loss of one's identity accompany loss of chief executive stature, but one's heroic mission remains unfulfilled, because the business, if abandoned, may die in the hands of a crude or careless successor.

Even at home, this confusion of identities and mission is involved, as the founder of the business can often confuse his or her role at work with serving as the head of the household outside of work. One son of a founder commented:

> My father refused to let go because he feared that after the retirement he would no longer be Papa. No longer the patriarch that all the children would look to and depend on. . . . He wanted to die ruling the family and the firm. . . . And unfortunately for all of us, he did.

The second set of challenges, those between the founder and the next generation, refer to heightened intergenerational tensions. Often the founder and his or her family deal better with the allocation of the assets in the estate than with the allocation of power once the founder leaves. Overt attention to succession planning seems to elicit from a parent deep fears of abandonment by children and even to presage death. The multiple leadership roles of founder-parents in family firms very much complicate the planning for a leader's exit.

Psychologists frequently emphasize the destructive oedipal competition for the business between father and son as the contest to determine which male has the primary relationship with the firm, which represents a feminine figure.[20] Research by John Davis of the University of Southern California indicates that life-stage clashes between father and son can exacerbate the tensions surrounding the leadership transition.[21] For example, when sons and their fathers are both in turbulent periods in life, animosity is far more likely. When the children are in the early twenties, they are struggling for independence. At that time fathers, in their forties, are very likely to be confronting the onset of mid-life anxieties, accompanied by the fear that time for new opportunity is running out. A son eager for a top position can easily be seen as a threatening force, out to usurp whatever opportunity is still rightfully the father's. Leaders in their sixties are often similarly anxious for a last chance to have impact as they confront the horror of their time running out, or the realization that the contributions made earlier in life are being eroded. But sometimes the life-stage differences are beneficial. Offspring in their early thirties tend to be attentive students, while parents in their fifties or seventies tend to be constructive teachers. Discussion of succession may be traumatic not only for parents; their children's childhood separation fears may also be rekindled. Researcher Ivan Landsberg of Yale commented that "deep down inside" the son fears a "discussion of succession would actually bring about his father's death."[22]

When the succession is between a father and daughter, or a mother and son, the transition may be free of rivalry, but it can be characterized by excessive paternal or maternal protection of the successor.[23] The struggle to break the suffocating "daddy's little girl" syndrome is becoming easier as more women become accepted in top management roles in general. The advantages are that each party seems more comfortable with the clear distinction about which leader is identified with what contribution. Hugh Hefner's transfer of command of Playboy Enterprises to his thirty-two-year-old daughter Christie made clear to all that there was a transition in power and in style from the creative, flamboyant founder to his tough, more systematic daughter. Barbara Pearce, the thirty-two-year-old chief operating officer of her father's real-estate development firm, H. Pearce Company of New Haven, feels that it was easier stepping in as a daughter than as a son. Her father readily attributes the growth of their business—from revenues of $37 million when she joined in 1981 to $200 million five years later—to her contribution. Barbara feels that he has more respect for her abilities than if she were his son, and she is quick to acknowledge his role as the business's entrepreneur and risk taker.[24]

We also see that sons differentiate their leadership style from that of their chief executive mothers. Many *Washington Post* insiders commented with surprise at how well the transition went between the paper's former publisher, Katherine Graham, and her son Donald Graham. Donald Graham became the third generation in the family to run the paper when he succeeded his mother in 1979. The *Post*, originally bought by Donald's banker grandfather, Eugene Meyer, at an auction in 1932, was then run by Meyer's brilliant but troubled son-in-law, Philip Graham. After Graham committed suicide, his widow, Katherine Graham, (Donald's mother) became publisher. Under her flamboyant and forceful leadership, the paper established a reputation as a leading investigative journal and prominent forum for social comment. With the different style of its new leader, Donald Graham, the paper has jettisoned much of its former scrappy image, as Donald deemphasized coverage of national controversy and emphasized news of the local community.[25] Similarly, Leonard Lauder's name may never replace his mother Estée's on their cosmetic products, but he has been able to make his own way as chief executive in the firm. It seems that the distinctions in styles and identities are crisper when the succeeding family leader is of the opposite gender.

A third set of challenges to the tranquility of leadership succession within family businesses has to do with the destructive intragenerational tensions among potential successors. Long-unspoken sibling resentment and the jealousy of cousins can erupt with such force that no action short of selling the business seems to be possible. The vicious fighting among members of the Bingham family, which had controlled the *Louisville Courier Journal*, is an example. Through the conspiracy of his sisters, from whom he was alienated, Barry Bingham, Jr., lost his position as the publisher and as the one to succeed his father, Barry Bingham, Sr. In a somewhat different twist, Sam Sebastiani of Sebastiani Vineyards worked hard as chief executive following the death of his father in August 1980, only to be dismissed later by family members angered by his treatment of them.[26] They questioned whether he was still an attentive brother and son. J. Willard Marriott discussed the importance of patience as he reported that it took twenty years to ease unproductive relatives out of the Marriott hotel chain.[27]

The selection of an intended successor from among siblings suggests favoritism, even when the management expertise of a given family member is clear and equality in parental treatment is intact. Furthermore, the inheritance of ownership shifts a more concentrated control from the parent-founder to a more disparate set of next-generation owners.[28] The warfare between management and nonmanagement family members among publisher Joseph Pulitzer's descendants tore at the seams of his newspaper empire and disturbed family relations well into the fourth generation. Those left out of management were eager to sell out their shares of the publishing firm.[29] The clarity of contribution from each sibling can be important as well if it appears that one brother or sister is usurping the credit or power that belongs to another. The tensions heightened by the press reports of the Corning Glass Works succession serve as a case in point. Their mother's emphasis upon cooperation as children helped the Houghton brothers through this challenge.

Finally, there are unanticipated challenges to family business leadership successions from more distant constituencies, such as long-term employees, customers, and suppliers. Some older managers were surprised and resentful when Bill Rosenberg appointed his son as president of Dunkin' Donuts. This is not an unusual reaction, regardless of the degree of competence of the family member promoted. Fifteen years after denouncing nepotism in management in his book, *The Corporate*

Oligarch, public relations wizard David Finn had placed three of his children in top management positions in his prominent public relations firm of Ruder-Finn, a fourth child worked in the research department, and his wife, daughter-in-law, and son-in-law held special vendor relationships. With the career prospects of many loyal employees dashed, this forty-year-old public relations firm suffered bad "P.R." in the wake of mass defections, sagging morale, and departing clients. One of Finn's daughters, Amy Binder, complained:

> It's very hard to be the child of a family-owned business. It is very hard to prove yourself and to prove that you're not there just because of nepotism. You get underpaid and work twice as hard.[30]

Thus the winning family successors and the outside parties that felt passed over need to develop relationships that respect each other's competence and career expectations. The founder can take the initiative in addressing the awkward feelings between these parties.

The founder's subordinates may grieve over the loss of a specific relationship with the chief executive. The successor may be seen as a presumptuous intruder. Many subordinates may have grown up with the business and with the founder. They may have shared victories and failures along the way. Their experiences and sacrifices may seem underappreciated by a new leader who seeks to make changes. Similarly, the firm's clients may feel that they had enjoyed a special relationship with the founder. The personal nature of their transactions with the firm may have ended and the new leader may terminate their direct link to the top.

These challenges can all be overcome if the people involved anticipate such problems. The response of the outgoing leader should include: (1) planning either a governor-like or ambassadorial departure; (2) initiating preparation within the firm for the leadership transition, particularly by bringing older employees into all planning; and (3) hiring outside counselors or advisers. Conferences and site visits to introduce successors to long-term customers and employees can provide stability and reassurance.

The personal preparation for a retiring leader often entails finding a new heroic mission and a new source of heroic stature. It is wrong to presume, as we often do, that entrepreneurs are locked in a lifelong oedipal battle with a long-gone father image and hence cannot exit gracefully. There are many who are confident of their abilities as creators and anxious for new adventure. Their contrasting comments were along these lines:

> I am an entrepreneur. I know my strengths and I also know my limits. I love creating things out of nothing, but I am bored by steady-state management. I get tired of the endless hand-holding and office politics of a big establishment. I like starting small and fresh and growing. I don't care

about leaving the mountain—it was my own creation. That's what I do best. I did it before and I'd like to show that I can do it again. I've worked my way up. Just wait and see; I'll do it again.

Such governor-like founders discovered that they had a knack for the franchising business, or the equipment-leasing business, or the restaurant business, or the financial deal-making business. In these industries, we have seen entrepreneurs excited by the prospects of proving themselves over and over. They can be superb governors in their exit pattern. To make this transition, the founder requires the self-awareness that his or her competence is symbolized by the firm, but is not bound by that past creation. Furthermore, the founder requires resources such as health, money, and ideas to start again.

If the departing leader is not the founder, he or she must work especially hard at identifying a way of maintaining a role within the family as well as the business that is acceptable to all parties. Frequently, this may mean that the nonfounder retiree follow the retirement style of an ambassador rather than of a governor. Should the transfer of power be between siblings, however, the best pattern may be one of a gradual plan for a complete exit. The close monitoring of a later-career older brother is bound to draw resentment.

The preparation of the family for the leader's exit requires a fair and systematic successor-selection process and a thoughtful program for the development of the successor. Other entrenched powers within the corporation can damage the business by trying to sabotage the careers of aspiring children of the boss working their way up in the organization. If these senior employees are to serve as mentors, they should be informed that they indeed have a secure role. A career plan for bypassed nonfamily members must be made explicit, otherwise valued managers may fear for the security of their own jobs and leave the firm. The departing leader should help to handle the explanation of the transition to clients and subordinates.

At this time, the successors are likely to want to make themselves known to shareholders.[31] There should be an open statement by the manager that the successor will be expected to take steps to distinguish him or herself from the departing leader and that he or she might make annoying changes and even some serious mistakes. It is important for the retiring family business leader not to appear to be an anxious parent looking out for comments on the performance of his or her child. The departing leader must be supportive of the change in command and confident in the selection. The length and criteria used in a trial period should not be a matter of negotiation for others beyond the outgoing leader and the incoming leader.

Lastly, the departing leader and the incoming leader can be well served by outside perspectives during this transition period. Other family members are still involved parties. A well-intentioned spouse of the departing leader may still be hiding some smothered grief over a loss of status. A parent or brother or sister or child has a unique and somewhat unconscious agenda in his or her relationship with both parties. The secrecy surrounding family businesses and the loneliness so common to entrepreneurs suggest that, while the wisdom of outside experience is particularly valuable at this time, those involved in a leadership transition are not likely to request such help. Founders are often most confident of their hunches and suspicious of outsiders. Anxious to keep embarrassing squabbles within the family, the key parties are trapped by their lack of either proper distance or skill to handle the explosive emotions and intertwined roles. The counsel of experienced consultants or peers who have triumphantly steered through succession crises themselves in other family businesses can be a useful addition to a board of directors or as part of a personal network of friendships.

The departure styles in family business successions can vary greatly according to the generational stage of the enterprise.[32] For first-to-second-generation transitions, we may expect monarch profiles of exit. Firms at this stage are likely to be led by figures with strong heroic needs to create. The intragenerational sibling and cousin warfare in the second to third generation of a family business may give rise to a greater likelihood of generals. The third to fourth generation of leadership transition is likely to display ambassador patterns, marked by feelings of obligation to continue family values and to cautiously preserve accumulated family wealth.

12

RIDING INTO THE SUNSET
AND THROUGH TO DAWN

**The light at the end of the tunnel is most
valuable to those just beginning.**

> Retiree named Nat on a park bench
> in the play, *I'm Not Rappaport,*
> by Herb Gardner

This book has examined the half of succession neglected by most literature on business, the retirement of the incumbent leader. A business leader's retirement is subject to the cultural paradox that traps many heroic leaders. Heroism is a confluence of societal as well as personal illusions. The societal illusion is that individuals can provide simplifying road maps to circumvent the barriers that block attainment of collective goals. Heroic leaders, in this vein, are the product of societies' needs and serve only as long as they satisfy that need. Thomas Jefferson remarked, "When a man assumes a public trust, he should consider himself a public property." The personal illusion is to see our heroes as those with near superhuman capabilities who have risen from humble childhood origins to achieve greatness in their careers. Some of these leaders have shaped not only their own careers, but also their constituents' collective well-being. Andrew Jackson commented, "One man with courage makes a majority." Scholars have long debated whether society creates the hero, or whether the great leader stamps his vision on society.

I believe that heroism is a consequence of both illusions. Great economic and social benefits can be viewed as the intended outcomes of master strategists, and great acts of corporate villainy and incompetence are seen as the result of corrupt or inept top leaders. Yet at the same time these corporate accomplishments can be achieved only by those leaders whose authority is granted from their constituents. The impact of a leader's exit from office demonstrates just how much leaders matter. A leader's late-career self-image, expressed in the departure style, fundamentally influences the firm's strategy and the livelihood of many. Such far-ranging aspects of corporate performance as the emphasis on sales over profits, the quality of management development, and the impact of the visions of top leadership are affected by how a leader departs. Next to our own there is no retirement more important to understand than that of our leaders.

Chief Executives as Aging Heroes

The basic purpose of this book has been to describe how leaders differ from other older workers and then to describe just why we should care about the difference. Leaders differ first, because their work defines their personal identity, and second, because their actions have a large impact on others. They have come to depend on their leadership role for an identity and for a life purpose. We must be concerned about this because the departure styles that follow from these self-concepts have a pronounced impact upon a corporation's strategy and the future supply of internal leaders. A leader's retirement is not a unique personal matter without pattern. It is a predictable public event with public consequences.

Chief executives in late career can form different self-concepts about their work because they serve as folk heroes on several levels. First, they have, in various periods in our history, served as national symbols of the triumphs of individual spirit amidst confusing social dislocation. Second, they can frequently serve as corporate rallying points for collective strategy and group loyalty, much the same as a team coach. Third, to themselves, leaders have so fused their personal dreams with the visions they deliver to their public following that their personal identity has often merged into their work roles. At times to a nation, frequently to their firms, and generally to themselves, the chief executives are heroes.

A hero makes personal sacrifices for the benefit of his or her constituents. Heroes do not accept traditional barriers in their striving. Their near superhuman confidence encourages us to overpower the restraints that keep us from achieving collective goals. But who liberates the hero? The heroe's imprisonment is self-imposed, as is his or her inability to escape the heroic role itself. The heroic self-concept does not welcome the prospect of retirement.

Society's Heroes

American folklorists stress the importance of legends in helping to develop a national identity, particularly legends that help us to triumph over ethnic and regional loyalties. It was not until the middle of the last century that the romanticization of early American heroes and the glorification of contemporary heroes led to national legend-building. Various cultural values—"common man ideal," "team players," "pride in work," "fearlessness in the face of danger," and "rugged individualism"— were projected onto our early heroes. The spotlight shifted across such occupations as frontiersmen, cowboys, mill hands, coal miners, oil drillers, railroaders, outlaws, soldiers, politicians, inventors, and business tycoons. The public's fascination with various types of folk heroes changed with the shift in location of greatest uncertainty, from the wilderness frontier to the battleground to the workplace.

Regardless of whether society is searching for its heroes from the leadership in a given period, many chief executives still fashion their images around a heroic self-concept. This is hinged upon five standard aspects of American heroism that we can apply to business heroism.

First, corporate heroes present themselves as self-made industrialists who rose from humble origins. This portrait is as true of today's H. Ross Perot, Lee Iaccoca, and An Wang as it was of such turn-of-the-century business leaders as Thomas Edison, Henry Ford, and Andrew Carnegie.

Second, these industrial heroes have conquered major career setbacks. Their resilience was the result of determination to prove invincibility and heroic valor.

Third, business heroes articulate visions that transform the nature of business conduct in their firms, in their industries, and even across industries. They champion new products, changes in technologies, market redefinition, regulatory changes, and other widely copied innovations.

Fourth, business heroes have rarely been humble, self-effacing fellows. Effective self-promoters, they have needed ego strength to stand up to the many critics of their new, destablizing visions.

Fifth, these leaders are guided by a sense of social responsibility manifested by a desire to make an even larger social impact than the enormous transformations that they have introduced at work. With intense emotional dedication, these leaders write books, deliver public addresses, and become prominent advocates of social causes.

Heroes of the Firm

Does the heroic character of business leaders unduly glorify them? It is true that the public considers only a small number of business leaders national folk heroes, yet audiences other than mass society construct more local heroic platforms. One audience is the business leader's own self-concept.

Robert Reich, John Kenneth Galbraith, and Joseph Schumpeter have argued against the glorification of the chief executive.[1] Such scholars have asserted that the days of the business hero are long past, gone with the turn-of-the-century entrepreneurial tycoon. They explain that the bureaucratic maze created by the success of capitalism mutes the voice of any single person. Individual initiative is blended into the blur of complex institutional dynamics. They describe today's business leaders as conformist bureaucrats who act merely as corporate caretakers. These critics see heroic firm leadership as mere symbolism, lacking substantive impact.

We can respond to this critique in several ways, one of which the underscores the heroism of leaders at least on level of the firm. Business leaders can revive old bureaucracies or else create new ones. Individual will has not necessarily been smothered. In addition, symbolic functions of leadership cannot be minimized, as they are inseparable from the substantive ones. Many of the heroic business leaders of the past were salaried employees and not owner-managers. Some of the greatest days of AT&T, Sears, General Motors, and IBM were during the reign of hired chief executives, long after their founding entrepreneurs departed. Leaders such as Theodore Vail, Robert Wood, Alfred P. Sloan, and Thomas Waston were neither founders, controlling owners, nor bureaucratic conformists, yet they changed their firms, their industries, and our world in profound ways. They led their firms to greatness by harnessing the potential of existing bureaucracies and steering them toward greater accomplishments.

Furthermore, it has certainly been premature of business critics to proclaim the demise of entrepreneurship, defining it as a lost historic curiosity. We can easily identify a long list of recently founded major enterprises that now dominate the U.S. economy. Our leading organizations are not merely bureaucratic remnants of turn-of-the-century creations. Especially in the high technology and service sectors, we can find new leading firms, such as Digital Equipment, Wang Laboratories, Hewlett Packard, Intel, McDonald's, Dunkin' Donuts, Texas Air, Capital Cities, CBS, Apple Computer, Control Data, Polaroid, Occidental Petroleum, and Wal-mart. Heroic individuals can still create and run large enterprises today, as was done in our past.

Last, we need to consider the distinction between symbolic and substantive leadership. The creation of meaning through symbolic behavior is one way the leader of a culture guides a group to collective action. Huge bureaucracies function via complex matrices of chains of command and by individual decree, but it is naïve to judge leaders' strength only by their effective utilization of formal command structures. A half-century of organizational research has continually supported the idea that symbolic acts of leadership have practical applications, and that leaders accomplish these symbolic goals by inspiring action, resolving conflicts, building political coalitions, and exchanging information in informal ways that bypass a formal chain of command. Leaders can reinforce collective values by designing membership rituals, allocating status, changing utilization of space, institutionalizing local myths, and delivering statements of mission at work. Through informal symbolic acts, leaders shape a culture and project individual personalities onto a group. Their influence is demonstrated by the profound impact of leadership succession on stock prices.

Current chief executives of firms with strong corporate cultures tackle threatening strategic and cultural changes by identifying with the wisdom of past corporate heroes. At IBM, changes are frequently accompanied by citations of the core principles articulated by Thomas J. Watson, Sr., and Thomas J. Watson, Jr. At the United Parcel Service, central corporate policies of founder Jim Casey are repeated in all important changes of technology, service, and strategy. A Policy Book and a Partnership Legacy Book serve as the bible of the organization. When UPS chairman Jack Rogers presented some dramatic changes in technology and in international operations at the eightieth annual management conference in 1987, he broke the news by conducting a simulated video dialogue with the deceased Casey through the use of old film segments and speeches. This seeming approval from the past reassured the 20,000 managers about the new goals and motivated them by making them see the importance of their roles in furthering the new corporate mission through new technologies, new international markets, and new services.

Self-Defined Heroes

Thus business leaders may, at times, serve as national heroes and frequently serve as heroes within their firms. The third level of heroism is within the leaders themselves. Heroes are anointed by their constituents, but to themselves they may already have assumed heroic ambitions. The group (whether a corporation, a nation, or a firm) confers the aura of heroism as an ultimate form of prestige to reward those who are most attentive to the group's needs, but a leader's self-concept may subtly lead to self-appointment. The heroic self-concept is not merely a superficial vanity, but the product of forceful drives to create and to serve.

One occupational hazard of top leaders is that the role of public figures threatens to overwhelm their other, more personal roles, such as that of parent, community member, or aging worker. Cognitive psychologists from Jean Piaget to Robert Keegan have theorized about the existence of a lifelong vacillation between individual and institutional identities as we progress through family, school, work, and community roles.[2] This movement is not as fluid for leaders, because leaders can become so encumbered by the responsibilities of office and the demands of constituents that they may fail to return to an inner, more autonomous sense of self. The trappings of office may become more than tools of leadership as a hero comes to identify with his or her public persona. Perhaps as compensation for low self-esteem from a deprived early life or perhaps due to unusually high self-esteem, the drive for status helps leaders rise above the crowd. As they achieve renown, the effort of fueling a public identity sometimes saps the resources used to fuel their private identities. *Heroic stature* refers to the aspect of a hero's self-concept that intertwines his or her personal identity with his or her occupational role as a leader.

The second aspect of heroic self-concept is that of purpose, or *heroic mission*. The drive to make an immortal contribution is, according to psychoanalyst Otto Rank, common to both artists and heroes.[3] Both set superhuman standards of accomplishment to leave a unique and lasting legacy. Their personal dreams of immortality, as fostered by their creative efforts, provide business leaders with an internal definition of heroism. Emerson suggested that we all seek to re-create the world as if others never existed. We want our existence to make a difference to the world. This desire to have a unique, lasting impact upon the world is not restricted to heroes. Psychoanalysts such as Otto Rank, Ernest Becker, and Robert Jay Lifton, however, have posited that top leaders have an unusually strong need to justify themselves as objects of primary value in the universe.[4] The quickness with which virtually each interviewed chief executive in this study equated retirement with death was a powerful support for Lifton's view. The chief executives wanted to be known as people who had both accomplished a great deal and still had more to contribute.

Heroic Self-Concept and Executive Retirement

When the constituency's definition of heroic roles clashes with the leader's definition of heroic self-concept, we find a leader at war with his or her own organization. Late-career heroes can inadvertently begin to resemble the villains they had sought to replace earlier in their careers.

Retirement is the time when we most often find a clash between the organization's goals and the leader's personal goals. The negotiation over the appropriate length of a leader's tenure is a difficult event. We considered three types of tensions that underlie this difficulty in timing a leader's exit: those within the individual over leaving unfinished business versus quitting while a winner; those between rising leaders and incumbents; and those between the leader and his or her following at large. Retirement for top leaders is different because they do not give up merely a livelihood; they give up an identity and a sense of purpose. The visions the leaders have sold their followers are personal dreams. The dream, once sold, is a public possession until it is eventually discarded.

This is not to suggest that other people retire from work without also leaving much behind. A study of the meaning of retirement is actually a study of the various meanings of work. For those whose work means more in their lives, retirement is all the more traumatic. In addition to material compensation, work provides many with a sense of purpose and self-esteem, a group membership, and a personal identity. Many, whether or not they are leaders, are reluctant to retire and walk away from their work. In Chapter 2, we looked at how latent and overt age bias in society has denied continued opportunity to many types of older workers. Retirement is not always a necessary or desirable institution. We saw that it was largely a twentieth-century creation to provide opportunity for younger workers and to protect older workers from stepped-up production technologies and provide them a retirement income. The creation of retirement was motivated by both well-intentioned concern for the elderly and substantial self-interest on the part of younger employees.

We now know that age is not an accurate or absolute indicator of an individual's ability to contribute at work. A challenging physical and psychological environment can minimize the effects of aging. Atrophy on the job is more a problem of poor human-resource development and the lack of planned career mobility than a product of age. Changes in legislation, prompted by an aging work force and labor shortages, have encouraged older people to remain on the job. Only now have we begun to look closely at the possible contribution that can be made by the appropriate matching of older workers and job responsibilities. Top political and corporate leaders have sometimes triumphed over barriers of age discrimination through their power to change or ignore retirement rules. When the heroic self-concept is absent or else under control, older workers offer valuable skills and wisdom.

Artists, performers, and politicians have been prominent among those who produced impressive late-career contributions. Artists and performers have often been able to transcend age discrimination because they work independently of formal organizational career paths. Artists

Grandma Moses, Pablo Picasso, and Marc Chagall displayed unbroken late-career productivity until their deaths at around age one hundred. Pianists Rudolf Serkin, Artur Rubinstein Vladimir Horowitz, and Claudio Arrau maintained active performance schedules through their eighties. Age-related declines in performance were sometimes a problem, however, because aging artists are unlikely to produce work that lives up to the peak of their past performances. While they may be free of the barriers of age discrimination, these figures frequently find themselves subject to another late-career barrier: that of their past reputations for greatness. They are haunted by the suspicion of being "has-beens" and are determined to prove otherwise.

The late Alan Jay Lerner had such a disappointing finish. In his late twenties and thirties he wrote or co-wrote such Broadway musical classics as *Brigadoon, Paint Your Wagon, Gigi, My Fair Lady,* and *Camelot.* In his fifties and sixties, however, his creative genius was suffocated by his own caution:

> The older a writer gets, the harder it is for him to write. This is not because his brain slows down; it is because his critical faculties grow more acute. If you're young, you have a sense of omnipotence. You're sure you're brilliant. Even if youth is secretly frightened, it assumes an outer assurance and plows right through whatever it is.[5]

Lerner's challenge in later career was not that the public held him up by comparing his later work to his earlier, but rather that he did this to himself. His own standards, he felt, paralyzed him.

Suspicions of faltering performance also haunt aging athletes, although many persevere into late career. At age sixty, Hall of Fame catcher Yogi Berra moved to Houston to take a job as coach with the Houston Astros after twice losing coaching positions in New York, where he had worn a baseball uniform for forty years.[6] Despite declining performance, baseball players Gaylord Perry of Seattle, Pete Rose of Philadelphia and Cincinnati, and Boston's Carl Yastrzemski, among others, continued to play well into their forties.[7] Satchel Paige pitched until he was sixty years old. Jim Kaat of the St. Louis Cardinals began his career playing for the Washington Senators in 1959. In 1983, still active, he commented on his participation:

> The game has gotten into my system and I can't get it out. It's like a blood condition. I feel challenged. At my age, the baseball people are waiting for you to fall apart at the seams. One short spell of failure and they may not give you more of a chance. With a younger player they'd say, "He's got a bright future, he'll come out of it." But someone like me, they say, "He's washed up." They can do you in in a hurry.[8]

Performers who do not submit to the discouraging pressures of age bias and charges of declining performance believe they still have more to give. Although these performers may realize that their contributions may not be immortal, and though they may be bothered that their fame may die with them, they still possess the ability to be net producers in life, and that is why they persist.

There are many such late-career workers who are driven to transcend late-career barriers. Unlike workaholics, these work-absorbed people, labeled *work-intensives* in Chapter 3, are not externally driven to keep up with others, but they have an internal compulsion to create. Common to artists, performers, professional workers, politicians, and business leaders are two sets of factors that keep them work absorbed. One set of factors has to do with the qualities of a work-intensive's job and the other set has to do with a work-intensive's character. Those qualities of the job that lead to work longevity include the degree of control and discretion available as well as the complexity of the work. The qualities of the work-intensive's character involve a personal motivation to achieve. Chief executives, of course, have a great deal of discretion, control, and challenge on the job and a tremendous amount of personal ambition and energy. Thus it is not surprising to find them among the categories of workers who are especially resistant to the notion of retirement.

In fact, in my own studies I found that chief executives were far less likely to plan for retirement than their top-level subordinates. They enjoyed their work and avoided any acknowledgment of an upcoming end to their reign.

Once retired, they were less likely than other top corporate officers to engage in recreation or relaxation. Instead, they continued to work within their old firms in various capacities or to seek out organizations willing to utilize their talents. In terms of heroic self-concept, the chief executives were far more likely than their subordinates to identify closely with the heroic stature of office.

While many late-career workers resist retirement, most try to find some way to come to terms with this final career stage. Those who continue to seek the same work tend to be highly ambitious people who work in occupations with high personal discretion over their conditions and a great deal of challenge. Such work-intensives as chief executives of corporations come to look forward to never-ending missions and enduring status. It is hard to obtain the immortality they seek, if indeed at all possible. However elusive the pursuit, the chief executive finds it difficult to exchange the hero's lofty quest for the image of a passive retiree.

Heroic Self-Concept and Heroic Context

The heroic self-concept combined with the corporate context produces four dominant departure styles. Attitudes regarding the fulfillment of one's career mission and one's attachment to one's identity as a leader were critical but not absolute determinants of one's exit behavior. Many financial, organizational, and cultural indices of the firm contributed to setting the stage for the heroes' grand exits. For example, exits from top office were more routine and organized in larger, more profitable firms, in firms with more outside directors, in firms where executives had spent less time than the other departure types in the specific firm they led, and in those firms where the chief executive was named to top office later in his or her career. We will review how the psychological and outside contextual forces combined for each departure style. Twenty-five years ago, sociologist Oscar Grusky found that the larger a firm's size, the greater its rate of chief executive turnover. Small firms had longer-reigning chief executives.[9] This is consistent with the present study, but such outside factors merely enhance or restrain more psychological features.

Monarchs' Exits

First, of the four types of leaders, the monarchs were the most attached to their roles as chief executives. The stature and the power were hard to relinquish. The monarchs were also most frustrated with their accomplishments. Their contributions, while impressive to outsiders, were seen by the monarchs as endangered by current business conditions. With a little more time, they felt they might turn a corner and bring the company to an immortal standing in industrial history. Their lesser emphasis on profits, as compared with that of the other types of leaders, reflected the typical monarchs' emphasis on building the institution, as seen by their firms' high sales growth, high asset growth, and high employment growth. In charge of relatively smaller firms with few outside directors, monarchs worked to shape their institutions in their own images. They did not leave office by their own choice, but led the company for two, three, or four decades. Fueled by their compelling vision, monarchs rule until death, until forcible removal by palace revolts of the board or their subordinates, or until the firm is sold.

In Chapter 6 we dispelled several common myths surrounding the monarchs. First, they are not necessarily evil or vain figures. In fact, they often had superior visions and led their firms to extraordinary growth in uncertain times. Second, they were not necessarily charismatic leaders or in less mature industries such as entertainment, communications, technology, or professional service. We found them in all industries. Third, they were not necessarily entrepreneurs, but could also be salaried managers with little or no ownership or identity as founders. Chapter 6 also questioned whether oedipal conflicts had as much impact on their departure style as some have intimated. Oedipal themes could be found in some cases in all the departure styles, but were absent in many cases in each departure style. Family intergenerational tensions, of course, were powerful factors in explaining the family business issues explored in Chapters 10 and 11.

If these factors underscore what was not true about monarchs, then what did they have in common? Successor selection was consistently weak, and monarchs frequently undermined successors. These pathbreaking leaders had frequently taken control of their firms at times when their industries were undergoing turbulent change. Whether in railroads, air travel, communications, finance, photography, consulting, or computers, these leaders had added valuable definitions of a business during uncertain times. Pan Am's Juan Trippe revolutionized the services, technology, image, and scope of air travel. J. P. Morgan had similarly reshaped the role of private financiers in public life. Bruce Henderson redefined the role of strategic consulting. Eastman Kodak's George Eastman and Polaroid's Edwin Land each brought industry-shaping change to photography. Armand Hammer built Occidental Petroleum into an independent oil giant by blending personal diplomacy with rugged determination and insightful deal-making. However, when times changed, the roles and visions of monarchical leaders were questioned.

Generals' Exits

The generals bore some likenesses to the monarchs, but there were also important differences. Unlike monarchs, these chief executives did not knowingly set up a weak succession plan. Instead, generals often developed strong leaders against whom they would eventually turn. They expressed a fairly strong attachment to heroic stature and were moderately frustrated by the loss of a heroic mission. The generals' firms were somewhat larger than those of the monarchs and had more outside directors. Thus they had less control over their firms than did the monarchs. They tended to have far less support from investors than the other groups. Profits were about median for the group, but overall firm performance was not as strong. In Chapter 7 we saw many generals who were institution builders in the tradition of monarchs, such as Robert Woodruff at Coca-Cola, William Paley at CBS, and Harold Geneen at ITT. The monarchs, by contrast, built institutions that faced external challenges, not internal warfare. As turnaround experts, the generals were used to using internal dissension to organize collective morale and mission around their presence. The generals, unlike monarchs, thought they would be able to leave their firms behind them when they retired. However, in retirement they mourned the respect and recognition once theirs and began to question the competence of their successors.

In office, the generals' charismatic powers transcended internal warfare to mobilize their firms to face external threats. Their skill in unifying disparate factions served as the instrument needed to orchestrate their return to power. The generals effectively offered themselves as symbols of a nearly lost time of corporate grandeur in the firm's history. Unlike the monarchs, these figures rarely created something brand new in their industry. They nonetheless radically reshaped their firms, placing a personal imprint on their triumphs. William Paley of CBS did not create the first broadcasting network. Harold Geneen of ITT did not create the first conglomerate. Robert Woodruff of Coca-Cola did not create the first beverage maker. But each of these people brought a novel vision to a troubled enterprise. The generals were highly committed leaders whose personal identities were closely intertwined with their positions as chief executives. Other roles in their family lives or community lives seemed less satisfying. The failure of a successor created an opportunity to return to greatness for both the individual leader and the troubled firm.

Ambassadors' Exits

The ambassadors expressed the greatest career contentment on leaving a firm and greeted their retirement with feelings of pride and pleasure. Psychologist Erik Erikson might have labeled this feeling of ambassadors as great late-life "integrity" and completeness. While they had a strong affinity for their firms, their identity did not hinge on their role as the leader. Their firms tended to be larger firms with moderate performance across the financial indices. Their accomplishments may have been no more modest than those of the monarchs or generals, but their attitudes were. Some, such as Thomas J. Watson, Jr., of IBM, Marvin Bower of McKinsey & Company, and Albert Gordon of Kidder Peabody, may have accomplished even more than many monarchs and generals. Unlike the monarchs and generals, however, ambassadors were not threatened by the firm's ability to carry on without them. The heroic myth of indispensability was most muted for the ambassadors. Their personal lives and their companies were relatively free of the external threat, internal turmoil, and distress that plagued the monarchs and generals. Unlike the governors, they did not feel a strong need to seek a new business adventure to demonstrate their continued heroic valor; as wise "elder statesman," they enjoyed sharing their insights with successors as mentors. They felt a sense of accomplishment from their career.

Governors' Exits

The last group of departing leaders, the governors, also led organizations through more tranquil times than did monarchs and generals. Their firms tended to be the largest, slowest growing, and most formal bureaucracies. Their heroic stature needs were low, but their drive to complete a heroic mission continued. This is the reverse protrait of the generals. While the governors had the lowest attachment to a leadership role in a given firm, they still longed for more opportunities to have an impact. They served as effective stewards to their firms through prescribed, and generally brief, terms of office before looking for alternative activities on the outside.

For the governors, retirement meant mostly a career switch. We saw three common paths taken by governors: (1) those who switched careers for top government service; (2) those who switched careers for start-up ventures; and (3) those who switched careers for turnaround challenges. Averell Harriman ran a railroad, founded and ran an investment bank, and then turned to public service as a governor and diplomat. James A. Ryder retired from Ryder Systems and founded a rival leasing and rental firm, Jartran. Jack Nash retired from Oppenheimer and founded the private firm, Odyssey Partners. Royal Little retired from Textron and founded a venture capital firm. Thornton Bradshaw retired from ARCO to help with the revival of RCA. Pepsi's Walter Mack retired to run other enterprises and founded two more soft-drink makers. Retired Southern Railroad chief executive L. Stanley Crane brought an amalgamation of old railroads back from the brink of disaster with his revival of Conrail. These leaders broke all former ties with their old firms. By the ends of their reigns, the governors had often become impatient for the next adventure.

Implications for Corporate Renewal

Each form of exit described above is marked by specific implications for corporate and for personal renewal. The issues regarding the corporation concern subsequent short-term firm performance, longer-term strategic responsiveness, and the development of future leaders. Key people in this planning include board members, other top officers, and the next cadre of leaders. The personal implications include the life stage of the leader at the time of exit, the degree of continued attachment to the firm, the impact on family members, and the creation of new life goals.

A critical goal of the monarch is to be central to the firm's vitality. A critical goal for the board of directors is to work with the monarch to try to limit that centrality. This is not easy because the monarchs often dominate their boards and maintain a strong appeal to investors. Monarchs place a disproportionate emphasis on long-term growth over current profitability. It is a testimony to their messianic salesmanship that they have been able to convince their constituents to share their monarchic vision. Not only do boards and subordinates follow along until death or mutiny, but even shareholders applaud the monarch's speeches, which bring order to their firms in times of turmoil. Would-be successors may have to prove that the monarchs have become obsolete as times have changed.

The eventual demise of the monarch may leave the firm without a substitute vision, since it lacks a next generation of strong leaders. The monarch's approach to succession is one of avoidance or of sabotage. Monarchs usually do not groom or name successors. If they do, they often nominate obviously flawed or physically ill candidates. As a last resort, they might set up contests among candidates in the hope that they might neutralize one another. Successors are often not found until six months before the monarchs retire. The monarchs even acknowledge in their retirement that they could have done a better job grooming their successors.

Thus boards of directors must pressure monarchs for realistic succession plans. The succession plan should include options for: (1) time frames of assignments; (2) candidates for key posts; and (3) development plans for assuming office, such as needed training and trial assignments.

Board members can also help the monarchs by developing a long-term exit plan that starts many years before retirement. The date may be flexible, but the gradual broadening of the authority and responsibility of the chief executive should not be. The chief executive should be more widely exposed to other models of succession and retirement by serving on a few outside boards and having more outside representation on the monarch's own board. Furthermore, chief executives should be encouraged to take outside special assignments and even leaves of absence to see how their skills can be usefully applied to an even broader domain in industries, in the government, or in community affairs. There are opportunities for institution-building elsewhere, but someone so absorbed in a given setting will not know where to look. With the awareness of the transferability of their skills, they will value the potential for their heroic career contributions elsewhere while allowing for new leadership in their firms.

The long reign of the monarchs necessitates that board members form a partnership with the chief executive in drafting a career development plan. Monarchs must be explicit about a reasonable term of office and aware of their own elusive definitions of success. Furthermore, the board must see that the chief executive is still being challenged by subordinates and still growing in his or her understanding of changing external events. As a work-intensive, insightful creator, the monarch should be encouraged to serve as a consultant to the board. This can also help a phased retirement. The monarch, however, may be far too personally invested in current strategies to serve as a constructive board member or officer.

Other officers and subordinates must be cautious about threatening monarchs, because they are quick to extinguish the potential flames of an uprising. The executives who serve a monarch are easily set up for destructive battles with each other, but they can overcome this trap by recognizing their common interests with their fellow subordinates. If they recognize their interdependence, they can be stronger, not as mutinous conspirators but as internal sources of candid feedback to the board and chief executive. They can also protect themselves by developing a familiar presence with the board of directors. The awareness of important backup candidates may embolden a more reticent board to take needed action.

Although monarchs' firms had the highest market-to-book ratio, the generals' firms had the lowest. Generals have led organizations with more internal dissension and executive turnover. When the board must shape the exit of a suspected general, the task is more subtle. The stubborn visions of the general may sometimes be interpreted by outsiders more as self-aggrandizement then heroic commitment to the common good. The generals have developed an expertise in trench warfare, although they have often camouflaged it with more congenial behavior. They have not actively neglected to train potential heirs. Nor have they willfully neutralized candidates for top leadership. With slightly greater feelings of fulfillment and less control over their boards, the generals acquiesce to retirement plans, at first outwardly resembling contented ambassadors. Eventually, however, their behavior comes to resemble that of the frustrated monarchs.

Before generals are given the chance to scheme for their return of office, they should be encouraged to develop leadership depth in the firm in case their preferred candidates do not work out as planned. Generals should consider possible transitional leaders in times of tragedy or a failure of the preferred candidates. They should clarify before they exit what performance failures by a successor they might find threatening. This should be shared with both the board and the successor before the appointment is announced. Specific criteria and time frames for succession should be spelled out so that all parties can see if there is sufficient allowance for opportunities to learn from some salvageable mistakes during a start-up and trial period.

Similarly, just before a general's return to command in the event of an unforeseen crisis, the board and the general should set a definite deadline for this extended assignment and establish mutually agreed upon objectives for stabilization. Jerome Gore's reluctant return to power at Hartmarx was an excellent model of the custodial role a former chief executive can play. Following the unanticipated exit of his initial heir, Richard Hamilton, the ambassador-like Gore returned for only three months until a new and stable leadership plan was developed with the board. Researchers John Gabarro and Richard Vancil have identified predictable stages in the "taking charge" process, each identifying steps, including intermittent periods of planning, action, and observation to learn about patterns of relationships and organizational response.[10] The general's impatience for results and insistence on strategic continuity can sabotage the successor's taking charge process.

Generals' successors should try to find post-retirement projects for the retiring general that provide status but not real influence over decision-making. Titles such as "chairman emeritus" can ease the loss of status. Generals seek to retain the dignity of their reputations and can serve as useful community representatives, but should not be allowed to intervene in corporate life. Given the politicized internal atmosphere, successors must be cautious as they distance their administration from that of the general. Board members and other peers are often divided along faction lines. Overreliance on the same sources for information and casting aspersions on the departing general may lead to greater dissension. The aftermath at ITT following Geneen's exit was a good example of this. Geneen loyalists were mobilized by Lyman Hamilton's open attacks. It is alleged that even the more cautious Rand Araskog was nearly ambushed by lingering Geneen loyalists.

The ambassadors can inadvertently be drawn into some of the dysfunctional behaviors of the generals. Through their continued presence in board meetings, executive conferences, company dining rooms, corridors, and employee events, they can begin to reclaim habitual old parts of their former roles. Ambassadors may offer impulsive unsolicited advice to successors on strategic as well as trivial issues. They may speak for the firm to outside parties. Ambassadors may intervene by counseling former subordinates or by responding to employee inquiries.

Ambassadors, however, do work hard to resist these temptations. Even so, the board can make it easier for them by sketching out clear lines of responsibility for retired chief executives who remain as chairman of the executive committee or some other such role. Old friends and employees are likely to want to continue old patterns of friendship with the retired chief executive, and he or she can become the rallying point for resistance to change and an accidental source of confidential information. Some remain attached to their old firm well into their ninth decade, with their interest in the company outlasting their physical energies or their mental alertness. Board members and successors to ambassadors sometimes find themselves caught in awkward conflicting loyalties to generous mentors. Embarrassment can be minimized by setting limits on the term of office for ambassadors as board members and by setting up anonymous mutual performance reviews on the board. This allows the firm to retain a valued elder statesman to provide the needed continuity and wisdom as long as desired while sparing a direct confrontation. An age gap of as much as a decade or more between mentor and protégé will produce less tension than if the two are closer in age.

In contrast, governors may rush out the door or be pushed out too quickly. Non-governor-style chief executives often faulted the governor style of exit as "hit-and-run" management or "assembly-line succession." Sometimes the governors served such brief terms in office that they left little imprint on their firms. At times, the overly formal succession processes may push along chief executives too quickly and too uniformly. Sometimes the governors were accused of being so captivated by outside interests that they were barely attentive to their own firm. This, of course, was Harold Geneen's complaint about Charles Percy of Bell & Howell.

Boards can encourage governors to remain in contact for a brief period of time after retirement by serving in transitional roles as short-term consultants. Eager to seek new adventures and to clear the deck for successors, the governors usually leave in a hurry. Those who are cajoled into remaining on the board often chafe under the assignment and resent having to watch the dismantling of their plans, even if they acknowledge that conditions necessitated it. Royal Little complained that the two post-retirement years he remained on the Textron board were two of the most painful in his seventy-year career. Rene McPherson, anxious to get out of Dana and move into the deanship of the Stanford Business School, found a consultant's role to be far more palatable. He stated, "I think that the chief executive should take credit when things go badly, share credit when things go well, and get the hell out of the way when it's someone else's turn." Robert Lear's board developed a plan under which he would take on just a few additional board memberships a year so that he could plan for his exit while still attending to the needs of Schaefer.

Boards and successors can also improve on the thoroughness of the grooming process offered by governors. Governors are not noted for the same skillful mentoring and sponsorship as the ambassadors. Frequently, the successors of the governors come from an internal contest or external selection. Providing little or no substantive post-retirement mentoring, the governors' valuable internal corporate insights and external networks of contacts can often be wasted. Richard Vancil found, as I did, that the "team" replacement concept common to the governors is not as predictable as the heir apparent grooming common among the ambassadors.[11]

Successors are often left on their own, somewhat underprepared for the office. Internal successors need assistance on how to work through frictions with peers who were fellow candidates in the "horse race" for the top job. Disappointments can be anticipated and overcome by a fair selection process. Externally hired successors also need assistance in learning about the company's culture and priorities. If the governor is not the one to provide this consultant assistance, two board members should be asked to spend extra time with governors' successors.

Overall, knowledge about a rising successor's self-concept, ambitions, and life stage can allow a board to anticipate likely departure styles years before retirement. Certainly once a chief executive is in office for a few years, a board can begin to expect what his priorities must be in helping in his or her eventual exit. I was regularly told that this is the most difficult task a board must manage. A company's size, maturity, and the formality of its culture can restrain or enhance tendencies toward given departure styles. The heroic context does not dictate the departure style, but it has a strong influence. Even corporate cultures that heavily favor a given departure style can be pushed toward another. A board that relies upon historic precedent and polite expectations may find itself dealing with a crisis. Firms can try to shape the values of their future leaders through selection and socialization, but regardless of industry, size, or company culture, all forms of departure styles are possible. The personal heroic leanings of the individual leader must be understood, as well as the succession systems (see Table 12.1). Rules can be changed and norms can be violated. An aware board and alert successors can build on the strengths and suppress the weaknesses of the various departure styles.

Implications for Personal Renewal

For most corporate heroes, "retirement" is a word they are quick to equate with death. Instead of seeing opportunity in retirement, many see it as the terminal point in a career that has known no limits. A leader's coming to terms with retirement first requires that he or she adjust to certain, non-negotiable limits, perhaps for the first time. These are not managers who had reached a plateau at mid-life. Now at later career they are wrestling with the dilemmas of mid-career and later life at the same time. These leaders were driven to make an immortal contribution through a lifetime commitment to a given path. They do not easily accept that the path is blocked. They often feel that their destination is just around the corner, even though as successful, achievement-oriented people they will always set the goals further off. Before these leaders can develop an effective detour, or a career change, they must be convinced that the dreaded roadblock is real.

Table 12.1   Corporate Renewal and CEO Departure Style

Advantages	Disadvantages
Monarchs' Departures	
Creates order amidst external turbulence	Restless in tranquil periods
Brilliant vision for institution building	Stubborn defense of old strategy
Growth in sales, assets, employees	Deemphasis on profitability
Long-term support from shareholders	Exit suggests firm instability
Complete personal dedication to business	Lack of outside management models
Assumes personal responsibility for problems	Reluctance to develop next generation
Generals' Departures	
Bridges internal factions	Fuels internal rivalries
Ready to return to office in crises	Leader encourages resistance to successor
Capable of building strong top leaders	Leader may undermine own successor
Cautious in leadership transitions	Leader attached to leadership identity
Ambassadors' Departures	
Continuity of command through long service	Maintains awkward continued presence, defends record
Available for elder statesman wisdom	Tense restraint of impulse to intervene, offer unsolicited advice, or public comments
Eager to accept assignments as external representative	Offers confusing statement on executive roles
Broad interests, community and outside boards	Encourages possible distraction of CEO from the company
Well informed on outside approaches to management	Replication of inappropriate fads
Governors' Departures	
Shorter terms of office, more opportunities	Little chance for lasting impact
Larger, more stable, and formal bureaucracies	Firms' performance lags over reign
Wide range of outside business interests	Possible distraction from office responsibilities
Freedom for successor to revamp strategy	CEO exit wastes accumulated wisdom
Complete break from firm on retirement	Old CEO offers little mentoring during "taking charge" of successor

The process for this acceptance is similar to the stages Elizabeth Kubler-Ross gleaned from her studies of adjustment of terminally ill patients to the prospect of death.[12] There is first a period of denial. The executives may feel, "This can't really be happening to me." We all feel ourselves to be uniquely immortal. The executives believe this especially strongly, or at least want to believe it. They cannot at first believe that their careers, after so many decades of preparation, are about to end. Second, there is a stage of anger, most often expressed as resentment of a next generation's opportunities. Successors have the future before them, once a possession of the outgoing leaders. Third, there is a stage of bargaining, in which they struggle with the board for an extended reign to clean up some old problems and leave a clean desk for their successor. This means an acceptance that the end is in sight. The fourth stage is one of depression. The leader feels defeated in the effort to leave a lasting monument. He or she contemplates the uncompleted projects, the long-forgotten files, the unrealized dreams, and wonders where the time went. Finally, he or she arrives at a stage of acceptance, where a feeling of contentment settles in. The degree of contentment may vary and the time it takes to get there may vary. Some may not live long enough to reach it. It requires that the leader reverse focus for the first time. Instead of looking at what is left to accomplish in a given job, they need to look back at how far they have come. Many can begin to appreciate their successful superhuman levels of accomplishment. Even the autobiographies of frustrated monarchs and generals show an eventual sense of pride of accomplishment. The exercise of writing memoirs, in fact, helps provide such a perspective.

To reach this point, the leaders have adjusted to many losses. Some of these losses include those relating to leadership stature, such as power, the comfort of group acceptance, the companionship of others with common interests, and the symbols of being an important person. Other losses include those concerning sense of mission, such as business goals, a sense of achievement, measurable outcomes, a daily routine, and scheduled events. Alone, stripped of an office, with once-rare blocks of time now suddenly stacked around like piles of old newspapers, the retired chief executive is rarely equipped for the trials of starting a career anew.

Many found ready solace in turning to family members. Some spouses had long awaited the day when the couple's daily schedule was not driven by business priorities. Travel with spouses, greater involvement with children and grandchildren, and just more time at home were mentioned by almost a quarter of the surveyed chief executives as one of the more rejuvenating aspects of their retirement. Many others, however, found that a patient, loving spouse was no longer there waiting for them. The death of a spouse, the prior neglect of family life, or the strains of high office blocked this avenue for adjustment as well. Some chief executives found that their spouses, already having full and independent lives, found it burdensome to have to accommodate a bored and lonely displaced leader. In a survey of two hundred spouses of retired executives at business school class reunions, almost 20 percent volunteered both serious and playful statements of complaint. One stated, "He has no one but me to order around now. I'm not his secretary, not even a temp." Another said, "Our kids are grown. I didn't want to care for another. It's just pathetic watching him try to figure out what to do at lunch time. No one to meet and trying to fix his own meal. It may not sound like real hardship, but he's lost."

By contrast, almost a third of the spouses volunteered comments that retirement had been a long-awaited time for sharing life adventures and common hobbies. While chief executives tended to identify their first year or two as the most difficult period after leaving office, spouses generally said the third and fourth years were more difficult. Much of their initial time is suddenly consumed by the logistics of sharing everyday life that they had previously been spared.

New Beginnings

Adjustment to loss is not the only process involved in personal renewal. The challenge for retiring leaders is not to conquer past problems, such as unresolved oedipal battles, but to recover from post-retirement emptiness. To do this, former chief executives must envision a new future. Grieving for the past or indulging in recreational pursuits will not lead these leaders to successful renewal. Their problems are not so much in coping with their pasts as in putting more meaning into their future. While counseling generally helped some to adjust, adjustment did not necessarily involve psychoanalytic diagnoses of the sources of their superhuman ambitions. The overt parental model was not a sufficient explanation for their different departure styles. Survey data and interviews revealed no distinctions in parental occupations, wealth, or types of childhoods that corresponded with departure styles.

Intimidatingly successful fathers were associated with each of the four departure styles. Similarly, many examples of fathers who were business failures were associated with each departure style. Nonetheless, it is important to know how, as adults, we use our memories and parental images. Bruce Henderson, Peter Grace, Baron Guy de Rothschild, J. P. Morgan, Thomas Watson, Jr., David Rockefeller, and Amory Houghton, Jr., enjoyed prominent careers despite the shadows cast by prior family successes. Such success may have served as an important yardstick of accomplishment, but it did not indicate which departure style they might follow in leaving office. Similarly, Harry Gray, Jack Nash, Irving Shapiro, and William Rosenberg all far surpassed their humble family origins, and yet they left office in quite different styles.

Furthermore, the reliance upon childhood retrospectives is suspect, since we have long known that our processes of recall are a mixture of stored experience along with active reconstruction to give those memories meaning.[13] Recently, psychological research has shown that our memories reflect some of our current views of ourselves.[14] The different adult memories siblings have of childhood family harmony, domestic affluence, and parental health often were best explained by the siblings' current life situations. In essence, happier adults may recall having been happier children. Those frustrated as adults may recall having been frustrated in childhood. The retired chief executives remembered having been inspired, diminished, or worshipped by their parents, depending on how they felt about themselves at the close of their careers.

For such reasons, the next step for successful personal renewal of top leaders is to look toward the future. As much as retirement is equated with death, it is not death. Once the retirees adjust to the present, they have to rebuild opportunities and dreams for the future. Chief executives plan less for their late-career moves than other workers because of their determination to avoid confronting the end of a chosen career. They avoid reminders of their mortality. The more it is denied, the more dreaded retirement becomes. Retirement planning is especially important for chief executives, even though they do it the least. This is because their initial years in retirement can be the most shocking. This is in striking contrast to the research on adaptation to retirement among other workers. Generally the first two years are a sort of honeymoon period during which retirees are consumed by the pursuit of all the things they have always wanted to do.[15] It is typically in the third and fourth years that disenchantment sets in as these indulgences provide insufficient joys to overcome the onset of financial stresses, health problems, and the loss of friends. The task then is to reorganize their lives and to provide some stability.

This sequence is usually the reverse for chief executives, because they generally do not have hobbies. Their greatest gratification was generally in the job they left and not in deferred recreation or outside organizations. They asked, "How much tennis can you play before you look for something bigger to do?" In the initial period after exit, some need a plan to manage all the distractions, while others need to find opportunities. Leaders deluged by post-retirement opportunities reported that their prior chief executive positions helped them to say no to the endless requests for their time, as previously their job demands were an acceptable excuse for saying "no."

This, then, raises the issue of what activities chief executives should say "yes" to and which opportunities they should seek out in retirement. Naturally these will vary by interest, personality, and health, but as a general rule, they should seek out those activities that will provide initial feelings of success. This means that they should try to learn new job skills in stages or build on familiar skills. While many highly driven workers in blue-collar occupations generally see retirement as an escape from pressure and hence become less driven after retirement, driven white-collar workers tend to seek out more driving work in retirement.[16] This transition for leaders means finding new involving and challenging tasks.

Ambassadors and governors reported the least difficulties in retirement, in part because they were more likely to plan for retirement than were the monarchs and generals. They also adjusted well because they managed to become involved in adventures that drew upon long-developed skills. Old interests and old work styles were projected into new settings. Winthrop Knowlton, a publisher, turned to education and writing. Irving Shapiro, a former corporate counsel at Du Pont, returned to the practice of law. Jack Nash of Oppenheimer redirected his great facility for deal-making and trading to another company. Marvin Bower of McKinsey focused again on consulting. Albert Gordon of Kidder Peabody drew on his interests and relationships linked to investment banking. Thornton Bradshaw, a skilled stabilizer at ARCO, helped lead a corporate turnaround for another company. Amory Houghton, Jr., of Corning Glass, long involved in New York State economic development, became a U.S. congressman. Thomas Carroll of Lever Brothers turned around to lead the International Executive Service Corps, one of a number of organizations that hires retired executives to contribute their time and insight to groups in need of assistance. Carroll had worked with this organization for many years before retirement. Each of these leaders also began reading more, learning new languages, and generally increasing their physical workouts. They also served on several boards each.

The challenge for the monarchs is to recognize broader interests beyond the firm. These interests need to be developed earlier in their careers so that they have a base on which to build new interests. Their ability to bring fresh insights to turbulent settings is certainly a desirable skill, as are their salesmanship and deal-making abilities. Generals need to find a role in post-retirement activities that affords them identification with a group and the stature they require. Cultural institutions are often the high-status organizations they energetically serve with pride and skill. Ambassadors tend to build on their long interests in community work and public service, and may hold a limited number of board directorships. They also tend to serve as exceptionally constructive "emeritus" leaders with reduced roles in their old firms. Governors often look for top-level positions in government, turnaround challenges, new business ventures, or extensive board directorships.

Retirement is not the end of a leader's career. It should be seen as a career change. It is not the end of opportunity, but a time for new opportunity. Some can seek a different schedule, some a different setting. Chief executive John Cullinane of Cullinet Software commented on his retirement at age fifty-three in 1987, "I wanted to look forward to a year of four seasons rather than four quarters." Ironically, he returned to office later that year. Retirement can lead to renewal if a realistic plan is developed that keeps challenge and growth alive. Heroes must believe in a chance for future contribution.

In Rod Serling's screenplay, *Requiem for a Heavyweight,* a boxing champ, Mountain McKlintock, is forced into retirement far earlier than he had anticipated. He is badly battered when he stays in the ring past his time. His manager and trainer no longer see any value in him as a boxer. They coax him to take demeaning work as a fake "professional" wrestler, but he is repulsed by this insulting suggestion that he has no marketable skills for a job that would give him a sense of dignity.

In a depressed state, he stops by a bar filled with retired boxers reenacting their greatest fights for one another. Mountain runs out shouting, "That's no way, that's no way at all!" At an employment office, he finds it hard to fit his credentials onto an employment application blank. In answering interview questions, which reveal his limitations, he explodes, and pounding his fist on a desk cries out, "I was almost the heavyweight champion of the world! I'm Mountain McKlintock. Where do I write that down on your form? Sure it hurts. Every punch along the way as you climb . . . you don't feel them . . . but now it all comes back to hurt and it hurts real bad."

At the end of the original TV version for "Playhouse 90," unlike the later movie version where he pathetically gives in to his manager's suggestion, Mountain is happy as an athletic camp counselor. The closing scene shows him eagerly teaching a young boy how to fight. Mountain has left his old peak and begun building a career using his old skills, maintaining his dignity, and making contact with a new generation. In the Hollywood remake, Mountain loses his dignity and, in shame, shuffles along in the wrestling ring where he stands sadly, dressed up as an Indian, to be laughed at by the crowds and told how to perform by the wrestling promoters. Between the two versions, we see a clear choice. In the later one, the champ continues to grieve for the past. In the other, he choses to seize opportunity and make a new future. Late-career champions in other fields have the same choice.

APPENDIX: CHIEF EXECUTIVE SUCCESSION SURVEY

\#_____   Year of Retirement_____

CHIEF EXECUTIVE SUCCESSION SURVEY

RETIREMENT SUGGESTIONS

PERSONAL PLANNING

1. What have been the most rejuvenating aspects of your retirement as CEO?

2. How did you prepare yourself for your own retirement?

3. What led you to try these particular preparatory steps?

4. What was most helpful about this preparation once you retired?

5. What was most difficult about this preparation (e.g., time demands, company events, etc.)?

6. Our records show that you retired as CEO in 19__. How did you decide exactly when to retire?
   Number first and second most important reasons.

   ( ) Company mandatory   ( ) Other business interests
        retirement policy   ( ) Community interests
   ( ) Company tradition   ( ) Recreational interests
   ( ) Personal health   ( ) Loss of pleasure in job
   ( ) Health of family   ( ) Other (please specify)
        member

7. Do you frequently regret your actual timing in leaving the CEO's position?

1	2	3	4	5	6	7
most times	very often	often	sometimes	not often	not very often	never

8. Do you have any comments on the above response on regrets?

9. When were the most difficult personal times for you after leaving office? Please rank list the top three.

( ) The first week   ( ) The second year   ( ) The fifth year
( ) The first month   ( ) The third year   and beyond
( ) The first year   ( ) The fourth year   ( ) Other

10. What characterized these times?

ORGANIZATIONAL PLANNING

11. What did you do to prepare the organization for your retirement as CEO?

12. Is there anything further which you would suggest that other leaders do to prepare their organizations for their retirement?

13. When did you feel most confident that the organization would adapt well to a new leader?

( ) Two years or more before   ( ) Six months after retiring
     retiring   ( ) One year after retiring
( ) One year before retiring   ( ) Two years or more after
( ) Six months before retiring   retiring
( ) At the time of retirement   ( ) Not yet confident

14. When did you feel least confident that the organization would adapt well to a new leader?

( ) Two years or more before   ( ) Six months after retiring
     retiring   ( ) One year after retiring
( ) One year before retiring   ( ) Two years or more after
( ) Six months before retiring   retiring
( ) At the time of retirement   ( ) Not yet confident

15. How long before you left did you identify your actual successor as the likely candidate to replace you?

( ) Two years or more   ( ) Six months before retiring
     before retiring   ( ) At the time of retirement
( ) One year before retiring   ( ) Not involved in identification

16. How long before your actual retirement did you announce the identity of your successor?

( ) Two years or more   ( ) Six months before retiring
     before retiring   ( ) At the time of retirement
( ) One year before retiring   ( ) Not involved in announcement

Why then?

17. What ongoing contact have you maintained with your firm since retiring?

Yes   No   (Please check yes or no for each line)

___ ___ Continued to hold an official position (e.g., chairman of executive committee)

___ ___ Continued to serve on the board for over two years

___ ___ Served on the board for less than two years

___ ___ Left the board immediately on retirement

___ ___ Continued to keep an office at the firm for over two years

___ ___ Continued to keep an office at the firm for less than two years

___ ___ Left your office at the firm immediately on retirement

___ ___ Continued to represent the firm externally at public events and with clients

___ ___ Continued to advise your successor on a regular basis

___ ___ Waited for solicitation of advice from successor

___ ___ Continued to advise other executives on a regular basis

___ ___ Waited for solicitation of advice from these executives

___ ___ Continued to appear at internal firm events

___ ___ Continued to respond to public inquiries about the firm

___ ___ Formal consultant relationship

DEPARTURE EXAMPLES

18. Did you have an example of a specific leader's retirement to emulate?

Yes____ No____
If yes, please state who and describe that retirement

19. Did you have an especially poor example of retirement which you hoped to avoid?

Yes____ No____
If yes, please state who and describe that retirement

20. Whan were your parents' occupations?

Father_____

Mother (if worked)_____

21. At what age did they retire?

Father_____ Mother (if worked)_____

CURRENT ACTIVITIES

22. Have you become involved in any of the following activities since retiring?

Possible Activity	Hours Per Month	Names of Key Organizations (if relevant)
Teaching	_____	
Consulting	_____	
Civic organizations (Museums, hospitals, charitable, etc.)	_____	
Political groups (Parties, causes)	_____	
Public office	_____	

22. Continued

Possible Activity	Hours Per Month	Names of Key Organizations (if relevant)
Corporate boards (please state if any are since retirement)	_____	
Started new business	_____	
New executive positions	_____	
Recreational pursuits (sports, study, hobby)	_____	

23. Did you decline opportunities in any of the above? If so, why?

    Activities   Reasons

24. What, if any, impact has your retirement had upon your family and friends?

    Family

    Friends

25. Have you any other comments to make as advice to other retiring leaders

26. Please provide the names of two executives who reported directly to you who also left the company due to retirement. (See cover letter for explanation.)

    Name

    Address

    Name

    Address

NOTES

Chapter 1

1. Otto Rank, *Art and Artist: Creative Urge and Personality Development* (New York: Knopf, 1932), esp. pp. 214–16.
2. Richard Tedlow, "Competing Against the Brand Beyond Competition," in *The History of Mass Marketing* (New York: Basic Books, in press).
3. Walter Mack with Peter Buckley, *No Time Lost* (New York: Atheneum, 1982), p. 177.
4. Warren Bennis and Burt Nanus, *Leaders: The Strategies for Taking Charge* (New York: Harper & Row, 1985).
5. Joseph E. Campbell, *The Hero with a Thousand Faces* (Princeton, N.J.: Princeton University Press, 1949), pp. 30–31.

Chapter 2

1. Lester B. Korn and Richard M. Ferry, *Korn/Ferry International's Executive Profile* (Los Angeles: Korn/Ferry, 1985).
2. "Americans Expect to Delay Retirement Says Harris Survey: Reversing Trend," *World of Work Report* 4, April 1979, pp. 1–3.

3. David J. Ross, Raymond Bosse, and Robert J. Glynn, "Period Effects on Planned Age for Retirement, 1975–1984," *Research on Aging* 3, 1985, pp. 395–407.

4. T. H. Holmes and R. H. Rahe, "The Social Readjustment Rating Scale," *Journal of Psychosomatic Research* 11, 1967, pp. 213–18.

5. Terry A. Beehr, "The Process of Retirement: A Review and Recommendations for Future Investigation," *Personnel Psychology* 39, 1986, pp. 31–35. See also S. V. Kasl, "The Impact of Retirement," in C. L. Cooper and R. Payne (eds.), *Current Concerns in Occupational Stress* (Chichester, U.K.: Wiley, 1980).

6. Ronald Blythe, *The View in Winter: Reflection on Old Age* (New York: Harcourt Brace Jovanovich, 1979), p. 73.

7. Benson Rosen and Thomas H. Jerdee, "Too Old or Not Too Old," *Harvard Business Review* 55, November–December 1977, pp. 97–106. See also Benson Rosen and Thomas H. Jerdee, *Older Employees, New Roles for Valued Resources* (Homewood, Ill.: Dow Jones-Irwin, 1985), pp. 34–50.

8. William Safire, "The Codgerdoggle," *New York Times*, Oct. 3, 1977, p. 29.

9. Norman Wexler comments on Mike Wallace interview, "The I. Magnin File," "60 Minutes," April 1984.

10. William Graebner, *A History of Retirement, The Meaning and Function of an American Institution, 1885–1978* (New Haven: Yale University Press, 1980), pp. 3, 56. See also Andrew N. Acherbaum, *Old Age in the New Land Since 1790* (Baltimore: Johns Hopkins University Press, 1978), pp. 20–22; and David Hackett Fischer, *Growing Old in America* (New York: Oxford University Press, 1977).

11. Quoted in Graebner, *A History of Retirement*, pp. 4–5.

12. Judith Treas, "The Historical Decline in Late Life Labor Force Participation in the United States," in James E. Birren, Pauline K. Robinson, and Judy E. Livingston (eds.), *Age, Health, and Employment* (Englewood Cliffs, N.J.: Prentice-Hall, 1986).

13. U.S. Bureau of the Census, *Historical Statistics of the United States, Colonial Times to 1970*, Bicentennial edition, Part 1 (Washington, D.C.: U.S. Government Printing Office, 1975), p. 132; U.S. Bureau of the Census, "Population Profile of the United States: 1980," *Current Population Reports*, Series P-20, No. 363 (Washington, D.C.: U.S. Government Printing Office p. 198.)

14. Edmund R. Hergenrather, "The Older Worker: A Golden Asset," *Personnel*, August 1985, p. 59.

15. U.S. Bureau of the Census, *Projection of the Population of the United States: 1971–2050*, Series P-25, No. 704, July 1977. In particular, see "Table H Estimates and Projections of the Population by Age: 1950–2000," pp. 10–11.

16. Madelyn Rosener and Linda R. Prout, "Targeting the Old Folks: Florida Leads the Way in Marketing to the Elderly," *Newsweek*, Jan. 6, 1986, p. 54.

17. Hank Gilman, "Marketers Court Older Consumers as Balance of Buying Power Shifts," *Wall Street Journal*, April 23, 1986, p. 33.

18. Aljean Harmetz, "NBC's Golden Girls' Gamble on Grown-Ups," *New York Times*, Sept. 22, 1985, pp. H-2, H-25.

19. Bernice Neugarten, "Acting One's Age," *Psychology Today*, April 1980, p. 66.

20. Hal Bodley, "Carlton Bows Out with His Mind at Ease," *USA Today*, Aug. 8, 1986, p. 5-C.

21. Oddessa M. Archibald, "Grandma High on Climbing: Mountain Kneels to 90-Year-Old," *USA Today*, Aug. 8, 1986, p. 5-C.

22. "Texas's Aging Angels," *Newsweek*, July 1, 1985, p. 45.

23. Edgar H. Schein, *Career Dynamics* (Reading, Mass.: Addison-Wesley, 1978).

24. Erik Erikson, *Childhood and Society*, 2nd ed. (New York: Norton, 1963); Daniel Levinson, with Charlotte N. Darrow, Edward B. Klein, Maria H. Levinson, and Braxton McKee, *Seasons of a Man's Life* (New York: Ballantine, 1978); and George E. Vaillant, *Adaptations to Life* (Boston: Little, Brown, 1977).

25. Pauline K. Robinson, "Age, Health, and Job Performance," in James E. Birren, Pau-

line K. Robinson, and Judy E. Livingston (eds.), *Age, Health, and Employment* (Englewood Cliffs, N.J.: Prentice-Hall, 1986).

26. Christopher Hallowell, "New Focus on the Old," *New York Times Magazine,* March 1985, pp. 48–50, 109–11. See also Harold M. Schmeck, Jr., "Expanding the Life Span May Just Be Impossible," *New York Times Magazine,* May 3, 1981.

27. Herbert de Vries, *Fitness After 50* (New York: Scribner's, 1986). See also Jane E. Brody, "Moderate Exercise Late in Life Is Found to Reverse Many of Effects of Aging," *New York Times,* June 10, 1986, pp. C1, C3.

28. A. T. Welford, "Thirty Years of Psychological Research on Age and Work," *Journal of Occupational Psychology* 49, 1976, p. 129.

29. William J. Hoyer and Dana J. Plode, "Attention and Perceptual Processes in the Study of Cognitive Aging," in Leonard W. Poon (ed.), *Aging in the 1980s* (Washington, D.C.: American Psychological Association, 1980).

30. J. E. Birren and K. W. Schaie (eds.), *Handbook of the Psychology of Aging* (New York: Van Nostrand Reinhold, 1977).

31. Richard C. Mog, Kenneth L. Davis, and Claire Parley, "Cholinergic Drug Effects on Memory and Cognition in Humans," in Leonard W. Poon (ed.), *Aging in the 1980s* (Washington, D.C.: American Psychologist Association, 1980), p. 150. See also Harold M. Schmeck, Jr., "Memory Loss Curbed by Chemical in Foods," *New York Times,* Jan. 9, 1979, pp. C1, C5.

32. "Data Point to Growth of Brain Late in Life," *New York Times,* July 30, 1985, pp. C1, C7.

33. Ellen J. Langer and Judith Rodin, "The Effects of Choice and Enhanced Personal Responsibility for the Aged," *Journal of Personality and Social Psychology* 34, 1976, pp. 191–98. See also Judith Rodin and Ellen J. Langer, "Long-Term Effects of a Control-Relevant Intervention with Institutionalized Aged," *Journal of Personality and Social Psychology* 35, 1977, pp. 897–902; and Ellen J. Langer, Pearl Beck, Cynthia Weinman, Judith Rodin, and Lynn Spitzer, "Environmental Determinants of Memory Improvements in Late Adulthood," *Journal of Personality and Social Psychology* 37, 1979, pp. 2003–13.

34. Special Committee on Aging, U.S. Senate, 98th Congress, *The Costs of Employing Older Workers* (Washington, D.C.: U.S. Government Printing Office, No. 37-1160, 1984).

35. John W. Hunt and Peter N. Saul, "The Relationship of Age, Tenure and Job Satisfaction in Males and Females," *Academy of Management Journal* 20, 1975, p. 690.

36. Linda A. Hill and Jeffrey A. Sonnenfeld, "Renewal Within Financial Service Firms: Managers' Reflections on Retraining," presented at Harvard Business School Colloquium on Contemporary Developments and Changes in the U.S. Financial Services Sector, Samuel L. Hayes III, chair, Boston, June 24, 1986.

37. D. A. Waldman and B. J. Avolio, "A Meta-Analysis of Age Differences in Job Performance," *Journal of Applied Psychology* 71, 1986, 33–38; and Glenn M. McEvoy and Wayne F. Cascio, "A Meta-Analysis of Age Differences in Job Performance: Replication and Extension," unpublished manuscript, University of Colorado, 1986.

38. J. L. Moore, "Unretiring Workers: To These Employees the Boss Is a Kid," *Wall Street Journal,* Dec. 7, 1977, p. 1.

39. S. Terry Atlas and Michael Rees, "Old Folks at Work," *Newsweek,* Sept. 26, 1977, p. 64.

40. See, for example, U.S. Department of Labor, *The Older American Worker, Report to the Secretary of Labor,* Title V., Sec. 715 of the Civil Rights Act of 1964 (Washington, D.C.: U.S. Government Printing Office, 1965); U.S. Department of Labor, Bureau of Labor Statistics, *Comparative Job Performance by Age: Office Workers,* Bulletin No. 1273 (Washington, D.C.: U.S. Government Printing Office, 1960); and Bureau of Labor Statistics, *Comparative Performance by Age, Large Plants in Men's Footwear and Household Furniture Industries,* Bulletin No. 1223 (Washington, D.C.: U.S. Government Printing Office, 1957).

41. William L. Cron and John W. Slocum, "The Influence of Career Stages on Salespeople's Job Attitudes, Work Perceptions, and Performance," *Journal of Marketing Research* 23, 1986, pp. 119–29. See also Carol H. Keller and Daniel A. Quirk, "Age, Functional Capacity, and Work: An Annotated Bibliography," *Industrial Gerontology* 19, 1973, p. 80.

42. Ronald C. Pelz, "The Creative Years in Research Environment, Industrial and Electrical Engineering: Transaction of the Professional Technical Group," *Engineering Management* 11, 1964, p. 23. and Wayne Dennis, "Creative Productivity Between the Ages of 20 and 80 Years," *Journal of Gerontology* 21, 1966, p. 1.

43. Victor H. Vroom and Bernt Pahl, "Age and Risk-Taking Among Managers," *Journal of Applied Psychology* 12, 1971, p. 22.

44. Craig C. Pinder and Patrick R. Pinder, "Demographic Correlates of Managerial Style," *Personnel Psychology* 27, 1974, pp. 257–70.

45. Bernard Holland, "Claudio Arrau: At Age 80, the Years Have Deepened His Art," *New York Times*, Feb. 20, 1983, pp. H1, H17.

46. E. B. Palmore, "Retirement Patterns Among Aged Men: Findings of the 1963 Survey of the Aged," *Social Security Bulletin* 27, 1964, pp. 3–10; and V. Reno, *Reaching Retirement: Findings From a Survey of Newly Entitled Workers, 1968–1970* (Washington, D.C.: Social Security Administration Report No. 47, U.S. Government Printing Office, 1976).

47. Thomas C. Nelson, "The Age Structure of Occupations," in Pauline K. Regan, (ed.), *Work Age and Retirement Policy Issues* (Los Angeles: Andrus Gerontology Center, University of Southern California, 1980). See also R. L. Kaufman and S. Spillerman, "The Age Structure of Occupations and Jobs," *American Journal of Sociology* 87, 1982, pp. 827–51.

48. Herbert S. Parnes and Lawrence Less, "Shunning Retirement: The Experience of Full-Time Workers," in Herbert S. Parnes (ed.), *Retirement Among American Men* (Lexington, Mass.: Lexington Books, 1985).

49. Mark D. Hayward and William R. Grady, "The Occupational Retention and Recruitment of Older Men: The Influence of Structural Characteristics of Work," *Social Issues* 64, 3, 1986, pp. 644–66; A. J. Jaffee, "The Retirement Dilemma," *Industrial Gerontology* 14, 1972, p. I-90; and P. L. Rones, "The Retirement Decision, A Question of Opportunity," *Monthly Labor Review* 103, 1980, pp. 14–17.

50. See Cynthia Dobson and Paula C. Murrow, "Effects of Career Orientation on Attitudes and Retirement Planning," *Journal of Vocational Behavior* 24, 1984, pp. 73–83; S. V. Kasl, "The Impact of Retirement: An Uncertain Legacy," *Journal of Health and Social Behavior* 22, 1984; J. T. McCune and N. Schmitt, "The Relationship Between Job Attitudes and the Decision to Retire," *Academy of Management Journal* 24, 1981, pp. 795–802; E. B. Palmore, L. K. George, and G. G. Fillenbaum, "Predictions of Retirement," *Journal of Gerontology* 37, 1982, pp. 783–92; and T. A. Beehr, "The Process of Retirement."

51. Quoted in Nan Robertson, "Artists in Old Age: The Fires of Creativity Burn Undiminished," *New York Times*, Jan. 22, 1986, p. C10.

52. Otto Rank, *Art and Artist: Creative Urge and Personality Development* (New York: Knopf, 1932).

53. Quoted in Nan Robertson, "Artists in Old Age," p. C-10.

Chapter 3

1. Dov Eden, "Propensity to Retire Among Older Executives," *Journal of Vocational Behavior* 8, 1976, pp. 145–54.

2. Harold Stieglitz, *Chief Executives View Their Jobs Today and Tomorrow* (New York: The Conference Board, Report No. 871, 1985).

3. Charles Margerison and Andrew Kakabudge, *How American Chief Executives Succeed:*

An AMA Survey Report (New York: American Management Association, 1984); Lester B. Korn and Richard M. Ferry, *Korn/Ferry International's Executive Profile* (Los Angeles: Korn/Ferry, 1985); and Gordon Donaldson and Jay W. Lorsch, *Decision Making at the Top* (New York: Basic Books, 1985).

4. Bryce Nelson, "Bosses Face Less Risk than the Bossed: Examining the Link Between Job Stress and Heart Disease," *New York Times*, April 3, 1983, p. B5; and Robert Karasek, Dean Baker, Frank Marxer, Anders Aldom, and Torres Theorell, "Job Decision Latitude and Cardiovascular Disease: A Prospective Study of Swedish Men," *American Journal of Public Health* 21, 1981, pp. 694–704.

5. Harry Levinson and Stuart Rosenthal, *CEO: Corporate Leadership in Action* (New York: Basic Books, 1984).

6. Donaldson and Lorsch, *Decision Making at the Top.*

7. Richard S. DeFrank, Michael T. Matteson, David Schweiger, and John M. Ivancevich, "The Impact of Culture on the Management Practices of American and Japanese CEOs," *Organizational Dynamics*, Spring 1985, pp. 62–76.

8. Stieglitz, *Chief Executives View Their Jobs.*

9. Korn and Ferry, *Korn/Ferry International Executive Profile.*

10. Stewart Toy, James P. Norman, and Terri Thompson, "Armand Hammer at 87: Still Showing Them How to Do Deals," *Business Week*, Jan. 20, 1986, pp. 68–71.

11. Pamela G. Hollie, "Well Past Age 65, They're Still Boss," *New York Times*, July 29, 1979, p. H1.

12. Robert Johnson, "Heineman Has a New Challenge at Northwest," *Wall Street Journal*, Dec. 7, 1983, p. 31.

13. Daniel J. Levinson, with Charlotte N. Darrow, Edward B. Klein, Maria Levinson, and Braxton McKee, *The Seasons of a Man's Life* (New York: Ballantine, 1978), pp. 35–36.

14. Joseph Wechsberg, *The Merchant Bankers* (New York: Simon & Schuster, 1966), pp. 176–77.

Chapter 4

1. Larry McMurtry, *Lonesome Dove* (New York: Simon & Schuster, 1984).

2. Robert Lacey, *Ford: The Men and the Machine* (Boston: Little, Brown, 1986), pp. 413–19. See also Allan Nevins and F. E. Hill, *Ford Volume I: The Times, the Man, and the Company* (New York: Scribner's, 1954); *Ford Volume II: Expansion and Challenge: 1915–1933* (New York: Scribner's, 1957); and *Ford Volume III: Decline and Rebirth: 1933–1962* (New York: Scribner's, 1967).

3. Ralph Waldo Emerson, "Self-Reliance," in *Essays: First Series* (Boston: James Munroe, 1841), pp. 35–73.

4. Robert B. Reich, "The Executive's New Clothes," *The New Republic*, May 13, 1985, p. 27.

5. John Kenneth Galbraith, "The Last Tycoon," *The New York Review of Books*, Aug. 14, 1986, p. 3.

6. Joseph E. Schumpeter, *Capitalism, Socialism, and Democracy* (New York: Harper & Brothers, 1942); and Max Weber, *Theory of Social and Economic Organization*, Talcott Parsons and A. M. Henderson, trans. (New York: Free Press, 1949).

7. Howard E. Aldrich, *Organizations and Environments* (Englewood Cliffs, N.J.: Prentice-Hall, 1979).

8. Jeffrey Pfeffer and Gerald Salancik, *The External Control of Organizations* (New York: Harper & Row, 1977).

9. Quotes from *Tolstoy* (New York: Doubleday, 1967), pp. 435–37.

10. Peter Petric, "America's Most Successful Entrepreneur," *Fortune*, Oct. 27, 1986, pp. 24–32.

11. Alfred D. Chandler, Jr., *The Visible Hand: The Managerial REvolution in American Business* (Cambridge, Mass.: Harvard University Press, 1977).

12. Ibid., pp. 459–65.
13. Ibid., pp. 201–3.
14. Ibid., pp. 9–14.
15. Harold C. Livesay, "Entrepreneurial Persistence Through the Bureaucratic Age," *Business History Review* 51, Winter 1977, in Richard S. Tedlow and Richard R. John, Jr. (eds.), *Managing Big Business* (Boston: Harvard Business School Press, 1986).
16. Rosabeth M. Kanter, *The Change Masters* (New York: Simon & Schuster, 1983); and Peter F. Drucker, *Innovation and Entrepreneurship* (New York: Harper & Row, 1985).
17. Stewart D. Friedman and Habir Singh, "It Makes a Difference: Letter to the Editor"; and John Kenneth Galbraith, "Response," *The New York Review of Books*, Oct. 23, 1986, p. 69. See also Stewart D. Friedman and Habir Singh, "Why He Left: An Explanation of the Succession Effect," presented at the Academy of Management, 50th Annual Meeting, Chicago, August 1986. Unpublished manuscript available through authors at the Wharton School of Management, University of Pennsylvania.
18. Richard E. Neustadt, *Presidential Power* (New York: Wiley, 1960), pp. 9–10.
19. Joseph L. Bower, *The Two Faces of Management* (Boston: Houghton Mifflin, 1983). See also Joseph L. Bower and Martha Weinberg, "Statecraft, Strategy and Corporate Leadership," Working Paper #1-785-058, Boston, Harvard Business School, 1985. For a theoretical discussion of organizations as political coalitions, see Richard M. Cyert and James March, *A Behavioral Theory of the Firm* (Englewood Cliffs, N.J.: Prentice-Hall, 1963).
20. Ken Auletta, *The Art of Corporate Success* (New York: Putnam's, 1984), p. 123.
21. Philip Selznick, *Leadership in Administration* (Englewood Cliffs, N.J.: Prentice-Hall, 1957).
22. See, for example, management theorist Elton Mayo, *The Human Problems of an Industrial Civilization* (New York: Macmillan, 1933); or New Jersey Bell CEO Chester Barnard, *The Functions of the Executive* (Cambridge, Mass.: Harvard University Press, 1938).
23. Henry Mintzberg, *The Nature of Managerial Work* (New York: Harper & Row, 1973).
24. John Kotter, *The General Managers* (New York: Free Press, 1982).
25. Fred Luthans, *Real Managers* (Cambridge, Mass.: Ballinger, 1987). See also Noel M. Ticky and Mary Anne Devanna, *The Transformational Leader* (New York: Wiley, 1986).
26. Edgar H. Schein, *Organizational Culture and Leadership* (San Francisco: Jossey-Bass, 1985).
27. Manfred F. R. Kets de Vries and Danny Miller, *The Neurotic Organization: Diagnosing and Changing Counterproductive Styles of Management* (San Francisco: Jossey-Bass, 1984).
28. See, for example, Elliot Jacques, *The Changing Culture of a Factory* (London: Tavistock, 1951); Abraham Zaleznik, *Human Dilemmas of Leadership* (New York: Harper & Row, 1966); and Michael Maccoby, *The Gamesman* (New York: Simon & Schuster, 1976).
29. Richard M. Dorson, *America in Legend* (New York: Pantheon, 1972); Richard M. Dorson, "The Question of Folklore in a New Nation," in Bruce Jackson, (ed.), *Folklore and Society* (Hatboro, Pa.: Folklore Association, 1966); and Dixon Wector, *The Hero in America* (New York: Scribner's, 1972).
30. Dorson, "Folklore in a New Nation," p. 33.
31. Dorson, *America in Legend*, p. 153.
32. Wector, *The Hero in America*, p. 147.
33. "The Vanishing American Hero," *U.S. News & World Report*, July 21, 1975, pp. 16–18. See also: J. H. Plumb, "Disappearing Heroes," *Horizon*, Autumn 1974, Vol. 4, pp. 48–52; "Where Have All the Heroes Gone?" *New York Times*, July 31, 1985, pp. C1, C10.
34. Benjamin DeMott, "Threats and Whimpers: The Business Heroes," *New York Times Book Review*, Oct. 26, 1986, pp. 1, 49; Bruce Nussbaum, John W. Wilson, Daniel Moskowitz, and Alex Beam, "The New Corporate Elite," *Business Week*, Jan. 21, 1985, pp. 62–80.
35. Gary Scharhost and Jack Bales, *The Lost Life of Horatio Alger, Jr.* (Bloomington: Indiana University Press, 1985), p. 155.

36. Ibid.
37. See N. R. Kleinfield, "The 'Irritant' They Call Perot," *New York Times*, April 27, 1986, pp. 3–1, 3–8.
38. Alfred P. Sloan, Jr., *My Years with General Motors* (Cambridge, Mass.: MIT Press, 1966).
39. Jonathan Hughes, *The Vital Few: The Entrepreneur and American Economic Progress* (New York: Oxford University Press, 1986), p. 295.
40. Ibid., pp. 165–66. See also George S. Bryan, *Edison: The Man and His Work* (New York: Knopf, 1926); and Matthew Josephson, *Edison: A Biography* (New York: McGraw-Hill, 1959).
41. Leo Braudy, *The Frenzy of Renown: Fame and Its History* (New York: Oxford University Press, 1986), pp. 37–41.
42. See reference in Steven Prokesch, "America's Imperial Chief Executive," *New York Times*, Oct. 12, 1986, pp. 3–1, 3–25. See also "Turnover at the Top," *Business Week*, Dec. 19, 1983, pp. 104–10.
43. Jeffrey Sonnenfeld, *Corporate Views of the Public Interest* (Boston: Auburn House, 1980); and Jeffrey Sonnenfeld, "Untangling the Muddled Management of Public Affairs," *Business Horizons*, December 1984.
44. "Executive Pay, Who Made the Most—And Why," *Business Week*, May 2, 1988, pp. 50–58.
45. For a fuller discussion of the debate on chief executive compensation, see Arch Patton, "Why So Many Executives Make Too Much," *Business Week*, Oct. 17, 1983, pp. 24, 26; Patricia O'Toole, *Corporate Messiah: The Hiring and Firing of Million-Dollar Managers* (New York: Signet, 1985); and "Who Gets the Most Pay," *Forbes*, June 4, 1984, pp. 98–146.
46. Thorstein Veblen, *A Theory of the Leisure Class* (New York: Macmillan, 1899).
47. Max Weber, in *From Max Weber: Essays in Sociology*, H. H. Gerth and C. Wright Mills, trans. (New York: Oxford University Press, 1947), p. 245, as quoted in Dankwart A. Rustow, *Philosophers and Kings: Studies in Leadership* (New York: George Grazellas, 1970), p. 15.
48. *From Max Weber*, p. 295.
49. William J. Goode, *The Celebration of Heroes* (Berkeley: University of California Press, 1978), pp. 344–45.

Chapter 5

1. For a fuller account, see Robert Rhodes James, *Anthony Eden—The Authorized Biography* (London: Weidenfeld and Nicholson, 1986).
2. Robert W. Creamer, *Stengel: His Life and Times* (New York: Simon & Schuster, 1985).
3. Joseph Campbell, *The Hero with a Thousand Faces* (Princeton, N.J.: Princeton University Press, 1949), p. 353.
4. Richard E. Neustadt, *Presidential Power* (New York: Signet, 1964), p. 83.
5. See Stanley Schacter's standard reference on group affiliation, *The Psychology of Affiliation, Experimental Studies of the Sources of Gregariousness* (Stanford, Calif.: Stanford University Press, 1959).
6. See Harold D. Lasswell, *Psychopathology and Politics* (New Haven: Yale University Press, 1930); James David Barber, *The Lawmakers: Recruitment and Adaptation to Legislative Life* (New Haven: Yale University Press, 1965); and Erik Erikson, *Young Man Luther: A Study in Psychoanalysis and History* (New York: Norton, 1958).
7. Barber, *The Lawmakers*, p. 17.
8. Leo Braudy, *The Frenzy of Renown: Fame and Its History* (New York: Oxford University Press, 1986).
9. Ibid., pp. 38, 43.
10. Robert Keegan, *The Evolving Self* (Cambridge, Mass.: Harvard University Press, 1985).

11. Terence Smith, "5 Leaders Emeritus Take a Look at the World," *New York Times*, Aug. 9, 1983, p. 1.
12. Ibid., p. 4.
13. D. C. Burnham, "Letter from the Chairman," *1974 Annual Report*, The Westinghouse Corporation, Pittsburgh, Pa., Jan. 31, 1975.
14. Guy de Rothschild, *The Whims of Fortune: The Memoirs of Guy de Rothschild* (New York: Random House, 1985), p. 135.
15. Ibid., p. 321.
16. Erik Erikson, *Childhood and Society*, 2nd ed. (New York: Norton, 1963).
17. Ernest Becker, *The Denial of Death* (New York: Free Press, 1973), p. 4.
18. Otto Rank, *Art and Artist: Creative Urge and Personality Development* (New York: Knopf, 1932).
19. Robert Jay Lifton, *Revolutionary Immortality: Mao Tse-tung and the Chinese Cultural Revolution* (New York: Random House, 1968).
20. Ibid., pp. 13–15.
21. Ibid., p. 151.
22. Please see questionnaire in Appendix.
23. Correlation of heroic mission and length of reign: $r = .19$, $p < .05$.
24. Correlation of heroic status and length of reign: $r = .21$, $p. < .01$.
25. CEO stature score $= -.87$, top officer stature score $= -.308$, $T = 6$, degrees of freedom $= 105$, $p < .0001$. The top officers were from the same firms as the CEOs. Both CEO samples and top officer samples yielded a 67 percent response rate. The CEO population sample was drawn from a random selection of one thousand companies: the *Fortune* 500 Industrials of 1984 and the *Fortune* 500 Service of 1984 (*Fortune*, April 29, 1985, and June 10, 1985). The population was reduced by such factors as mergers or if the firms were founded since 1960. Out of 674 firms, 227 were drawn at random. Of these 227, roughly 150 had living retired chief executives. Out of this sample of 150, 100 replied, for a response rate of 67 percent. Nonrespondent firms showed no differences by size, industry, or board. The score was composed of the subtraction of a twelve-item scale corresponding with low heroic stature needs from a nine-item scale, reflecting high heroic stature needs. Thus, CEOs had a higher score than did their subordinates, indicating greater identification with heroic stature in the leadership role. There was no significant difference between the two groups regarding heroic mission.
26. Correlation of age when appointed and length of reign: $r = -.29$, $p < .01$.
27. Correlation of company service and length of reign: $r = .18$, $p < .05$.
28. Correlation of percentage of outside directors and length of reign: $r = .24$, $p < .05$.
29. In a median split on employment growth by departure style, the percentages in the "high" group versus the "low" group were: Monarchs 100%, Generals 20%, Ambassadors 44%, Governors 31%.
30. Correlation of change in earnings-per-share by promptness in leaving office: $r = .44$, $p < .001$. Correlation of change in income with reluctance to advise successor without solicitation: $r = .27$, $p < .01$.
31. Correlation of length of chief executive reign with income growth over two years prior to retirement: $r = .18$, $p < .05$.
32. Correlation of age and income growth over two years prior to retirement: $r = .19$, $p < .05$.
33. Analysis of variance of likelihood of keeping an on-site office by departure style: $F = 5.095$, $p < .001$, degrees of freedom $= 3,92$. Monarchs and were governors more likely to keep an office, ambassadors and generals far less likely to keep an office.
34. Analysis of variance of timing of retirement seen as "too early" by departure style: $F = 3.32$, $p < .05$, degrees of freedom $= 3,92$; seen as much too early for monarchs and generals.
35. Analysis of variance of likelihood of keeping a post-retirement position in the firm:

$F = 11.46$, $p < .01$, degrees of freedom = 3,89. Generals were most likely, followed by monarchs and ambassadors with governors least likely. Analysis of variance of retirement planning by departure style: $F = 2.87$, $p < .05$, degrees of freedom = 3,92. Monarchs and generals were found least likely to plan.

36. Analysis of variance of likelihood of planning retirement, $F = 2.87$, $p < .05$, degrees of freedom = 3,92. Monarchs and generals were least likely to plan for retirement.

37. Analysis of variance of timing of retirement, same as note 34.

38. Analysis of variance of likelihood of remaining on board over two years by departure style: $F = 15.57$, $p < .001$, degrees of freedom = 3,93. Ambassadors and generals were most likely to remain on the board, governors least likely to remain on the board.

39. Analysis of variance of retirement regrets over loss of power by departure style: $F = 4.21$, $p < .01$, degrees of freedom = 3,92. Generals were far more likely to express regret over loss of power. Analysis of variance of retirement regrets over loss of prestige by departure style: $F = 3.80$, $p < .01$, degrees of freedom = 3,92. Generals were far more likely to express regret over loss of prestige. Analysis of variance of retirement regrets over loss of being center of attention: $F = 12.862$, $p < .001$, degrees of freedom = 3,70. Generals were far more likely to express regret over loss of being center of attention.

40. Analysis of variance of likelihood of keeping a formal position after retirement by departure style: $F = 11.46$, $p < .001$, degrees of freedom = 3,92. Generals were most likely, followed by monarchs, then ambassadors, and lastly governors.

41. Analysis of variance of retirement seen as reduction in stress by departure style: $F = 5.45$, $p < .01$, degrees of freedom = 3,92.

42. Analysis of variance of likelihood of awaiting solicitation of advice by successor by departure style: $F = 4.28$, $p < .01$, degrees of freedom = 3,92. Monarchs and generals were unlikely to wait for solicitation.

43. Analysis of variance of involvement in civic affairs by departure style: $F = 4.58$, $p < .01$, degrees of freedom = 3,88. Ambassadors most involved.

44. Analysis of variance of prompt exit from board by departure style: $F = 2.43$, $p < .05$, degrees of freedom = 3,87. Governors left most promptly with monarchs the next most likely.

45. Analysis of variance of involvement in new business activities for rejuvenation by departure style: $F = 4.58$, $p < .01$, degrees of freedom = 3,88.

46. Analysis of variance of retirement seen as too late by departure style: $F = 2.83$, $p < .05$, degrees of freedom = 3,88. Governors were far more likely to report a desire to have retired earlier.

Chapter 6

1. Clyde Haberman, "Hirohito (1901–?) Takes a Bow as Oldest Emperor," *New York Times*, April 28, 1982, p. A-2.

2. Richard Tedlow and Henry Feingold, "Interview with Leonard Goldenson: March 21, 1981," *American Jewish History* 72, No. 1, September 1982.

3. Lenore Hershey, *Between the Covers: The Ladies Own Journal* (New York: Coward-McCann, 1983), p. 11.

4. Robert Bonner, "Stormy Voting Session for Chock-Full-o-Nuts," *New York Times*, Dec. 12, 1982, p. F7.

5. Sandra Salmans, "Victor Potamkin The Salesman," *New York Times*, Sept. 26, 1985, pp. D1, D5.

6. Ibid.

7. Victor F. Zonard, "Paul Kalmanovitz Uses Offbeat Tactics to Build a Stable Beer Empire," *Wall Street Journal*, April 2, 1983, pp. 11, 20.

8. William Cellis, III, "Coleman Faces Big Transition in Leadership," *Wall Street Journal*, Sept. 18, 1984, p. 34.

9. Ken Auletta, "Power, Greed and Glory on Wall Street," *New York Times Magazine*, Feb. 24, 1985, pp. 45–48, 60–65.

10. Michael Blumstein, "Gentle Transition at Lehman," *New York Times*, July 29, 1983, p. D1.

11. Kendall J. Wills, "Every 30 Years or So a Long Vacation," *New York Times*, March 2, 1986, p. D7.

12. Kendall J. Wills, "From Story Lines to Value Line," *New York Times*, March 2, 1986, p. D7.

13. Robert Lenzer, *The Great Getty* (New York: Crown, 1986); and Leslie Wayne, "The Tangled Fight for Getty Oil," *New York Times*, Dec. 11, 1983, pp. F2, F8.

14. Thomas C. Hayes, "Unocal's Chairman Digs In," *New York Times*, April 16, 1985, p. D1.

15. Frederick Rose, "Unocal Struggles on with Attempt to Get Crude Oil from Shale," *Wall Street Journal*, May 14, 1986, p. D-1.

16. Haynes, "Unocal's Chairman Digs In."

17. Stewart Toy, James R. Norman, and Terri Thompson, "Armand Hammer at 87: Still Showing Them How to Do Deals," *Business Week*, Jan. 20, 1987, pp. 68–71.

18. Joseph Finder, "Dr. Armand Hammer's Medicine Show," *Harpers*, July 1983, pp. 30–42.

19. Ibid., and correspondence with Armand Hammer, Oct. 31, 1987.

20. Correspondence with Armand Hammer, Oct. 31, 1987.

21. Christopher S. Wren, "Occidental China in Coal Pact," *New York Times*, April 30, 1984, pp. D1, D4; and correspondence with Armand Hammer, Oct. 31, 1987.

22. David Pauly, Doug Tsuruoko, and Elizabeth Bailey, "Occidental's One-Man Show," *Business Week*, Sept. 10, 1984, p. 57; and correspondence with Armand Hammer, Oct. 31, 1987.

23. Robert J. Cole, "Wall Street Stunned as Shamrock Cancels Giant Occidental Merger," *New York Times*, Jan. 8, 1985, p. A1.

24. Arie Gelman and Madelyn Rosener, "Armand Hammer Is Left at the Altar," *Newsweek*, Jan. 21, 1985, p. 60; and correspondence with Armand Hammer, Oct. 31, 1987.

25. Winston Williams, "The Uneasy Peace at Occidental," *New York Times*, Sept. 9, 1984, pp. F1, F8; and Stephen J. Sansweet, "Power Struggle at Occidental Pits Hammer Against Biggest Holder," *Wall Street Journal*, March 30, 1984, p. D-.

26. Toy, Norman, and Thompson, "Armand Hammer at 87, pp. 68–71.

27. Ibid.

28. Armand Hammer and Neil Lydon, *Hammer* (New York: Putnam's, 1987).

29. Marilyn Bender and Selig Altschul, *The Chosen Instrument* (New York: Simon & Schuster, 1982), p. 295.

30. Ibid., p. 297.

31. Robert Daley, *An American Saga: Juan Trippe and His Pan Am Empire* (New York: Random House, 1980), pp. 253–54.

32. Ibid., p. 374.

33. Ibid., p. 409.

34. Ibid., p. 503.

35. Interview with former Pan American director Charles Adams, Feb. 1, 1983.

36. *Newsweek*, April 3, 1972, p. 67.

37. *Fortune*, Aug. 27, 1979, p. 3.

38. *Wall Street Journal*, Aug. 3, 1981, p. 1.

39. Richard J. Kirkland, Jr., "How Much Longer For Pan Am?" *Fortune*, March 2, 1987, p. 8.

40. Geraldine Fabrikant, "The Orderly World of Martin Davis," *New York Times*, Feb. 23, 1986, p. F9.

41. Board member Henry Walker quoted in Laura Landro, "Gulf & Western Chief Moves Quickly to Cast Company in His Image," *Wall Street Journal*, March 16, 1983, p. 2.

42. Fred R. Bleakley, "United Technologies President Out," *The New York Times*, Sept. 19, 1984, pp. D-1, D-2.

43. William M. Carley, "United Technologies in a Buzz over Charges of Bugging Devices," *Wall Street Journal*, Nov. 2, 1984, pp. 1, 29.

44. Ibid.

45. Ibid.

46. Lee A. Daniels, "United Technologies Top Post," *New York Times*, Oct. 16, 1984, pp. D1, D6.

47. "A Change May Mean No Change at United Technologies," *New York Times*, Oct. 29, 1984, p. 46.

48. Thomas J. Lueck, "Gray Still Dogged by Same Charges," *New York Times*, Nov. 30, 1984, pp. D1, D5.

49. Thomas J. Lueck, "Chief's Post Given Up by Gray," *New York Times*, Sept. 24, 1985, pp. D1, D15; Resa King, "Is Harry Gray Really Making Room at the Top?" *Business Week*, Oct. 7, 1985, pp. 40–41; and Hank Gilman, "United Technologies Appoints Daniell Chief Executive; Gray Stays Chairman," *Wall Street Journal*, Sept. 24, 1985, p. 22.

50. Howard Banks, "Holding Action at United Technologies," *Forbes*, July 1, 1985, pp. 32–33.

51. Charles Stein, "What Would Harry Gray Think Now?" *Boston Globe*, Dec. 14, 1986, pp. A-1, A-3.

52. William Carley, "How Dissension Jolted United Technologies, Led to Carlson's Exit," *Wall Street Journal*, May 20, 1986, pp. 1, 25.

53. David Remnick, "Grace Under Pressure," *Manhattan Inc.*, January 1987, pp. 55–63.

54. C. Alexander G. de Secada, "Arms, Guano, and Shipping: The W. R. Grace Interests in Peru, 1865–1885," *Business History Review* Winter 1985, pp. 592–621.

55. "Key Points from Letter on Waste," *New York Times*, Jan. 13, 1984, p. A14.

56. Chris Welles, "Inside the Troubled Empire of Peter Grace," *Business Week*, June 16, 1986, p. 68.

57. Ibid., p. 69.

58. "J. Peter Grace Is Swallowing His Pride and Shifting Course—Well Sort Of," *Business Week*, Dec. 10, 1984, pp. 99–100.

59. Remnick, "Grace Under Pressure," p. 60. See also Daniel F. Cuff, "Grace's Uncertain Successor," *New York Times*, March 14, 1987, p. D1.

60. Remnick, "Grace Under Pressure," p. 62.

61. Ibid., pp. 62–63.

62. Ibid., p. 692.

63. Cuff, "Grace's Uncertain Successor," p. D-1.

64. David Finn, "A Computer Pioneer's Deals and Ideals," *Across the Board*, April 1986, pp. 20–28.

65. Charles F. McCoy, "Control Data Cuts Its Earnings in SEC Review," *Wall Street Journal*, Aug. 7, 1985, p. 3.

66. Personal correspondence from William Norris, Oct. 26, 1987.

67. Richard Gibson, "Control Data's Price in Top Posts Must Prove Quickly He Can Revive Firm," *Wall Street Journal*, Jan. 10, 1986, p. 4.

68. James C. Worthy, *William C. Norris: Portrait of a Maverick* (Cambridge, Mass.: Ballinger, 1987).

69. Finn, "A Computer Pioneer's Deals and Ideals," p. 32.

70. Peter C. Wensberg *Land's Polaroid* (Boston: Houghton Mifflin, 1987), pp. 227–29.

71. Peter W. Bernstein, "Polaroid Struggles to Get Back in Focus," *Fortune*, April 7, 1980, p. 66.

72. From interview with two board members who preferred anonymity.

73. Bernstein, "Polaroid Struggles," p. 66.

74. William M. Bulkeley, "Losing Its Flash: As Polaroid Matures Some Lament a Decline

in Creative Excitement," *Wall Street Journal*, May 10, 1983, p. 1; Mitchell Lynch, "Polaroid Tries to Get Itself in Focus," *New York Times*, May 19, 1983, p. D4; "Polaroid Can't Get Its Future in Focus," *Business Week*, April 4, 1983, p. 31.

Chapter 7

1. General Douglas MacArthur, Address to Joint Meeting of Congress, April 19, 1951.
2. William Manchester, *American Caesar: Douglas MacArthur* (Boston: Little, Brown, 1978).
3. Quoted in "An Old Soldier Dies," *Newsweek*, April 13, 1964, pp. 34–35.
4. Martin Blumenson, *Patton: The Man Behind the Legend* (New York: William Morrow, 1985).
5. Alexander Werth, *De Gaulle: A Political Biography* (Harmondsworth, U.K.: Penguin Books, 1969). See also Harold Callende, "Crisis Arises as De Gaulle Resigns Post," *New York Times*, Jan. 2, 1946. pp. 1, 4.
6. Stanley Hoffman and Inge Hoffman, "De Gaulle as a Political Artist: The Will to Grandeur," in Stanley Hoffman, (ed.), *Decline or Renewal: France Since the 1930s* (New York: Viking, 1979), p. 243.
7. Robert J. Schoenberg, *Geneen* (New York: Norton, 1985), p. 80.
8. Ibid., p. 20, and correspondence with Geneen's attorney Phil Gilbert, Dec. 21, 1987.
9. Ibid., p. 42.
10. Ibid., pp. 49–52.
11. Ibid., pp. 56–76. This rationale is disputed by Geneen's attorney Phil Gilbert.
12. Ibid., p. 78.
13. Ibid., pp. 82–83, 93.
14. Ibid., pp. 99, 200; personal interviews with Charles F. Adams.
15. Schoenberg, *Geneen*, pp. 108–9, 333.
16. Ibid., pp. 198–202.
17. Ibid., pp. 211–19.
18. Ibid., p. 271.
19. Ibid.
20. Ibid., pp. 282–85.
21. Ibid., pp. 311–12.
22. Ibid., p. 313.
23. Ibid., p. 321. Geneen's attorney Phil Gilbert claimed that Dunleavy had denied making this statement.
24. Ibid., p. 327.
25. Ibid., pp. 327–31.
26. Ibid., p. 333.
27. "How Cleaning House May Help ITT Clean Up," *Business Week*, March 23, 1987, p. 64. See also Janet Guyon, "Telephone Switch: ITT-CGE Deal Shows the Change Buffeting Telecommunications," *Wall Street Journal*, April 30, 1987, pp. 1, 20.
28. Arie L. Priest, "Irv Jacobs' Raid Could Force a Break Up of ITT," *Business Week*, Dec. 24, 1984, p. 31.
29. Schoenberg, *Geneen*, p. 333.
30. Peter Barnes, "CBS's Wyman Forced to Quit, Sources Assert," *Wall Street Journal*, Sept. 11, 1986, p. 3.
31. Bill Powell and Jonathan Alter, "The Showdown at CBS," *Newsweek*, Sept. 22, 1986, pp. 54–60.
32. Peter J. Boyer, "At CBS News, A Feeling of Relief," *New York Times*, Sept. 11, 1986, p. D6.
33. See David Halberstam, *The Powers That Be* (New York: Knopf, 1979).
34. "Bill Paley: Reliving History," *Newsweek*, Sept. 22, 1986, p. 56.

35. Halberstam, *The Powers That Be.*
36. "Bill Paley: Reliving History," p. 56.
37. Sally Bedell, "Paley Grip Cited in CBS Ouster," *New York Times,* May 10, 1980, p. 1.
38. Sally Bedell, "What's Gone Wrong at Black Rock?" *New York Times,* Oct. 31, 1982, pp. F1, F8.
39. Albert Scardino, "Behind the Revolt at CBS: An Erosion of Confidence," *New York Times,* Sept. 16, 1986, p. 1.
40. Ibid.
41. Bill Powell and Jonathan Alter, "Civil War at CBS," *Newsweek,* Sept. 15, 1986, pp. 46–56; Powell and Alter, "The Showdown at CBS," pp. 54–58.
42. Peter W. Barnes, Laura Landro, and James B. Stewart, "How the CBS Board Decided Chief Wyman Should Leave His Job," *Wall Street Journal,* Sept. 12, 1986, p. 1.
43. Ken Auletta, "Gambling on CBS," *New York Times Magazine,* June 8, 1986, p. 106.
44. Pat Watters, *Coca-Cola: An Illustrated History* (New York: Doubleday, 1978). See also E. V. Kahn, Jr., *The Big Drink: The Story of Coca-Cola* (New York: Random House, 1960).
45. Richard Tedlow, "Competing Against the Brand Beyond Competition," in *The History of Mass Marketing* (New York: Basic Books, in press).
46. "Robinson of Coca-Cola: A Yankee Salesman for a Southern Institution," *Fortune,* September 1955, p. 122; and Brian McGlynn, "The Strategy That Refreshes," *Forbes,* Nov. 11, 1981, pp. 81–84.
47. Peter W. Bernstein, "Coke Strikes Back," *Fortune,* June 1, 1981, pp. 30–36.
48. John Huey and John Koten, "Former Coke Chairman Reasserts His Power Shaking up the Troops," *Wall Street Journal,* June 10, 1980, p. 1.
49. Bernstein, "Coke Strikes Back," p. 32.
50. Ibid., p. 33.
51. Huey and Koten, "Former Coke Chairman Reasserts His Power," p. 1.
52. John Koten and Scott Kilman, "How Coke's Decision to Offer 2 Colas Undid 4½ Years of Planning," *Wall Street Journal,* July 15, 1985, p. 1.
53. "Amerada Chairman Takes Added Title," *New York Times,* Jan. 9, 1986, p. D2.
54. "Hess Holders Pass Measures to Block Hostile Takeover," *Wall Street Journal,* May 10, 1985, p. 5.
55. James R. Norman, "Leon Hess: Can the Bottom-of-the-Barrel Oil Baron Get Back on Top?" *Business Week,* June 29, 1987, pp. 50–55.
56. Ibid., p. 55.
57. Steven Greenhouse, "Managing by Tumult at Winnebago," *New York Times,* May 10, 1986, pp. F1, F29.
58. Ibid.
59. Ibid.
60. Ibid., p. F-29.
61. Clyde H. Farnsworth, "A Troubled Rule at the World Bank," *New York Times,* Sept. 2, 1984, p. F1. See also Peter T. Kilborn, "Clausen Departing as U.S. Role Grows, *New York Times,* Oct. 9, 1985, p. D22.
62. "Clausen's Court Recrowns Its King: A Look at Bank America's Board of Directors," *Bankers Monthly.* November 1986, pp. 37–38.
63. Jonathan B. Levine and Sarah Bartlett, "Bank America's New Tight Spot," *Business Week,* June 22, 1987, p. 50. See also G. Christian Hill and Richard B. Schmitt, "Autocrat Tom Clausen Faces Formidable Task to Save Bank America," *Wall Street Journal,* Oct. 17, 1986, pp. 1, 19.
64. John N. Frank, "MGIC Rises from the Ashes of Baldwin United," *Business Week,* March 4, 1985, pp. 92–93.
65. Alfred D. Chandler, Jr., *The Visible Hand: The Managerial Revolution in American Business* (Cambridge, Mass.: Harvard University Press, 1977), pp. 210–12.

66. Kenneth Dreyfack, "Why Beatrice Had to Dump Dutt," *Business Week*, Aug. 19, 1985, pp. 94–95; see also "Beatrice Shake-Up Seen as Helpful," *New York Times*, Aug. 6, 1985, p. D5.
67. Dreyfack, "Why Beatrice Had to Dump Dutt," p. 95.

Chapter 8

1. Stephen E. Ambrose, *Eisenhower: The President* (New York: Simon & Schuster, 1985), esp. pp. 594, 600, 602, 638, and 656. See also Carl M. Brauer, *Presidential Transitions* (New York: Oxford University Press, 1986).
2. Harry Levinson and Stuart Rosenthal, *CEO Corporate Leadership in Action* (New York: Basic Books, 1985), p. 85.
3. Katherine Davis Fishman, *The Computer Establishment* (New York: Harper & Row, 1984), pp. 85–87.
4. Vincent P. Carosso, *More Than a Century of Investment Banking* (New York: McGraw-Hill, 1979).
5. Ibid.
6. David Ogilvy and Joel Raphaelson, *The Unpublished Ogilvy* (New York: Crown, 1986), p. 161.
7. John Rossant, "Advertising's Grand Old Man Stays Plugged In—From a Distance," *Business Week*, Jan. 20, 1986, p. 49.
8. Ibid.
9. Ogilvy and Raphaelson, *The Unpublished Ogilvy*, p. 160.
10. Ibid., p. 161.
11. Ibid., p. 174.
12. Lee Israel, *Estée: Beyond the Magic: An Unauthorized Biography* (New York: Macmillan, 1985).
13. Estée Lauder, *Estée: A Success Story* (New York: Random House, 1986).
14. Joan Kron, "The Book World Is Abuzz Over Lives of Estée Lauder," *Wall Street Journal*, Sept. 26, 1985, p. 1.
15. Otto J. Scott, *The Creative Ordeal: The Story of Raytheon* (New York: Atheneum, 1974), p. 191.
16. Robert J. Schoenberg, *Geneen* (New York: Norton, 1985), p. 82.
17. Lois Therrien, "Raytheon May Find Itself on the Defensive," *Business Week*, May 21, 1986, pp. 72, 74.
18. Michael Tushman, William H. Neuman, and Elaine Romanelli, "Convergence and Upheaval: Managing the Unsteady Face of Organization," *California Management Review* 29, 1986, pp. 29–84.

Chapter 9

1. "Chief Dan George, 82, Dies; Appeared in 'Little Big Man,' " *New York Times*, Sept. 24, 1981, p. 42.
2. Edgar Driscoll, Jr., "Ellsworth Bunker, 90; Was Top Diplomat, U.S. Ambassador to South Vietnam During the War," *Boston Globe*, Sept. 28, 1984.
3. "Bowles Dies; Diplomat, Politician, Advertising Executive," *Newsweek*, June 9, 1986, p. 54.
4. Walter Isaacson and Evan Thomas, *The Wise Men* (New York: Simon & Schuster, 1986), pp. 47–49.
5. Ibid., p. 45.
6. Alan S. Oser, "Ex-Gov. Averell Harriman, Advisor to Four Presidents, Dies," *New York Times*, July 27, 1986, pp. 1, 23.

7. Lynn Langway and David T. Friendly, "Marketing: Cola Wars," *Newsweek*, Sept. 25, 1978, p. 79.
8. "Execution Hall of Fame: Forrest Mars," *Fortune*, April 2, 1984, p. 110.
9. Paul Engelmayer, "Developer of Festive Market Places Sets Up Foundation to Renovate Inner-City Homes," *Wall Street Journal*, Dec. 29, 1983, p. 35.
10. "Ryder Retires at Truck Concern," *New York Times*, June 17, 1979, p. D2.
11. Leonard Sloane, "Ryder's Founder Starts a Rival," *New York Times*, June 27, 1979, p. D2.
12. Leonard Sloane, "Working for Mr. Ryder a Second Time Around," *New York Times*, June 6, 1980, p. D2.
13. Thomas L. Friedman, "The Truck-Leasing Triangle," *New York Times*, Jan. 7, 1982, pp. D1, D4.
14. Ibid., p. D-4.
15. Fred Pillsbury, "Amtrak Profitless but Improving," *Boston Globe*, Nov. 25, 1984, p. A-47.
16. Winston Williams, "Turning a Railroad Around," *New York Times Magazine*, Jan. 13, 1985, pp. 32–74.
17. Ibid., p. 71.
18. Bill Richards, "Speculation at Standard of Indiana Favors President as Next Chairman," *Wall Street Journal*, May 5, 1983, p. 37; Daniel F. Cuff, "Indiana Standard Names a Chairman," *New York Times*, July 29, 1983, p. D1.
19. Fred S. Worthy, "Can an Oilman Re-energize Continental Bank?" *Fortune*, Nov. 26, 1984, pp. 156–63.
20. John Frank and Steve Crock, "At Continental, What a Difference a Year Makes," *Business Week*, May 6, 1985, p. 48.
21. Royal Little, "I Lost $100 Million and Had Fun Doing It," *Fortune*, Aug. 27, 1979, pp. 106–14.
22. Royal Little, *How to Lose $100,000,000 and Other Valuable Advice* (Boston: Little, Brown, 1979), p. 173.
23. Ibid., p. 273.
24. Ibid.
25. Peter Collier and David Horowitz, *The Rockefellers: An American Dynasty* (New York: Holt, Rinehart and Winston, 1976). See also Kathleen Teltsch, "The Cousins: The Fourth Generation of Rockefellers," *New York Times Magazine*, Dec. 30, 1984, pp. 12–17, 30–31.
26. Chester Bouroki and Alan Lafely, "Strategic Staffing at the Chase," in Charles Fombrun, Noel Tichy, and Mary Anne Devanna (eds.), *Strategic Human Resource Management* (New York: Wiley, 1984).
27. Carol J. Loomis, "The Three Year Decline at David's Bank," *Fortune*, July 1977, pp. 70–80.
28. Cary Reich, "Chase After Rockefeller," *Institutional Investor*, November 1979, pp. 33–44.
29. Carol J. Loomis, "It's a Stronger Bank that David Rockefeller Is Passing on to His Successors," *Fortune*, Jan. 14, 1980, pp. 38–45.
30. Ibid.
31. Cary Reich, "Chase After Rockefeller," *Institutional Investor*, November 1979, pp. 33–44.
32. Ibid., p. 43. See also Loomis, "It's a Stronger Bank."
33. Carol J. Loomis, "The End of a Dynasty," *Fortune*, Aug. 4, 1986, pp. 26–38.
34. For more background, see, "David's Connections," *Institutional Investor*, May 1981, pp. 117–53.
35. Personal correspondence with author, April 8, 1986.
36. Peter Nulty, "A Peacemaker Comes to RCA," *Fortune*, May 4, 1981, pp. 149–53.

37. Eric N. Berg, "Orderly Transition at RCA: But Frederick Faces Hurdles," *New York Times*, March 7, 1985, p. 54.
38. "RCA: Will It Ever Be a Top Performer?" *Business Week*, April 12, 1984, p. 53.
39. Laura Landro, "Fine Tuning: As Robert Frederick Takes to Job at RCA, Picture Looks Brighter," *Wall Street Journal*, March 6, 1985, p. 1.
40. Berg, "Orderly Transition at RCA." p. 1.
41. Janet Guyon, "AT&T Picks Olson to Succeed Brown as Chairman, Names Allen President," *Wall Street Journal*, May 22, 1986, p. 42; David E. Sanger, "AT&T Changes at the Top," *New York Times*, May 22, 1985, p. D-1; Calvin Sims, "Robert Allen Is on the Line," *New York Times*, April 24, 1988, p. F5.
42. Richard F. Vancil, *Passing the Baton: Managing the Process of CEO Succession* (Boston: Harvard Business School Press, 1987).
43. "Management Succession at General Electric—Question and Answer with Reginald Jones," Richard F. Vancil (ed.), Boston, Harvard Business School Case Series, Videocassette #5-882-054.

Chapter 11

1. See, for example, Robert Lenzer, *The Great Getty* (New York: Crown, 1986). See also Leslie Wayne, "The Tangled Fight for Getty Oil," *New York Times*, Dec. 11, 1983, pp. F2, F8.
2. John L. Ward, *How to Plan for Continuing Growth, Profitability and Family Leadership* (San Francisco: Jossey-Bass, 1987).
3. See Thomas Goldwasser, *Family Pride* (New York: Dodd, Mead, 1986), pp. 203–16. See also Stephen Prokesch, "When the Relatives Fall Out," *New York Times*, June 11, 1986, pp. D1, D15.
4. Ann Hughey, "With New Chairman, Corning Tries to Get Tough and Revive Earnings," *Wall Street Journal*, June 22, 1983, p. 31; Myron Magnet, "Corning Glass Shapes Up," *Fortune*, Dec. 13, 1982, pp. 90–109.
5. Jonathan Hughes, *The Vital Few: The Entrepreneur and American Economic Progress* (New York: Oxford University Press, 1986), p. 295; Robert Lacey, *Ford: The Men and the Machine* (Boston: Little, Brown, 1986); David Halberstam, *The Reckoning* (New York: William Morrow, 1986); and Peter Collier and David Horowitz, *The Fords: An American Epic* (New York: Summit, 1987).
6. Lacey, *Ford: The Men and the Machine*, pp. 411–12.
7. Ibid., p. 418.
8. Ibid., pp. 555–56.
9. Collier and Horowitz, *The Fords*, p. 259.
10. Halberstam, *The Reckoning*, pp. 376–84. See also Lacey, *Ford: The Men and the Machine*, p. 557; and Collier and Horowitz, *The Fords*, pp. 288–304.
11. Halberstam, *The Reckoning*, pp. 383–84. Collier and Horowitz, *The Fords*, pp. 338–57.
12. Collier and Horowitz, *The Fords*, p. 343.
13. Lacey, *Ford: The Men and the Machine*, pp. 411–12.
14. Ibid., pp. 621–23.
15. Halberstam, *The Reckoning*, pp. 511, 541.
16. Ibid., pp. 552–60.
17. Donald F. DeScenza, "Management Changes at Ford: Probable Causes and Implications," *Research Bulletin*, Donaldson, Lufkin & Jenrette Securities Corporation, July 1978.
18. James Burrow, "Caldwell to Peterson at Ford," *New York Times*, Oct. 30, 1984, p. D1.
19. William J. Hampton and James R. Norman, "General Motors: What Went Wrong?" *Business Week*, March 16, 1987, pp. 102–10.

20. Harry Levinson, "Don't Choose Your Own Successor," *Harvard Business Review,* November–December 1974, pp. 53–62.

21. John A. Davis, "The Influence of Life Stage on Father–Son Relationships in the Family Firm," Ph.D. dissertation, Harvard Business School, 1982, available through University Microfilms, Ann Arbor, Michigan.

22. Ivan Landsberg, "The Succession Conspiracy: Resistance to Succession Planning in First Generation Family Firms," *Working Paper Series A,* No. 73 (New Haven: Yale School of Organization and Management, 1986), p. 10.

23. Steven Prokesch, "Daughter Always the Little Girl," *New York Times,* June 11, 1986, pp. D1, D15.

24. Personal interviews, see also Carol B. Higgins, "Honor Thy Father, Join His Corporation," *Intercorp,* Jan. 23, 1986, pp. 1, 30, 31; "Outstanding Young Working Women," *Glamour,* February 1987, p. 23.

25. Walter S. Mussberg and Alan L. Otten, "Washington Post Cuts Flash, Turns Inward Under Donald Graham," *Wall Street Journal,* Sept. 3, 1986, pp. 1, 18.

26. Prokesch, "When the Relatives Fall Out," p. D15.

27. Steven Prokesch, "Rediscovering Family Values," *New York Times,* June 10, 1986, p. D10.

28. Landsberg, "The Succession Conspiracy."

29. Alex S. Jones, "And Now the Pulitzers Go to War," *New York Times,* April 13, 1986, p. F4.

30. Joanne Lipman, "Family Affair: Ruder-Finn P.R. Firm Is Roiled by Defections Amid Nepotism Issue," *Wall Street Journal,* July 2, 1986, p. 1.

31. Louis B. Barnes and Simon A. Hershon, "Transferring Power in the Family Business," *Harvard Business Review* 54, 4, November–December, 1976, pp. 105–14.

32. See Richard Beckard, Peter Davis, and Barbara Hollander, "Perpetuation, Continuity and Change," in *Managing the Dynamics of the Family Firm* (San Francisco: Jossey-Bass, in press). See also W. Gibb Dyer, Jr., *Cultural Change in Family Firms* (San Francisco: Jossey-Bass, 1987).

Chapter 12

1. John Kenneth Galbraith, "The Last Tycoon," *The New York Review of Books,* Aug. 14, 1986, p. 3; Robert B. Reich, "The Executive's New Clothes," *The New Republic,* May 13, 1985, pp. 22–28; and Joseph E. Schumpeter, *Capitalism, Socialism, and Democracy* (New York: Harper & Brothers, 1942).

2. Robert Keegan, *The Evolving Self* (Cambridge, Mass.: Harvard University Press, 1985).

3. Otto Rank, *Art and Artist: Creative Urge and Personality Development* (New York: Knopf, 1932).

4. Ernest Becker, *The Denial of Death* (New York: Free Press, 1973); Robert Jay Lifton, *Revolutionary Immortality: Mao Tse-tung and the Chinese Cultural Revolution* (New York: Random House, 1968); and Rank, *Art and Artist.*

5. Samuel G. Freedman, "Alan Jay Lerner, the Lyricist and Playwright, Is Dead at 67," *New York Times,* June 15, 1986, pp. 1, 31.

6. Beth Miller, "Yogi More Colorful than Ever," *USA Today,* May 28, 1986, p. 8-C.

7. Ira Berkow, "Baseball: The Game Is Entering Golden Age," *New York Times,* April 3, 1983, pp. J1 and J10.

8. Ibid., p. J-10.

9. Oscar Grusky, "Administrative Succession in Formal Organizations," *Social Forces* 39, 2, December 1960, pp. 105–15. Oscar Grusky, "Corporate Size, Bureaucratization, and Managerial Succession," *American Journal of Sociology* 67, 3, November 1961, pp. 263–69; and Oscar Grusky, "Managerial Succession and Organizational Effectiveness," in Amitai Etzioni (ed.), *A Sociological Reader in Complex Organizations,* 2nd ed. (New York: Holt, Rinehart and Winston, 1969), pp. 398–409. See also Gene F. Brady

and Donald Helmich, *Executive Succession: Toward Excellence in Corporate Leadership* (Englewood Cliffs, N.J.: Prentice-Hall, 1984), especially pp. 232–51, for an interesting discussion on the association between rates of chief executive turnover and company performance.

10. John J. Gabarro, *The Dynamics of Taking Charge* (Boston: Harvard Business School Press, 1987); and Richard F. Vancil, *Passing the Baton: Managing the Process of CEO Succession* (Boston: Harvard Business School Press, 1987).

11. Vancil, *Passing the Baton.*

12. Elizabeth Kubler-Ross, *On Death and Dying* (New York: Macmillan, 1969).

13. R. C. Bartlett, *Remembering* (Cambridge: Cambridge University Press, 1932).

14. David C. Rubin, *Autobiographical Memory* (Cambridge: Cambridge University Press, 1987). See also Daniel Goleman, "In Memory, People Re-create Their Lives to Suit Their Image, the Present," *New York Times,* June 23, 1987, pp. C1, C9.

15. R. C. Atchley, *The Sociology of Retirement* (Cambridge, Mass.: Halsted Press, 1976), R. C. Atchley, *The Social Forces in Later Life* (Belmont, Mass.: Wadsworth, 1972). See also Larry G. Peppers, "Patterns of Leisure and Adjustment to Retirement," *The Gerontologist,* 16, 5, 1976, pp. 441–45, for a research report on the importance of continuity of activity for personal satisfaction in retirement.

16. John A. Howard, Peter A. Rechnitzer, David A. Cunningham, and Allan P. Donner, "Change in Type-A Behavior a Year After Retirement," *The Gerontologist* 26, 6, 1986, pp. 643–49.

NAME INDEX

SUBJECT INDEX